~~Rich Aal~~

WENDY ROSS

EYEWITNESSES to Jewish History

Edited by

AZRIEL EISENBERG

HANNAH GRAD GOODMAN

ALVIN KASS

EYEWITNESSES TO JEWISH HISTORY

From 586 B.C.E. to 1967

Union of American Hebrew
Congregations, New York, N.Y.

LIBRARY OF CONGRESS CATALOGING IN PUBLICATION DATA

Eisenberg, Azriel Louis, 1903– comp.
Eyewitnesses to Jewish History, 586 B.C.E.–1967.

SUMMARY: Selections from the Tanach, the Bible, the Dead Sea Scrolls, newspapers, radio programs, and other sources trace Jewish history from 586 B.C.E. to 1967.
Includes bibliographical references.
1. Jews—History—Sources. 2. Jews—History—Juvenile literature. [1. Jews—History—Sources]
I. Goodman, Hannah Grad, joint comp. II. Kass, Alvin, joint comp. III. Title.
DS118.E378 910'.039'24 72–1898

PRODUCED IN THE U.S. OF AMERICA

To Estelle and David Perl with
affection and gratitude

To my mother, Ida Reiser Grad

To my children, Sarah Ann and
Jonathan Kass, in the hope that
this volume will whet their
appetites for the further study
of Jewish history

CONTENTS

FOREWORD

This book is a first attempt to present Jewish history through the eyes of the men and women who saw it happen, from the destruction of the First Temple in 586 B.C.E. to the Six Day War in 1967—a span of over 2,500 years.

These eyewitness accounts are drawn from books, diaries, travelers' notes, letters, memoirs, poems, newspaper reports, magazine articles. Introduced by explanatory material, they provide a fresh look at events and key personalities with which the reader may already have some acquaintance. History textbooks of necessity consist of highly condensed, emotionally-dehydrated generalizations. They are important in presenting series of facts and for providing summaries and reviews of events. By their very nature—their responsibility to objectivity—they cannot transmit the emotional impact and tone of a happening. The eyewitness approach of on-the-spot stories adds flesh to the dry skeleton of history and infuses it with life and spirit. It gives new meanings to facts, imparts insights and attitudes, provides a mood, conveys an emotional impact.

The seventy-seven compiled selections have been written by some of our greatest writers and most intriguing personalities. It is hoped that they will enliven the study of Jewish history and that the reader will delve into them for a matchless experience in living through some of these epic experiences.

The idea for this book was suggested by Dr. Emil Feuerstein of Israel, who is an outstanding writer and critic. Dr. Jack D. Spiro, director of the Commission on Jewish Education, and Mr. Abraham Segal, associate director, were most helpful and cooperative as editor and advisor. Sincere thanks are due also to Mr. Ralph Davis who saw the book through the process of design and production; Miss Patricia Pierce and Mrs. Diana Schoolman for their devoted and meticulous preparation of the manuscript; Mrs.

Josette Knight for her excellent copy editing; Mrs. Jacqueline L. Bergman, who assiduously read proof; and to the readers for the Commission on Jewish Education: William Hallo, Alan Bennett, Albert Lewis, Max Shapiro, Leon Fram, and Samuel Glasner. The Library of the Jewish Theological Seminary provided the documentary photographs.

The editors also express their deep appreciation to the publishers and authors who gave their generous permission to reprint the selections included in this book.

A.E., H.G.G., A.K.

EYEWITNESSES to Jewish History

BARUCH BEN NERIAH Describes the Fall of Judah, 586 B.C.E.

The fall of Judah in 586 B.C.E. was the first of a series of separations of the Jewish people from its land. It was the beginning of the 2,500-year struggle for survival and return which is the epic of the Jew.

Jewish history is the saga of a people's will to live as Jews, of their steadfast devotion to the God of their fathers. Part of it is the remarkable story of return—again and again, individually and *en masse*—to *Eretz Yisrael,* the Land of Israel.

The destruction of the second Jewish kingdom (the northern kingdom, Israel, had been destroyed by the Assyrians in 722 B.C.E.) marked the end of Jewish independence. Eleven years before, Nebuchadnezzar, the mighty monarch of Babylonia, had conquered the southern kingdom, Judah. He had sent many of its leading families into exile and set the puppet, Zedekiah, on the throne. But when Zedekiah conspired with Egypt to shake off the Babylonian yoke, Nebuchadnezzar's armies overran Judah and destroyed its capital, Jerusalem. They laid the countryside in ruins, slaughtered thousands, and exiled thousands more.

This terrible destruction appeared to be the last act in the drama of Jewish history. By all the laws of logic, it was impossible to revive the Jewish faith, the Jewish people, or the Jewish state.

But several dedicated Jews refused to let physical defeat mean spiritual destruction. They refashioned Jewish practices and institutions so that their religion could be practiced even on alien soil, without the Holy Temple. The exiled Judeans clung to the faith of their fathers amid strange surroundings until the opportunity arose in 539 B.C.E. (with the reign of Cyrus of Persia) to return to Judea.

Our chief source of information on the destruction of the First Commonwealth is the *Tanach* (the Hebrew Bible). The *Book of Jeremiah,* which was recorded by Jeremiah's scribe and loyal friend, Baruch, contains a full description of the catastrophe which he lived through. It appears in *Nevi-im* (*Prophets*), the second section of the *Tanach.*

"So Judah was carried away captive out of his land."

AND ZEDEKIAH rebelled against the king of Babylon. And it came to pass in the ninth year of his reign, in the tenth month, in the tenth day of the month, that Nebuchadnezzar king of Babylon came, he and all his army, against Jerusalem, and encamped against it; and they built forts against it round about. So the city was besieged unto the eleventh year of King Zedekiah. In the fourth month, in the ninth day of the month, the famine was sore in the city, so that there was no bread for the people of the land. Then a breach was made in the city, and all the men of war fled, and went forth out of the city by night . . . and they went by way of the Arabah. But the army of the Chaldeans pursued after the king and overtook Zedekiah in the plains of Jericho; and all his army was scattered from him. Then they took the king and carried him up unto the king of Babylon to Riblah in the land of Hamath; and he gave judgment upon him. And the king of Babylon slew the sons of Zedekiah before his eyes; he slew also all the princes of Judah in Riblah. And he put out the eyes of Zedekiah; and . . . bound him in fetters, and carried him to Babylon, and put him in prison till the day of his death.

Now in the fifth month, in the tenth day of the month, which was the nineteenth year of King Nebuchadnezzar, king of Babylon, came Nebuzaradan the captain of the guard . . . into Jerusalem; and he burned the house of the LORD and the king's house; and all the houses of Jerusalem, even every great man's house, burned he with fire. And all the army of the Chaldeans, that were with the captain of the guard, broke down all the walls of Jerusalem round about. Then Nebuzaradan the captain of the guard carried away captive of the poorest sort of people, and the residue of the people that remained in the city, and those that fell away, that fell to the king of Babylon, and the residue of the multitude. But Nebuzaradan the captain of the guard left of the poorest of the land to be vinedressers and husbandmen. And the pillars of brass that were in the house of the LORD, and the bases and the brazen sea that were in the house of the LORD, did the Chaldeans break in pieces and carry all the brass of them to Babylon . . . and all the vessels of brass wherewith they ministered, took they away . . . that which was of gold, in gold, and that which was of silver, in silver. The two pillars, the one sea, and the twelve brazen bulls which King Solomon had made for the house of the LORD—the brass of all these was without weight. . . .

And the captain of the guard took Seriah the chief priest, and Zephaniah the second priest, and the three keepers of the door and . . . an officer that was set over the men of war; and seven men of them that saw the king's face, who were found in the city; and the scribe of the captain of the host, who mustered the people of the land; and threescore men of the people of the land, that were found in the midst of the city. And Nebuzaradan the captain of the guard took them, and brought them to the king of Babylon at Riblah. And the king of Babylon smote them and put them to death at Riblah in the land of Hamath. So Judah was carried away captive out of his land.

The Holy Scriptures
Jeremiah 52:3–27

JEREMIAH Grieves over the Destruction of Jerusalem, 586 B.C.E.

The *Book of Lamentations* provides us with some reliable eyewitness accounts of events. We find a vivid and heart-rending first-hand picture of fallen Jerusalem and of the feelings of those who lived through those tragic days.

Lamentations is one of the five *Megillot* in *Ketuvim* (*Writings*), the third section of the *Tanach*. It was composed, according to Jewish tradition, by the prophet Jeremiah. It is read in the synagogue on Tishah b'Av (the Ninth of *Av*), anniversary of the destruction of the Temple, which has been for 2,500 years a day of fasting and mourning to the Jews.

Jeremiah had foreseen the disaster and had long warned the people that God would punish them for their sins. Now his worst fears had come to pass. With a breaking heart he saw the Temple gutted by flames, the city burnt to the ground, thousands of his fellow Jews slain, and Judah's best citizens taken into exile. The Jewish state had come to an end.

Jeremiah put his utter woe and desolation into words, and the result was an enduring masterpiece. Throughout the long ages to this day, Jews have turned to *Lamentations* to express their most bitter sorrows. They have drawn upon his deep reservoirs of faith, remembering how the aged prophet had refused to give up and what he had done to save what was left of his people and their religion.

When we read the following excerpt from this great classic, we share Jeremiah's grief and horror at the fulfillment of his dread prophecies.

". . . Our days are numbered and over;
for our end has come."

AH! how the gold is dimmed
the gold so pure!
the sacred gems are scattered
over every street;

the priceless sons of Sion,
worth their weight in gold,
count no more than crockery,
mere pots of clay!

Even jackals give the breast,
their whelps they suckle;
but cruel are the women of my people
as the ostrich wild;

for the tongue of the nursling cleaves for thirst
to the roof of its mouth,
the children beg for food,
and no one gives it.

Those who fared on dainties
rot upon the street;
those who lay on scarlet rugs
huddle on an ash-heap.

The guilt of my people was greater
than even the sin of Sodom—
Sodom that fell in a flash,
ere any could wring his hands.

Her headmen were brighter than snow,
and whiter than milk,
ruddier than rubies,
their bodies veined like sapphires;

and now they look more darksome than the night—
none knows them as they pass—
their skin drawn tight over the bone,
dry as a stick.

Better to die by the sword
than by starving,
stabbed to death by hunger
suddenly in the field!

The hands of tender women
have sodden their own children—
making that their food,
amid the wreck.

The Eternal has carried out his fury,
venting his hot anger;
he has lit a fire in Sion
that burns her to the base.

None could believe, no king,
no man in all the world,
that foe or enemy could ever enter
inside Jerusalem.

It was all for the sin of her prophets,
for the crime of her priests,
who shed in her
the blood of the just.

Now, stained with blood, they wander
blindly about the streets,
brushing against men
they once avoided.

Men shout to them, "Begone! you are unclean!
begone! avoid us!"
So they stagger and wander abroad,
finding no shelter;

the Eternal himself has scattered them,
caring nothing for them,
regardless of the priests,
and heedless of the prophets.

Our eyes are strained and failing,
as we look for aid unavailing;
we are watching for a nation
that has never brought salvation.

Foes dog our steps,
we dare not walk abroad;
our days are numbered and over,
for our end has come.

More swift were our pursuers
than eagles of the air,
hunting us over the hills,
ambushing us on the wolds;

they trapped the king, the Eternal's choice,
the very breath of our lives,
of whom we said, "Under his reign
we shall hold out, among the nations!"

Rejoice and be glad in your home-land,
O maiden Edom!
But the cup will come round to you,
and leave you drunk and dishevelled.

Sion, your guilt is over and gone—
no more exile for you!
But, Edom, your guilt shall be punished,
your sins laid bare!

The Bible, A New Translation, by James Moffat
The Book of Lamentations 4:1–22

THE EXILES Return to Judea, 538 B.C.E.

The Jew of the twentieth century can well understand the excitement of a return to the Holy Land. Having witnessed the rebirth of the Jewish state in 1948, which opened the doors of Palestine to Jews scattered all over the globe, he can picture the emotions of that small band of Jews who undertook the long and hazardous journey to Judea in 538 B.C.E.

The returnees showed that love and dedication of the Jew to Zion survived time and distance. As in our own time, not all Jews returned to the Land of Israel. Many had attained wealth and position in Babylonia and established businesses or farms. Furthermore, the practical problems of rebuilding a land desolate for 48 years, since it was destroyed by Babylonia, were appalling. In view of the luxuries of life in Babylonia and the hardships and perils in Judea, it is remarkable that 48,000 Jews uprooted themselves from their homes of half a century to return to the land of their forefathers.

The return had been made possible by the decree in 539 B.C.E. of the great Cyrus of Persia, who had conquered Babylonia. The long hard journey took several months. Mainly on foot, their possessions loaded on donkeys and camels, the Jews traveled the long reaches between Judea and Babylonia, most of it barren, burning desert. When they finally reached their destination, they burst into songs of jubilation and thanksgiving. Not long after, they met great hardship in trying to restore the ruined land, but their faith held firm.

All this is recalled in Psalm 126, the song which was on the lips of the Jews who had come home.

*"They that sow in tears
shall reap in joy."*

WHEN the LORD brought back those that returned to Zion,
We were like men who dream.
Then was our mouth filled with laughter,
And our tongue with singing;
Then said they among the nations:
"The LORD has done great things for them."
Yes, the LORD has done great things for us;
And we are rejoiced.
Change our captivity, O LORD,
As the streams change the dry land.
They that sow in tears
Shall reap in joy.
Though he goes weeping as he bears the seed to the field,
He shall come home with joy, bearing his sheaves.

The Holy Scriptures
The Book of Psalms 126

NEHEMIAH Rebuilds the Wall of Jerusalem, 445 B.C.E.

The task of reclaiming a country is not easy. Indeed, the Babylonian Jews who returned to Judea after Cyrus' edict found it extremely difficult to restore fruitfulness to a land that had grown wild during their absence. The interference of hostile neighbors also went far towards dashing their hopes and dreams. Gradually, reports leaked back to Babylonia that the Jewish community in Judea was slowly dying.

Nehemiah, a Jew who occupied the high post of cupbearer to the Persian king, Artaxerxes, yearned to help his brethren in Judea. The king reluctantly granted him a leave of absence and gave him the title of military governor of Judea.

The new governor soon realized that the surrounding nations must be kept from entering the unwalled city of Jerusalem at will, free to interfere and disrupt. Nehemiah mobilized the Jews for the rebuilding of the wall. Nobles, priests, and even women joined in the work with a "sword by their side" to protect themselves against attack. Their enemies, led by Sanballat the Samaritan (the Horonite), Tobiah the Ammonite, and Geshem the Arabian, tried in vain to prevent the construction of the wall.

The wall was a necessary first step in restoring the Jewish state. It was soon followed by other religious, social, and economic reforms.

In the following selection from Nehemiah's autobiography, found in the biblical volume called by his name, the great military governor recounts the saga of the rebuilding of the wall of Jerusalem.

". . . Each of them worked with one hand and held a weapon in the other."

I SAID to them then, "You see the plight we are in, Jerusalem lying waste and the gates burned with fire. Come, let us rebuild the wall of Jerusalem, and we shall no longer be scoffed at." And I told them of God's kind favour to me, and also of what the king had said to me. So they said, "Let us start and build." And they set their hands bravely to the good work.

When Sanballat the Horonite and Tobiah the Ammonite slave and Geshem the Arabian heard it, they derided and despised us. "What are you doing?" they asked. "Are you rebelling against the king?" But I replied, "The God of heaven, He will give us success; so we His servants will start to build. But there is no property, no rights, no memorial for you in Jerusalem."

. . . When Sanballat heard that we were building the wall, he was angry and furious and scoffed at the Jews. He addressed his fellows and the army of the Samaritans thus: "What are these feeble Jews doing? Will they complete the rebuilding and then offer sacrifice? Can they do it all in a day? Can they recover stones from the rubbish heaps, when the stones are burned?" And Tobiah the Ammonite, who was beside him, added, "Let them build. If a fox stepped up, he would knock down that stone wall of theirs!"

Hear, O our God—for we are scorned—and turn their scoffs back upon their own heads; leave them to be plundered in the land of their exile; forgive not their iniquity, and let not their sin be blotted out before thee; for the builders have heard them provoking thee.

So we built the wall to half its height all round, for the heart of the people was in their work. But when Sanballat and Tobiah and the Arabians and the Ammonites and the Ashdodites heard that the repairs upon the walls of Jerusalem went forward, and that the breaches were being closed, they were extremely angry; they all conspired together to go and attack Jerusalem and make confusion in the city. But we offered prayer to our God and posted guards to watch them day and night. Judah said, "The strength of the labourers is giving way; the rubbish is great; we will never be able to build the wall." . . . And when the Jews who lived beside our enemies came in, they kept telling us, "They are gathering against us from all quarters."

The foe placed themselves in the low ground behind the wall, at the breaches; but I posted the people by companies, armed with sword and spear and bow. As I saw that they were afraid, I rose and addressed the authorities and the deputies and the rest of the people: "Have no fear of them, remember the Lord, who is great and terrible, and fight for your kinsfolk, your sons and your daughters, your wives and your homes."

Our foes heard that we knew of their plan, and God defeated their purpose; so we all went back to the wall, every man to his work. After that, half of my retinue went on with the work, and half wore their spears and shields and bows and coats of mail, to support all the community of Judah who were building the wall. The labourers were armed; each of them worked with one hand and held a weapon in the other. The masons were each girded with a sword, as they built. And the bugler stood beside me. I told the people, "The extent of the work is great, and we are far apart from each other on the wall; so, wherever you hear the bugle sounding, rally to us there. Our God will fight for us." This was how I and my men did our work; half held their spears from dawn until the stars appeared. I also told the citizens, "Let each of you, man and servant alike, keep inside Jerusalem, to provide us with guard duty at night and with labour during the day." As for myself and my retinue and the guard who followed me, none of us took off our clothes; each kept his weapon in his hand.

Now when Sanballat and Tobiah and Geshem the Arabian and the rest of our enemies heard that I had built the wall and that there was no breach left in it (though I had not yet erected the doors in the gateways), Sanballat and Geshem sent to ask me, "Come, let us meet at some village in the plain of Ono." They meant harm to me. But I sent messengers to them, saying, "I am doing a great work, and I cannot come down. Why should the work stop, while I leave it and come down to you?" They sent four times, to the same effect, and I answered them to the same effect. The fifth time Sanballat sent, his servant brought me an open letter. He wrote: "It is reported among the nations, and Geshem says so, that you and the Jews mean to rebel, and that this is why you are building the wall; you are to be their king—so people say. Now the king will be told what people say. So come and let us talk over the matter." Then I sent him this message: "Nothing of what you say has taken place; you are making it up, yourself!" (For they all wanted to terrify us; they thought, "Their hands will drop the work, and it will never be done." But now, strengthen Thou my hands!)

When I went to the house of Shemaiah the son of Delaiah, the son of Mehetabel, who kept himself apart, he said, "Let us meet in the house of God, in the temple, with shut doors, for they are coming to kill you—yes, coming to kill you by night!" But I said, "Is a man like me to run away? Besides, who would go into the temple, simply to save his life? I will not go in!" I detected at once that he had no mission from God; he was acting as a prophet against me, for Tobiah and Sanballat had bribed him, to terrify me into this act of sin, that it might be a scandal, and that they might sneer at me. O my God, remember all this against Tobiah and Sanballat and the prophetess Noadiah and the rest of the prophets who would have scared me!

On the twenty-fifth day of *Elul*, the wall was finished, in fifty-two days.

The Bible, A New Translation, by James Moffat
Nehemiah 2:17–4:23; 6:1–15

EZRA Reads the Torah to the Judeans, 444 B.C.E.

Because of their love of learning the Jews have been called the "People of the Book." No man was more responsible for this love than that pious Babylonian Jew, Ezra. A priest by descent and a scribe (which also meant "teacher") by profession, he moved to Judea about 458 B.C.E.

Ezra was shocked at the level of Jewish life he found there. The Jews were disrespectful toward the priests and neglectful of the temple service. Widespread intermarriage with pagan neighbors had introduced pagan ways.

As a scholar and teacher, Ezra believed that Judaism could be saved only by knowledge—knowledge of Torah and other sacred literature of the Jews. He started what amounts to the first public education program in history. On the first of *Tishri* (Rosh Hashanah), 444 B.C.E., he assembled the Jews and read the Torah to them. Until that time, knowledge had been the special province only of the priests.

Ezra proved himself a consummate teacher, second only to Moses himself. The people listened raptly for hours as he read to them of their history, obligations, and God-given destiny. Many wept when they realized how far they had strayed from the Law, and resolved to fulfill God's commandment thereafter.

That was the beginning of public reading of the Torah on Sabbath, Monday, and Thursday, festival and fast days, which became a fixed part, the "portion of the week," of Jewish religious services. Ezra's gift of knowledge to every Jew—a "second giving of the Torah"—changed Jewish history. A first-hand account of the event is in the biblical *Book of Nehemiah*.

". . . The joy of the LORD *is your strength."*

AND WHEN the seventh month was come, and the children of Israel were in their cities, all the people gathered themselves together as one man into the broad place that was before the water gate; and they spoke unto Ezra the scribe to bring the book of the Law of Moses, which the LORD had commanded to Israel. And Ezra the priest brought the Law before the congregation, both men and women, and all that could hear with understanding, upon the first day of the seventh month. And he read therein before the broad place that was before the water gate from early morning until midday, in the presence of the men and the women, and of those that could understand; and the ears of all the people were attentive unto the Book of the Law. And Ezra the scribe stood upon a pulpit of wood, which they had made for the purpose . . . And Ezra opened the book in the sight of all the people —for he was above all the people—and, when he opened it, all the people stood up. And Ezra blessed the LORD, the great God. And all the people answered: "Amen, Amen," with the lifting up of their hands; and they bowed their heads and fell down before the LORD with their faces to the ground. Also . . . the Levites caused the people to understand the Law; and the people stood in their place. And they read in the Book, in the Law of God, distinctly; and they gave the sense and caused them to understand the reading.

And Nehemiah, who was the Tirshatha [governor], and Ezra the priest the scribe, and the Levites that taught the people, said unto all the people: "This day is holy unto the LORD your God; mourn not, nor weep." For all the people wept when they heard the words of the Law. Then he said unto them: "Go your way, eat the fat, and drink the sweet, and send portions [charity] unto him for whom nothing is prepared; for this day is holy unto our LORD; neither be ye grieved, for the joy of the LORD is your strength." So the Levites stilled all the people, saying: "Hold your peace, for the day is holy; neither be ye grieved." And all the people went their way to eat, and to drink, and to send portions, and to make great mirth, because they had understood the words that were declared unto them.

The Holy Scriptures
Nehemiah 8:1–12

THE MISHNAH Depicts the Festival of the First-Fruits, Period of the Second Temple

Color, drama, and pageantry make up the fabric of traditional Jewish life. Through the centuries such festive ceremonials have enabled Jews to express in a concrete way the values and feelings that were important to them. The pilgrimage to Jerusalem bearing the first-fruits at Shavuot was one of the most notable.

In cities large and small, near and far, the bringing of the first-fruits to the Temple filled men with pious yearnings and eager anticipation. It was a time for dancing, singing, and praying. The nearer one came to the Holy City, the larger and more enthusiastic were the crowds. The roads became congested with travelers driving oxen and decorated cattle to be sacrificed. Numerous languages and dialects merged as Jews gathered from all over the world.

Now that the Temple is no more, the bringing of first-fruits as an expression of gratitude to God is a distant memory. The motivations for it—the desire to share one's bounty with others, to draw closer to God, and to acknowledge appreciation and dependence upon Him—remain, however, as the basic needs of the Jewish people, who seek to fulfill them in other ways.

The best description of the festival of the first-fruits comes from the *Mishnah,* a compendium of traditional Jewish doctrines, practices, and laws edited about 200 C.E. The following account of the festival in the days of the Second Temple conveys its excitement and color.

"Arise, and let us go up to Zion,
to the house of the Lord our God."

IN WHAT manner were the first-fruits [of the crop, an offering to the Temple] brought up? All the inhabitants of the towns of a district assembled in the principal city of the district; they spent the night in the market place of the city and entered no house. Early in the morning the appointed officer would proclaim: "Arise, and let us go up to Zion, to the house of the Lord our God."

They that lived in the vicinity would bring fresh figs and grapes; they that came from afar would bring dried figs and raisins. The bull [to be sacrificed] went before them, its horns overlaid with gold, and a garland of olive leaves on its head. The flute played before them. . . . When they drew near Jerusalem, they sent messengers before them. . . . The governors, deputies, and treasurers came out to meet them; according to the rank of those that entered did they come out. All the craftsmen of Jerusalem stood up before them and greeted them, saying: "Our brethren, ye men of such and such a place, ye are welcome."

The flute played before them, until they reached the temple mount. When they reached the temple mount, each man (even King Agrippa) put his basket upon his shoulders. Then they went in as far as the temple court. When they reached the temple court, the Levites recited the song: "I will extol Thee, O Lord, for Thou hast raised me up, and hast not suffered mine enemies to rejoce over me." [*Psalms* 30:2]

The pigeons which were fastened to the baskets were offered as sacrifices, while those which they held in their hands were given to the priests. . . .

The wealthy would bring their first-fruits in baskets of silver or of gold, while the poor would bring them in wicker baskets made of peeled willow twigs. The baskets and the first-fruits were given to the priests.

Post-Biblical Hebrew Literature, by Ben-Zion Halper
Mishnah Bikkurim 3:1–5; 8

AN UNKNOWN AUTHOR Writes about the Translating of the Septuagint, Third Century, B.C.E.

The tremendous impact of the Bible upon world civilization results in large measure from its translation into many languages. One of the earliest translations, the Greek rendering called the *Septuagint,* opened the study of the Hebrew Scriptures to the Western world. Allegedly it was commissioned by Ptolemy II, king of Egypt (285–245 B.C.E.), at the request of Demetrius, librarian of the Royal Library at Alexandria, in order to complete what was regarded as the finest library in the world.

After lengthy correspondence with the High Priest Eleazar, legend has it that Ptolemy sent his trusted officer Aristeas to Jerusalem to bring back a copy of the *Five Books of Moses,* along with men who could translate them into Greek. Aristeas brought back a scroll and 72 wise and saintly scribes who greatly impressed the Egyptian court with their learning and wisdom. The 72 scholars were placed in separate rooms and each undertook the entire translation by himself, a task that by coincidence took 72 days. When the 72 translations were compared, the allegedly miraculous outcome was that they all were identical, without the slightest divergence in letter or word. The proud king proclaimed the anniversary of the completion of the *Septuagint* (which means "seventy," in honor of the more than 70 scholars who worked on it) an annual holiday.

The story of this translation is found in a document called *The Letter of Aristeas,* which the king's officer is supposed to have written to his brother Philocrates. It is believed, however, to belong to a body of literature called the *Pseudepigrapha,* whose writers usually ascribed authorship of their works to better-known people so that the books would have greater influence. *The Letter of Aristeas* is thought to have been written by a Jew who credited it to a Greek in the hope that it would be more readily accepted. Here are excerpts from this fascinating tale.

"It was right, men of God, that I should first of all pay my reverence to the books . . ."

THE HIGH PRIEST selected men of the finest character and the highest culture, such as one would expect from their noble parentage. They were men who had not only acquired proficiency in Jewish literature but had studied most carefully that of the Greeks as well. . . . And one could observe how they loved Eleazar by their unwillingness to be torn away from him and how he loved them. For, besides the letter which he wrote to the king concerning their safe return, he also earnestly besought Andreas [chief of Ptolemy's bodyguard] to work for the same end and urged me, too, to assist to the best of my ability. And, although we promised to give our best attention to the matter, he said that he was still greatly distressed, for he knew that the king out of the goodness of his nature considered it his highest privilege, whenever he heard of a man who was superior to his fellows in culture and wisdom, to summon him to his court . . . But it was for the common advantage of all the citizens that he was sending them. For, he explained, the good life consists in the keeping of the enactments of the law, and this end is achieved much more by learning than by reading. . . .

And Eleazar, after offering the sacrifice, and selecting the envoys, and preparing many gifts for the king, despatched us on our journey in great security. And, when we reached Alexandria, the king was at once informed of our arrival . . . Andreas and I warmly greeted the king and handed over to him the letter written by Eleazar. The king was very anxious to meet the envoys and gave orders that all the other officials should be dismissed . . . Now this excited general surprise, for it is customary for those who come to seek an audience with the king on matters of importance to be admitted to his presence on the fifth day, while envoys from kings or very important cities with difficulty secure admission to the court in thirty days—but these men he counted worthy of greater honour, since he had held their master in such high esteem, and so he immediately dismissed those whose presence he regarded as superfluous . . . When they entered with the gifts . . . and the valuable parchments, on which the law was inscribed in gold in Jewish characters, for the parchment was wonderfully prepared and the connexion between the pages had been so effected as to be invisible, the king as soon as he saw them began to ask them about the books. And, when they had taken the rolls out of their coverings and unfolded the pages, the king stood still for a long time, and then making obeisance about seven times he said: "I thank you, my friends, and I thank him that sent you still more, and most of all God, whose oracles these are." And, when all the envoys, and the others who were present as well, shouted out at one time and with one voice: "God save the King!" he burst into tears of joy. For his exaltation of soul and the sense of the overwhelming honour which had been paid him compelled him to weep over his good fortune. He . . . said: "It was right, men of God, that I should first of all pay my reverence to the books for the sake of which I summoned you here and then, when I had done that, to extend the right-hand of friendship to you . . . I have enacted that this day, on which you arrived, shall be kept as a great day and it will be celebrated annually throughout my lifetime. It happens also that it is the anniversary of my naval victory over Antigonus. Therefore I shall be glad to feast with you to-day. . . ." After they had expressed their delight, he gave orders that the best quarters near the citadel should be assigned to them . . . And Nicanor summoned the lord high steward, Dorotheus, who was the special officer appointed to look after the Jews, and commanded him to make the necessary preparation for each one. . . .

. . . They met together daily in the place which was delightful for its quiet and its brightness and applied themselves to their task. The work of translation was completed in seventy-two days, just as if this had been arranged of set purpose.

When the work was completed, Demetrius collected together the Jewish population in the place . . . and read it over to all, in the presence of the translators, who met with a great reception also from the people, because of the great benefits which they had conferred upon them. They bestowed warm praise upon Demetrius, too, and urged him to have the whole law transcribed and present a copy to their leaders.

. . . The priests and the elders of the translators and the Jewish community and the leaders . . . said, that since so excellent and sacred and accurate a translation had been made, . . . no alteration should be made in it. And, when the whole company expressed their approval, they bade pronounce a curse . . . upon any one who should make any alteration either by adding or changing in any way whatever any of the words . . . or making any omission. This was a very wise precaution to ensure that the book might be preserved for all the future time unchanged.

"The Letter of Aristeas," translated by Herbert T. Andrews,
from *The Apocrypha and Pseudepigrapha of the Old Testament,*
edited by R. H. Charles

BEN SIRACH Reminisces on the Glory of the High Priest's Service, Second Century, B.C.E.

Most modern Jews feel that their forefathers' practice of sacrificing animals in the Holy Temple in Jerusalem can no longer be regarded as a meaningful or desirable way to worship God. Yet, in its day, it was a much more humane and sophisticated mode of worship than the idolatrous and often barbaric religious practices of the heathen peoples.

The ancient sacrificial cult was an impressive spectacle. A vivid and enthusiastic account of the temple service was penned by the scribe Joshua ben Sirach, in a book full of pithy and wise sayings which gave practical advice on how to live. Writing at a time when Greek influence had eroded the values and way of life of many Jews, Joshua ben Sirach tried to show the wisdom behind the old customs and traditions. Alarmed by the degeneration of the high priests, he held up as a model the brilliant record of Simon the Just, high priest from 300 to 270 B.C.E.

Simon the Just ranks as one of the most distinguished of Jewish leaders. He rebuilt the walls of Jerusalem, renovated the Temple, and assured the city's water supply even during drought or siege. Highly esteemed as a man of learning, he is credited with some of the most famous sayings in the *Talmud,* including the maxim, "The world rests on three things, on the Law, on Divine Service, and on Charity." (*Avot* 1:2)

In the following selection, recorded from authentic recollections of his period, Joshua ben Sirach describes Simon's august conduct of the temple worship.

"He made the court of
the sanctuary glorious."

IT WAS Simon, the son of Onias, the great priest,
Who in his lifetime repaired the house,
And in his days strengthened the sanctuary.
He laid the foundation for the height of the double wall,
The lofty substructure for the temple inclosure.
In his days a water cistern was hewed out,
A reservoir in circumference like the sea,
He took thought for his people to keep them from calamity,
And fortified the city against siege.
How glorious he was, surrounded by the people,
As he came out of the sanctuary!
Like the morning star among the clouds,
Like the moon when it is full;
Like the sun shining forth upon the sanctuary of the Most High;
Like the rainbow, showing itself among glorious clouds . . .
When he assumed his glorious robe,
And put on glorious perfection,
And when he went up to the holy altar,
He made the court of the sanctuary glorious.
And when he received the portions from the hands of the priests,
As he stood by the hearth of the altar,
With his brothers like a wreath about him,
He was like a young cedar on Lebanon,
And they surrounded him like the trunks of palm trees,
All the descendants of Aaron in their splendor,
With the Lord's offering in their hands,
Before the whole assembly of Israel;
And when he finished the service at the altars,
To adorn the offering of the Most High, the Almighty,
He stretched out his hand to the cup,
And poured out some of the blood of the grape;
He poured it out at the foot of the altar,

A fragrant odor unto the Most High, the King of All.
Then the descendants of Aaron shouted;
They sounded the trumpets of beaten work;
They made a great sound heard,
For a reminder, before the Most High.
Then all the people made haste together,
And fell upon their faces on the ground,
To worship their Lord,
The Almighty, the Most High.
The singers too praised him with their voices;
They made sweet music in the fullest volume.
And the people intreated the Lord Most High,
With prayer before him who is merciful,
Until the worship of the Lord should be finished,
And they completed his service.
Then he came down and lifted his hands,
Over the whole assembly of the descendants of Israel,
To pronounce the blessing of the Lord with his lips,
And to exult in his name.
And they prostrated themselves a second time,
To receive the blessing from the Most High.

Now bless the God of all,
Who in every way does great things;
Who exalts our days from our birth,
And deals with us according to His mercy.
May He give us gladness of heart,
And may there be peace in our days
In Israel, and through the days of eternity.
May He intrust His mercy to us,
And let Him deliver us in our days.

With two nations my soul is vexed,
And the third is no nation;
They who live on the mountain of Samaria, and the Philistines,
And the foolish people that live in Shechem.

Instruction in understanding and knowledge

Has Joshua, son of Sirach, son of Eleazar, of Jerusalem,
Written in this book,
Who poured forth wisdom from his mind.
Happy is he who concerns himself with these things,
And he that lays them up in his mind will become wise.
For if he does them, he will be strong for all things,
For the light of the Lord is his path.

The Wisdom of Ben Sirach 50:1–29,
from *The Apocrypha,* edited by Edgar J. Goodspeed

A HISTORIAN Recounts the Beginning of the Maccabean Revolt, 168 B.C.E.

Wherever human beings struggle for freedom, they can find courage in the story of the Maccabees. That small band of guerillas battled against huge odds for the right to live by their ancestral faith. Their revolt erupted after the anti-Jewish decrees of Antiochus IV, the Syrian monarch who controlled Judea.

The rebellion was born in 168 B.C.E. in the small town of Modin, when an aged Jewish priest named Mattathias refused to follow Syrian orders to sacrifice a pig to the pagan god Jupiter. The struggle that ensued was the first war for religious freedom in human history. Mattathias died not long after the rebellion began, but his five sons took up the cause. The eldest, Judah, called the *Maccabee* (meaning "hammer") because of his strength, became the leader. Within three years his forces had pushed the Syrians back on every front and recaptured the Temple in Jerusalem. After cleansing the Temple of paganism, the Jews rededicated it, beginning on the 25th of *Kislev* in 165 B.C.E., with an eight-day celebration which is the foundation of the observance of Chanukah today.

The Maccabean struggle was recorded in the *First Book of the Maccabees* by an eyewitness. It is part of a body of literature called the *Apocrypha,* which consists of Jewish religious books not included in the *Tanach.* The following selection from the *First Book of Maccabees* tells how the revolt began.

Modin, site where the Hasmonean rebellion began. (Israel Office of Information)

"Yet will I and my sons and my brethren walk in the covenant of our fathers."

IN THOSE days arose Mattathias the son of John, the son of Simeon, a priest of the sons of Joarib, from Jerusalem, and dwelt in Modin.

And he had five sons, Joannan, called Caddis: Simon, called Thassi: Judas, who was called Maccabeus: Eleazar, called Avaran: and Jonathan, whose surname was Apphus.

And when he saw the blasphemies that were committed in Judah and Jerusalem, he said, "Woe is me! Wherefore was I born to see this misery of my people, and of the Holy City, and to dwell there, when it was delivered into the hand of the enemy, and the sanctuary into the hand of strangers?

"Her temple is become as a man without glory.

"Her glorious vessels are carried away into captivity, her infants are slain in the streets, her young men with the sword of the enemy.

"What nation hath not had a part in her kingdom, and gotten of her spoils?

"All her ornaments are taken away; of a free woman she is become a bond slave.

"And, behold, our sanctuary, even our beauty and our glory, is laid waste, and the Gentiles have profaned it.

"To what end therefore shall we live any longer?"

Then Mattathias and his sons rent their clothes, and put on sackcloth, and mourned very sorely.

In the meanwhile the king's officers . . . came into the city Modin, to make them sacrifice.

And when many of Israel came unto them, Mattathias also and his sons came together.

Then answered the king's officers, and said to Mattathias on this wise, "Thou art a ruler and an honourable and great man in this city, and strengthened with sons and brethren:

"Now therefore come thou first, and fulfill the king's commandment, like as all the heathen have done, yea, and the men of Judah also, and such as remain at Jerusalem: so shalt thou and thy house be in the number of the king's friends, and thou and thy children shall be honoured with silver and gold, and many rewards."

Then Mattathias answered and spake with a loud voice, "Though all the nations that are under the king's dominion obey him, and fall away every one from the religion of their fathers, and give consent to his commandments:

"Yet will I and my sons and my brethren walk in the covenant of our fathers.

"God forbid that we should forsake the law and the ordinances.

"We will not hearken to the king's words, to go from our religion, either on the right hand, or the left."

Now when he had left speaking these words, there came one of the Jews in the sight of all to sacrifice on the altar which was at Modin, according to the king's commandment.

Which thing when Mattathias saw, he was inflamed with zeal, and his reins trembled, neither could he forbear to shew his anger according to judgment: wherefore he ran, and slew him upon the altar.

Also the king's commissioner, who compelled men to sacrifice, he killed at that time, and the altar he pulled down.

And Mattathias cried throughout the city with a loud voice, saying, "Whosoever is zealous of the law, and maintaineth the covenant, let him follow me."

So he and his sons fled into the mountains, and left all that ever they had in the city.

Then many that sought after justice and judgment went into the wilderness, to dwell there.

The First Book of Maccabees 2:1–29,
from *The Apocrypha and Pseudepigrapha of the Old Testament,*
edited by R. H. Charles

PHILO Reveals the Existence of the Therapeutae, First Century, B.C.E.

Today, when many young people choose to live in communes, we can understand why groups of Jews in Roman times isolated themselves in order to lead mystic and religious ways of life.

The first century before the Common Era was a period of great religious ferment. Partly in reaction to the harsh Roman rule, partly because of disappointment in Greek rationalism, a wave of Jewish mysticism arose, emphasizing the End of Days, an afterlife, and the coming of a Messiah who would bring about a better world.

About half of the world's Jews were living in Palestine (the name the Romans gave to Judea), the others in large metropolises of the Roman Empire—Rome, Damascus, Antioch, and Alexandria. The Diaspora Jews came to Jerusalem for the three major holidays and maintained close ties with their brethren in Palestine.

Religiously, Jews were of two major schools of thought: the Saducees, of the priestly aristocracy and the rich, and the Pharisees who were mainly the laity, democratic, progressive in the interpretation of the Law. The emerging communities of mystics were probably an offshoot of the Pharisees. Among them were the Essenes (a word that may mean "pious ones"). These fellowships generally tended toward asceticism, self-discipline, Torah study and prayer, and renunciation of private property. From this religious and social ferment arose the followers of Jesus, devout Jews who had no intention of starting a new religion.

Near Alexandria, Egypt, where over a million Jews lived, there was a sect known as the Therapeutae (Greek for "worshipers of God"). Fortunately, we have a first-hand account of the Therapeutae left by Philo, an Alexandrian Jewish philosopher who lived about 20 B.C.E. to 40 C.E. Member of a wealthy and aristocratic family in government circles, a statesman, philosopher, and writer, Philo was the foremost Jew of the Hellenistic period. His book, *On the Contemplative Life,* provides the only record we have of the Therapeutae and their life of mystic devotion and asceticism.

"They keep the memory of God alive . . ."

THE VOCATION of these philosophers is at once made clear from their title of Therapeutae . . . a name derived from a verb used in the sense of "worship" because nature and the sacred laws have schooled them to worship the self-existent . . .

They settle in a certain very suitable place which . . . is situated above the Mareotic Lake [south of Alexandria] on a somewhat low-lying hill very happily placed . . . The houses of the society thus collected are exceedingly simple, providing protection against two of the most pressing dangers, . . . the fiery heat of the sun and the icy cold of the air. They are neither near together as in towns, since living at close quarters is troublesome and displeasing to people who are seeking to satisfy their desire for solitude, nor yet at a great distance, because of the sense of fellowship which they cherish and to render help to each other if robbers attack them. In each house there is a consecrated room which is called a sanctuary or closet, and closeted in this they are initiated into the mysteries of the sanctified life. They take nothing into it, either drink or food or any other of the things necessary for the needs of the body, but laws and oracles delivered through the mouth of prophets and psalms and anything else which fosters and perfects knowledge and piety. They keep the memory of God alive and never forget it so that even in their dreams the picture is nothing else but the loveliness of divine excellences and powers . . . Twice every day they pray, at dawn and at eventide; at sunrise . . . they pray for a fine bright day, fine and bright in the true sense of the heavenly daylight which they pray may fill their minds. At sunset they ask that the soul may be wholly relieved from the press of the senses and . . . pursue the quest of truth. The interval between early morning and evening is spent entirely in spiritual exercise. They read the Holy Scriptures and seek wisdom from their ancestral philosophy by taking it as an allegory since they think that the words of the literal text are symbols of something whose hidden nature is revealed by studying the underlying meaning. They have also writings of men of old, the founders of their way of thinking . . . And they . . . also compose hymns and psalms to God in all sorts of metres and melodies which they write down with the rhythms necessarily made more solemn. For six days they seek wisdom by themselves in solitude in the closets mentioned above, never passing the outside door of the house or even getting a distant view of it. But every seventh day they meet together as for a general assembly and sit in order according to their age in the proper attitude, with their hands inside the robe, the right hand between the breast and the chin, and the left withdrawn along the flank. Then the senior among them who also has the fullest knowledge of the doctrines which they profess comes forward and with visage and voice alike quiet and composed gives a well-reasoned and wise discourse . . . This common sanctuary in which they meet every seventh day is a double enclosure, one portion set apart for the use of the men and the other for the women. For women, too, regularly make part of the audience with the same ardour and the same sense of their calling. The wall between the two chambers rises up from the ground to three or four cubits built in the form of a breastwork, while the space above up to the roof is left open. This arrangement serves two purposes; the modesty becoming to the female sex is preserved while the women sitting within earshot can easily follow what is said since there is nothing to obstruct the voice of the speaker.

They lay self-control to be as it were the foundation of their soul and on it build the other virtues. None of them would put food or drink to his lips before sunset since they hold that philosophy finds its right place in the light, the needs of the body in the darkness, and therefore they assign the day to the one and some small part of the night to the other. Some in whom the desire for studying wisdom is more deeply implanted even only after three days remember to take food; others . . . hold out for twice that time and only after six days do they bring themselves to taste such sustenance as is absolutely necessary . . . But to the seventh day as they consider it to be sacred and festal in the highest degree they have awarded special privileges as its due . . . Still they eat nothing costly, only common bread with salt for a relish flavoured further by the daintier with hyssop and their drink is spring water . . .

I will now describe the festal meetings . . . First of all these people assemble after seven sets of seven days have passed . . . This is the eve of the chief feast which Fifty (i.e. the feast of Pentecost) takes for its own . . . So then they assemble, white-robed and with faces in which cheerfulness is combined with the utmost seriousness, but before they recline . . . they take their stand in a regular line in an orderly way, their eyes and hands lifted up to heaven . . . and pray to God that their feasting may be acceptable and proceed as He would have it. After the prayers the seniors recline according to the order of their admission, since by senior they do not understand the aged and grey-headed . . . but those who have spent their prime in pursuing the contemplative branch of philosophy which indeed is the noblest and most godlike part. The feast is shared by women also, most of them aged virgins who have kept their chastity . . . of their own free will in their ardent yearning for wisdom. Eager to have her for their life mate they have spurned the pleasures of the body and desire no mortal offspring but those immortal children which only the soul that is dear to God can bring to the birth unaided because the Father has sown in her spiritual rays enabling her to behold the verities of wisdom. The order of reclining is so apportioned that the men sit by themselves on the right and the women by themselves on the left . . . Their seats are plank beds of the common kinds of wood, covered with quite cheap strewings of native papyrus, raised slightly at the arms to give something to lean on . . . They do not have slaves to wait upon them as they consider that the ownership of servants is entirely against nature. For nature has borne all men to be free, but the wrongful and covetous acts of some who pursued that source of evil, inequality, have imposed their yoke and invested the stronger with power over the weaker. In this sacred banquet there is as I have said no slave, but the services are rendered by free men who perform their tasks as attendants not under compulsion not yet waiting for orders but with deliberate goodwill anticipating eagerly and zealously the demands that may be made. For it is not just any free men who are appointed for these offices but young members of the association chosen with all care for their special merit who as becomes their good character and nobility are pressing on to reach the summit of virtue. They give their services gladly and proudly like sons to their real fathers and mothers, judging them to be the parents of them all in common, in a closer affinity than that of blood, since to the right-minded there is no closer tie than noble living. And they came in to do their office ungirt and with tunics hanging down, that in their appearance there may be no shadow of anything to suggest the slave . . . No wine is brought (abstinence from wine is enjoined to them for their lifetime) but only water of the brightest and clearest, cold for most of the guests but warm for such of the older men as live delicately. The table, too, is kept pure from the flesh of animals; the food laid on it is loaves of bread with salt as a seasoning, sometimes also flavoured with hyssop as a relish for the daintier appetites. . . . Such are the preliminaries. But when the guests have laid themselves down arranged in rows, as I have described, and the attendants have taken their stand with everything in order ready for their ministry, the president of the company, when a general silence is established . . . discusses some question arising in the Holy Scriptures or solves one that has been propounded by someone else. His instruction proceeds in a leisurely manner, he lingers over it and spins it out with repetitions, thus permanently imprinting the thoughts in the souls of the hearers . . . His audience listens attentively . . . signifying comprehension and understanding by nods and glances, praise of the speaker by the cheerful change of expression . . . difficulty by a gentler movement of the head and by pointing with a finger tip of the right hand. The young men standing by show no less attentiveness than the occupants of the couches. The exposition of the Sacred Scriptures treats the inner meaning conveyed in allegory. For to these people the whole law book seems to resemble a living creature with the literal ordinances for its body and for its soul the invisible mind laid up in its wording. It is in this mind especially that the rational soul begins to contemplate the things akin to itself and looking through the words as through a mirror beholds the marvellous beauties of the concepts, unfolds and removes the symbolic coverings, and brings forth the thoughts and sets them bare to the light of day for those who need but a little reminding to enable them to discern the inward and hidden through the outward and visible. When then the president thinks he has discoursed enough and both sides feel sure that they have attained their object . . . universal applause arises showing a general pleasure in the prospect of what is still to follow. Then the president rises and sings a hymn composed as an address to God, either a new one of his own composition or an old one by poets of an earlier day who have left behind them hymns in many measures and melodies . . . After him all the others take their turn as they are arranged and in the proper order while all the rest listen in complete silence except when they have to chant the closing lines or refrains, for then they all lift up their voices, men and women alike. When everyone has finished his hymn the young men bring in the tables mentioned a little above on which is set the truly purified meal of leavened bread seasoned with salt mixed with hyssop, out of reverence for the holy table enshrined in the sacred vestibule of the temple on which lie loaves and salt without condiments, the loaves unleavened and the salt unmixed . . .

After the supper they hold the sacred vigil which is conducted in the following way. They rise up all together and standing in the middle of the refectory form themselves first into two choirs, one of men and one of women, the leader and precentor chosen for each being the most honoured amongst them and also the most musical. Then they sing hymns to God composed of many measures and set to many melodies, sometimes chanting together, sometimes taking up the harmony antiphonally, hands and feet keeping time in accompaniment, and rapt with enthusiasm reproduce sometimes the lyrics of the procession, sometimes of the halt and of the wheeling and counter-wheeling of a choric dance. Then . . . they mix and both together become a single choir, a copy of the choir set up of old beside the Red Sea in honour of the wonders there wrought. For at the command of God the sea became a source of salvation to one party and of perdition to the other. As it broke in twain and withdrew under the violence of the forces which swept it back there rose on either side, opposite to each other, the semblance of solid walls, while the space thus opened between them broadened into a highway smooth and dry throughout on which the people marched under guidance right on until they reached the higher ground on the opposite mainland. But when the sea came rushing in with the returning tide, and from either side passed over the ground where dry land had appeared, the pursuing enemy were submerged and perished. This wonderful sight and experience, an act transcending word and thought and hope, so filled with ecstasy both men and women that forming a single choir they sang hymns of thanksgiving to God their Saviour, the men led by the prophet Moses and the women by the prophetess Miriam. It is on this model above all that the choir of the Therapeutae of either sex, note in response to note and voice to voice, the treble of the women blending with the bass of the men, create an harmonious concert, music in the truest sense. Lovely are the thoughts, lovely the words, and worthy of reverence the choristers, and the end and aim of thought, words, and choristers alike in piety. Thus they continue till dawn, drunk with this drunkenness in which there is no shame, then not with heavy heads or drowsy eyes but more alert and wakeful than when they came to the banquet they stand with their faces and whole body turned to the East and when they see the sun rising they stretch their hands up to heaven and pray for bright days and knowledge of the truth and the power of keen-sighted thinking. And after the prayers they depart each to his private sanctuary once more . . . So much then for the Therapeutae who have taken to their hearts the contemplation of nature and what it has to teach and have lived in the soul alone . . .

From *On the Contemplative Life,* by Philo,
as quoted in *Philosophical Writing,*
Philo Selections, edited by Hans Lewy

OUR SAGES Tell of the Founding of the Academy at Yavneh, 70 C.E.

If not for the foresight of Johanan ben Zakkai, one of the greatest of Jewish statesmen, the destruction of Jerusalem by the Romans in 70 C.E. might have meant the end of Judaism. Believing that political independence was not as important as the spiritual task—the preservation and teaching of the *Torah*—this wise teacher disapproved of the revolt against Rome in 66 C.E.

During the siege of Jerusalem, Johanan ben Zakkai made a daring plan to ensure that physical defeat would not mean spiritual destruction. He determined to ask the Roman general, Vespasian, to let him start an academy where he could teach the *Torah* after Jerusalem fell. Since the Jewish zealots allowed only the dead to leave Jerusalem, Johanan's disciples announced that he had died, and they got permission to bury him outside the city. Once through the city gates, Johanan rose from his coffin and journeyed to the Roman camp. He persuaded Vespasian to let him open a school in the coastal town of Yavneh. After Jerusalem had been reduced to stubble and ashes, it was this school that sparked a national revival, transmitted Jewish teachings, and created new ways to meet the changed circumstances, so that Jewish life could survive. Johanan ben Zakkai's statesmanship was as essential to the preservation of Judaism as were the deeds of Moses, Joshua, and David.

The fascinating account of Johanan ben Zakkai's escape and of his dialogue with Vespasian is contained in the talmudic tractate of *Gittin,* of which a portion is presented here.

"Give me Yavneh and its Wise Men."

THE *biryonim* [rebels, terrorists] were then in the city. The rabbis said to them: "Let us go out and make peace with them [the Romans]." They would not let them, but on the contrary said, "Let us go out and fight them." The rabbis said: "You will not succeed." They then rose up and burnt the stores of wheat and barley so that a famine ensued. . . .

Abba Sikra, the head of the *biryonim* in Jerusalem, was the son of the sister of Rabban Johanan ben Zakkai, who sent to him saying, "Come to visit me privately." When he came he said to him, "How long are you going to carry on in this way and kill all the people with starvation?" He replied: "What can I do? If I say a word to them, they will kill me." He [Johanan ben Zakkai] said: "Devise some plan for me to escape. Perhaps I shall be able to save a little." He [Abba Sikra] said to him: "Pretend to be ill, and let everyone come to inquire about you. Bring something evil-smelling and put it by you so that they will say you are dead. Let then your disciples get under your bed, but no others, so that they shall not notice that you are still light, since they know that a living being is lighter than a corpse." He did so, and Rabban Eliezer went under the bier from one side and Rabban Joshua from the other. When they reached the door, some men wanted to put a lance through the bier. He said to them: "Shall [the Romans] say, 'They have pierced their Master?' " They wanted to give it a push. He said to them: "Shall they say that they pushed their Master?" They opened a town gate for him and he got out.

When he [Johanan ben Zakkai] reached the Romans he said, "Peace to you, O king, peace to you, O king." He [Vespasian] said: "Your life is forfeit on two counts, one because I am not a king and you call me king; and again, if I am a king, why did you not come to me before now?" He replied: "As for your saying that you are not a king, in truth you are a king, since, if you were not a king, Jerusalem would not be delivered into your hand, as it is written, 'And Lebanon shall fall by a mighty one.' 'Mighty One' [is] applied only to king, as it is written, 'And their mighty one shall be of themselves'; and Lebanon refers to the Sanctuary, as it says, 'This goodly mountain and Lebanon.' As for your question, 'Why if you are a king, did I not come to you till now?' the answer is that the *biryonim* among us did not let me." He [Vespasian] said to him: "If there is a jar of honey around which a serpent is wound, would they not break the jar to get rid of the serpent?" He [Johanan] could give no answer. Rabban Joseph, or as some say Rabban Akiba, applied to him the verse, "[God] turneth wise men backward and maketh their knowledge foolish." He ought to have said to him: "We take a pair of tongs and grip the snake and kill it, and leave the jar intact."

At this point a messenger came to him [Vespasian] from Rome saying, "Up! For the Emperor is dead, and the notables of Rome have decided to make you head [of state]." He had just finished putting on one boot. When he tried to put on the other he could not. He tried to take off the first, but it would not come off. He said: "What is the meaning of this?" Rabban Johanan said to him: "Do not worry: the good news has done it, as it says, 'Good tidings make the bones fat.' What is the remedy? Let someone whom you dislike come and pass before you, as it is written, 'A broken spirit drieth up the bones.' " He did so, and the boot went on. He [Vespasian] said to him: "Seeing that you are so wise, why did you not come to me till now?" He said: "Have I not told you?" He retorted: "I, too, have told you."

He [Vespasian] said: "I am now going, and will send someone to take my place. You can, however, make a request of me and I will grant it." He said to him: "Give me Yavneh and its Wise Men" [that is, give me leave to found a school at Yavneh], and the family chain of Rabban Gamaliel [that is, spare the dynasty of the House of David] . . . Rabban Joseph, or some say Rabban Akiba, applied to him the verse, "[God] turneth wise men backward and maketh their knowledge foolish." He ought to have said to him: "Let them [the Jews] off this time." He, however, thought that so much he would not grant, and so even a little would not be saved.

Seder Nashim, Gittin 5, edited by Rabbi Dr. I. Epstein,
from *The Babylonian Talmud*

JOSEPHUS Views the Sacking of the Second Temple, 70 C.E.

The destruction of Jerusalem by the Romans in 70 C.E. was the greatest calamity in Jewish history. In its wake came slaughter, famine, and exile. It was responsible for the historic tragedy of Jewish dispersion, 2,000 years of hapless and helpless wandering over the face of the globe, and the spectres of homelessness and anti-Semitism that left no Jew untouched. The Jewish people has never gotten over this tragedy nor ceased to mourn the loss of its Temple. Commemorated in the observance of Tishah b'Av, it is remembered to this day with fasting, prayer, and mourning.

The Roman triumph was hard-won. It was no token resistance that the vastly outnumbered Jews offered. Victory came only after seven years of bitter fighting in which the Jews hurled themselves again and again against the Roman legions with such ferocity that more than once the tide of battle nearly turned. A record of this long and fearful struggle was made by the Roman historian, Flavius Josephus, who was born a Jew and lived through many of the battles.

For almost 2,000 years Josephus has been a great riddle. Was he a renegade, or merely prudent? Did he sacrifice his honor for self-preservation, or to preserve the reputable name of the Jews? Did he write as a Jewish patriot, or as an apologist for his people?

Born Joseph ben Mattathias in 37 B.C.E., he lived through a period of upheaval and change. In his lifetime he was patronized by the Romans; after his death he was exalted by the Christians, who have regarded him as *the* historian of the Jews *par excellence*. And in recent times, Josephus, long anathematized by his people for his despicable and traitorous conduct, has been readmitted into the gallery of Jewish notables and has become a subject of careful study.

During the ill-fated rebellion against Rome which began in 66 C.E., Josephus, just 21, was commander of the Galilee. Suspected of duplicity, he was almost removed from his post. He led the defense of Jodephath, an important fort, but the legions of Vespasian prevailed. Josephus hid in a cave with forty companions who would not let him surrender. They decided to die together, each by the hand of his brother, the last to take his own life. Josephus managed to be last, and then gave himself up to the Romans. He prophesied that Vespasian would be emperor, which proved correct, winning him the imperial favor. He returned in honor to Rome with Titus, received a pension, and lived in the imperial palace.

Taking the name of Flavius in gratitude to the Flavian emperors, he wrote several important works about the Jews. His book, *The Wars of the Jews,* from which the excerpt below is taken, blames a few fanatics for the rebellion of 66. *Against Apion* effectively refutes allegations against the Jews made by the anti-Semite Apion. In *Antiquities of the Jews* he tells the story of his people with great affection and reverence. Although his history does not meet modern scientific standards, his embellishments of the biblical narrative and his taking of excerpts from earlier works without citation were common in his day. He was a learned man and, but for him, much of Jewish history would have been forgotten.

"And now they spared not their lives any longer, nor suffered anything to restrain their force, since that holy house was perishing . . ."

SO TITUS resolved to storm the Temple next day early in the morning with his whole army, and to encamp round about the holy house; but, as for that house, God had for certain long ago

Arch of Titus, Rome, Italy. (Photo, F. Lli Alinari)

Procession of Roman soldiers carrying the seven-branched candlestick, the table of the shewbread, and the silver trumpets taken at the capture of Jerusalem, by Titus. (From a marble relief on the Arch of Titus)

doomed it to the fire; and now that fatal day was come: . . . it was the tenth day of the month *Lous* [*Ab*] upon which it was formerly burnt by the king of Babylon; . . . the seditious [the rebels] . . . attacked the Romans again, when those that guarded the holy house fought with those that quenched the fire that was burning in the inner court of the Temple; but these Romans put the Jews to flight, and proceeded as far as the holy house itself. At which time one of the soldiers, without staying for any orders, and . . . hurried on by a certain divine fury, snatched somewhat out of the materials that were on fire, and . . . set fire to a golden window. . . . As the flames went upward the Jews made a mighty clamour . . . and ran together to prevent it; and now they spared not their lives any longer, nor suffered anything to restrain their force, since that holy house was perishing, for whose sake it was that they kept such a guard about it.

And now a certain person came running to Titus, and told him of this fire; . . . whereupon he rose up in great haste and, as he was, ran to the holy house. . . . Then did Caesar [Titus] both by calling to the soldiers that were fighting, with a loud voice, and by giving a signal to them with his right hand, order them to quench the fire; but they did not hear what he said . . . having their ears already dinned by a great noise another way; nor did they attend to the signal he made . . . ; but as for the legions that came running hither, neither any persuasions nor any threatenings could restrain their violence, but each one's own passion was his commander . . . many of them were trampled on by one another, while a great number fell among the ruins of the cloisters, which were still hot and smoking, and were destroyed in the same miserable way with those whom they had conquered. . . . As for the seditious . . . they were everywhere slain and everywhere beaten; and as for a great part of the people, they were weak and without arms, and had their throats cut wherever they were caught. Now, round about the altar lay dead bodies heaped upon one another; as at the steps going to it ran a great quantity of blood, whither also the dead bodies of those that were slain on the altar above rolled down.

And now, since Caesar was in no way able to restrain the enthusiastic fury of his soldiers, and . . . he went into the holy place of the Temple, with his commanders, and saw it, with what was in it, which he found to be far superior to what the relatings of foreigners contained . . . and he came in haste and endeavoured to persuade the soldiers to quench the fire, and gave orders to . . . beat the soldiers that were refractory with their staves, and restrain them! Yet were their passions too hard . . . as was their hatred for the Jews . . . Moreover, the hope of plunder induced many of them to go on, as having this opinion, that all the places within were full of money . . .

While the holy house was on fire, everything was plundered that came to hand and ten thousand of those that were caught were slain; nor was there a commiseration of any age, or any reverence of gravity; but children, and old men, and profane persons, and priests, were all slain in the same manner; so that this war went round all sorts of men, and brought them to destruction. . . . And because this hill was high . . . one would have thought that the whole city was on fire. Nor can any one imagine anything either greater or more terrible than this noise; for there was at once a shout of the Roman legions . . . and a sad clamour of the seditious, who were now surrounded with fire and sword. . . . The multitude also that was in the city joined in this outcry . . . and besides many of those that were worn away with the famine . . . when they saw the fire of the holy house, they exerted their utmost strength, and broke out into groans and outcries again. . . . Yet was the misery itself more terrible than the disorder, for one would have thought that the hill itself, upon which the Temple stood, was seething hot . . . that the blood was larger in quantity than the fire and those that were slain more in number than those that slew them; for the ground did nowhere appear visible, for the dead bodies that lay upon it: but the soldiers went over the heaps of these bodies, as they ran upon such as fled from them.

From *The Wars of the Jews*, by Flavius Josephus

JUSTINIAN Proscribes Interpretation of the Torah, 553

Justinian I (527–565), emperor of the Eastern Roman (or Byzantine) empire, tried to make the practice of Judaism so difficult that the Jews would give up their ancient faith. Attacks on synagogues were permitted to occur with great frequency, while the law forbade the construction of new synagogues and allowed only repair of the old. Jews could not hold high office and were placed at a disadvantage in non-Jewish courts of law. They were forbidden to proselytize, even among their own slaves.

Even worse, Justinian interfered with what went on inside the synagogue. He told the Jews which Greek translation of the *Tanach* they could use. He prohibited interpretation of the Bible—a particularly odious decree, since the imaginative, hope-inspiring interpretations known as *Midrash* helped Jews persevere even in the face of oppression. Because the *Midrashim* conflicted with the Church's interpretations of the Bible, they aroused the ire of the emperor and the Christian clergy whose bidding he was always prepared to do.

Despite Justinian's ban, the Jews managed to keep alive this essential facet of biblical study.

In the selection below, Justinian, in his own words, proscribes scriptural interpretation.

". . . Beware of the wickedness of their interpreters."

THE EMPEROR Justinian to Aerobindus, the most honourable Praefectus Praetorio.

Preamble

The Jews, when they heard the *Holy Scriptures,* ought not to have clung to the mere letter but should have turned their attention to the hidden prophecies which foretell the great God and Saviour of the human race, Jesus Christ. But although they have given themselves over to irrational explanations and have, to this day, gone astray from the true interpretation, when we heard they were divided among themselves we could not leave their differences unresolved. For we have learned that some hold to the Hebrew language and wish to use it alone for the reading of the *Holy Scriptures* whereas others wish to use the Greek language as well. . . . We have found those more praiseworthy who wish to have the assistance of the Greek language for the reading of the *Holy Scriptures* (or, indeed, any language which . . . is better understood by the audience).

Chapter I

We therefore decree that, wherever there are Jews who so desire, the *Holy Scriptures* may be read in the synagogues in Greek (or in our mother tongue [that is, in Latin] or in any other language which suits the place where the reading is given) so that the text may be understood by those present. . . . The Jewish interpreters . . . shall not be allowed to corrupt the Hebrew text on account of their being the only ones who understand it. . . . Those, however, who read in Greek are to use the *Septuagint,* the most accurate translation of all, which is to be preferred especially because of the miracle which occurred when it was made, the translators, working only in pairs and in different places, producing one and the same text. . . . But we strictly forbid what they call *Deuterosis* [biblical interpretation], as it is neither included in the *Holy Scriptures* nor transmitted of old through the Prophets but is an invention of men who spoke merely with earthly wisdom and were not divinely inspired. They shall read the holy words themselves, opening the *Holy Scriptures* with their own hands, and hiding nothing of what is written by adding worthless and vain phrases of their own. . . . Nor shall those called Archipherekitae or elders or teachers be entitled to prevent this by cunning or by curse, unless they wish to be made wise by corporal punishment and to forfeit their property to us. . . .

Chapter II

But if any of them dare introduce godless and vain teachings denying the Resurrection, the Last Judgement, or that the angels are the work and creation of God, it is our will that he shall be expelled from every place. . . . For those who dare say such things shall be subjected to the most severe penalties so that we may thereby purge the Jewish people of the error thus introduced.

Chapter III

We wish to admonish those who hear the *Holy Scriptures* read . . . to beware of the wickedness of their interpreters; they should not cling to the letter, but penetrate into the matter itself and grasp the truly divine sense so that they may come to know what is better, and finally cease to err and sin. . . . For everybody will agree that a man who has been brought up in the *Holy Scriptures* . . . will be much more able to distinguish and choose what is better than one who knows nothing of Scripture but only clings to the name of divine service, . . . believing to be divine doctrine what in reality must be termed sheer heresy.

Epilogue

This our will and what is decreed by the present sacred law is not only to be observed by your Highness and those under you but by everyone who holds the same office. Under no circumstances shall he permit the Jews to undertake anything against it; he shall rather subject those who dare to resist it or hinder it in any way to corporal punishment first, then force them to live in exile and confiscate their property. . . . He shall also send orders to the provincial prefects, commanding them to obey our law and to publish it in every town when they have realized that everybody must necessarily observe it for fear of arousing our displeasure.

Given at Constantinople, 13th February, in the 26th year of the reign of the Emperor Justinian, in the 12th of the consulate of Basilius, V.CL. (=AD 553).

Novella 146, from the year 553,
from *The Cairo Geniza,* by Paul E. Kahle

A KARAITE Explains How the Sect Was Born, Eighth Century

During the long years of the Diaspora, different schools of thought arose in Judaism. Some left an indelible mark on Jewish practice, while others were shortlived.

The Karaites were a sect which denied the authority of all religious teaching since the *Tanach*. The very name, "Karaite," means "scripturalist" (from the Hebrew word for Bible, *mikra*), one who believes solely in the Bible.

According to this sect, the rabbis and the *geonim* (heads of the academies) had distorted the meaning of many biblical statements and every Jew should study the *Tanach* carefully in order to ascertain for himself its true meaning. As they saw it, every Jew had a right to interpret the Bible in his own way. Hence, each man constituted for himself the ultimate authority for understanding *Torah.*

Although Karaism still survives in a few isolated communities, it declined sharply in the tenth century after Saadia Gaon pointed out its fallacies and contradictions. He showed, for example, that, although condemning the rabbis for developing traditions outside the *Tanach,* the Karaites did the same thing, except that their traditions were inferior. Moreover, by resting the final authority for interpreting the Bible in each individual Jew, they threatened to undermine Jewish unity and replace it with anarchy and chaos.

The Karaitic movement was founded in the eighth century by Anan ben David, a nephew of the exilarch in Babylonia. Annoyed that on the death of his uncle he was passed over for the post of exilarch in favor of a younger brother, Anan criticized the *geonim,* the *Talmud,* and the rabbis in general. As a result, he was thrown into prison as a rebel against the caliph's government. To save himself, Anan argued that he was not opposing the organized Jewish community but founding a new religion. The caliph accepted this contention and freed Anan, who then undertook his battle against traditional Judaism in earnest.

The story of the founding of the Karaitic sect is contained in a tract by a twelfth-century Karaite, Elijah ben Abraham. Although some claim that Saadia Gaon is its true author, there is no definite internal evidence to support that assumption.

"Anan undertook also to deceive his own followers."

ANAN HAD a younger brother named Hananiah. Although Anan exceeded this brother in both learning and age, the contemporary rabbanite scholars refused to appoint him exilarch, because of his great lawlessness and lack of piety. They therefore turned to his brother Hananiah, for the sake of the latter's great modesty, retiring disposition, and fear of Heaven, and they set him up as exilarch. Thereupon Anan was seized with a wicked zeal—he and with him all manner of evil and worthless men set up a dissident sect—in secret, for fear of the Moslem government which was then in power—and they appointed Anan their own exilarch.

On a certain Sunday, however, the affair was discovered by the government, and the order was given that Anan be imprisoned until the following Friday, when he was to be hanged on the gallows as a political rebel. In prison Anan came upon a Moslem scholar who was also confined there and was likewise to be hung on the same Friday, as a violator of the Mohammedan faith. This scholar advised Anan, saying, "Are there not in the Law ordinances admitting of two contradictory interpretations?" "Indeed there are," answered Anan. "Observe then," said the Moslem scholar, "the interpretation accepted in the teaching of those who follow your brother and take the other interpretation for yourself, providing that those who follow you will back you up in it. Then give a bribe to the viceroy so that you might perchance be permitted to speak in your defense, after which prostrate yourself before the caliph and say: 'O my Lord the King! Did you set up my brother to rule over one religion or over two?' Upon his replying: 'Over one religion only,' say to him further: 'But I and my brother belong to two different religions!' Of a certainty you will save yourself, providing you explain to him the difference between your religion and that of your brother, and providing your followers back you up. Say these things, and when the king hears them he will say nothing further about your execution."

Anan undertook also to deceive his own followers and said to them: "Last night Elijah the prophet appeared before me in a dream and said to me, 'You deserve to be put to death for violating that which is written in the Law.'" [Presumably, for not breaking openly with rabbanite synagogue.] He spoke thus to them in order to entice them with his crafty argumentation and out of fear for his life so that he might save himself from a cruel death and might perpetuate his name in eternity. He also expended a great sum of money in bribes, until the king gave him permission to speak, whereupon he said, "The religion of my brother employs a calendar based upon calculation of the time of the new moon and intercalation of leap years by cycles, whereas mine depends upon actual observation of the new moon and intercalation regulated by the ripening of new grain." Since the king's religion likewise employed the latter method, Anan thus gained his favor and good will.

From the *Karaite Anthology,* by Leon Nemoy

AMRAM GAON Sets a Formal Order of Prayers, 869

How the Jewish people retained its unity despite its dispersion to the four corners of the earth is one of the marvels of history. One factor was the practice of referring questions to the greatest rabbis of the time, which provided to Jews scattered across the globe uniform guidance by a central authority. Thus, the *responsum* to a Spanish congregation in 860 C.E. by Rav Amram, *gaon* (head) of the Sura academy (the preeminent teacher of his generation), established an order of prayer that was followed until about a century ago by all Jews everywhere.

Although the arrangement of many of the basic prayers had been formulated many centuries before, local communities had continuously inserted additional psalms and original poetic compositions, causing a great deal of confusion. The inquiry of a community, bewildered over what prayers to say and in what order, occasioned the arrangement of prayers that became known as the *Siddur* or *Seder* of Rav Amram.

The answer was sent to other Jewish settlements for an authoritative statement on the order of prayer.

Rav Amram based part of his answer on a *responsum* by his predecessor, Gaon Natronai. Similarly, the later *gaon,* Rav Saadia, leaned heavily on Rav Amram's *responsum.* Although Amram's answer was referred to by all later religious leaders, the *responsum* itself was not available in modern times until a copy was chanced on in Hebron in the nineteenth century. The section which follows deals with the hundred benedictions that observant Jews are supposed to recite every day.

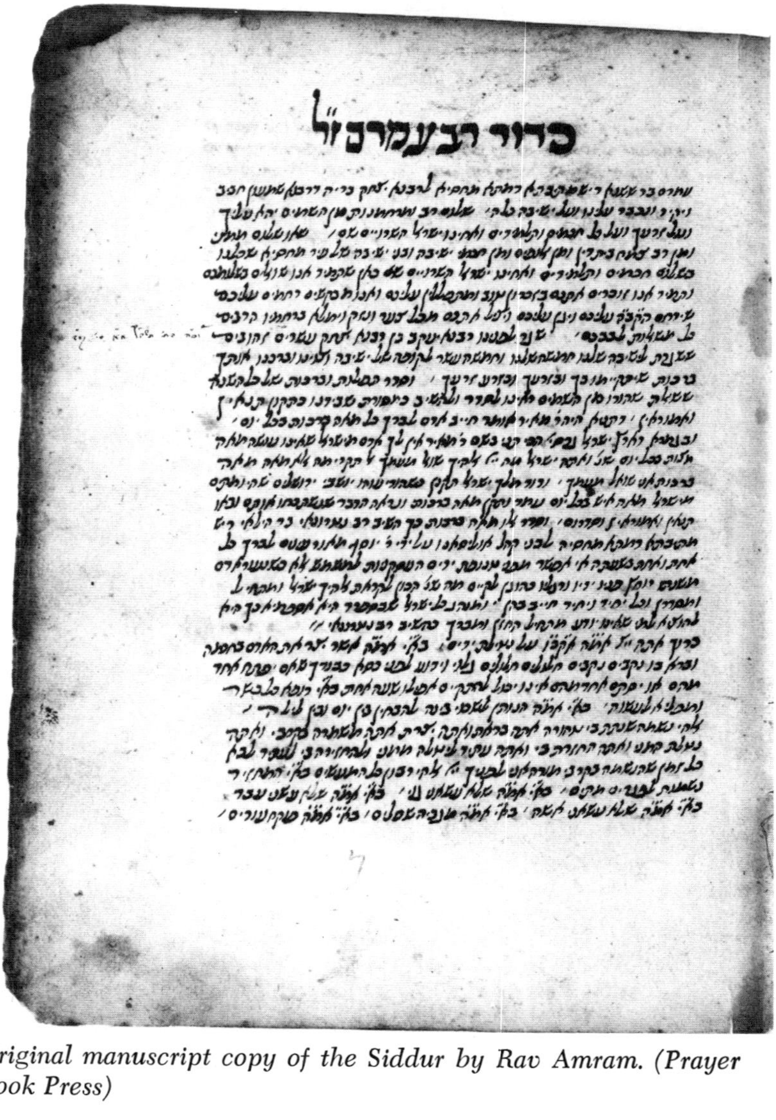

סדור רב עמרם ז"ל

Original manuscript copy of the Siddur by Rav Amram. (Prayer Book Press)

"We give you answer according to the tradition which exists in our possession."

AMRAM, the son of Sheshna, head of the school at Mata Mehasia [Sura], to Rabbi Isaac, the son of the teacher and rabbi, Simon, beloved, dear and honored by us and the entire college. Great peace from the Mercy of Heaven be upon thee and all thy seed and upon all the sages and scholars and our brethren of Israel who dwell there. Accept greetings of peace from me and Rab Zemah, the chief judge of Israel, and from the comrades and sages of the college and the members of our college and of the city of Mehasia, and the sages and the scholars and the children of Israel who dwell here . . . May He in His great mercies fulfill all the desires of your heart. Rabbi Jacob, the son of Isaac, has transmitted to us the ten gold-pieces which you have sent to the *yeshivah,* five for us and five for the treasury of the *yeshivah,* and we have ordained and blessed you with blessings that will be fulfilled for you and your seed for generations.

As for your questions about the order of prayers and blessings for the entire year . . . and which they have shown us from Heaven [that is, the answer which God has vouchsafed to us], we . . . give you answer according to the tradition which exists in our possession and as arranged by the *Tannaim* and *Amoraim* [teachers of the *Mishnah* and the *Talmud*] . . . Rabbi Meir said, "Every man is in duty bound to pronounce a hundred blessings every day." . . . and it was King David himself who arranged [these hundred blessings]. When they informed him that the inhabitants of Jerusalem were dying at the rate of a hundred a day, he arose and ordained these hundred blessings.

It seems that these blessings were then forgotten and the *Tannaim* and *Amoraim* arose and reestablished them.

Now as to the order of these hundred blessings; thus has already answered Rav Natronai, the son of Rav Hillai, head of the college of Mata Mehasia, to the congregation of Lucena [Spain] . . . It is impossible for a person to pronounce each of the hundred blessings at its appropriate time because of the uncleanness of the hands which are wont to keep busy and touch things: but when a person awakens from his sleep, he shall wash thoroughly his face and hands and feet to fulfill the verse: "Prepare to meet thy God, O Israel." [*Amos* 4:12] Each and every individual is in duty bound to recite them; and it is the custom of all Israel in Sefarad [Spain] for the cantor to read them aloud in order to discharge the obligation of anyone who cannot say them for himself. Thus answered Rav Natronai bar Hillai.

From *The Responsa Literature,* by Solomon B. Freehof

SAADIA GAON Discusses the Jewish Calendar Controversy, 921

At first glance, the calendar might seem a petty reason for a bitter argument. However, when you stop to think about it, the calendar is basic to our whole way of life. If people observed the major occasions on different days, there would be utter chaos, making organized communal life impossible.

A difference in calculating the calendar produced an acrid dispute between Saadia, the great Egyptian Jewish scholar who became *gaon* of the Babylonian academy at Sura, and Aaron ben Meir, head of a Palestinian school.

The conflict revolved about whether the Hebrew months, *Cheshvan* and *Kislev*, should be full (30 days) in the year 1233 or deficient (29 days). The decision depended on which method of computation was used, and this was the nub of the controversy. The disagreement, however, was only a symptom of a deeper conflict that shook world Jewry in the tenth century: namely, whether Babylonia or Palestine should be the center of religious authority. For several hundred years Babylonia had occupied the place of leadership because of its great scholars, and now Aaron ben Meir hoped to reestablish the supremacy of Palestine. But Saadia's calendar system won the support of the entire Jewish community and Babylonia retained her leadership.

In the letter below, Saadia writes to his Egyptian pupils of his disagreement with Aaron ben Meir.

"May it be the will (of the Lord) that there be no stumbling-block and no pitfall in your place . . ."

[*Somewhere in Babylonia, about January, 922*]

MAY the Lord grant me a worthy place among His sages. I am unable to praise His glory sufficiently. My love and affection for you, my three dear pupils, has never waned, for educating the young leaves indelible traces on the heart, the more when it has been undertaken for the sake of the fear of God and the glorification of His Name.

As I have been desolate ever since I left my wife and children, so I have grieved over my separation from you. May it be the will of the Almighty that I see you again in health and happiness. . . . Only recently I was told by our friend R. David, son of Abraham, that you had written to him and requested him to secure the opinions of the heads of the academies regarding the fixing of the months *Marcheshvan* and *Kislev* of the year 1233 (Sel.). I presume that you wrote to him, and not to me, only because, in accordance with previous reports, you thought I was still in Palestine. He himself suggested that you seem to have thought so. He further requested me to write to you and inform you.

Know that when I was yet in Aleppo some pupils came from Baal Gad and brought the news that Ben Meir intends to proclaim *Cheshvan* and *Kislev* deficient. I did not believe it, but as a precaution I wrote to him in the summer [not to do so]. The exilarch, the heads of the academies, all the *alufim,* teachers and scholars, likewise agreed to proclaim *Cheshvan* and *Kislev* full, and that Passover be celebrated on Thursday. In conjunction with their letters I too wrote to most of the great cities, in order to fulfill my duty. Persist ye also in this matter and close up this breach, and do not rebel against the command of God. None of the people dare to profane the festivals of God willfully, to eat leavened bread on Passover, and eat, drink, and work on the Day of Atonement. May it be the will [of the Lord] that there be no stumbling-block and no pitfall in your place or in any other place in Israel. Pray, answer this letter and tell me all your affairs and your well-being. May your peace grow and increase forever!

From *Saadia Gaon,* by Henry Malter

NATHAN HA-BAVLI Narrates the Conflict between Saadia and the Exilarch, 937

Late in the sixth century, a new type of Jewish religious leader had developed in Babylonia—the *gaon*. Head of the academy at Sura or at Pumbedita (*gaon* is short for the Hebrew meaning "head of the academy which is the excellency of Jacob"), he was the religious authority of Babylonia Jewry for 450 years.

Most famous of all *geonim* was Saadia (882–942), a man of prodigious energy and a leader of men as well as a scholar. This lover of combat once antagonized the Exilarch David, son of Zakkai. In the seven years of their strife, David deposed Saadia, who promptly ordered his removal. He also battled the Karaites, the Jewish sect which did not recognize rabbinic tradition.

Saadia is known to posterity for his profound scholarship. The first to codify the whole of Jewish law, he also edited an *Order of Prayers*, wrote the first Hebrew grammar, produced a rhyming dictionary, translated the *Tanach* into Arabic, and presented basic Jewish doctrine in *Beliefs and Opinions*, which shows the harmony between Revelation and Reason.

Another noted *gaon* from Sura was Sherira, famous for an epistle showing how Jewish tradition was transmitted from its beginnings to his own day. His work safeguarded important facts that might otherwise have been lost for all time.

The last *gaon*, Hai, came from Pumbedita. In authority forty years (998–1038), he codified all civil laws of the *Talmud*, answered nearly 1,000 queries, and established the preeminence of the Babylonian *Talmud* over the Palestinian.

"Make your peace with him and don't cherish any grudge against him."

THE ROOTS of the quarrel between Saadia and the exilarch were some property that belonged to some men who were within the jurisdiction of the exilarch. . . . The exilarch's share amounted to seven hundred goldpieces, so he issued the documents for them, sealed them, and ordered them to go to the heads of the academies who would confirm them. [Legal papers of the exilarchs had to be confirmed by heads of the great academies of Sura and Pumbedita.] . . . Saadia examined them and saw things in them that did not seem right to him. Nevertheless he spoke to the men courteously: "Go to Kohen Zedek, the head of the Pumbedita academy, and let him sign this document first; then I will do so." Now he only said this in order to cover up the unseemly thing . . . which he did not wish to make public. They . . . went to Kohen Zedek . . . and he put his seal on them.

They came back to Saadia to have him also sign and confirm them. "Why do you want my signature?" asked Saadia of them. "You already have the signatures of the exilarch and of Kohen Zedek, the head of the Pumbedita academy. You don't need my signature." "Why don't you sign?" they countered. . . . He refused to reveal the reason until they adjured him many times to tell them . . .

They then returned to the exilarch and told him about it, so he sent for Judah, his son, and said to him: "Go tell Saadia, in my name, that he should sign the documents." Judah . . . went and told Saadia . . . "Return and tell your father," Saadia answered, "that it is written in the Bible [*Deuteronomy* 1:17] you must never show partiality in a case." So the son went back and his father said to him: "Tell Saadia to sign the papers and not to be a fool." . . . But Saadia refused.

The exilarch sent to him many times but the son . . . made every effort to . . . avoid a break between Saadia and his father. . . . However, when his father tired him out with all this coming and going, he became angry and raised his hand against Saadia saying: "If you don't sign the papers . . . I'll hit you."

No sooner had the words left the mouth of the youth than the servants of Saadia dragged him outside the door and closed the gates in his face. With tears streaming down his cheeks he came back to his father. . . . He told him the whole story. As soon as his father heard this he deposed Saadia. . . . But Saadia . . . in turn excommunicated the exilarch and sent for Hasan, that is Josiah, the brother of David ben Zakkai, to be exilarch in place of his brother.

This brother held the office for three years and died, but the quarrel between Saadia and the exilarch was dragged out for seven years, until a certain case turned up between two men. . . . The one chose Saadia as judge, the other selected the exilarch. The exilarch sent for the man who had chosen Saadia . . . and they beat him badly. [The exilarch's ban against Saadia forbade anyone to employ him as a judge.]

With his clothes torn, the wounded man went about crying to the whole community telling them what had happened to him . . .

Since this man was not under the jurisdiction of the exilarch, the community was incensed. . . . All of them went to Bishr ben Aaron, the father-in-law of Caleb ibn Sargado . . . and they told him . . . "Do something. It all depends on you," they said to him. "We're with you. Perhaps we'll be able to stop this quarrel which is only being kept up by your son-in-law, Caleb ibn Sargado." [Sargado had written a diatribe against Saadia . . . Saadia called him *celeb,* dog, instead of Caleb . . . Street-brawls between the two factions were frequent. Saadia himself was assaulted.]

Bishr went to the most prominent Jews . . . and in the presence of them all spoke to the exilarch . . . "What is this that you are doing? How long will you persist in this dispute and not fear divine punishment? Fear your God and stay out of trouble, for you know how far a quarrel can go. Now consider how you can improve your relations with Saadia. Make your peace with him and don't cherish any grudge against him."

The exilarch responded with a peaceful answer that he would do as advised. Then Bishr brought Saadia to his house and repeated to him the very words he had spoken to the exilarch, and he also responded favorably. The exilarch with his adherents . . . were in one house, and our master, Saadia, with his party . . . were in another house . . . in the courtyard of this Bishr, who went from one to the other with words of peace.

Then leaders of the community . . . escorted the exilarch and . . . Saadia; and these two marched from their respective sides until they met. Then they kissed and embraced each other. . . .

From *The Jew in the Medieval World,* by Jacob R. Marcus

HASDAI IBN SHAPRUT and JOSEPH, King of the Khazars, Correspond, about 960

Hasdai, son of Isaac ibn Shaprut, who served two caliphs of Cordova in the tenth century as both physician and inspector-general of customs, was one of Spanish Jewry's most commanding figures. A man of high position and intense love of learning, he protected and helped his fellow Jews.

His Moslem masters admired his shrewd and subtle diplomacy. His mastery of languages enabled him to translate Greek and Latin works into Arabic for them. His greatest joy, however, was in Hebrew letters, and he attracted Jewish scholars and writers to his court and patronized their cultural activities.

Hasdai's fervent commitment to Judaism is seen in his persistent efforts to contact a Jewish kingdom in the land of the Khazars near the Black Sea. His efforts to send a letter to the Jewish sovereign were thwarted by suspicious Byzantine officials. He finally managed to get the letter of the Khazar king via a German Jew who carried it through Germany, Hungary, Bulgaria, and Russia.

The letter expresses Hasdai's joy at learning of an independent Jewish state, and his willingness to give up all his power and influence for the privilege of living in a sovereign Jewish kingdom. In reply, King Joseph invited him to come to the Khazar kingdom and there occupy a position of importance and honor. Soon after, however, the Jewish kingdom was destroyed by nearby Kiev and Hasdai was forever deprived of the realization of his dream to be part of an independent Jewish state.

The correspondence remains as an eloquent testament to the strong bond between Jews all over the world and to their unquenchable yearning to live in a sovereign state, free from persecution and masters of their own destiny.

Hasdai's moving letter and King Joseph's reply are quoted below.

"I would go over mountains and hills, through seas and lands, till I should arrive at the place where my Lord the King resides, that I might see not only his glory and magnificence but also the tranquillity of the Israelites."

From *Hasdai ibn Shaprut to the King of the Khazars*

I, HASDAI, son of Isaac, son of Ezra, belonging to the exiled Jews of Jerusalem, in Spain, a servant of my Lord the King, bow to the earth before him and prostrate myself towards the abode of your Majesty, from a distant land. I rejoice in your tranquillity and magnificence, and stretch forth my hands to God in Heaven that He may prolong your reign in Israel. But who am I . . . ?

Praise be to the beneficent God for his mercy towards me! Kings of the earth, to whom His magnificence and power are known, bring gifts to him [the king of Spain]. . . . All their gifts pass through my hands and I am charged with making gifts in return. . . . I always ask the ambassadors of these monarchs about our brethren the Israelites, the remnant of the captivity, whether they have heard anything concerning the deliverance of those who have pined in bondage and had found no rest. At length mercantile emissaries of Khorasan told me that there is a kingdom of Jews who are called Khozars (and between Constantineh [Constantinople] and that country is a sea voyage of fifteen days, by land many nations dwell between us and them). But I did not believe these words, for I thought that they told me such things

A Khazar document found by Dr. Solomon S. Schechter in the Cairo Genizah. (Jewish Theological Seminary)

to procure my goodwill and favour. I was, therefore, hesitating and doubtful till the ambassadors of Constantineh came. . . . They answered me, "It is quite true; there is in that place a kingdom, Alcusari, distant from Constantineh a fifteen days' journey by sea; . . . the name of the king now reigning is Joseph: ships sometimes come from their country bringing fish, skins, and wares of every kind; the men are our brethren and are honoured by us; there is frequent communication between us by embassies and mutual gifts; they are very powerful; they maintain numerous armies. . . ." This account inspired me with hope, wherefore I bowed down and adored the God of Heaven.

I now looked about for a faithful messenger whom I might send into your country. . . . The thing seemed impossible to me, owing to the very great distance of the locality, but at length by the will and favour of God, a man presented himself to me named Mar Isaac, the son of Nathan. He put his life into his hand and willingly offered to take my letter to my Lord the King. I gave him a large reward, supplying him with gold and silver . . . and with everything necessary. Moreover, I sent out of my own resources a magnificent present to the king of Constantineh, requesting him to aid this my messenger in every possible way. . . . Accordingly this messenger set out, went to the king and showed him my letter and presents. The king, on his part, treated him honourably, and detained him there for six months. . . . One day he told my messenger to return, giving him a letter in which he wrote that the way was dangerous, that the peoples through whom he must pass were engaged in warfare, that the sea was stormy. . . . When I heard this I was grieved even to death, and took it very ill. . . .

Afterwards I wished to send my letter by way of Jerusalem, because persons there guaranteed that my letter should be dispatched from thence to Nisibis, thence to Armenia, from Armenia to Berdaa, and thence to your country. While in this state of suspense, behold ambassadors of the king of Gebalim [the Slavonians], arrived, and with them two Israelites; the name of one was Mar Saul, of the other Mar Joseph. These persons . . . comforted me, saying, "Give us your letter, and we will take care that it be carried to the king of the Gebalim, who for your sake will send it to the Israelites dwelling in the land of the Hungarians, they will send it to Russ, thence to Bulgar, till at last . . . its destination."

. . . I did none of these things for the sake of mine own honour, but only to know the truth, whether the Israelitish exiles, anywhere form one independent kingdom and are not subject to any foreign ruler. If, indeed, I could learn that this was the case, then, despising all my glory, abandoning my high estate, leaving my family, I would go over mountains and hills, through seas and lands, till I should arrive at the place where my Lord the King resides, that I might see not only his glory and magnificence . . . but also the tranquillity of the Israelites. On beholding this . . . my lips would pour forth praises to God, who has not withdrawn his favour from his afflicted ones.

Now, therefore, let it please your Majesty, I beseech you . . . to send back a reply . . . to inform me fully concerning the condition of the Israelites, and how they came to dwell there. . . .

One thing more I ask of my Lord . . . whether there is among you any computation concerning the final redemption which we have been awaiting so many years, whilst we went from one captivity to another, from one exile to another . . . And oh! how can I hold my peace and be restful in the face of the desolation of the house of our glory and remembering those who, escaping the sword, have passed through fire and water, so that the remnant is but small. We have been cast down from our glory, so that we have nothing to reply when they say daily unto us, "Every other people has its kingdom, but of yours there is no memorial on the earth." Hearing, therefore, the fame of my Lord the King, as well as the power of his dominions, . . . we lifted up our head, our spirit revived . . . Blessed be the Lord of Israel who has not left us without a kinsman as defender nor suffered the tribes of Israel to be without an independent kingdom. May my Lord the King prosper for ever. . . .

"I therefore choose the religion of Abraham."

King Joseph's Reply to Hasdai ibn Shaprut

WE ARE of the posterity of Japhet and the descendants of his son Togarma. We read in the genealogic books of our forefathers that Togarma had ten sons; we are the issue of Khozar, the seventh. It is set down in our chronicles that from his days onward our ancestors had to fight against peoples more numerous and more powerful than they. . . . Some centuries later there came a descendant of Khozar, King Bulan, a wise man and God-fearing. . . . The kings of Edom [Christians] and of Ishmael [Mohammedans] sent their ambassadors to him with great treasures, and also sent their learned men to convert them to their religions. But the king, in his wisdom, also sent for a learned Israelite . . . and he then had them as it were compete, so that each one expounded with fire the principles of his own religion and sought to refute the arguments of his antagonists. . . . Then the king said to the monk: "Of the two religions, that of the Israelite and that of the Ishmaelite, which is to be preferred?" The priest replied: "That of the Israelite." Then he asked the cadi: "Between the faith of the Israelite and the faith of the Edomite, which is to be preferred?" The cadi replied: "The religion of the Israelite is much to be preferred to the religion of the Nazarenes." To this the prince answered: "You both acknowledge that the faith of the Israelites is the wiser and the better; I therefore chose that religion, the religion of Abraham." From that time on God always helped him and strengthened him, and he and his people were all circumcized. . . . From that time on we have followed this religion: God be praised for it eternally. . . .

With reference to your question concerning the marvelous end [the restoration to former glory by the Messiah] our eyes are turned to the Lord our God and to the wise men of Israel who dwell in Jerusalem and Babylon. Though we are far from Zion, we have heard that because of our iniquities the computations are erroneous. . . . But, if it please the Lord, He will do it for the sake of His great name; nor will . . . all the troubles which have come upon us be lightly esteemed in His sight. He will fulfil His promise, and "the Lord whom ye seek shall suddenly come to His temple, the messenger of the covenant whom ye delight in: behold he shall come, saith the Lord of Hosts." [*Malachi* 3:1] Besides this we have only the prophecy of Daniel. May God hasten the redemption of Israel, gather together the captives and dispersed, you and I, and all Israel that love His name, in the lifetime of us all.

Finally, you mention that you desire to see my face. I also long and desire to see your honoured face, to behold your wisdom and magnificence. Would that it were according to your word, and that it were granted me to be united with you, so that you might be my father and I your son. All my people would pay homage to you: according to your word and righteous counsel we should go out and come in. Farewell.

From *The Jew in the Medieval World,* by Jacob R. Marcus

EPHRAIM BEN JACOB Describes the Fate of the Jews in the First Crusade, 1096

The First Crusade unleashed a torrent of anti-Jewish persecutions and fostered hatred for generations to come, thanks to the zeal and fanaticism of Church officials.

The Crusade was originally proclaimed by Pope Urban II, in 1096, to rally European Christians to wrest Palestine from the Moslems. The call evoked an enthusiastic response from multitudes of Christians, many of whom sincerely desired to free the Holy Land from "infidels." There were others, however, who joined for lesser reasons: to seek adventure, to escape daily routine, and to find a fortune. Since the "soldiers of the Cross" were poorly organized and lacking in adequate leadership they were difficult to control. It did not take long for the Crusade to turn into a holy war against the Jews.

Jewish wealth and property were a continuing temptation to those who sought booty. Furthermore, the crusaders argued that before killing God's enemies in a distant land they should destroy those in their midst. As a result, thousands upon thousands of Jews were robbed and murdered.

The events of 1096 are nevertheless a proud chapter in Jewish history, for the Jews responded heroically to their unmerited suffering. Unflinchingly they gave their lives for *Kiddush ha-Shem,* "the sanctification of the Name" of God. Ephraim ben Jacob, a noted talmudist and poet, penned a dramatic account of the Crusades, which he viewed first-hand.

Tomb of St. Hugh in Lincoln Cathedral. His death was used to foment a charge of ritual murder against the Jews of Lincoln in 1255. (The Jewish Encyclopedia, *Funk & Wagnalls)*

Clifford's Tower, York, England, where the Jews took refuge during the twelfth-century riot, and then unable to defend themselves against the mob killed themselves. (The Jewish Encyclopedia, *Funk & Wagnalls)*

"Their one deep fear was that the weakness of human flesh under the extremity of torture might keep any from sanctifying the ineffable Name."

AND NOW I shall begin to relate how destruction came upon the congregations who let themselves be slain for the sake of the name of the Eternal, and how with their whole souls they clung to the Eternal, the God of their fathers, and acknowledged Him, the One, with their last breath.

It came to pass in the year 4856, which is the year 1096 according to the calendar of the nations. . . .

It was the impious Pope of Rome who arose and issued a call to all the peoples, the sons of Edom [Christians], who believed in Christ, bidding them to gather and fare forth toward *Yerushalayim* [Jerusalem] and conquer the city. . . . The command was obeyed; the nations gathered. . . .

First came an insolent rabble of Christians, a raging mob of Frenchmen and Germans. . . . They fastened a cross upon their garments, both men and women, and they were numerous as locusts. . . .

Whenever upon their way they came into cities in which Jews had their dwellings, each said to the other, ". . . Behold, in our very midst dwell the Jews who hung Him innocent upon the cross and slew Him. Let us . . . revenge ourselves first upon them. . . . Or else let them become even as ourselves and accept our faith."

When the Jewish communities heard such speech, they did after the manner of our fathers, . . . with penitence and prayer and charitable deeds. . . . And He had chosen this generation because it had the strength to bear witness in His temple, to fulfill His word, to sanctify the ineffable Name. It is concerning such that David spoke: Praise the Lord, ye messengers, ye heroes who are mighty to fulfill His word.

It came to pass on the day of the new moon of the month of *Sivan* that Count Emicho, the oppressor of all Jews—may his bones be ground in a mill of iron!—came with mercenaries and crusaders and villagers and set up his tents outside the walls of the city, for the gates had been barred. He . . . had mercy neither on old men nor virgins nor suckling babes nor the sick . . . and he put our youths to the sword and ripped open the bellies of our women who were with child. He wore the crusader's cross and was a leader of armies. . . . Learning of the arrival of this impious one, the elders of the congregation of Mainz hastened to the bishop and bribed him with three hundred marks of fine silver, beseeching him to remain in the city. . . . He invited all the congregation into the great hall of his palace and vowed to stand by them. The count of the citadel, too, declared that he would protect the Jews . . . but stipulated that the Jews were to bear the costs. To this the Jews agreed and both the bishop and the count declared that they would, if need be, die with them. Furthermore, the congregation determined to give money to the impious Emicho as well, and to assure him in a writing that the other congregations upon his way would pay him equal honors. . . . But it was all of no avail.

It was on that third day of *Sivan* which once, when the *Torah* was given us, was a day of sanctification . . . upon this day it was also granted to the saints of the congregation of Mainz, separated and purified, to ascend unto God together. In their death they were not divided. All were in the bishop's great hall. . . . With them were the *Torah* and greatness of soul, wealth and honor, wisdom and humility, charity and faith. . . .

At the hour of noon the cruel Emicho moved against the city with his hordes, and the citizens opened the gates. . . . With fluttering banners the army drew up before the bishop's castle. But the sons of the holy covenant knew no trembling in the face of these mighty numbers of the enemy. All of them, strong or weak, put on armor and girded swords. Rabbi Kalonymos ben Meshullam led them. And Rabbi Menachem ben David Halevi, one of the great of his age, said, "Do you sanctify the ineffable Name in perfect devotion!" Thereupon they proceeded towards the gate in order to fight against the crusaders and the townsmen . . . But . . . our enemies prevailed against us and streamed into the castle. The bishop's men, pledged to help us, fled. . . . The bishop himself fled into his church, for they threatened him because he had spoken in favor of the Jews. . . .

When the sons of the holy covenant saw that their fate was about to be fulfilled . . . their one deep fear was that the weakness of the human flesh under the extremity of torture might keep any from sanctifying the ineffable Name.

Therefore they all cried . . . "We dare delay no longer, for the enemy is upon us. Let us hasten and sacrifice ourselves to the Lord. Whoever has a knife, let him first slay us and then himself."

In that year the Passover fell upon a Thursday and the first day of the new moon of the month of *Iyar* that the judgment came upon us. The crusaders, joining themselves with the townsfolk, arose first against the holy and pious congregation of Speyer, thinking to catch all in the house of prayer. But the Jews, getting word of this, rose early on the Sabbath, prayed hurriedly, and left the house of prayer. The enemies, seeing that their plan had failed, fell upon the Jews and slew eleven of them. . . .

When the evil news came to Worms that eleven men of Speyer had been slain . . . the congregation divided itself into two parts; one part fled into the bishop's castle; the other remained in their houses because the townsmen had promised them protection. But . . . the townsmen had an understanding with the crusaders . . . "Fear them not," they spoke to us, "for whoever slays one of you will have to answer with his life." By fair speeches they made all flight impossible. Relying on their faith, the Jews put into their hands all their goods and precious things, for the sake of which the townsmen betrayed them afterwards.

On the tenth day of *Iyar* those wolves of the desert attacked those who had remained in their houses and exterminated them —men, women, and children, young and old; they hurled them down the stairs and hacked down the houses and plundered and looted . . . and left death and horror behind them. . . .

On the twenty-fifth of *Iyar* the terror came over those who had taken refuge in the house of the bishop . . . But they had been fortified by the example of their brethren and accepted death and sanctified the Name . . . One slew his brother, another his kinsman or his wife and his children; bridegrooms slew their brides and tender mothers their little ones . . . The enemies stripped them naked and dragged and hurled them about; they left none save a few whom they forced to accept baptism. Eight hundred was the number of the slain on these two days; naked they were thrown into a common grave. . . .

Now when the pious men of the great congregation of Mainz, shield and refuge of our exile, famous through many lands—when they heard of the slaughter of the saints in Speyer and in Worms . . . the heads of the congregation who were well seen at the bishop's court went thither and . . . asked them what they should do to escape the fate of their brethren in Speyer and Worms. The answer was, "Take our advice. Bring all your fortunes into our treasuries and . . . come into the house of the bishop and stay there until the crusaders have passed by. Thus you will be secure." . . . But their words were lies. They brought us into their power; they caught us as fisherman catch fishes in a net in order to rob us of our money . . . Only the bishop was honestly inclined to put forth his power in our favor . . . The first upon whom the enemies came in the courtyard were some of the most devout, among them that great scholar, Rabbi Yitzchak ben Moshe. These pious men had disdained to flee into the inner chambers in order to buy one more hour of life. Nay, they sat wrapped in their praying shawls ready to fulfill the will of their Maker. The enemies first overwhelmed them with stones and arrows and then hewed them down with their swords. When those in the inner chambers saw the great patience of these saints they cried, "The time has come!" The women girded their loins with strength and slew first their sons and their daughters and then themselves. Many men, too, plucked up courage and slew their wives and their children. . . . And young men and women who were betrothed looked out of the window and cried, "Behold, O God, what we do to sanctify Thy holy Name and to avoid being forced to acknowledge the Crucified!" . . . And the blood of men was commingled with that of their wives, of . . . children and babes with that of their mothers. All were slaughtered upon that day for the sake of the Oneness of the dreadful Name of God. He who hears thereof, is not his very soul shaken? For what has man seen in all ages like unto this thing? . . . Eleven hundred were sacrificed on one day . . . Why then did not the heavens grow dark and the light of the stars go out and the sun and the moon die in their stations . . . when eleven hundred souls were slain in martyrdom—children among them, oh so many, and the little babes, the poor innocents who had not yet sinned? Canst Thou let such things be, O Lord? Were they not slain for the sake of Thee?

Avenge, O Lord, the blood of Thy servants soon, in our days, for our eyes to behold! Amen!

Has human ear heard a tale like unto that . . . of that young woman named Rachel . . . ? "I have four children," she said . . . "Spare them not for the Christians to catch them alive and make renegades of them. Let them, too, sanctify the Name!" But when one of her friends took up the knife to slay the children, the young mother cried aloud and beat her head and breasts. "Where is Thy loving kindness, O Lord?" she cried. And in despair she spoke to her friend, "Oh, do not kill Isaac before the eyes of Aaron . . ."

. . . The woman also had two very lovely young daughters, Bella and Madrona. These . . . bent back their white throats and besought her to sacrifice them . . . Rachel called to her last child, to Aaron, "Where are you, my son? I dare not spare you!" And she drew him forth from behind the chest where he was hidden and sacrificed him unto God. When her husband saw the death of his four lovely children he cast himself upon a sword . . . But the mother hid her dead children two in each of her wide sleeves, and sat her down and lamented. When the enemies came into the room they roared, "Give us the gold, Jew wench, which is doubtless hidden in thy sleeves." But when they saw the dead children they struck down Rachel with one blow, so that she perished without a moan.

From *The Island Within,* by Ludwig Lewisohn

A MOSLEM Mocks at David Alroy, 1147

The lot of Jews all over the world deteriorated tragically after the Crusades. Only one hope was left to them in their despair—that the Messiah would come to rescue them.

There was no lack of would-be bearers of the messianic banner to try their hand at convincing Jews, who were eager to believe, that they were the Chosen One. Motivated by the desire to escape from oppressive rulers, from religious fanatics, and from exorbitant taxation, many Jews flocked to the side of one or another of the messianic pretenders.

David Alroy, who arose in Persia at the time of the Second Crusade (1146–1147), is one of the best-known of the false messiahs. He persuaded a band of Jewish warriors in the mountains of northern Persia to join him in war against Moslem domination, after which they would return in triumph to Jerusalem. Although murder cut short Alroy's brief career, many devoted followers continued to believe in him and to venerate his memory for years.

A Moslem physician and mathematician of the time, Samuel ibn Abbas, an apostate from Judaism, wrote *The Silencing of the Jews and the Christians through Rational Arguments*, a book whose primary purpose was to mock his former coreligionists. As an example of Jewish inferiority he cites the influence of David Alroy. Despite the author's obvious prejudice, his is the most accurate contemporary account available.

"This occurrence is sufficient to cover them with lasting disgrace and eternal shame."

WE ARE going to tell a story of the haste with which the Jews accepted the false and the fictitious, which shows how little discernment they have. The following incident happened in our time among the finest, cleverest, and shrewdest among them, namely, the Jews of Bagdad. A swindler, a young Jew, a man of fine features, whose name was Menahem ben Solomon but who was known by the name of Ibn al-Ruhi, grew up in the neighborhood of Mosul. [As a messianic pretender he took the name of David. "*Al-Ruhi*" (Alroy) may mean "the inspired."]

. . . The commandant of the citadel there was very fond of this rogue and liked him because he held a good opinion of him, and because he considered him as well-versed in religious matters as Alroy wished to appear. . . . This gave the rogue the desire to secure the position of this officer, whom he considered such an imbecile that he imagined he could attack the citadel, take it, and make a fortress out of it. [Alroy, a cultured man, was more likely a patriot than a rogue.]

He therefore wrote to the Jews who live in the territory of Azerbaijan and its borders, since he knew that the Jews of Persia were more ignorant than all others. He mentioned in his letters that he had arisen in order to free the Jews from the power of the Moslems. [Alroy was really leading a rebellion of the desperate Persian Jews against their Moslem overlords.]

In his approach he made use of all sorts of cunning and deceit . . . I have seen that which has in substance the following meaning: "Perhaps you will say: Why is our help called for? Is it for battle or for war? No, we do not want you for battle or for war. You merely have to appear before this commander in order that the envoys of the princes . . . may see you." At the end of the letters there was written: "It is proper that every one of you have a sword or some other weapon . . . concealed under his clothes."

. . . The Jews of Persia and . . . of Amadia and . . . of Mosul consented, and they came to him with their sharpened weapons so that he had a large force. The commandant . . . thought all these people had come merely to . . . visit this scholar whose fame, he fancied, had reached them. He finally discovered their intentions, but . . . killed only the swindler who had incited the revolt. [Benjamin of Tudela, however, indicates that Alroy was successful until betrayed for a huge reward.]

As obvious as these facts are to every intelligent person, they are nevertheless not yet clear to the Jews, and the Jews of Amadia hold Alroy even today in higher esteem than many of their prophets. Many consider him to be the expected Messiah himself.

About the time that the people in Bagdad heard of Menahem, two crafty deceivers among the Jewish scholars forged letters in his name in which they announced . . . the redemption which they had been awaiting of old, and designated a night in which they would all fly to Jerusalem together. The Bagdad Jews, in spite of their supposed intelligence and their boasted critical spirit, listened to this and allowed themselves to be misled into accepting it as the truth. Their wives brought their possessions and jewelry to both men . . . that these might distribute them in their name to those who in their judgment were worthy of them. . . .

They procured green garments [green was a symbol of resurrection] for themselves, and they came together that night on the roofs, waiting for the moment, when . . . they would fly to Jerusalem on angels' wings. The women began to scream . . . for fear that they would fly away before their children, or their children before them . . . The Moslems there were amazed at this, wondering what could have happened to the Jews. . . .

The Jews . . . were disillusioned by the break of dawn and by the departure of the deceivers who had already left with their riches. . . . This year was called the "Year of Flying Away." . . . [This story seems mythical as a similar story was told of Jews and of Moslem heretics in earlier centuries.]

This occurrence is sufficient to cover them with lasting disgrace and eternal shame . . . and will suffice to silence them and to shut their mouths. . . .

From *The Jew in the Medieval World,* by Jacob R. Marcus

BENJAMIN OF TUDELA Describes Jewish Autonomy in Bagdad, 1168

Benjamin of Tudela (a town in northern Spain) was a wealthy merchant who liked to travel. In 1160 he set out on a 13-year trip through southern France, Italy, Greece, Asia, and North Africa. Wherever he went he was warmly greeted by local Jewish communities, testifying to the deep bond between all Jews, no matter how far apart their wanderings had taken them.

Fortunately, Benjamin kept a diary. Its wealth of information on the various Jewish settlements makes it one of our most important sources of Jewish history of that period.

Among the places Benjamin of Tudela visited was the city of Bagdad, where Jews had lived since the Babylonian Exile (586 B.C.E.). At a very early date the Babylonian Jews had been granted the right to govern themselves. At the time of Benjamin's stay, their political leader was called the exilarch or "head of the exile." Reputedly a descendant of the House of David, he was deeply admired by the Jews and represented them at the court of the caliphs. He was given a vast domain of authority over the Jewish population, including the power to tax and to sit in judgment.

Religious leadership was vested in the *gaon*. Although there was occasional conflict between the *geonim* and the exilarchs, by and large mutual respect and harmony prevailed.

Without Benjamin of Tudela's excellent description of Jewish self-government in twelfth-century Bagdad, our knowledge of this era would be much poorer. Here is a portion of his personal account.

"The sceptre shall not depart from Judah . . ."

IN BAGDAD there are about forty thousand Jews, and they dwell in security, prosperity, and honor under the great caliph, and amongst them are great sages. . . . At the head of the great academy is the chief rabbi, Rabbi Samuel the son of Ali. He is the "head of the academy which is the excellency of Jacob." He is a Levite, and traces his lineage back to Moses our teacher. [Nine other scholars are listed.]

These are the ten scholars, and they do not engage in any other work than communal administration. . . .

And at the head of them all is Daniel the son of Hisdai [exilarch about 1160–1174]. He possesses a book of pedigrees going back as far as David, king of Israel. The Jews call him "our lord, head of the exile," and the Mohammedans call him *saidna ben Daoud* (noble son of David), and he has been invested with authority over all the congregations of Israel by the Emir al Muminin, the lord of Islam [the caliph of Bagdad]. For thus Mohammed commanded concerning him and his descendants; and he granted him a seal of office over all the congregations that dwell under his rule, and ordered that every one, whether Mohammedan or Jew or belonging to any other nation . . . should rise up before the exilarch and salute him, and that anyone who should refuse to rise up should receive one hundred stripes.

And every Thursday when he goes to pay a visit to the great caliph, horsemen—non-Jews as well as Jews—escort him and heralds proclaim: "Make way before our Lord, the son of David, as is due unto him." . . . He is mounted on a horse, and is attired in robes of silk and embroidery with a large turban on his head, and from the turban is suspended a long white cloth adorned with a chain upon which the seal of Mohammed is engraved.

Then he appears before the caliph and kisses his hand, and the caliph rises and places him on a throne . . . and all the Mohammedan princes rise up before him. And the exilarch is seated on his throne opposite to the caliph, in compliance with the command of Mohammed to give effect to what is written in the law: "The sceptre shall not depart from Judah, nor the ruler's staff from the obedience of the peoples be." [*Genesis* 49:10]

The authority of the exilarch extends over all the communities of Babylon, Persia, Khorasan, and Sheba which is El-Yemen, and Diyar Kalach [Bekr] and all the land of Mesopotamia, and over the dwellers in the mountains of Ararat and the land of the Alans [in the Caucasus].

. . . The exilarch gives the communities power to appoint rabbis and overseers who come unto him to be consecrated and to receive his authority. He owns hospices, gardens, and plantations in Babylon, and much land inherited from his fathers, and no one can take his possessions from him by force. He had a fixed weekly revenue arising from the hospices of the Jews, the markets and the merchants, apart from that which is brought to him from far-off lands. The man is very rich, and wise in the Scriptures as well as in the *Talmud*, and many Israelites dine at his table. . . .

At his installation, the exilarch gives much money to the caliph, to the princes, and the officials. On the day that the caliph performs the ceremony . . . the exilarch rides in the second of the royal equipages, and is escorted from the palace of the caliph to his own house with timbrels and fifes. The exilarch appoints the head of the academy. . . .

In Bagdad there are twenty-eight synagogues, situated either in the city itself or . . . on the other side of the Tigris; for the river divides the metropolis into two parts. The great synagogue of the exilarch has columns of marble . . . overlaid with silver and gold, and on these columns are sentences of the *Psalms* in golden letters. And in front of the ark are about ten steps of marble; on the topmost step are the seats of the exilarch and of the princes of the House of David. The city of Bagdad is twenty miles in circumference, situated in a land of palms, gardens, and plantations. . . . People come thither with merchandise from all lands. Wise men live there, philosophers . . . and magicians expert in all manner of witchcraft.

From *The Jew in the Medieval World,* by Jacob R. Marcus

MAIMONIDES Comments on the Decline of Jewish Learning, Twelfth Century

It is said that even an "ill wind" carries with it some good. Thus, the bitter deterioration of Jewish life in the twelfth century brought about a brilliant legal work for which all later generations are profoundly grateful. Moses Maimonides, one of the foremost scholars in Jewish history, was moved by the sorrowful situation of his fellow Jews to write the *Mishneh Torah* (literally, "Repetition of the Law"), a work that summarized and codified all the religious duties of the Jews in an easily understandable form.

The widespread persecution of the Jews reached its climax in Yemen, where the Jews were faced with the blunt choice of conversion to Islam or death. Talmudic study, the foundation of the Jewish way of life, was seriously hampered, for it required time, concentration, and peace of mind, all of which grew increasingly scarcer. There was danger that the Jewish people would forget their laws, since the *Talmud* was the only source of information about the *mitzvot* (commandments). Maimonides undertook the monumental task of organizing the content of the *Talmud* and deciding the law in the many instances where rabbinic debates failed to indicate whose position was ultimately accepted as binding. As a result of his labors, people could find what they wanted to know about Jewish law without consulting any other book. The *Mishneh Torah* became a model for all subsequent codes and is regularly consulted to this day by all students of Jewish law.

Born in Cordova in 1135, Moses Maimonides died in Palestine in 1204. The world has not ceased to marvel at the depth and breadth of his knowledge. A famous doctor, he wrote treatises on medicine and other secular subjects. His great Judaica classics include *The Luminary,* a commentary on the *Mishnah,* and *The Guide to the Perplexed,* a systematic philosophic statement which attempts to harmonize Judaism with the teachings of Aristotle. No wonder he is called "the greatest of the great men" that the Jews produced in the Middle Ages!

The following documents show Moses Maimonides' deep concern for the state of Jewish learning in the twelfth century.

"Endeavor to be men of valor, for eveything depends on you . . ."

To the Scholars of Lunel [France]

MY DEAR friends, let me tell you that, except for your community and the neighboring cities, there is no group that would bear the banner of Moses' teachings and engage in talmudic studies in these difficult times. You are the only ones, of whom I know, who pursue regular studies of Jewish and other sciences. In our communities the study of *Torah* is no longer fostered; most of the larger communities are inactive, the others are declining. In all of Palestine there are only three or four communities left, and they are laid low. In Syria, Aleppo is the only city where there are students of the *Torah,* but they would not stake their lives for it. In the Babylonian diaspora two or three fragments are left; in Yemen and other Arabian countries there is but a limited study of the *Talmud.* However, three well-to-do men from there have sent messengers and bought three copies of my *Mishneh Torah* and presented them to communities in three parts of their country. This expanded their views and restored Jewish activities in the communities as far as India. The Jews of India know of the Written Law and practice only the ordinances con-

Responsum by Maimonides found in the Cario Genizah. (British Museum)

Portrait of Maimonides with autograph. (The Jewish Encyclopedia, *Funk & Wagnalls)*

cerning the observance of the Sabbath and circumcision. The Jews of the Islamic Barbary States [in Northwestern Africa] study the Written Law and live according to its literal interpretation. As to the communities in Northern Africa, you know what was decreed against them [conversion to Mohammedanism]. You, our brothers, are the only ones of whom help and rescue can be expected.

"Be of good courage, and let us prove strong for our people, and for the cities of our God." [*II Samuel* 10:12] Endeavor to be men of valour, because everything depends on you; the decision lies in your hands. Do not rely upon me in this struggle; I can no longer be as active as I would like to be, for I am an old man, not because of advanced age but as a result of a weak state of health. May God help you and bless you.

"No one should find it necessary to consult other books for information on any of the laws of Israel."

On His Code of Laws

OURS IS a time of great disasters; everybody feels the stress of the present hour. The wisdom of our wise men is lost, and the counsel of our scholars is hidden. Therefore, the commentaries, codes, and decisions of the *geonim,* which they thought to be generally intelligible, are not understood in our days; only a few are able to comprehend them perfectly. I need not say that this is also true of the *Talmud*—the Babylonian and the Palestinian alike—and other rabbinic texts. Wide knowledge, wisdom, and much study are necessary to deduce from them the right understanding of the observance of the laws and commandments.

Therefore, I, Moses ben Maimon from Spain, trusting in God, girded my loins to study all these works, and I decided to compile the conclusions to be deduced from them pertaining to all the laws of the *Torah*. This presentation is put forward in simple style and in a concise manner, so that the Oral Law may become familiar to all; no reference is made to arguments and discussion of points of law. No one should find it necessary to consult other books for information on any of the laws of Israel. This work aims to be a compendium of the Oral Law as a whole, and lists ordinances, customs, and decisions, introduced from the times of Moses, our teacher, to the redaction of the *Talmud*.

I, therefore, named this work *Repetition of the Law* (*Mishneh Torah*). He who studies the Written Law and then this work will know the entire Oral Law and need not read any other book.

From *Maimonides Said*, translated and edited by Nahum N. Glatzer

THE RASHBA Answers Questions on Jewish Life, Thirteenth Century

How does a religion stay alive and modern? In the case of Judaism the answer is simple: *responsa.* From medieval times forward, Jews who wanted answers to concrete problems would address questions to the leading rabbis of their generation. This exchange of questions and answers (known in Hebrew as *she-elot u-teshuvot*) make up what is called the *responsa* literature, of which there are over a thousand extant collections.

These *responsa,* which helped to keep the legal decisions of the *Bible* and *Talmud* current, also strengthened the unity of the far-flung Jewish communities by insuring similarity of observance and practice. To this day *responsa* are being written by outstanding religious authorities who recognize their responsibility to make the Jewish faith relevant to the needs of this century.

With the passing of time, *responsa* of outstanding rabbis have been compiled into books, and studied as a supplement to the *Talmud* and the Codes of Law. They not only are an extremely important repository of wisdom but also provide insight into the life of the Jews of their day.

Among the great rabbis of medieval times was Solomon ibn Aderet (1235–1310), also referred to as the Rashba. The spiritual leader of Barcelona Jewry, he had influence far beyond the borders of his native Spain as a result of the many *responsa* that he wrote. In the following two examples, the Rashba deals with the proper way for a community to take care of its poor and with the legality of gambling.

"Charity is to be so dispensed as to rob no man of his dignity."

How Should a Community Levy Taxes for the Support of Its Poor?

Question: The poor of the city are many and the government taxes are exorbitant. . . . The wealthy say, "Let the poor go begging at the doors and all will contribute toward their daily bread, for the middle class is just as obligated to support as we, the rich." The middle class, however, insist that the poor should stay at home and not go begging at the doors, for they are our brothers, our own flesh and blood. The burden of their sustenance should rest upon the community as a whole and each should contribute according to his wealth. This is feasible because the *bet din* [Jewish court] has the right to enforce the collection of its assessments in accordance with the precedent established by Rabbah. [*Babylonian Talmud,* Tractate *Baba Batra* 8b] On whose side is the law?

Answer: The law is on the side of the middle class, because charity and support of the poor is not to be borne equally by all members of the community, but is to be based on their relative possessions. . . . Every poor man should be provided for according to his needs. Our rabbis of the *Talmud* teach that if a man is too proud to accept charity, his needs are to be supplied in a subtle manner, either through "gifts" or "loans" . . . and that the charity is to be so dispensed as to rob no man of his dignity. Thus, if a man is of noble descent, he is to be given a larger grant. Under no circumstances is a poor man to be forced to go begging at the doors. . . . The practice everywhere is to provide the poor from the community fund, and the assessments for this fund are apportioned according to the possessions of the residents of this city. If the poor, after receiving their allowance, wish to go begging at the doors, they may do so and everyone is to give them according to his disposition.

How the Jewish Communities Proscribed Gambling

Question: A community agreed to excommunicate anyone who gambled. Later a part of the community wanted to lift the ban but the rest opposed them, some of the outstanding members of the community publicly voicing their opposition to such a procedure. But the former group paid no attention to this opposition and declared the ban lifted. On that very day one vile fellow took advantage of this lifting of the ban and was therefore punished and excommunicated.

Does this lifting the ban [by a part of the community] have any validity?

Answer: The prohibition of gambling is not new. It is an important ordinance originating with our distinguished scholars of old. To allow gambling was therefore sinful to the extreme. Whoever attempts to permit it opens the way to lawlessness. . . .

Even if a whole community agreed to lift such a ban, gambling would still be prohibited by rabbinic law. Now that there is an additional prohibition by a local ordinance and a ban of excommunication, how can anyone possibly permit it? . . . Whoever . . . agrees to permit this is like one who agrees to transgress a religious prohibition in the company of a crowd of accomplices. The larger the number of accomplices, the greater the sin and the greater the confusion.

Moreover, I contend that when part of a community opposes the lifting of a ban . . . the excommunication still holds good because of the biblical law that oaths and bans can be nullified only if provisions for retracting them were made at the very outset, and then only through the agency of a scholar. . . .

In our days, however, because of the general practice of lifting community bans when there is a unanimous demand, no loopholes are needed. . . . It is assumed that there is a tacit understanding that the excommunication become null and void whenever the whole community so desires. . . . In any case the prevalent custom is that if even a single member dissents no retraction can take place. . . . It is therefore clear that the lifting of the ban by a part of your community has no validity whatever. . . .

From *An Anthology of Medieval Hebrew Literature,*
by Abraham Millgram

TWO CONTEMPORARIES View the Burning of the Talmud, 1244

During the Middle Ages not only were the Jews physically attacked, but their sacred literature as well. In 1239, for example, Pope Gregory IX ordered the kings and archbishops of Christian Europe to confiscate all copies of the *Talmud,* and, if it was found to contain statements which offended the Church, to condemn it and all its commentaries.

On Saturday, March 3, 1240, the French police seized these books while their owners were in the synagogue. A trial of the *Talmud* was held in Paris, with the apostate Jew, Nicholas Donin, as prosecutor and Rabbi Yehiel of Paris as chief defense attorney. The queen-mother of France presided, and a group of bishops were the judges. The prosecution ridiculed the folklore of the *Talmud* and twisted many statements out of context to prove that it was blasphemous. Rabbi Yehiel's defense was restricted to reinterpretation of the passages which Donin chose. Although he did his best, the judges did not seriously consider his arguments, since they had already determined that the *Talmud* must be classified as dangerous.

The tribunal brought in a verdict of guilty, and twenty-four carloads of the *Talmud* were burned in a giant bonfire in the public square of Paris in 1244. The tragic occurrence shook the Jews of France and Germany who expressed their grief in moving elegies and lamentations. One of the best-known was composed by Rabbi Meir of Rothenburg, who witnessed the conflagration, and is recited to this day on the Ninth of *Av.* Pope Gregory's order is also presented here.

"That is the main reason that heresy has such a hold on the obstinate Jews."

IF IT IS true what they tell about the Jews who live in the kingdom of France and in the other countries, then no punishment will be sufficient and fitting for them. For indeed we have heard that they are not satisfied with the old *Torah* that God gave to Moses in writing; on the contrary, they neglect it altogether and they say that God gave Moses another *Torah* that is called *Talmud,* which means "study," and transmitted it to him orally; and they delude themselves with the belief that this *Torah* which is engraved on their souls was preserved for a long time, until there came some, who are called by them sages or scribes [men of letters], and these put it in a written form, the volume of which surpasses immeasurably the text of the sacred writings. These writings contain words of slander and abuse, of vanity and evil, which are a disgrace to those who express them and a horror to those who hear them.

Now since it is said that that is the main reason that heresy has such a hold on the obstinate Jews, we are of the opinion that your feelings of brotherly love should be aroused and we hereby send you this communication by messenger. On the first Saturday, on the morning of the great fast, when the Jews are assembled in the synagogues, all the books of the Jews in your country shall be seized, in accordance with our authority, and these books are to be faithfully held by the priests or acolytes [the Dominican or Franciscan monks]. To this end, you are, if necessary, to avail yourself of the help of the secular arm; and you have permission to excommunicate those priests and laymen under your jurisdiction who may refuse to hand over the Hebrew books which are in their possession, even after being asked to do so either privately or by the churches.

From *The Church and the Jews in the Thirteenth Century,*
by Solomon Grayzel

"And thou revealed amid a heavenly fire by earthly fire consumed . . ."

ASK, is it well, O thou consumed of fire,
With those that mourn for thee,
That yearn to tread thy courts, that sore desire
Thy sanctuary;
That, panting for thy land's sweet dust, are grieved,
And sorrow in their souls,
And by the flames of wasting fire bereaved,
Mourn for thy scrolls;

And thou revealed amid a heavenly fire,
By earthly fire consumed,
Say how the foe unscorched escaped the pyre
Thy flames illumed!

O Sinai! was it then for this God chose
Thy mount of modest height,
Rejecting statelier, while on thee arose
His glorious light?

Moses; and Aaron in the mountain Hor;
I will of them inquire:
Is there another to replace this Law
Devoured of fire?

In sackcloth I will clothe and sable band,
For well-beloved by me
Were they whose lives were many as the sand—
The slain of thee.

I am astonished that the day's fair light
Yet shineth brilliantly

On all things:—it is ever dark as night
  To me and thee.
E'en as thy Rock has sore afflicted thee
  He will assuage thy woe;
Will turn again the tribes' captivity,
  And raise thee low.

My heart shall be uplifted on the day
  Thy Rock shall be thy light,
When He shall make thy gloom to pass away,
  Thy darkness bright.

The Burning of the Law, by Meir of Rothenburg,
translated by Nina Davis in *Songs of Exile*

ABU ASTRUC Reports a Medieval Christian-Jewish Disputation, 1413

The Tortosa disputation of 1413, like other medieval debates between Jews and Christians, was an attempt to humiliate the Jewish faith. The antipope Benedict XIII ordered it upon the agitation of Vincent Ferrer, a Dominican preacher who sought to exclude the Jews from Spain's social and economic life. Since the rules of the debate made free and open discussion impossible, it was a chance for Benedict to add to his reputation throughout Christendom. The topic was whether or not the *Talmud* itself says that the Messiah has already come.

The debate dragged on for two years. The Christian side was led by an apostate Jew, Joshua Lorki (or Geronimo de Santa Fe), Benedict's personal physician. Representing the Jewish community were the leading Jewish scholars of Spain, including Vidal Benveniste, Rabbi Zerahiah ha-Levi, Rabbi Matatiah, Rabbi Abu Astruc, and Rabbi Todros.

The predictable results were a law banning study of the *Talmud* and enactment of Vincent Ferrer's entire anti-Jewish program. Governmental pressure, coupled with the danger of violence, forced many Spanish Jews to give up their ancestral faith.

Solomon ibn Verga, the prominent fifteenth-century Jewish historian, in his classic work, *Shebet Yehuda,* which tells of the sufferings of the Jews, quotes a letter from one of the participants, Abu Astruc, to the Jews of Gerona. The following excerpt from it demonstrates the perils and the pathos of the occasion as well as the humor of the Jews which made the episode bearable.

Polemical treatise between a Christian and a Jew. (Halberstam Collection, Goldblum)

"But if ye refuse and rebel,
ye shall be devoured with the sword."

YOU, who are esteemed among the sons of Israel, you, the nobles in Judah . . . may you always keep alive the courage in your hearts. What you have known previously, know it now as well—that our helper "doth neither slumber nor sleep," but saves us from those who scheme evil toward us. A shoot that came forth from among us thought to destroy us . . . For he, Joshua ha-Lorki, invented thoughts to lead us astray, and to demonstrate that he was in truth a Christian . . . And so he asked the pope to bid the chief among the wise men of Jewry to come before him, for it was his purpose to prove to us from our own *Talmud* that the Messiah had already come. And he told the pope that after he had proved this it would be legitimate to force the Jews to accept the religion of Jesus. . . . Know then that we have indeed escaped a danger that cannot be gauged, for . . . many were eager to find us guilty. . . .

The delegates . . . decided that Don Vidal Benveniste was to begin, because he is versed in all manner of knowledge, and can use the Latin language. They also decided not to behave like the learned Jews in the academies, where each interrupts the other's word and scoffs at him if he does not agree, lest the pope hold them in contempt, and also that they would address Joshua ha-Lorki and the bishops with calm and courtesy. None was to grow violent, not even if he were derided, and each was to strengthen the courage of the other so that his heart might not sink.

Then we . . . who were the delegates went to the pope with the help of God, "who delivereth the poor from him that is too strong for him," and the pope received us with an agreeable countenance, and . . . asked each as to his name and commanded all to be written down. At this we were greatly alarmed and tried to discover the reason for it from the scribe. He, however, told us that it boded no ill, for popes and kings were wont to have everything . . . written down in books. . . .

Then the pope said to us: "You, who are esteemed among the people of the Jews, a people that was chosen by a Chooser who has existed from time immemorial, and that, if it was rejected, was rejected because of its own failings—have no fear of this debate, for no wrong and no insult shall be done to you in my presence. Calm your thoughts and speak with a firm heart; have no fear and do not despair.

"Maestro Geronimo . . . wishes to prove that the Messiah has already come . . . from your own *Talmud.* In our presence will it be shown whether truth abides with his word, or whether he has dreamed a dream. But you must not be afraid of him, because in a debate there is one law for both sides. Go then, rest in your lodgings, and come to me again early tomorrow."

And forthwith he gave orders that we be given suitable lodgings and . . . food . . . And some of us rejoiced at the pope's words, and others were sad thereat—as is usual with Jews.

On the second day we came before the pope and found the entire great hall . . . tapestried in many colors, and seventy chairs set up for the bishops . . . and all of these wore raiment embellished with gold. All the great men of Rome were there . . . almost a thousand persons . . . And then our "hearts melted and became as water." Notwithstanding we said: "Blessed be he who has accorded of his glory to flesh and blood" [the benediction on seeing a king].

Then the pope began to speak, saying: "You, who are the wise men among the Jews, know that I have not come here . . . to decide which of the two religions is the true, since I am well aware that my religion and my faith are the true, and that your *Torah,* while it once was true, has ceased to be so. You have been summoned only because Geronimo said he wanted to prove that the Messiah has already come, from the *Talmud* of your masters, who knew better than you. Therefore, speak only of this matter." . . . And Maestro Geronimo began: "Come now, and let us reason together, saith the Lord . . . But if ye refuse and rebel, ye shall be devoured with the sword."

Then Don Vidal Benveniste began the *harenga* [argument] in the Latin tongue, and the pope took pleasure in his wisdom and his language. And . . . Don Vidal complained of Geronimo, saying that it was not right for one who wishes to debate, to begin by using hostile words . . . "But if ye refuse and rebel, ye shall be devoured with the sword." He had proved nothing for the time being, and yet was setting himself up as a judge and avenger.

At that the pope interposed: "You are right, but you must not be astonished at this evil way of his, for he was one of you."

The third day was the beginning of the debate proper, and Maestro Geronimo began, saying: "In your *Talmud,* it is said: 'Six thousand years is the span of the world—chaos [without knowledge of the law, until Abraham, the first worshiper of God], two thousand years; *Torah,* two thousand years; and two thousand years, days of the Messiah' [designated by the *Talmud* as coming from the school of the prophet Elijah]. From this it is evident that the Messiah has come within the last two thousand years, and who could he be but our Savior?"

Ha-Lorki took a long time in talking on this subject . . . until the pope said to him: "Geronimo, it has been known to me for a long time that you are a great preacher; yet not because of this have we come together, but to hear you prove what you have promised. Therefore, have a care that you lose not yourself in preaching."

Then he turned his countenance upon the delegates and said: "Reply to the passage he cited."

And Don Vidal Benveniste spoke: "Sir, let us first consider the characteristics of the Messiah, and then it will become evident whether he has already come. . . ."

And the pope said: "That is no answer to the question put to you. . . . You are following the manner of contentious Jews, who when one asks them about one thing, slip over to the next."

Thereupon Don Vidal answered him: "Sir, our beginning was in the manner of wise men, for it is proper to speak first of the nature of the matter in hand, and then of the particular circumstances; scientists also follow this rule. But if this way does not please you, our Lord, we shall not take it. And so I shall now speak of the passage itself, and say that wise Geronimo extracted from it what he pleased, and what supports his point, but disregarded what contradicts it. For toward the end of the passage, we read: 'But because of our iniquities, which were many, as much time has passed as has passed,' and this clearly proves that he has not come."

Then Geronimo replied: "According to this, you have not understood the words, or you pretend not to . . . For 'and two thousand years, days of the Messiah' is the pronouncement of the prophet Elijah . . . as a passage in the *Tanna debe Eliyahu* proves, and the talmudists know this; now those . . . are the ones who added, 'But because of our iniquities, which were many,' . . . to substantiate their belief that Jesus was not the Messiah. But the prophet Elijah, being a prophet and knowing what was true, said only, 'And two thousand years, days of the Messiah,' . . .

And Rabbi Zerahiah ha-Levi replied, saying: "It is probably more correct to assume that a passage originated with one man, rather than with two. When such is the case, the *Talmud* usually says: 'Rab Ashi, however, says,' or this one or that one says, 'But because of our iniquities, which were many.' That is why at the outset we said . . . that we wanted to see if the characteristics of the Messiah apply . . . to him who has come. . . . If the characteristics do apply to this person, then we will accept . . . Geronimo's interpretation; if not . . . our interpretation is the true one."

And Geronimo replied: "But Elijah came long before the Jews went into exile, therefore . . . the passage, 'Because of our iniquities, which were many,' was spoken by another, by one who was in exile. And so it originated with the talmudists . . ."

Then Rabbi Joseph Albo argued: "The talmudists . . . would not have taken into it [the *Talmud*] anything that was contrary to their views. Therefore, they believed that there were two possible periods of time for the Messiah—the time God has promised, or the time when Israel will be prepared and will turn to God. That is why the passage sets no time limit . . . but speaks of 'two thousand years, days of the Messiah'—in other words, days prepared for the coming of the Messiah. If the Jews are worthy of him, he will come at the beginning; if they . . . grow worthy within the period of time, the Messiah will come then. If they do not grow worthy within the period, but at the very end, then the Messiah will come at the end. But the two thousand years will not pass without his coming."

And the pope said: "Why do you not say that if the Christians are worthy of it he will come at once, but if not, that he will tarry until the end of the two thousand years?"

The delegates replied: "We believe that the redeemer will come only for the sake of those who are in exile. For he who lives in peace, does he require a redeemer? . . ."

Then Rabbi Matatiah said to Geronimo: "My wise sir, you prove from the *Talmud* that the Messiah has already come. Why . . . do you not prove the contrary from that selfsame *Talmud:* For it says: 'Let the spirit of those breathe its last, who seek to calculate the end.' " [*Sanhedrin* 97b]

But here the pope interposed, saying: "I have heard this before and should like to know what it is interpreted to mean."

And Rabbi Mattatiah replied: "We . . . follow the plain meaning in the words themselves: A curse be upon him who makes calculations and declares precisely when the Messiah will come. This is very harmful to the people. For when the appointed time arrives, and he does not come, they fall into despair . . . God has hidden this thing from all peoples and from all prophets—yet this man is counting upon revealing it."

At this the pope was greatly angered, and said: "O people of fools, O foolish and despicable talmudists! Does Daniel, for example, who calculated the term, deserve that it be said of him, 'Let his spirit breathe its last'? Truly, it appears that you are as sinful and rebellious as they."

Here Don Todros broke in, saying: "O sir, if the talmudists are so foolish in your eyes, why do you refer to them to prove that the Messiah has already come? 'Nothing can be proved by fools.'" [*Shabbat* 104b]

But at that the pope became still angrier. So Don Vidal . . . said conciliatingly: "It is not like His Holiness to be angered because of a matter that is being debated, especially since we were given freedom of speech. But we must have been guilty of some other thing, and so our words erred. And that is why we beg you, O lord, to give us your favor."

. . . But when we arrived in our lodgings, a bitter quarrel broke out between us and Rabbi Matatiah and Rabbi Todros, because they had . . . failed to rein their tongues.

Geronimo began with a passage [*Yerushalmi Berachot* II] of which Rabbi Judah says: "It is written in Scriptures: 'And Lebanon shall fall by a mighty one. And there shall come forth a shoot out of the stock of Jesse.' This clearly demonstrates that . . . the day the Temple was destroyed, the Messiah was born."

And the wise Abu Astruc replied: "This passage has been discussed by great men, in the debate belween Maestro Moses [Moses ben Nachman, Nachmanides] and Fra Paolo [in Barcelone, 1263]." And Don Vidal said that . . . the maestro explained that it did not mean the Messiah had actually been born. But even if we did say that . . . it would be possible for him to be born on that day, but to live in the Garden of Eden . . . Maimonides also writes that the Messiah was not born on the day of the destruction of the Temple, but that the passage means that from that day on a man is born in every generation worthy to be the Messiah, if Israel were worthy. And . . . that the purpose of these words is to goad hearts to turn to God, and to expound that the Messiah was not dependent upon a fixed time . . ."

The pope replied angrily: ". . . Of what interest to me [is] all this vain and idle quibbling that he was born, but is not as yet come! . . . [Then] why was he born at all? . . . He might have been born on the day on which they were prepared and worthy!"

And the delegates replied: "If they were worthy this very day, and if the Messiah were born this very day, could a child who is one day old lead them?"

The following morning the pope said: "You Jews say terrible things. What sensible man would say that the Messiah was . . . born, but lived in the Garden of Eden . . . for fourteen hundred years?"

Then Rabbi Astruc jumped up and said: "Sir, since you believe so many improbable things about your Messiah, let us believe this one about our Messiah."

And the pope was so aroused by this that we feared his bitter anger would break forth like a fire, and we said to him: "Lord, what our comrade spoke was not fairly spoken and not in agreement with all the rest of us, and he spoke in jest, when he should not have done so, since the pope is not one of us."

We went to our lodgings and we all screamed at Rabbi Astruc, saying: "Our wrong be upon you! For you have put the sword in the hands of our foes. We agreed not speak in the manner you have spoken. See, the pope was favoring our cause, and he came to our assistance more than to Geronimo's. But now that the pope is angered, who will protect us, if not heaven in its mercy? But 'we must not rely on miracles' [talmudic saying] where our own merit is so dubious."

. . . The following morning we returned in great fear and distress. But God granted that we were in favor, and we found the pope with unclouded countenance . . .

From *A Jewish Reader: In Time and Eternity,*
edited by Nahum N. Glatzer

DON ISAAC ABRAVANEL Flees from Portugal, 1483

The misfortunes that befell the Jews of the Iberian Peninsula are typified in the life of Don Isaac Abravanel (1437–1508). He was born to wealthy and prominent parents in Lisbon, Portugal, to which his grandfather had fled from his home in Castile, Spain, after the calamitous anti-Jewish acts of 1391.

Both father and grandfather had held important posts in the Portuguese government. Isaac, too, was gifted both as a scholar and a financier, and was soon made secretary of the treasury by King Alfonso of Portugal. He not only executed his official duties with great skill but also used his prestige to strengthen the Jewish community's adherence to its faith. Revered for his knowledge of Bible and philosophy and for his devotion to his people, Abravanel represented the finest qualities of fifteenth-century Jewry.

In 1483, however, after King Alfonso died, Abravanel was falsely accused of conspiring against the new monarch, Juan II, Alfonso's son. As a result, Isaac's property was confiscated and he and his family had to flee to Spain for their lives.

In Spain also his abilities were quickly recognized, and King Ferdinand appointed him secretary of the treasury. The expulsion of the Jews from Spain in 1492 caused Abravanel to pull up roots once again. He moved first to Naples, and later to Venice, where he remained until his death.

The following is Isaac Abravanel's own account of his flight from Portugal.

Abravanel's Commentary on the Torah, Venice, 1579. (Jewish Theological Seminary)

"God's compassion protected me and they could not find me."

I WAS very happy in my home in Lisbon, the capital of Portugal. I was rich and well-esteemed, living in a beautiful castle where the intellectuals and the pious gathered, as was the custom during the reign of King Alfonso the Great, who ruled with love, and who was fortunate in all his enterprises. The Jews lived in peace and happiness and I was under his special protection. And being very close to him, he made use of my ability and knowledge.

Suddenly, the day of calamity and punishment struck the people of God, the children of Jacob. It was a day of darkness and misfortune when the king became sick and died. The Jews lost their protector. . . . Their streets were full of wailing, fasting and grieving people. I became ill, my pains were unbearable. His son Don Juan, who succeeded to the throne, was suspicious and hostile towards . . . his father's friends. . . . "You deserve to be killed because you plotted against me and against my country to deliver us into the power of the king of Spain," he said.

The king also directed his spite against me. . . . In better times, I had been on friendly terms with the princes who were now persecuted, and who had often solicited my advice. He therefore directed his wrath against me, since he believed that I was one of those who had intrigued against him. . . . Unworthy people, who wanted to oust me in order to appropriate my fortune, schemed against me. They sharpened their tongues like snakes and accused me of misdeeds that had never entered my mind.

During this confusion I received an order to present myself before the king. I started out at once to the palace . . . for I was sure of my innocence. As I was passing an inn, a man approached me and said, "Do not go any further! Save yourself! These are unfortunate times."

Then I understood that my life was in danger . . . I had witnessed with my own eyes how many mighty and pious men were expelled and had to abandon their fortunes to others. I asked myself, "Where to? I know that they are after my wealth. The king wants to get me; so what use are gold and silver to me, all my vineyards? My substance is my misfortune. I have to save my life, even if I have to stay poor and miserable for the rest of my life." So I left my wife, children, and fortune and escaped during the night. . . .

At daybreak, the news of my disappearance reached the palace. The king sent soldiers after me, to bring me back, dead or alive. That day and night the cavalry was seeking me, but God's compassion protected me and they could not find me. In the middle of the night I crossed the frontier of Egypt, that is, the frontier of Portugal. I arrived in the border-city of Segura Della Arden. When the king of Portugal learned that he could not get me, he confiscated all my goods, my whole fortune, the movables and the immovables.

Introduction to *Commentary on the Book of Joshua*,
by Isaac Abravanel

AN ITALIAN JEW Reports the Expulsion from Spain, 1492

On March 31, 1492, the drama of Jewish life in Spain came to its tragic end as King Ferdinand and Queen Isabella signed the decree expelling all Jewish inhabitants.

Although Jews everywhere in Europe were suffering oppression, the events in Spain were especially shocking and poignant—for Spanish Jews had risen to great heights, were eminent in public life, had contributed to Spanish culture, and developed a magnificent culture of their own. All this was ended with one stroke of the pen. Prohibited from exporting any precious metals and limited to what they could carry, multitudes were suddenly impoverished. The hardships were too much for the sick and aged; the rest faced a hopeless wandering in search of refuge.

The Jews sent a delegation to Ferdinand and Isabella, hoping that either sympathy or bribery might change their minds. The delegates were Abraham Senior, secular leader of the Jews of Castile, and Isaac Abravanel, for many years financial advisor to the throne. The pleas of these two court favorites failed to move the monarchs. Senior subsequently converted to Christianity. Abravanel, however, remained steadfast in his faith and chose exile with his brethren, even when the king and queen offered to make an exception of him and to permit him to live in Spain as a Jew.

The selection here was written by an anonymous Italian Jew of the period.

"Because they fled to glorify God's name, only a small number were converted."

IN THE YEAR 1492 during the reign of Ferdinand, God again punished the remnant of the Jewish people, by having them expelled from Spain. Ferdinand had wrested the city of Granada from the Moslems on January 7 [actually January 2nd] and soon thereafter ordered all Jews to be deported from Castile, Catalonia, Aragon, Galicia, Majorca, Minorca, the Basque provinces, Valencia and Alusia, and the islands of Sardinia and Sicilia. The king gave them three months' time to leave the country. On May 1st the edict was read in every city [the nineteenth day of the *Omer* and expired one day before Tishah b'Av] . . . I would estimate that around 50,000 families were affected. They owned homes, land, vineyards, and cattle. The majority however were artisans. There were many *yeshivot* in Spain, and some of the heads were Rabbi Isaac Aboab in Guadalajara. Rabbi Isaac Bezodo in Leon, and Rabbi Jacob Habib in Salamanca. In the latter city lived the great mathematician, Abraham Zacuto, whose advice was sought on all mathematical problems that could not be solved by the Christian scholars.

During the three months left to them, the Jews tried everything in their power to reverse the decree. . . . Their leaders were: the Rabbi Don Abraham Senior, the head of the Spanish communities, who always traveled with a train of thirty mules; Rabbi Meir Hamelamud, the king's secretary [a son-in-law of Abraham Senior]; and Don Isaac Abravanel, who had escaped from the Portuguese king, and was appointed to the same post in the Spanish court . . . Don Isaac Abravanel was later exiled to Naples where he was held in high esteem by the king of Naples . . . Isaac Abravanel used to call Don Abraham Senior *"Soneh Or"* ["Hater of Light," a pun on Senior] because he was an *epicurus* [a heretic]. He was correct, for at the age of eighty, Senior and his whole family [except his brother Samuel] were converted.

Don Abraham had arranged the match between the king and the queen. . . . Because of this, he had been appointed rabbi of the Spanish Jews, but without their consent. An agreement was almost reached that the Jews would pay an enormous amount of money and be permitted to stay, but it was thwarted by an official [supposedly, Torquemada, the Grand Inquisitor] who reminded the queen of the story of the cross. The queen then gave an answer, similar to the saying of King Solomon [*Proverbs* 21:1], . . . adding "Do you believe, that this was brought on you by us? It is God who controls the king's heart."

The Jews realized then that the king was out to harm them and they abandoned all hope. . . . There was little time left, and . . . they sold their homes, their land, and their cattle for paltry sums. As the king did not allow the export of gold or silver, they had to convert their money to textiles, furs, and other articles.

One hundred and twenty thousand persons left for Portugal, following an agreement between the king of Portugal and a . . . certain Don Vidal bar Benevenesti del Cavallaria. . . . The Jews had to pay one ducat for each person admitted and one quarter of their goods in order to stay six months. . . . After the six months had elapsed, he [the king] enslaved them all and deported 700 children [some say 1,400] to the island of St. Thomas where they perished. . . . And so it came to pass, as it is said, "Your sons and daughters will be given to another people . . ." [*Deuteronomy* 28:32]

Many of the exiles went to Moslem countries, to Fez and to the Berber provinces, which were under the rule of the king of Tunis. The Moslems did not admit the Jews to their cities, and many died of starvation, many were devoured by lions and bears while lying exhausted on the outskirts of the cities. A Jew of Tiemsen named Abraham, who was viceroy to the king, admitted many of the exiles into the country, spending a fortune on their behalf. The Jews of North Africa were very helpful. But many of the exiles, finding no place that would receive them, returned to Spain and embraced Christianity. . . . Because they had fled to glorify God's name, only a small number were converted. . . .

When the edict became known in other countries, ships arrived from Genoa to transfer the Jews. The sailors on these ships behaved atrociously towards them, robbing them and delivering most of them to the notorious pirate called the "Corsair of Genoa." Those who managed to escape to Genoa were mercilessly mistreated by the populace, who went so far as to tear children from their mothers' breasts, and to convert them.

Many boatloads of Jews from Sicily arrived in Naples. The king of Naples was friendly to the Jews, behaved mercifully and gave them financial assistance. The Jews of Naples provided the sufferers with good as much as they could, and dispatched messengers throughout Italy to collect money to sustain them. The Marranos in the city lent them money without interest. Even the Dominicans showed human sympathy. But all this was not sufficient to keep them alive. Many died of starvation, others sold their children to Christians to keep them alive. Finally, a plague spread among them, and many died, and those who remained alive were too tired to bury the dead.

Some of the exiles sailed to Turkey. Many of them were thrown overboard and drowned, but those who managed to reach Turkey were warmly received by the sultan because they were artisans. He lent them money and enabled them to settle on an island where they received land and homes.

A few of the exiles settled in the various cities of Italy. . . .

From *The Jew in the Medieval World*, by Jacob R. Marcus

A DISCIPLE Follows Rabbi Obadiah of Bertinoro to Palestine, 1495

Traditionally, the relationship of rabbi and disciple was far more than the usual association of teacher and student. A combination of love, admiration, and reverence bound the disciple to his master in bonds akin to those between parent and child. The student aspired not only to the learning which his teacher expounded, but also to the piety and goodness of his life. To be under the influence of such a noble personality was considered the highest privilege, and a disciple would travel from one end of the world to the other to find such a teacher.

Rabbi Obadiah of Bertinoro (1470–1520), who had emigrated from Italy to Palestine as a young man, personified the virtues of the great teacher. A brilliant scholar whose popular commentary on the *Mishnah* is an indispensable tool of study, he exerted even greater influence by the example of his conduct. For over twenty years his kindness, gentleness, and piety set the moral tone of Jewish life in Jerusalem. His modest and genial demeanor won the unqualified backing of Jew and non-Jew alike, enabling him to reorganize communal life in the Holy City, and to establish a great center of rabbinic learning there.

One young disciple, who had studied with Obadiah in Italy, undertook to follow him to Jerusalem. The student, whose identity is unknown, has left an account of his trip as well as his impressions of life in Palestine, from which the following selection is taken.

". . . Yet he is extremely humble and modest and his words are sweet."

ON the fifth of August 1495, we departed from Venice with gladness, rejoicing to set out on our way peacefully and directly [the direct sea route was again available for Jews].

On the Sabbath day at the twenty-second hour we reached Pola. There we spent two days in the magnificent house of Jacob Ashkenazi, may his Rock and Maker guard him, who graciously led us to his house and prepared a feast. . . .

We set sail with a following wind, and reached Corfu on Monday, the seventeenth of August. Corfu is a large city but . . . mean and dirty, particularly the Jewish quarter. . . . The city is six hundred miles from Pola. . . .

We set out from Corfu with a strong and favorable wind, and reached Modone on Friday morning, the twenty-first of the month. This is also a large city. . . . It has many merchants and is a land of olives, oil and wines, figs and pomegranates. However, the countryside is not as beautiful as your region, and those who dwell in it may be compared to cattle. From Corfu to Modone is a distance of five hundred miles.

We set out from Modone and arrived at Rhodes on Friday, the twenty-seventh of the month, and nobody descended from the ships for some time, for fear of the corsairs, the reason being that Rhodes is a city of refuge for pirates . . . five hundred miles from Modone.

We departed from Rhodes at noon on the twenty-ninth and reached Famagusta on Thursday, the third of September 1495 . . . it is a fine city full of good things. Never in my life have I seen such plenty of bread and meat and everything else. A man can maintain himself honorably and well there on six ducats a year . . . It is true that this is a land that consumes its inhabitants, for the air is very bad and the water too is not good, for which reason the inhabitants are few . . . Famagusta is in Cyprus, three hundred miles distant from Rhodes.

The evening of the sixth of September 1495 we departed from Famagusta, and reached the coast of Beirut on Tuesday the eighth . . . From Venice to Beirut took us thirty-four days. . . .

We took a house in the company of the exalted and saintly man, our master Rabbi Joseph Saragossi, a Sephardic [Spanish] Jew. . . .

The Venetians bring to Damascus and Beirut silver and gold, tin, wrought and beaten copper, and sundry thick garments. On their return they fetch pepper, ginger, and all kinds of spices, silk and Cordovan fabrics, and sometimes precious stones . . . At Beirut we reached an agreement with a donkey driver to take us to Damascus . . . The agreement was drawn up by a scribe there. On the night of Wednesday, the sixteenth of September 1495, we departed from the city to a distance about a bow-shot away . . . and delayed there in order to evade the *kafar* [taxes or other charges on the road]. At midnight we rose and continued on our way all night long without mishap, thank God, and we passed two *kafar* posts without paying them.

In the morning we reached the third *kafar* post, where they treated us very well and sold us bread and grapes, so that we ate till we were full . . . Thus we continued all day and all night long . . . In all that region there are no inns . . . that have rooms—beds and tables; but . . . a tumbledown roofless caravansary called a *khan* may sometimes be found. . . There is no place to lodge, so that people remain outside in the courtyard together with their donkeys.

On Friday morning, which was the eve of the new year, we arrived in Damascus hale and hearty, praise God. We stayed in the house of Rabbi Moses Makran . . . for five days. In none of the places are there innkeepers to furnish food . . . When a stranger . . . arrives in Damascus not a man will budge to take any steps on his behalf save our master Moses Makran. May the Name reward him as befits his good deeds.

On Wednesday, the fifth day of October 1495, we departed from Damascus . . . and reached Safed on Friday, and there took a small room in the house of a poor and needy Jew. . . .

Safed is built on the slopes of a mountain and is a great city. The houses are small and mean, and when the rain falls it is impossible to walk about town on account of the dirt . . . It is also difficult to go out . . . for you must always be climbing up or down. However, the land is good and healthgiving . . . And this is the absolute truth; I saw men in Safed who are far older than sixty or seventy years. Among them was an old man aged a hundred and thirty, who was still flourishing, strong and healthy. The holy congregation numbers about three hundred householders, and most of the Jews have shops of spices, cheese, oil, and . . . fruits. I have heard that a man can make twenty-five ducats out of one of those shops, on which five people can live. . . . Our wise and learned master Rabbi Peretz Colombo, may he see children and length of days, Amen, is the head of this city and showed us favor . . .

. . . Near the Jewish quarter is the burial place of the prophet Hosea ben Beeri of blessed memory. There is no tomb-stone or inscription above it, and only a large stone at the cave mouth; and as soon as I reached Safed I said prayers at this grave. About as far from Safed as one may walk on a Sabbath is the grave of the talmudic master Rabbi Judah bar Ilai . . . and there I prostrated myself and lit candles.

About six miles from Safed is a village called Meron, where very great and pious saints . . . are buried. . . . A little farther away is the burial place of Rabbi Tarphon of saintly and blessed memory, with a handsome monument above it. A little farther yet is the grave of Rabbi Jose ben Kisma of saintly and blessed memory. . . .

After this we reached the village itself and saw the cave of Hillel and his disciples of saintly and blessed memory . . . and they number twenty-four. We entered a cave nearby in which twenty-two scholars lie . . . the disciples of Rabbi Simeon bar Yohai of saintly and blessed memory . . .

On Friday, the twelfth day of the month *Marcheshvan* 5256

[October, 1495], we left Safed . . . with a caravan of donkey drivers, Jews and Christians and Ishmaelites [Arabs]. Their pay was one hundred and two pieces of silver per person to bring them to Jerusalem the Holy. . . .

On Friday, the Sabbath eve, we reached the village of Kana . . . From . . . Kana to Jerusaelm the Holy the way is exceedingly dangerous because of the robbers and the *kafar*, for the *kafar* collectors may take a man's life and none dare protest.

On Tuesday we proceeded all night without a word. . . . We passed the Dothan way, and I saw the pit into which the saintly Joseph of blessed memory was flung . . . During the second night we passed Shechem . . . We journeyed only by night for fear of the *kafar* . . . but . . . the men of the *kafar* of Shechem caught us . . . and took us back to a camp . . . where we remained all night in fear and dread. On Thursday morning the Jews agreed . . . to pay fourteen ducats; and as my share I had to pay fourteen silver pieces. On Thursday night we set out . . . in fear and trembling, for we were afraid that the men of Shechem would pursue us, since most of them are men of violence; but the Lord led us in the ways of truth. By the time the morning star arose, our feet stood before the gates of Jerusalem the Holy City, on Friday morning, the eighteenth day of the month *Marcheshvan.*

When I saw the desolate and ruined city from a distance, and Mount Zion lying waste, a habitation for jackals and a lurking place for young lions . . . my spirit overflowed, my heart mourned . . . I sat down and wept, and rent my garment in two places as is required; and I prayed facing our Temple. May the Lord in His lovingkindness bring back the captivity of Jacob speedily and in our days . . . Amen.

After I entered the town we went to the home of that awesome and famous man, that lofty and exalted light of the Exile . . . my master and teacher Rabbi Obadiah, may his Rock and Maker guard him. To him I made known . . . my abject petition; telling how . . . I had forsaken my family and the land of my birth to take shelter under his shadow . . . Rabbi Obadiah appeared before me, an old man and full of mercy and he said: "I shall keep my eyes upon you like a beloved son and treat you well." . . .

He is a great man and the whole land obeys his words. No one will lift a hand without him, and people inquire often after his opinion from the ends of the earth . . . Even the Ishmaelites honor and fear him . . . yet he is extremely humble and modest and his words are sweet. . . .

In Jerusalem the Holy there are about two hundred householders who refrain from any sin or transgression and are heedful . . . of the commandments. Evening and morning and noon they gather together, rich and poor alike, to pray. . . . An aged, wise, and understanding man of eighty years named Rabbi Zechariah Sephardi, may he see length of days, Amen, delivers a sermon after the morning prayer . . . as well as after the evening prayer . . . But the great light, Rabbi Obadiah, speaks only two or three times a year. . . .

Every day after the prayer and the sermon, people stay in the house of study . . . and afterward they "go from strength to strength," visiting the sick and giving gifts to the poor, each one giving what his heart counsels him. The people give much alms although they have little themselves, and there are many poor folk in this city, so that most of the congregation are supported by charity.

There is little to be earned here in Jerusalem the Holy. . . . Any handicraftsman, such as a goldsmith or blacksmith, or a flax-weaver or a tailor, will earn his needs, albeit scantily. . . .

The houses in Jerusalem the Holy are all of stone and do not have many floors. . . . Indeed, wood in this city is extremely expensive. . . . Nor does this city have any wells of fresh water. Instead, every courtyard has a single pit full of rain water, and if there is no rain, the water in these pits is used up; and sometimes the Ishmaelites gather together to pour out Jewish wine and smash Jewish vessels, for they say that the rain does not fall on account of the sin of the Jews in drinking wine. . . .

In the city . . . there is an empty place to which all the congregation go after prayers in order to pray facing the Temple. . . . Near this is the El Aksa Mosque, "the school of King Solomon," may he rest in peace, but only Ishmaelites enter there. . . . And I have heard . . . that the building is made of extremely beautiful stones, radiant and pure as the very heavens, and covered over with pure gold . . . and the Ishmaelites gather there every Friday at noon and say their prayers. . . .

Below is the valley of Jehoshaphat and the valley of ben Hinnom, and beyond . . . a building like a tower called the Pillar of Absalom. It is half-hidden by stones which have been thrown at it, because . . . of Absalom who rebelled against his father. . . .

On the Mount of Olives there is a large cave in which are buried the prophets Haggai, Zechariah, and Malachi, of blessed memory. About half a day's journey is the burial place of the prophet Samuel of Ramah, of saintly and blessed memory . . . on top of the mountain and there is a fine synagogue there. . . . The burial place of the patriarchs in Hebron is a day's journey and on that road is the Tomb of Rachel, may she rest in peace. But I have not been there, as the roads are not safe on account of the Arabs.

From *Roads to Zion,* by Kurt Wilhelm

AN INQUISITOR Details Proceedings of the Inquisition, 1567-69

In the thirteenth century, the pope established the Inquisition—an office for the suppression of beliefs and practices contrary to the will of the Church. Although the Inquisition fulfilled the wishes of devout Christians to destroy heresy, its secret investigations and merciless prosecutions of anyone who deviated from official Catholic doctrine filled the people with fear and trembling. It also antagonized civil government, since it was a law unto itself. Moreover, the property it confiscated went to the Church instead of to the king or his barons. Local bishops resented it because it diminished their own authority. But, it was throughout the Middle Ages the Church's most effective weapon against heterodoxy (unaccepted doctrines).

Technically, the Inquisition had jurisdiction only over Christians, so that Jews were outside the scope of its authority. It had control, however, over the Marranos, converts to Christianity who secretly continued to practice Judaism. The populaces of Spain and Portugal hated the Marranos, not only for their attachment to Judaism, but because as equal members of society they were economic competition. The desire to persecute the Marranos was responsible for the establishment of the Inquisition in many places. As a result, thousands upon thousands of Jews suffered the agonies of the torture chamber and ended their lives on burning pyres.

The following excerpt from the official records of the Inquisition describes only the beginning of the ordeal of Elvira del Campo, a Marrano who subsequently confessed whatever was demanded of her.

Various tortures during the Inquisition. (The Jewish Encyclopedia, *Funk & Wagnalls*)

Procession of the Inquisition at Goa which was the chief seat in South India. (*After Picart,* The Jewish Encyclopedia, *Funk & Wagnalls*)

"Lord, you are witness that if I knew how to say anything else I would say it."

SHE WAS carried to the torture chamber and told to tell the truth, when she said that she had nothing to say. She was ordered to be stripped and again admonished, but was silent. When stripped, she said "Señores, I have done all that is said of me and I bear false-witness against myself, for I do not want to see myself in such trouble; please God, I have done nothing." She was told not to bring false testimony against herself but to tell the truth. The tying of the arms commenced; she said, "I have told the truth; what have I to tell?" She was told to tell the truth and replied, "I have told the truth and have nothing to tell." One cord was applied to the arms and twisted and she was admonished to tell the truth but said she had nothing to tell. Then she screamed and said, "I have done all they say." Told to tell in detail what she had done she replied, "I have already told the truth." Then she screamed and said, "Tell me what you want for I don't know what to say." She was told to tell what she had done, for she was tortured because she had not done so, and another turn of the cord was ordered. She cried: "Loosen me, Señores, and tell me what I have to say: I do not know what I have done, O Lord have mercy on me, a sinner!" Another turn was given and she said, "Loosen me a little that I may remember what I have to tell; I don't know what I have done; I did not eat pork, for it made me sick; I have done everything; loosen me and I will tell the truth." . . . She was told to tell what she had done contrary to our holy Catholic faith. . . . She was told to tell in detail truly what she did. She said, "What am I wanted to tell? I did everything—loosen me for I don't remember what I have to tell—don't you see what a weak woman I am? Oh! Oh! my arms are breaking." More turns were ordered and as they were given she cried, "Oh . . . Oh, my arms! I don't know what I have to say—If I did I would tell it." The cords were ordered to be tightened when she said, "Señores have you no pity on a sinful woman?"

She was told, yes, if she would tell the truth. She said, "Señor tell me, tell me it." The cords were tightened again, and she . . . was ordered to tell in detail, to which she said, "I don't know how to tell it señor, I don't know." Then the cords were separated and counted, and there were sixteen turns, and in giving the last turn the cord broke.

She was then ordered to be placed on the *potro* [frame]. She said: "Señores, why will you not tell me what I have to say? Señor, put me on the ground—have I not said that I did it all? I have said I did all that the witnesses say. Señores release me, for I do not remember it." She was told to tell it. She said, "I do not know it. Oh, Oh, they are tearing me to pieces—I have said that I did it —let me go." She was told to tell it. She said: "Señores, it does not help me to say that I did it, and I have admitted that what I have done has brought me to this suffering—Señor, you know the truth—Señores, for God's sake have mercy on me. Oh Señor, take these things from my arms—Señor, release me, they are killing me." . . . The garrotes were ordered to be tightened. She said, "Señor, do you not see how these people are killing me? Señor, I did it—for God's sake let me go." She was told to tell it. She said, "Señor, remind me of what I did not know. . . . She was told to tell the truth or the cords would be tightened. She said, "Remind me of what I have to say for I don't know it—I said that I did not want to eat it—I know only that I did not want to eat it," and this she repeated many times. She was told to tell why she did not want to eat it. She said, "For the reason that the witnesses say—I don't know how to tell it—miserable that I am that I don't know how to tell it. I say I did it, and my God how can I tell it?" Then she said that, as she did not do it, how could she tell it—"They will not listen to me—these people want to kill me—release me and I will tell the truth." . . . She was told to declare it. She said, "I don't know how to say it—I have no memory—Lord, you are witness that if I knew how to say anything else I would say it. I know nothing more to say than that I did it and God knows it." She said many times, "Señores, Señores, nothing helps me. You, Lord, hear that I tell the truth and can say no more—they are tearing out my soul—order them to loosen me." Then she said, "I do not say that I did it—I said no more." Then she said, "Señor, I did it to observe that law." She was asked what law. She said, "The law that the witnesses say—I declare it all Señor, and don't remember what law it was—O, wretched was the mother that bore me." She was asked what was the law she meant and what was the law she said the witnesses say. This was asked repeatedly, but she was silent and at last said that she did not know. She was told to tell the truth or the garrotes would be tightened but she did not answer. Another turn was ordered on the garrotes and she was admonished to say what law it was. She said, "If I knew what to say I would say it. Oh Señor, I don't know what I have to say—Oh, Oh, they are killing me—if they would tell me what—Oh, Señores! Oh, my heart!" Then she asked why they wished her to tell what she could not tell and cried repeatedly "O, miserable me!" Then she said, "Lord, bear witness that they are killing me without my being able to confess." She was told that if she wished to tell the truth before the water was poured she should do so and discharge her conscience. She said that she could not speak and that she was a sinner. Then the linen *toca* [funnel] was placed [in her throat] and she said "Take it away, I am strangling and am sick in the stomach." A jar of water was then poured down, after which she was told to tell the truth. She clamoured for confession, saying that she was dying. She was told that the torture would be continued till she told the truth and was admonished to tell it, but though she was questioned repeatedly she remained silent.

Then the inquisitor, seeing her exhausted by the torture, ordered it to be suspended.

From the official records of the Holy Office of the Inquisition, as quoted in *A History of the Marranos*, by Cecil Roth

A JEWISH MYSTIC Speaks of Kabalism, 1607

Safed, set in the inspiring hills of northern Israel, became the center of Jewish mysticism in the sixteenth and seventeenth centuries. Dismayed by the misfortunes of European Jewry, which were climaxed by the expulsion from Spain in 1492, many sensitive Jews migrated to Safed where they delved into *Kabalah* (Jewish mysticism). They tried to understand the reasons for Jewish suffering as well as, all-important, the time and circumstances of their redemption.

The Kabalists ardently sought to understand God's mysteries and to use that knowledge to save the world. Study, prayer, fasting, and the faithful performance of all of God's commandments, both ethical and ritual, were the means they used. Their saintliness was revered by Jews everywhere.

The most prominent Safed mystic was the German scholar Rabbi Isaac Luria, who founded a school for the study of his own brand of Kabalism which believed in such unusual ideas as the transmigration of souls. His immersion in Jewish mysticism was so esteemed that many Jews left their homes to come to Safed to pursue the pious life led by Luria and his followers. Among them was Solomon Meinsterl, who gave up his wife and daughter when they refused to uproot themselves from their home in eastern Europe in order to settle in Safed.

In the letter reprinted here, Solomon Meinsterl gives insight into the saintly and scholarly life of the Safed Kabalists.

Safed, entrance to a synagogue. (Israel Office of Information)

"So now I have no other business than the business of the Torah and the service of the blessed Name."

THE DAY I became twenty-two my Maker moved me and awakened my heart and said unto me: "How long, O sluggard, wilt thou sleep in the slumber of idleness? Rise now, gird up thy loins like a warrior and pursue the knowledge of the *Torah* and of the commandments . . ."

Thereupon I arose and took courage and put away all worldly affairs from me; and I prepared myself to seek and know the God of my fathers . . .

And when my Maker brought me to my twenty-eighth year, tidings reached me of the awesome, holy, and wonderful wisdom to be gained in the Land of the Living, where are to be found the seats of *Torah* and Testimony . . . At once I girded my loins to run the course; and I sent my wife away with a divorce as she did not wish to go with me [Jewish law in cases where a husband or wife did not wish to emigrate to the Land of Israel with his partner]. I also paid her all that was due her in accordance with her marriage contract, and also left our one daughter who was at that time thirteen years old with her. So, of all that had been mine not so much as a hair was left, not even my clothes and books, for I left them behind for her alimony and for the dowry of my daughter; but I trusted in the God of Jacob . . . So I did depart from the land of my birth, in complete destitution.

So I arrived in the holy city of Safed in the mid-days of the Feast of Booths of 5363 [autumn, 1602], arriving in peace and finding a holy congregation. For this is a great city before God with close on to three hundred great rabbis . . . Eighteen talmudic academies I found here, as well as twenty-one synagogues and a large house of study with close on to four hundred children in the charge of four teachers, who give them free instruction. For there are wealthy folk in Constantinople who pay the hire of the teachers, and likewise send them clothes every year.

And in all the synagogues, after the morning and evening prayer, the entire congregation gather together and sit before their rabbis, five or six groups in every synagogue, each group engaging in study . . .

In this way there is no one who goes forth in the morning to his trade or business without having first learned his measure of the *Torah*. Everybody does the same . . . after the evening prayer. Then on the Sabbath day all the people go to hear the sermons of the rabbis. And every Thursday they all gather together in one great synagogue after the morning prayer, where they pray to his Name; an awesome prayer for the welfare of all Israel . . . and mourn the Exile . . . and the destruction of the house of our God. And they bless all those who send their money to aid the poor of the Land of Israel . . .

Before they begin to pray, the great and pious rabbi, our master Rabbi Moses Galante, may his Rock and Maker guard him, ascends the pulpit and utters mighty words . . . Afterward there ascend two heads of academies, great and pious scholars and men of good deeds.

Then they begin to pray in awe and fear and great dread, their eyes weeping like two fountains of water. Who has ever seen the like of those great and bitter prayers and outcries of all Israel that weep and as one man let tears fall over the Exile and the Destruction . . .

Then every new moon's eve they follow the practices of the eve of the Day of Atonement until midnight . . . And all Israel gather together in one great synagogue or proceed to the grave of Hosea ben Beeri the prophet . . . or to the cave of the divine teacher, Abba Saul, may he rest in peace; or . . . before the grave of Rabbi Judah bar Ilai . . . There they pray an awesome prayer . . .

Now the Gentiles . . . are all subject to the holiness of Israel . . . Not a single Gentile would dare approach a congregation of Jews praying, or open his mouth to mock . . . On the contrary, they hold the graves of our holy masters in great reverence, as well as the synagogues; and they kindle lights at the graves and vow to supply the synagogues with oil.

The villages of En Zetim and Meron contain ruined synagogues, but because of our many sins no Jews dwell there. There are countless Torah scrolls . . . in the synagogues which the Gentiles treat with much honor. The keys to the synagogues are in their hands, and they clean them and light candles before the arks, and no one would dare to touch a Torah scroll. Sometimes we go to pray . . . in those synagogues.

The entire Holy Land is filled with the blessing of the Lord, with great plenty . . . Now when I . . . saw all this bounty is being consumed by the nations of the world while Israel are dispersed . . . I wept greatly and I said: "Would that our brethren, the children of Israel, knew but a tenth of all this plenty and goodness . . . to be found in the Land of Israel! For then they would weep day and night over their exile . . ."

Poultry and eggs are very cheap . . . The mutton is good and fat, and each sheep has a fatty tail weighing seven pounds . . . Beef costs a pound for three *kreutzer,* and fish one pound for our smallest coin . . . Rice is cheaper, as well as sundry kinds of beans and peas and lentils . . . There are also sundry sweets, . . . the like of which you have never tasted . . . Then there are the fine fruits: carobs, oranges, lemons, and melons and watermelons which are as sweet as sugar, and cucumbers, and pumpkins, and lettuces and all sorts of other greens which are unknown to you, so there is no advantage in my mentioning them.

. . . He who has merited of the Name, be it blessed, to make his home in the Land of Israel, and has a little money . . . happy is he and happy his portion . . . Apart from this, there are the clear and wholesome air and the healthgiving water which prolong a man's days. For this reason most of the inhabitants . . . live to eighty, ninety, a hundred, or a hundred and ten years.

Now the Lord who is the true God and King of the universe

. . . had appointed for me as my helpmeet a good and God-fearing woman, the daughter of a great and very exalted and pious scholar . . . Rabbi Israel Sarug of blessed memory.

The Holy One, blessed be He, has given me the merit of possessing all the writings prepared by that holy and godly man and teacher of all Israel, our master Rabbi Isaac Luria of blessed memory . . . I came to them through the wife I married in the Land of Israel, who inherited them from her honored father . . . who tirelessly sought them out all his life and expended more than two hundred *thalers* until he obtained them all.

I now have them, praise God, and delight in them every day.

So now I have no other business than the business of the *Torah* and the service of the blessed Name . . . The woman whom your servant married did not bring me gold or silver, but a house and its vessels and the *Kabalah* writing of our master Rabbi Isaac Luria of blessed memory . . . For I married the daughter of a pious scholar for the sake of heaven, to obtain those holy writings, for without her I could never have obtained them at all . . . The Holy One, blessed be He, has caused me to find favor and friendship in the eyes of all the sages of Safed . . . and they do not withhold from me any of the secrets concealed in the *Torah,* praise God.

Written by Solomon Schloemel, son of my noble father, Rabbi Hayyim, known as Meinsterl, of blessed memory, and written in haste here at Safed, may she be rebuilt and established speedily and in our days, in the Upper Galilee, which is in "the Land of Beauty," on the twenty-fourth day of *Tamuz* 5367 [1607].

From *Roads to Zion,* by Kurt Wilhelm

RABBI NATHAN HANOVER Sees the Massacres at Nemirow, 1648

The bloodiest massacres that befell the Jews of Europe occurred in Poland in 1648 during the Cossack rebellion against the Poles. The Cossacks, a sturdy and contentious band of Ukrainian peasants, originally organized in defense against the Asian Tatars, resented Polish rule which they accused of economic oppression, political tyranny, and religious heresy. The Jew, whose faith was alien both to Polish Catholic and Greek Orthodox Cossack, was hated by both. As renting agent and overseer of the large Polish estates, which exacted oppressive fees from the Ukrainian peasants, he was associated in the popular imagination with the despised Polish nobles. Consequently, when the Cossacks raised the banner of insurrection under Bogdan Chmielnitzki, they perpetrated atrocities on Jews and Poles alike.

Cossack barbarism knew no limits. Beautiful estates were burned to the ground. Human beings, whether Jews or Poles, were flayed like fish, mutilated, and often left to a slow and agonizing death. Women were taken captive, others violated in the presence of their families. Children were ripped from their mothers' breasts and drowned in wells. To escape death, many Jews fled to the Tatars, who did nothing worse than enslave them.

One of the worst assaults occurred in Nemirow, whose Jews were treacherously delivered into enemy hands. The heart-rending story is contained in this on-the-spot account by Rabbi Nathan Hanover. The disorders continued for almost three years, a period in Jewish history referred to as "The Black Years."

"They perished by all sorts of terrible deaths . . . May God avenge their blood."

THE OPPRESSOR Chmiel, may his name be blotted out, heard that many Jews had gathered in the holy community of Nemirow, and that they had a great deal of silver and gold with them. He knew that the holy community of Nemirow was distinguished for its great riches. It had been a great and important community replete with scholars and scribes, a city full of justice, the abode of righteousness . . .

Accordingly, Chmiel sent a leader, an enemy of the Jews, and about 600 swordsmen with him, to attack this noble community. In addition, he wrote to the city heads to help the band. The city leaders readily responded . . . not so much out of love for the Cossacks, but because of hatred of the Jews.

And it came to pass on a Wednesday, the 20th of *Sivan,* that Cossacks approached the city of Nemirow. When the Jews saw the troops from afar, their hearts trembled from fright . . . All the Jews went with their wives, and infants, with their silver and gold, into the fortress, and locked and barred the doors, prepared to fight them. What did those evil-doers, the Cossacks do? They devised flags like those of the Poles, for there is no way to distinguish between the Polish and the Cossack forces except through their banners. The people of the city were fully aware of this trickery, and nevertheless called to the Jews in the fortress: "Open the gate. This is a Polish army which has come to save you . . ." The Jews standing guard on the wall, seeing the flags of Poland, believed that the people of the city spoke the truth . . . No sooner had the gate been opened than the Cossacks entered with drawn swords, and the townspeople, too, armed with swords, spears, and scythes, and some only with clubs, and they killed the Jews in large numbers. Women and young girls were ravished, but some of the women and maidens jumped into the moat surrounding the fortress in order that the uncircumcized should not defile them. They drowned in the waters. Many of them who were able to swim, jumped into water, believing they would escape the slaughter, but the Ukrainians swam after them with their swords and their scythes, and killed them in the water. Some of the enemy shot with their guns into the water . . . until the water became red with blood . . .

The head of the rabbinical academy of Nemirow was also there, . . . our master and teacher, Rabbi Yechiel Michael, son of our great teacher, Rabbi Eliezer, of blessed memory. He knew the whole of rabbinic writings by heart and was proficient in all the worldly sciences. On the Sabbath before . . . he had preached and admonished the people that if the enemy should come (God forbid), they should not change their faith, but rather be martyred for the sanctification of His Name. This the holy people did. A Ukrainian seized him . . . but the scholar implored him not to kill him, for which he would compensate him with a great deal of gold and silver. The Ukrainian consented, and he led him to the house, where his silver and gold were hidden, and the Cossack released him. The rabbi . . . and his mother hid in a certain house all that night . . .

On the morrow, the 22nd of *Sivan*, the Ukrainians searched the houses . . . The rabbi and his mother fled to the cemetery . . . But near the cemetery, a Ukrainian shoemaker, one of the townspeople, pursued the rabbi with club in hand . . . The rabbi's mother pleaded with the Ukrainian to be killed instead of her son, but he . . . proceeded to kill first the rabbi and then the mother, may God avenge their blood . . .

It happened there that a beautiful maiden, of a renowned and wealthy family, had been captured by a certain Cossack who forced her to be his wife. But, before they lived together she told him with cunning that she possessed a certain magic and that no weapon could harm her. She said to him, "If you do not believe me, just test me. Shoot at me with a gun, and you will see that I will not be harmed." The Cossack, in his simplicity, . . .

shot at her, and she fell and died for the sanctification of the Name, to avoid being defiled by him, may God avenge her blood.

Another beautiful girl, about to be married to a Cossack, insisted that their marriage take place in a church across the bridge. He granted her request, and with timbrels and flutes, attired in festive garb, led her to the marriage. As soon as they came to the bridge she jumped into the water and was drowned for the sanctification of the Name. May God avenge her blood . . . The number of the slain and drowned in the holy community of Nemirow was about 6,000. They perished by all sorts of terrible deaths . . . May God avenge their blood. Those who escaped fled to the holy community of Tulczyn, for there, outside the city, was a very strong fortress.

From *Abyss of Despair*, by Nathan Hanover

MENASSEH BEN ISRAEL
Intercedes with Cromwell, 1655

Since the Jews had been banned from England in 1290, that country was closed to the desperate refugees fleeing the Inquisition. In 1649, however, the English monarchy was overthrown by Oliver Cromwell and his Puritans, who were devoted to the Bible and held the Chosen People of God in high esteem.

Hoping that the Puritans might reverse the ban on the Jews, the noted Amsterdam rabbi, Menasseh ben Israel (1604–1657), made an appeal to Cromwell. The son of Portuguese Marranos who had found haven in Holland, Menasseh was a cultured and cosmopolitan man. He was drawn to the speculations of the Christian Millenarians (believers in the messianic era of the prophesied millennium) that the end of days was at hand. Prerequisite, however, was the return of the Jews to the Land of Israel and the reunion of the Ten Lost Tribes with the remnant of Judah.

A Marrano named Antonio de Montezinos declared that he had met American Indians who claimed descent from the tribe of Reuben. The rabbi investigated and reported his findings in *The Hope of Israel,* a tract in Spanish on the theory that the lost tribes had wandered from Tartary across China to the New World. Hence, the Jews had been dispersed to every land but England, and the biblical prophecy was almost fulfilled.

Cromwell saw the potential value of the Jews to British commerce. His interest led Menasseh to rewrite his book in Latin with a special dedication to the English Parliament, appealing for good will to the scattered remnants of his people. Cromwell invited him to England in 1652, but hostilities between England and Holland interfered. A second invitation in 1655 gave Menasseh the chance to appeal in his *Humble Addresses* for readmission of the Jews to England. His case was based on both the messianic and the practical. First, complete dispersion of the Jews throughout the world, which was indispensable to redemption, required their presence in England. Second, the Jews could enrich England's commercial wealth.

Although Cromwell personally favored Menasseh's cause, the Parliament turned it down. Nevertheless, a conference of lawyers at Whitestone in 1655 declared that there was nothing in English law to prevent Jews from settling there. Gradually Jews returned to the island.

Although Menasseh died believing that he had failed, he had made it possible for the Jews to return "by the back door." In a few years, English Jewry formed a community which held religious services and acquired a cemetery.

The letter which follows, written in Portuguese by Menasseh on the eve of his trip, shows his emotions as he set out on his mission.

"Moved only by zeal and love of my people . . . I am setting out today on this enterprise."

The Chacham Menasseh ben Israel to all persons of the Hebrew nation living in Asia and in Europe, especially to the Holy Synagogues of Italy and Holstein, S.P.D. [salutem plurimam dicit, bids abundant peace]

IT IS notorious to all of our nation how (moved not only by the merit of the case, but also by certain letters from virtuous and prudent individuals) I have labored for a long time past in order that there should be conceded to us in the most flourishing Commonwealth of England the right of public exercise of our

To His Highnesse Oliuer Lord Protector of The Commonwelth of England, Scotland, and Ireland, & the Dominions thereof

The Humble Petition of The Hebrews at Present Reziding in this citty of London whose names ar Vnderwritten

Humbly sheweth

That Acknowledging The Manyfold fauours and Protection yor Highnesse hath bin pleased to graunt Vs in order that wee may with security meete priuatley in our particular houses to our Deuotions, And being desirous to be fauoured more by yor Highnesse, wee pray with all Humblenesse yt by the best meanes which may be such Protection may be graunted Vs in Writting as that wee may therewth meete at our said priuate deuotions in our Particular houses without feere of Molestation either to our persons famillys or estates, our desires Being to Liue Peaceably under yor Highnes Gouernement, And being wee ar all mortall wee allsoe Humbly pray yor Highnesse to graunt Vs Lisence that those which may dey of our nation may be buryed in such place out of the cittye as wee shall thinck Conuenient with the Proprietors Leaue in whose Land the place shall be, and soe wee shall as well in our life tyme as at our death be highly fauoured by yor Highnesse for whose Long Life and Prosperity wee shall continually pray To the allmighty God &c.

Menasseh ben Israel
David Abrabanel
Abraham Israel Caruajal
Abraham Coen Gonsales
Jahacob de Caceres
Abraham Israel de Brito
Isak Lopes Chillon

HER MAJESTY'S STATE PAPER OFFICE

Petition
of Commiss.

Menasseh ben Israel, by Rembrandt. (Foto-Commissie Rijksmuseum, Amsterdam)
Petition to Cromwell, 1655–56.

religion; as also how . . . on two occasions, I was persuaded by my relatives, for certain political reasons, to postpone the journey . . . Now therefore do I once more make known to all how, although not yet fully recovered from a long illness, moved only by zeal and love of my people and (as I have signified) neglecting all of my private interests, I am setting out today on this enterprise; which I pray may be to the service of God and to our common good. It is true that certain persons who are in the employment and under the protection of divers most clement princes and magistrates little esteem this perpetual care of mine. Nevertheless, considering the general approval, the common good, the affliction of those of our people who are today so oppressed, who could find refuge and remedy in that most puissant Commonwealth, without prejudice to any other; having regard, too, for the many souls who, dissimulating their religion, dwell scattered in so many parts of Spain and France; it was impossible for me to neglect an affair of such merit, even though it be at the cost of my faculties. I have been informed by letters, and by faithful correspondents, that today this English nation is no longer our ancient enemy, but has changed the papistical religion and become excellently affected to our nation, as an oppressed people whereof it has good hope. Nevertheless, since there is nothing sure or certain in this world, I supplicate all of the holy congregations that in their orisons they pray affectionately to God to give me grace in the eyes of the most benign and valorous Prince, his Highness, the Lord Protector, and in those of his most prudent Council, that he may give us liberty in his land, where we may similarly pray to the most high God for his prosperity. Farewell!

The *Chacham* Menasseh ben Israel, Amsterdam, 2nd September 5415 (1655)

From *Anglo-Jewish Letters*, edited by Cecil Roth

A BRITISH DIPLOMAT Comments on Sabatai Zevi, 1626-1676

What was Sabatai Zevi—a scoundrel, an idealist, a deluded mystic? We may never answer this question, but we do know that he wielded tremendous influence in his day and, for a few years, brought solace and hope to a generation of Jews mired in misery and despair.

A number of historical accidents conspired towards his acceptance by the Jewish masses as their Messiah. First, Sabatai Zevi arose in the third quarter of the seventeenth century, a time when both Jewish and Christian mystics had predicted that the Messiah would arrive. The tragic persecutions of the Jews of central and eastern Europe seemed to correspond to the war and pestilence which Jewish tradition said were to precede the Messiah's coming. He was born on the Ninth of *Av*, and an ancient legend connected the Messiah's birth with the date of the destruction of the Temple. Finally, his physical attractiveness, his magnetic personality, his profound knowledge of the *Zohar*, his exalted self-image and bold actions evoked widespread support.

Nathan of Gaza, a young man of supposed prophetic powers, announced that Sabatai Zevi was the Messiah. Then the latter's marriage to a girl named Sarah, who had been predicting that she would marry the Messiah, aroused the expectations of Jewish multitudes from one end of Europe to the other. Women reacted hysterically wherever he preached. Sensible men sold their property in preparation for the trip to Palestine. Even Christians stood by in astonishment, waiting for the final redemption.

Their hopes, however, were doomed to disappointment. The Turkish sultan arrested Sabatai Zevi.

Threatened by death, the supposed messiah not only repudiated all previous claims and promises, but even converted to Islam. This shocking turn of events disillusioned all but a few diehards.

Sir Paul Rycault (1628–1700) was secretary at the British embassy to the Ottoman court from 1661 to 1667, and from 1667 to 1668, consul at Smyrna, Sabatai Zevi's birthplace. He wrote in great detail about the affair, compiling material gathered from distinguished Jews and non-Jews of the time. His report is presented in his own words.

"And here I leave the reader to consider how strangely this deceived people was bemused . . ."

Anno 1666

WE SHALL begin this year with the strange disturbance of the Jews concerning Sabatai Zevi, their pretended messiah.

According to the predictions of several Christian writers, who comment on the *Apocalypse* or *Revelations,* 1666 was to prove a year of wonders, and of blessing to the Jews . . . Whereupon strange reports flew from place to place, of the march of multitudes of people into remote deserts of Arabia, supposed to be the Ten Tribes and a half, lost for so many ages. That a ship was arrived in Scotland, with sails and cordage of silk, navigated by marriners who spoke only *Hebrew,* and with this motto on their sails, *The Twelve Tribes of Israel.* These reports, agreeing to former predictions, put the wild sort of the world into an expectation of strange accidents this year . . . regarding the *Jewish* monarchy.

. . . Sabatai Zevi first appeared at Smyrna, and published himself to the Jews for their Messiah, relating the greatness of their approaching kingdom, that God was about to deliver them from

Collection of prayers in Sabatai Zevi's honor, published in Amsterdam, 1666. (Jewish Theological Seminary)

Sabatai Zevi. From an old print. (The Jewish Encyclopedia, *Funk & Wagnalls)*

bondage, and gather them from all parts of the world. It was strange to see how fast the report of Sabatai flew . . . I perceived a strange transport in the Jews, none of them attending to any business, unless to wind up negotiations, and to prepare for a journey to Jerusalem.

Sabatai Zevi was son of Mordecai Zevi, an inhabitant and natural [native] broker to an English merchant . . . But his son Sabatai Zevi . . . became a notable proficient in the Hebrew and Arabick languages; and especially in divinity and metaphysicks . . . and drew so many disciples, as one day raised a tumult in the synagogue; for which afterwards he was by censure of the *kochams* [*chachams,* literally, "wise men"] (who are the expounders of the law) banished out of the city.

During the time of his exile he travelled to Thessalonica, now called Salonica, where he married a very handsum woman; but . . . she was divorced from him. Again, he took a second wife more beautiful than the former; but he . . . obtained another divorce. And . . . his wandring head moved him to travel through the Morea, thence to Tripoli in Syria, Gaza, and Jerusalem, and by the way picked up a Ligornese lady, whom he made his third wife . . . And at Jerusalem . . . meeting with a certain Jew called Nathan, a proper instrument to promote his design, he told him his . . . intentions to declare himself the Messiah of the world, so long expected and desired by the Jews. This design took wonderfully with Nathan; and because it was thought necessary, according to Scripture and ancient prophecies, that Elias [Elijah] was to precede the Messiah, Nathan thought no man so proper to act the part of the prophet as himself; and so no sooner had Sabatai declared himself the Messiah, but Nathan discovers himself to be his prophet . . . and to confirm this belief the more . . . the rumour of the Messiah had flown so swift that intelligence came from all countries, where the Jews sojourn, by letters to Gaza and Jerusalem, congratulating the happiness of their deliverance . . . To which they adjoyned other prophecies . . . that for nine months the Messiah was to disappear;

. . . but then returning again should be acknowledged for the sole monarch of the universe . . . And here I leave the reader to consider, how strangely this deceived people was bemused . . .

. . . Sabatai Zevi resolved to travel toward Smyrna, the country of his nativity, and thence to Constantinople . . .

And now all the cities of Turkie, where the Jews inhabited, were full of the expectation of the Messiah, no trade was followed; every one imagined that daily provisions, riches, honours, and government were to descend upon him by some miraculous manner . . . The Jews at Thessalonica . . . to purifie their consciences from all sins . . . applied themselves to fastings, and some having for seven days taken no sustenance were famished; others buried themselves in their gardens, their heads only excepted . . . until their bodies were stiffened with cold; others would roul themselves in the snow . . . All business was laid aside . . . unless to clear merchandise at any price . . .

In the heat of all this talk and rumour came Sabatai Zevi to Smyrna . . . but by the *kochams* or doctors of their law, who gave no credence to what he pretended, was ill received . . . took boldness to enter into dispute with the Grand *Kocham* (who is chief expositor of their law, and superintendent of their civil government) . . . and the Grand *Kocham,* losing both the affection and obedience of his people, was displaced from his office . . . No invitation . . . nor marriage, nor circumcision held, where Sabatai was not present, accompanied with multitudes of his followers, and the streets covered with carpets for him to tread on; but his humility appeared such that he would stoop and turn them aside . . .

Notwithstanding . . . many opposed his doctrine, publickly avouching that he was an impostor, amongst which was one Samuel Pennia, a man of good estate and reputation in Smyrna; who . . . raised such a sedition and tumult amongst the Jews, as not only prevailed against his arguments, but had also against his life, had he not timely conveyed himself out of the synagogue . . . But howsoever it fell out, Pennia in a short time became a convert and not only he, but his whole family, fell into strange ecstasies: and not only this house, but above four hundred men and women prophesie of the growing kingdom of Sabatai, and young infants who could scarce yet stammer out a syllable to their mothers, repeat and pronounce clearly the name of Sabatai . . . All being effects of diabolical delusions, as the Jews themselves since have confessed to me . . .

In this manner things ran to strange height of madness amongst the Jews at Smyrna, that no comedy could equal . . .

Sabatai Zevi . . . declared that he was called by God to visit Constantinople . . . whereunto he privately shipped himself with some few attendants on a Turkish saike in the month of January 1665, lest the crowd of his disciples should endanger him in the eyes of the Turks . . . Yet multitudes of Jews traveled over land to meet him again at Constantinople . . . The great vizier then also at Constantinople, having heard some rumours of this man, and the disorder and madness he had raised amongst the Jews, sent two boats . . . with commands to bring him up prisoner to the port, where accordingly Sabatai being come was committed to the most loathsome and darkest dungeon in the town . . . The Jews were not at all discouraged at this ill treatment of their prophet, but rather confirmed in their belief of him, as being an accomplishment of the prophecy of those things which ought to precede his glory and dominion; which induced the chiefest persons amongst the Jews to make their visits and addresses to him with the same ceremony and respect in the dungeon as they would have done had he then sate exalted on the throne of Judah . . .

Sabatai Zevi remained a prisoner at Constantinople for two months; at the end of which the vizier having designed his expedition for Candia . . . thought it not secure to suffer him to remain in the imperial city, whilst both the grand signior and himself were absent; and therefore changed his prison to the Dardanelli, otherwise called the Castle of Abydos, being on the Europe side of the Hellespont . . . This confirmed the Jews of his being the Messiah, supposing that had it been in the power of the vizier . . . to have destroyed his person, they would never have permitted him to live . . .

The Jews flocked in great numbers to the castle, where he was imprisoned, not only from neighbouring parts, but also from Poland, Germany, Ligorn, Venice, Amsterdam, and other places . . . So great was the confluence of the Jews to this place that the Turks thought to make their advantage thereof, and so not only raised the price of their provisions, lodgings, and other necessaries, but also denied to admit any to Sabatai, unless for money . . .

Howsoever some of the Jews remained in their wits all this time, amongst which was a certain *kocham* at Smyrna, one zealous of his law, and of the good and safety of his nation . . .

Another Jew at Constantinople reported, That he met Elias in the streets, habited like a Turk . . . and that he injoin'd the observation of many neglected ceremonies, and particularly the *zezit* [*tzitzit*] [*Leviticus* 15:38] . . . Also the *peotz* [*peot*] [*Leviticus* 19:27] . . . every one nourished a lock of hair on each side, which was visible beneath their caps, which soon after began to become a sign of distinction between the believers and the *koparims* [*epicurus*], a name of dishonour, signifying as much as unbelievers or heretick . . .

But to return again to Sabatai Zevi himself, we find him . . . visited by pilgrims from all parts . . . amongst which one from Poland named Nehemiah Cohen was of special renown, learned in the Hebrew, Syriack, and Chaldee, and versed in the doctrine and *Kabalah* of the rabbins, as well as Sabatai himself: One of whome it was said esteemed himself as able a fellow for to act a messiah as the other. . . . These two great rabbins being together, a hot dispute arose between them. For Cohen alledged, That according to Scripture and exposition of the learned thereupon there were to be two messiahs, one called Ben Ephraim, and the other Ben David . . . Nehemiah was contented to be Ben Ephraim, the afflicted and poor messiah, and Sabatai was well enough contented he should be so; but Nehemiah accused him for being too forward in publishing himself the latter messiah, before Ben Ephraim had first been known to the world. Sabatai took this reprehension so ill . . . or that he suspected Nehemiah, being once admitted for Ben Ephraim, would quickly, being a subtle and learned person, perswade the world that he was Ben David . . . And thereupon the dispute grew so hot, and the controversie so irreconcilable, as was taken notice of by the Jews . . . but Sabatai prevailed, and Nehemiah was rejected as an enemy to the Messiah, which afterwards proved the ruine and downfal of this imposture. For Nehemiah being a person of authority, and a haughty spirit, meditated nothing but revenge; to execute which he took a journey to Adrianople, and there informed the chief ministers of state and officers of the court . . . of prophecies [made by Nathan] of the revolt of the Jews from their obedience to the grand signior . . .

The grand signior having by this time received divers informations of the madness of the Jews, and the pretences of Sabatai, grew big with desire to see him; so that he was brought before the grand signior. Sabatai appeared much dejected, and failing of that courage which he shewed in the synagogue. And he would not trust so far to the vertue of his messiahship, as to deliver himself in the Turkish language, but desired a doctor of physick (who had from a Jew turned Turk) to be his interpreter, which was granted to him, but not without reflection of the standers by, that had he been the Messiah . . . his tongue would have been loosed into eloquence and perfection of languages. But the grand signior would not be put off without a miracle, and it must be one of his own chusing; which was that Sabatai should be stripped naked, and set as a mark to his archers; if the arrows passed not his body . . . he would believe him to be the messiah . . . But now Sabatai renounced all his title—alledging that he was an ordinary Jew . . . The grand signior notwithstanding declared, That . . . his crime could not be expiated without becoming a Mahometan convert: Which if he refused, the stake was ready at the Gate of the Seraglio to impale him. Sabatai being now reduced to his last extremity, not being in the least doubtful what to do . . . replied that he was contented to turn Turk, and . . . having been long desirous of so glorious a profession, he esteemed himself honoured . . . to owe it first to the grand signior . . . And now contemplate the consternation, shame, and silence to which the Jews were reduced . . .

The news of Sabatai turning Turk, and of the Messiah to a Mahometan, quickly filled all parts of Turkie; the Jews became the derision of the towns, where the boys shouted after them, coining a new word (*Pouftai*) which every one seeing a Jew, with a finger pointed out, would pronounce with contempt; so that this deceived people for a long time after remained with confusion, silence, and dejection of spirit . . .

And thus ended this mad phrensie amongst the Jews, which might have cost them dear, had not Sabatai renounced his messiahship at the feet of Mahomet. These matters were transacted in the years 1665 and 1666; since which Sabatai hath passed his time devoutly in the Ottomon court . . .

From *The History of the Turkish Empire,* by Paul Rycault, 1687

RHODE ISLANDERS Report on the Dedication of the Touro Synagogue, 1763

While the fires of the Inquisition burned in Europe, Jews struck out desperately in search of refuge. A few Marranos (some with Columbus) braved the long and dangerous voyage across uncharted seas to the New World, hoping to find a place where they could live in peace. By the sixteenth century, venturesome Jews had made their way to Brazil, the West Indies, Mexico, and North America. In the American colonies they came at last to a land of religious and political freedom. And here they started to build a new life for themselves.

The colony of Rhode Island, which made no distinction among the settlers it admitted, was particularly hospitable to Jews. The fifteen families who came there in 1658 grew into a thriving community, the hub of which was the city of Newport. Although a congregation had been in existence for several decades, the Jews of Newport built their first synagogue in 1763.

The dedication of the Touro Synagogue was a big event in the life of the community, attended by Jews and non-Jews. Led by the congregation's rabbi, Reverend Isaac Touro, it was held on the first day of Chanukah, the day on which, according to Jewish tradition, Judah Maccabee rededicated the Holy Temple in Jerusalem in 165 B.C.E.

The edifice was designed by the famous architect and builder, Peter Harrison, an associate and pupil of Christopher Wren. It combined the classic colonial style, for which Harrison was noted, with traditional synagogue architecture of the Spanish-Portuguese Jews. It included school facilities, sexton's quarters, and an oven to bake *matzah* (unleavened bread) for Passover; the courtyard contained wells and cisterns connected with a *mikvah* (ritual bath). A fascinating part of the synagogue was the secret passage which led to the sea, a remnant of the Marrano practice of providing a place to hide or a means of escape in time of danger.

Today the Touro Synagogue is the oldest (though not the first) synagogue in America. In 1967 it was designated a national historic shrine.

The following are contemporary comments about the Newport synagogue. Of special interest are the observations of the famous Protestant divine, Dr. Ezra Stiles, who was known for his knowledge of Hebrew and his interest in Judaism.

". . . could not but raise in the mind a faint ideal of the majesty and grandeur of the ancient Jewish worship mentioned in the Scripture."

IT WILL BE extremely elegant within, when completed, but the outside is totally spoiled by a school which the Jews would have annexed to it for the education of their children!

From notes of a traveler passing through Newport, 1760
in *The Jews of Newport*, by Morris A. Gutstein

IN THE AFTERNOON was the dedication of the new synagogue in this town. It began by a handsome procession in which were carried the Books of the Law to be deposited in the ark. Several portions of Scripture, and of their service with a prayer for the

To the Hebrew Congregation in Newport
Rhode Island.

Gentlemen

While I receive, with much satisfaction, your Address replete with expressions of affection and esteem; I rejoice in the opportunity of assuring you, that I shall always retain a grateful remembrance of the cordial welcome I experienced in my visit to Newport, from all classes of Citizens.

The reflection on the days of difficulty and danger which are past is rendered the more sweet, from a consciousness that they are succeeded by days of uncommon prosperity and security. If we have wisdom to make the best use of the advantages with which we are now favored, we cannot fail, under the just administration of a good Government, to become a great and a happy people.

The Citizens of the United States of America have a right to applaud themselves for having given to mankind examples of an enlarged and liberal policy: a policy worthy of imitation. All possess alike liberty of conscience and immunities of citizenship. It is now no more that toleration is spoken of, as if it was by the indulgence of one class of people, that another enjoyed the exercise of their inherent natural rights. For happily the Government of the United States, which gives to bigotry no sanction, to persecution no assistance requires only that they who live under its protection should demean themselves as good citizens, in giving it on all occasions their effectual support.

It would be inconsistent with the frankness of my character not to avow that I am pleased with your favorable opinion of my administration, and fervent wishes for my felicity. May the Children of the Stock of Abraham, who dwell in this land, continue to merit and enjoy the good will of the other Inhabitants; while every one shall sit in safety under his own vine and figtree, and there shall be none to make him afraid. May the father of all mercies scatter light and not darkness in our paths, and make us all in our several vocations useful here, and in his own due time and way everlastingly happy.

G Washington

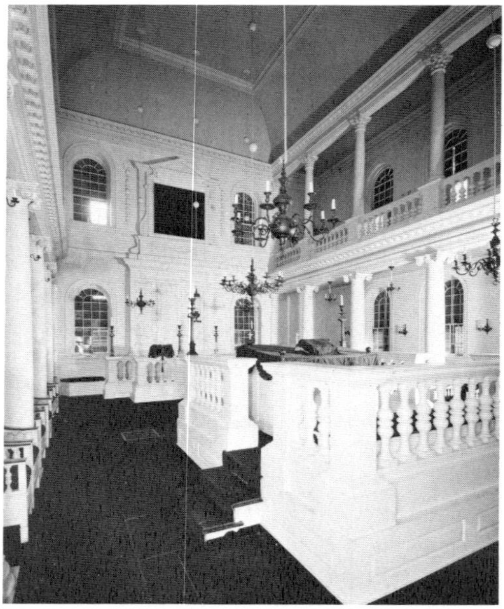

Touro Synagogue, Newport, Rhode Island. Pulpit and gallery. (Library of Congress)

royal family were read and finely sung by the priest and the people. There were present many gentlemen and ladies. The order and decorum, the harmony and solemnity of the music, together with a handsome assembly of people, in an edifice the most perfect of the temple kind perhaps in America, and splendidly illuminated, could not but raise in the mind a faint idea of the majesty and grandeur of the ancient Jewish worship mentioned in the Scripture. Dr. Isaac de Abraham Touro performed the service.

From the *Newport Mercury*, December 5, 1763,
as quoted in *The Jews of Newport.*

THE SYNAGOGUE is about perhaps forty foot long and thirty wide, of brick on a foundation of free stone; it was begun about two years ago, and is now finished except the porch and the capitals of the pillars. The front representation of the holy of holies, or its partition veil, consist only of wainscotted breast work on the east end in the lower part of which four long doors cover an upright square closet the depth of which is about a foot or the thickness of the wall, and in the apartment (. . . called the ark) were deposited three copies and rolls of the *Pentateuch*, written on vellum or rather tanned calf skin: one of these rolls I was told by Dr. Touro was presented from Amsterdam and is two hundred years old; the letters have the rabbinical flourishes.

A gallery for the women runs around the whole inside, except east end, supported by columns of the Ionic order, over which are placed correspondent columns of the Corinthian order supporting the ceiling of the roof. The depth of the Corinthian pedestal is the height of the balustrade which runs around the gallery. The pulpit for reading the law is a raised pew with an extended front table; this placed about the center of the synagogue or nearer the west end, being a square balustrading comporting with the length of the indented chancel before the end of the foot of the ark.

On the middle of the north side and affixed to the wall is a raised seat for the *parnas* or ruler, and for the elders: the breast and back interlaid with Chinese mosaic work. A wainscotted seat runs around sides of the synagogue below, and another in the gallery. There are no other seats or pews.

A report by Dr. Ezra Stiles, 1763, in *The Jews of Newport*

SOLOMON MAIMON Meets Moses Mendelssohn, about 1780

For many centuries the Jews of Europe lived within the confines of their ghetto communities. The ghettos isolated them not only physically, but also culturally, sharply restricting their intellectual outlook. In the late eighteenth century there arose a small group of Jews who sought to widen their cultural horizons. Among them was Solomon Maimon (1753–1800), a Polish Jew who migrated to Germany and became a highly esteemed philosopher, friend of such men of letters as Goethe and Schiller.

Solomon Maimon venerated Moses Maimonides, who had successfully harmonized the Jewish and Greek civilizations. Indeed, the surname, Maimon, was deliberately assumed. At twenty-five, Maimon left for Berlin to devote himself to serious scientific study. He soon encountered problems, for he was at first refused permission to live in Berlin.

A high point of his arrival was the meeting with Moses Mendelssohn, who symbolized the wholesome integration of Jewish and general cultures. Mendelssohn extended a generous helping hand to Maimon, offered to counsel him on his writings, and introduced him to the most distinguished members of Berlin's Jewish community.

Maimon's *Autobiography* was a success in both Jewish and non-Jewish circles. It dealt with his personal development as well as the character of the Polish Jews among whom he grew up. It contains an account of his momentous meeting with Moses Mendelssohn, from which the following selection is taken.

Moses Mendelssohn. (The Jewish Encyclopedia, *Funk & Wagnalls*)

"He assured me that, if I went on in this way, I should in a short time make great progress in metaphysics."

AS I CAME to Berlin this time by post, I did not require to remain outside the Rosenthaler Gate to be examined by the Jewish elders; I proceeded without any difficulty into the city, and was allowed to take up my quarters where I chose. To remain in the city, however, was a different thing. The Jewish police officers . . . made inquiry into the quality and occupation of newcomers, as well as the probable length of their stay, and allowed them no rest till they had either found some occupation in the city, or were out of it again . . . As I had learnt that there was a Polish Jew, a man of talent, residing in Berlin for the sake of study, and received with esteem in the best families, I paid him a visit.

He received me as a countryman in a very friendly manner . . . When I told him . . . that from my childhood I had discovered an inclination to the sciences, had already made myself acquainted with this and that Hebrew work which touches upon these, and now had come to Berlin in order to be *ma-amik bechochmah* [absorbed in the sciences], he smiled at this quaint rabbinical phrase, but gave me his full approval; and after conversing with me for some time, he begged me to visit him often, which I very willingly promised to do, and went away rejoicing in spirit.

The very next day I visited my Polish friend again, and found with him some young people belonging to a prominent Jewish family, who visited him often, and conversed with him on scientific subjects . . . And when I made known my fear about the above-mentioned police officer, they made me pluck up courage by promising to obtain protection for me from their family, so that I might remain in Berlin as long as I chose.

They kept their word, and Herr D——— P—, a well-to-do man of excellent character . . . and fine taste, an uncle of these young men . . . procured for me a respectable lodging, and invited me to the Sabbath dinner. Others of the family also sent me meals at my room on fixed days . . .

As I now had permission to remain in Berlin, I thought of nothing but how to carry my purpose into effect. Accidentally one day I went into a butter-shop, and found the dealer in the act of anatomising a somewhat old book for use in his trade. I looked at it, and found, to my no small astonishment, that it was Wolff's *Metaphysics, or the Doctrine of God, of the World, and of Man's Soul.* I could not understand how, in a city so enlightened as Berlin, such important works could be treated in this barbarous fashion. I turned therefore to the dealer, and asked him if he would not sell the book. He was ready to part with it for two groschen . . . I gave the price at once, and went home delighted with my treasure.

At the very first reading I was in raptures . . . Not only this sublime science in itself, but also the order and mathematical method of the celebrated author—the precision of his explanations, the exactness of his reasoning, and the scientific arrangement of his exposition—all this struck a new light in my mind.

With the ontology, the cosmology, and the psychology all went well; but the theology created many difficulties, inasmuch as I found its dogmas, not only not in harmony, but even in contradiction, with the preceding propositions . . .

I resolved therefore to set forth these doubts in the Hebrew language, and to send what I wrote to Herr Mendelssohn, of whom I had already heard so much. When he received my communication, he was not a little astonished at it, and replied to me at once, that in fact my doubts were well founded, that I should not however allow myself to be discouraged on their account, but should continue to study with zeal . . .

Encouraged by this, I wrote in Hebrew a dissertation in which I brought into doubt the foundations of revealed as well as of natural theology. All the thirteen articles of faith, laid down by Maimonides, I attacked with philosophical arguments, with the exception of one, namely the article on reward and punishment, which I conceded merely . . . as referring to the natural consequences of voluntary actions. I sent this dissertation to Mendelssohn, who was not a little amazed . . . He invited me to visit him, and I accepted his invitation. But I was so shy, the manners and customs of the Berliners were so new to me, it was not without fear and embarrassment that I ventured to enter a fashionable house. When therefore I opened Mendelssohn's door, and saw him and other gentlefolks who were there, as well as the beautiful rooms and elegant furniture, I shrank back, closed the door again, and had a mind not to go in. Mendelssohn however had observed me. He came out and spoke to me very kindly, led me into his room . . . and paid me many compliments about my writing. He assured me that, if I went on in this way, I should in a short time make great progress in metaphysics; and he promised also to resolve my doubts. Not satisfied with this, the worthy man looked after my maintenance also, recommended me to the most eminent, enlightened and wealthy Jews, who made provision for my board and other wants. Their tables I was at liberty to enjoy when I chose, and their libraries were open to my use.

From *An Autobiography*, by Solomon Maimon,
translated by J. Clark Murray

THE TANYA Tries to Make Peace with the Vilna Gaon, 1789

Judaism continued to be creative in the Diaspora. Over the centuries, new forms emerged, various sects developed, and a rich cultural and religious life was created by different Jewish communities.

In the eighteenth century a new religious movement arose out of the poverty and persecution of east European Jewry. Chasidism (Pietism) helped Jews forget their miseries in a joyous, emotional worship of God that stressed spirit more than formal prayers or talmudic learning. Started by Rabbi Israel (1700–1760), known as the Ba-al Shem Tov, a saintly man who was supposed to be a miracle worker, Chasidism swept through the Ukraine northward to southern Poland.

Further north, Chasidism met the opposition of rabbinical Judaism, which was centered in Lithuania and White Russia. Those who resisted the new movement were known as *Mitnagedim* (literally, "opponents"). Led by the Gaon Elijah, of Vilna in Lithuania, one of the most brilliant scholars in Jewish history, the *Mitnagedim* condemned the chasidic disregard of learning, the liberties taken with prayers by ordinary citizens, and the elevation of second-rate scholars to positions of leadership.

Hostility reached the point where the Ba-al Shem Tov's books were burned and the *Chasidim* were excommunicated. The enraged *Chasidim,* in turn, arranged a great celebration when the Gaon Elijah died. The conflict raged until the early nineteenth century, when the two groups finally learned to live with each other.

One of those who helped make peace between

them was Rabbi Schneur Zalman of Ladi, in the north, where Chasidism was more rational and sophisticated. Equally at home in chasidic teachings and in talmudic study, Rabbi Zalman agreed with the *Chasidim* that God should be served with joy, but maintained that such joy should come from study of the *Torah.* He contended that religious leaders should be learned men, but sympathetic to the unlettered. His moderation led to a version of *Chasidim* called *Chabad,* since it was based on *chochmah* (wisdom), *binah* (understanding), and *da-at* (knowledge). Rabbi Zalman, the Tanya to his followers, was the founder of the Lubavicher dynasty which now makes its headquarters in Brooklyn.

Chasidism left a distinct mark on present-day Jewish worship, and still has thousands of adherents all over the world.

In the following letter, the Tanya describes his efforts to make peace between the *Chasidim* and the *Mitnagedim.*

"Let me caution you against arousing further controversy."

MY BELOVED brothers and friends, *Chasidim* of Vilna, whose foundation is the *Torah* and the worship of God: may God give you eternal life.

There is indeed no greater commandment than that which enjoins us to establish peace in Israel. But what can we do that we have not yet done? All our efforts have come to nothing. Before God and Israel, we are guiltless.

I went to the house of the Gaon, the light of Israel, in the company of the late Rabbi Mendel Horasner . . . We had sent word that we were coming to discuss his complaints against us . . . Twice he shut the door in our face. The leading men of the city begged him to see us: "Rabbi," they said, "their most famous rabbi has come to debate with Your Honor. Defeat him and there will be harmony in Israel." Yet he put them off. When they persisted, he left the city . . .

Soon after this incident, we made a journey to the community of Shklav, again hoping to engage in a discussion—and again we failed. Moreover . . . they broke their promise not to harm us. For when they realized there was no valid reply to our arguments, they were forced to resort to violence—and they justified their conduct by citing the words of the "great tree"—the pious Gaon—may God keep him.

In all fairness, we must not be too harsh in our judgment of the Gaon. The matter had been settled in his mind beyond any doubt: evidently, he based himself on the reports of witnesses whom he took to be reliable. A witness, however, "sees only with his eyes." . . .

You tell me that the book, *Gathering of Sayings,* was burned because it interprets the phrases, "Who fills all the worlds" and "There is no place empty of Him," as literal descriptions. According to the Gaon, it is utter heresy to suggest that God actually exists in lower and unworthy things. But there is an inner, deeper meaning . . . which the Gaon refuses to see. For example, the phrase "the whole world is full of His glory" affirms the existence of a Providence. Would that I were able to explain and present our opinions before the Gaon, to refute once and for all these complaints and philosophical charges, which, according to his pupils, he accepts—attempting to know God through the mind of man.

But if he should find it difficult to change the ways in which he has been raised from childhood, and if my words offend him, then let him at least have the humility (which must surely be an element of his greatness) to bring his indictment against us clearly and in writing. Let him sign the bill of grievances himself, and I shall . . . reply to his charges and also sign it with my hand. Let these two letters be printed and sent to every qualified scholar throughout the world, and let them decide between us . . .

As for the burning of the above-mentioned book, let me caution you against arousing further controversy. It is not for you to fight the battle of the Ba-al Shem Tov. This is not the place, and this is not the way which God desires. Remember that though this burning may seem a new thing to you, it is really old. Who was greater in his generation than the Rambam [Maimonides], a man whose glory and holiness and piety were recognized in his native Spain while he still lived. Yet in distant lands . . . they condemned him as a heretic and a desecrator of the holy *Torah.* They burned his books in the streets of the city on the authority of certain sages who, because of their limited learning and unsure grasp, were unable to understand what the Rambam had written on the laws of repentance. However, just as those days passed and along with them their hatred—"so truth shall spring up from the earth and all Israel shall know that Moses was with truth." May it be soon and in our own days. Amen.

Schneur Zalman

Translated by Herbert Weiner,
as quoted in *Commentary,* January, 1956

AN ITALIAN JEW Exults at the Emancipation from the Ghetto, 1798

The French Revolution in 1789 was one of the great turning points in Jewish history. Its slogan. "Liberté, Egalité, Fraternité," brought a measure of liberation not only to Frenchmen, but also to the Jews who had been walled up in ghettos throughout much of Europe during the Middle Ages. In France itself, the Jews were admitted to citizenship in the republic on an equal basis with everyone else. The French armies, moreover, carried the ideals and principles of the revolution to other parts of Europe.

In Italy, particularly, the Jews welcomed the French armies with open arms, and for good reason. Compelled to reside in ghettos in most of the Italian cities, they had endured many other forms of humiliation and persecution—heavy taxes, limitations on their social and economic pursuits, forced conversions to Christianity, and the kidnapping of their children. Conditions changed in 1798, after the arrival of the French armies. The gates of the ghetto were thrown open and the badge of shame removed.

Although reactionary forces led to withdrawal of the privileges within a few months after they had been granted, the course initiated by the French Revolution would not be permanently stayed, and continued to move forward until most European Jews had been fully emancipated.

How to describe the excitement and exultation of the Jewish community of Ancona, Italy, upon the arrival of the French armies! The following lines, penned by an Italian Jew, convey some of the feeling.

". . . For surely joy such as ours will not again come to Israel except with the coming of the Messiah."

FOR, PRAISED be the Almighty, the French have entered the city with great speed, swifter than on the wings of eagles, and more powerful than lions. Immediately they inquired the whereabouts of the Jewish ghetto, and . . . entered the ghetto, and said to the Jews: "Jews, our brothers, fear no longer the wicked Christians who seek to harm you! We have come to save you, for God has shortened our journey so we might rescue you from the hands of these people!" And the Jews, seeing this great deliverance, raised their voices with cries of joy: "God bless you, who come in peace, our brethren, our flesh and blood! [for the Frenchmen who had come to the ghetto were Jews] O may the French nation which saved us from our enemies live forever and ever!" And they kissed and embraced each other with great affection, and many of the Jews, because of their great happiness, went to the synagogue and recited the *Song of the Sea* in strong, loud voices, for the portion of the Bible read in the synagogue that week dealt with the liberation of the Jews from Egypt and their crossing of the Red Sea.

With no interference on the part of the officials of their community, they issued an order at the command of the city authorities—that the candles in every house be lighted outside of the windows, in honor of the French army, and since outside of the ghetto not all the people lit their candles, and inside the ghetto there wasn't a single house where the candles were not burning, the saying, the "Jews had light and joy and happiness and pleasure" [*Book of Esther*], was materialized. And every member of our congregation, each according to his own understanding and ability, praised and thanked God for the liberation and freedom, for replacing sadness with joy, slavery with freedom . . .

And now things are different—for all the Christians were very much afraid upon seeing the Frenchmen, and there was no spirit left in them, and their hearts sank and their faces turned dark as soot when they saw the Jews happy and in good spirits. Therefore, we, the sons of Ancona, feel it our duty to thank God, blessed be his name, for all his kindness to us. Blessed is the God of Israel, who alone works such miracles, for surely joy such as ours will not again come to Israel except with the coming of Messiah, which we hope will be in our day, and bring us a complete deliverance.

From *Jewish Survival in the World Today,*
by Abraham Duker

THE SECRETARY Reports the Convening of Napoleon's Sanhedrin, 1806

The emperor Napoleon used Jewish emancipation for his own ends. Since he knew little about the Jews, he reflected the prevailing prejudices of the time—particularly the peasants' claims that they were losing their land because of Jewish usury. Napoleon, who did not hesitate to deprive all Frenchmen of their personal freedom, found Jewish financial operations morally offensive. He believed that the "repugnance" and "repulsiveness" of the Jews would disappear if barriers to their assimilation were removed. Hence, he gave them rights not to encourage their distinctive way of life but so they would abandon it.

Napoleon invited France's Jewish communities to send delegates to a special council to discuss Jewish-French relations. The Assembly of Notables, as the meeting was called, met in Paris in 1806. Delegates were asked a series of questions testing their loyalty.

Satisfied, Napoleon proceeded to revive the Sanhedrin, the ancient legislative body of the Jews, in full accordance with Jewish law.

He took care that delegates were selected who would support his views. As a result, the Great Sanhedrin, organized ostensibly to revitalize Jewish life, promulgated doctrines meant to destroy it. The Sanhedrin resisted Napoleon on only one point: the rabbis refused to officiate at mixed marriages.

Napoleon's hypocrisy is evident in his "Infamous Decrees," published soon after, which essentially cancelled out rights gained by the Jews as a result of the French Revolution.

The Sanhedrin convened by Napoleon, 1807. From an old print. (The Jewish Encyclopedia, *Funk & Wagnalls*)

"Long live the Emperor and King!"

TRANSACTIONS
OF THE
PARISIAN SANHEDRIN
OR
ACTS OF THE ASSEMBLY
OF
ISRAELITISH DEPUTIES OF FRANCE AND ITALY
CONVOKED AT PARIS BY AN IMPERIAL AND ROYAL DECREE
DATED MAY 30, 1806.

QUESTIONS PROPOSED to the Assembly of the Jews by the Commissioners named by His Majesty the Emperor and King, to transact whatever concerns them.

1st. Is it lawful for Jews to marry more than one wife?

2nd. Is divorce allowed by the Jewish religion?
Is divorce valid, although not pronounced by courts of Justice, and by virtue of laws in contradiction with the French code?

3rd. Can a Jewess marry a Christian, or a Jew a Christian woman?
Or has the law ordered that the Jews should only intermarry among themselves?

4th. In the eyes of Jews, are Frenchmen considered as brethren or as strangers?

5th. In either case, what conduct does their law prescribe towards Frenchmen not of their religion?

6th. Do the Jews born in France, and treated by the law as French citizens, acknowledge France as their country? Are they bound to defend it?
Are they bound to obey the laws, and to follow the directions of the civil code?

7th. What kind of police-jurisdiction have the rabbis among the Jews?

8th. What judicial power do they exercise among them?

9th. Are the forms of the elections of the rabbis and their police-jurisdiction regulated by the law, or are they only sanctioned by custom?

10th. Are there professions from which the Jews are excluded by their law?

11th. Does the law forbid the Jews from taking usury from their brethren?

12th. Does it forbid or does it allow usury towards strangers?

During these questions, the assembly manifested by unanimous and spontaneous emotions, how deeply it was affected by the doubt which the questions seemed to convey, as to the attachment of Frenchmen who followed the Law of Moses, for their fellow citizens, and for their country, and as to their sense of the duty by which they are bound to defend it.

The assembly was not able to conceal the emotions caused by the sixth question, in which it is asked if Jews born in France and treated by the law as French citizens, acknowledge France as their country, and if they are bound to defend it. The whole assembly unanimously exclaimed, "Even to death!" . . .

The assembly had unanimously resolved to set apart the whole day of the 15th of August for prayers, thanksgivings, and all the demonstrations of a pure and lively joy.

M. Rodrigues, of *La Gironde,* had been directed by the Committee of Five to give in his report on the means best calculated to fulfil, to the utmost, the intentions of the assembly.

He gave it in on the 12th of August, and it was adopted by the assembly . . .

In consequence, on the 15th of August, at ten o'clock in the morning, the deputies met . . . The bust of his Majesty the Emperor adorned the hall. At this sight, cries of "Long live the Emperor!" burst from everyone.

The president presented to the assembly an ode in Hebrew composed by M. J. Mayer on the Festival of Napoleon the Great . . . At eleven o'clock the deputies began their procession for the grand synagogue; they walked in silence, in the greatest order, with the president at their head. The temple was ornamented with taste. The name of Jehovah, the cyphers, and the arms of Napoleon and of Josephine shone on every side. The ark, which contained the Book of the Law, was surrounded and overshaded by shrubs and flowers; seats were prepared for the president and the officers of the assembly, for the rabbis, and others. The deputies formed a circle, into which were admitted many Jewish and Christian spectators, from among the most distinguished citizens. The ladies, according to custom, had a separate gallery. Order and serenity prevailed everywhere: every countenance exhibited the most heartfelt satisfaction, manifesting, on so glorious, so fortunate a day, our gratitude to a monarch who, amidst so many labours, has made the fate and the social happiness of the descendants of Israel the special object of his attention. Choruses and hymns began the ceremony. The president, M. Furtado, afterwards delivered a discourse, tracing a rapid sketch of the persecutions which the Jews had had to encounter during two thousand years, till the epoch when, recalled in France to the enjoyment of their civil and political rights, they saw the first dawn of their complete regeneration. He concluded by exhorting his brethren to bestow the greatest care on the education of their children, in order to enable them to repay to the country the manifold benefits conferred upon them . . .

MM. Segre, Zinzheimer, and Andrade, rabbis and deputies, delivered sermons: the first in Italian, the second in German, and the third in French. M. Segre clothed the sentiments of a mild and persuasive morality in elegant language. The sermon of M. Andrade was marked by numerous and appropriate quotations from the Holy Writ. M. Zinzheimer traced a more detailed picture of the different epochs of Jewish history. The same rabbi, in taking from the ark the Book of the Law, and in presenting it round the temple, pronounced a prayer for the happiness of all Frenchmen, which excited the liveliest emotion. Psalms and hymns were afterward sung; and when they came to the prayer which Jews are accustomed to put up for sovereigns, enthusiasm knew no bounds.

Cries of "Long live the Emperor and King," in Hebrew and in French, proceeded from every mouth. Thus has this festival been rendered remarkable by all the peculiarities which characterise the most ancient people on earth, blended with the patriotic effusions so natural to all Frenchmen. During a symphony of Haydn, collections were made by Mlles. Julie-Theodore Cerf-Berr, Caroline Wolf, and Schmoll, accompanied by MM. Avigdor, Rodrigues, senior, and Castro, junior. The produce was distributed among the poor of all persuasions . . .

From *Transactions of the Parisian Sanhedrin Convoked at Paris by an Imperial and Royal Decree,* translated by F. D. Kirwan

A WITNESS Describes the Dedication of the First Reform Temple, 1810

Seesen, Germany, was the site of the first Reform Jewish temple in history. Founded in 1810, it aspired to make Judaism attractive and meaningful to emancipated Jews who found certain traditional religious practices to be outmoded, irrelevant, or ineffective. Its moving spirit was Israel Jacobson (1768–1828), a businessman who later became official head of Westphalian Jewry under Napoleon.

Among the changes Jacobson introduced were the ceremony of confirmation, sermons in the German language, a few prayers in the vernacular, a mixed choir and instrumental music in the service. Although his innovations were relatively mild, they deviated from traditions hallowed by centuries and, consequently, evoked storms of protest from the bulk of German Jewry. Nevertheless, as time passed, the wisdom of many of his reforms was recognized, and they won widespread acceptance throughout Germany.

The dedication of the Temple of Jacob, as Jacobson's synagogue was called, drew hundreds of people from all over Germany. Clergymen of all faiths participated, initiating an ecumenical interest which is still a dominant feature of Reform Judaism. The dedication service also showed the reforms that Jacobson sought to establish in the new synagogue. An anonymous eyewitness has left a description of this historic occasion, which was to profoundly affect Jewish religious thought and practice.

"Where would one have seen a similar day on which Jews and Christians celebrated together in a common service. . . ?"

THE MANY hundreds of persons who had been invited came from Brunswick, Kassel, Halberstadt, Gottingen, Goslar, Helmstadt, and all surrounding places . . . Some of them lodged in the ample buildings of the president [Israel Jacobson], and others . . . were put up in the inn, and all costs were borne by Mr. Jacobson. In the evening he entertained everyone for dinner.

On the day of the dedication itself, on the seventeenth of July, at 7:00 in the morning, lovely music resounded from the roof of the temple (which was flat like a platform) and announced to the city the approaching festivities. At 8:00, all who had come to participate . . . assembled in the school hall of the well-known educational institution which President Jacobson had founded in Seesen. One could see persons of distinguished rank, scholars, Jewish, Protestant, and Catholic clergymen, officials, businessmen of all kinds, all walking together in complete concord; and uniform tolerance seemed to permeate all members of this numerous company. Here friends met, acquaintances and comrades from university days who had not seen each other for a long time . . .

At 9:00, the ringing of bells announced that the ceremonies would begin . . . Thereafter, everyone began the solemn processional under the ringing of bells. The procession was led by two flags and by the students of the Jacobson Institute and the teachers. Then followed President Jacobson, the prefect of the Department of Oker, Mr. Hanneberg, and the clerics and lay members of the Israelite Consistory from Kassel. Then came all the rabbis present, walking in pairs, in their clerical robes, and the Christian clergymen similarly. The mayor of the town and the deputy mayor came in their robes, the count of Brabeck, public officials of the kingdom who were present, and all the other invited persons appeared in their best clothes. Finally, there came many other people from all classes and all faiths, who had come . . . to observe the festivities. In solemn silence the long procession went from the auditorium of the school into the halls, through the doors into the street, and again through the doors of another house, and through this house into the court to the temple. Special admission cards had been printed . . .

After the procession had entered the temple proper, there came from the organ loft lovely music by sixty to seventy musicians and singers, and this put all hearts into the most solemn mood. After everyone had taken his seat, a cantata composed especially for this celebration by Dr. Heinroth, one of the teachers in the Jacobson Institute, was sung splendidly to the accompaniment of the rousing sound of the instruments.

The Jewish ritual now began, with Mr. Jacobson himself being the chief officiant and the rabbis assisting him. At the end, President Jacobson gave an address . . . After the scrolls of the *Torah,* which were elaborately ornamented, had been taken from the ark with great ceremony, they were carried around the temple seven times, preceded by boys with burning wax candles. Then several chapters of the *Pentateuch* were read, first in Hebrew and at once in German, publicly and with a loud voice. Mr. Schott, director of the educational institution, then mounted the rostrum and talked to the assembled multitude. Then came a chorale accompanied by organ and full orchestra, . . . sung first in Hebrew and then in German. At the end of this song, in which the Christians and Israelites participated with deep emotion, Church Counselor Heinemann delivered an address befitting the occasion.

The temple was richly and tastefully illuminated. Its architectural beauty, its decorations and gilded pieces . . . the graceful columns and antique chandeliers, the flower garlands which hung everywhere, the colorful mixture of people, all this presented a most beautiful and interesting view. At the end of the service, President Jacobson elaborately entertained at a table of two hundred in the school auditorium, in adjoining rooms for his seventy musicians, and in other rooms for an additional one hundred persons. The students of the Institute ate in the open, in the courtyard.

The festivities were original and unique. Where would one have seen a similar day on which Jews and Christians celebrated together in a common service in the presence of more than forty clergymen of both religions, and then sat down to eat and rejoice together in intimate company?

From *The Rise of Reform Judaism,* by W. Gunther Plaut

ALEXANDER HERZEN Sees a Group of Cantonists, 1835

Perhaps the cruelest and most wicked technique by which Czar Nicholas I (1825–1855) tried to eliminate Judaism in Russia was the recruitment of young Jewish boys for service in the army. Although the normal age for conscription was eighteen, the Jewish boys, who were called "cantonists," had to enroll as young as age eight. Still malleable and unformed, they were easier to change than eighteen-year-olds whose rearing made them more unwilling to abandon their faith for Christianity. Since conscription was for twenty-five years, to draft a boy at such a tender age was to deprive him of parental guidance and instruction during the entire period of his young manhood. By the time he returned home, if he ever did, he would probably be completely alienated from his parents.

Innumerable Jewish families suffered the tragedy of having their children kidnapped or forcibly torn from them. Placed in a hostile environment, many of the children died from malnutrition, overwork, or beatings. Thousands of Jewish youths perished as a result of the czar's endeavors to secure a few additional converts for the Russian Church. Moreover, the spectre of having possibly to provide a "cantonist" for the army filled Jewish parents with unfathomable torment and anguish.

The following description is taken from the memoirs of the famous Russian writer and freedom-fighter, Alexander Herzen (1812–1875?), who in 1835 was deported from Feom to Wiatka, deep inside Russia, because of his criticism of czarist oppression. On his way he met a party of cantonists, who left a deep impression on him.

"Half of them will not get to their destination."

"WHOM DO you carry and to what place?"

"Well, sir, you see, they got together a bunch of these accursed Jewish youngsters between the age of eight and nine. I suppose they are meant for the fleet, but how should I know? At first the command was to drive them to Perm. Now there is a change. We are told to drive them to Kazan. I have had them on my hands for a hundred *versts* [about .6629 mile] or thereabouts. The officer that turned them over to me told me they were an awful nuisance. A third of them remained on the road (at this the officer pointed with his finger to the ground). Half of them will not get to their destination," he added.

"Epidemics, I suppose?" I inquired, stirred to the very core.

"No, not exactly epidemics; but they just fall like flies. Well, you know, these Jewish boys are so puny and delicate. They can't stand mixing dirt for ten hours, with dry biscuits to live on. Again everywhere strange folks, no father, no mother, no affection. Well then, you just hear a cough and the youngster is dead. Hello, corporal, get out the small fry!"

The little ones were assembled and arrayed in a military line. It was one of the most terrible spectacles I have ever witnessed. Poor, poor children! The boys of twelve or thirteen managed somehow to stand up, but the little ones of eight and ten . . . No brush, however black, could convey the terror of this scene on canvas.

Pale, worn out, with scared looks . . . they stood in their uncomfortable, rough soldier uniforms, with their starched, turned-up collars, fixing an inexpressibly helpless and pitiful gaze upon the garrisoned soldiers, who were handling them rudely. White lips, blue lines under the eyes betokened either fever or cold. And these poor children, without a kind gesture, exposed to the wind which blows unhindered from the Arctic Ocean, were marching to their death. I seized the officer's hand, and, with the words: "Take good care of them!" threw myself into my carriage. I felt like sobbing, and I knew I could not master myself.

From *A Source Book on Jewish History and Literature*, edited by Julius Hoexter and Moses Jung

AN EYEWITNESS Regards the Damascus Blood Libel, 1840

In 1840, an occurrence took place in Damascus, Syria, which shook world Jewry—a revival of the "blood libel." Jews, who had lulled themselves into believing that nineteenth-century liberalism made it impossible to revive the baseless medieval charge of Jewish ritual murder, were shocked into awareness that modern enlightenment was only a thin veneer.

The disappearance of a Christian monk, Padre Tommaso, and his servant aroused the rumor that Jews had committed murder to obtain Christian blood for their wine. In truth, it was clear that the monk had been killed by a Moslem with whom he had argued bitterly. The other monks, however, fearful of reprisals from the Moslem community, accused the Jews, who were helpless to defend themselves. Several Jewish artisans, such as Solomon Murad and Meyer Farki, were tortured into "confessions." France, the alleged champion of human rights, gave credence to these charges, further disillusioning liberal thinking people everywhere. Despite protests, the French government, concerned with its influence in the Near East, refused to retreat from its position.

In this letter an eyewitness advises the great English statesman Sir Moses Montefiore not to go to Damascus. Subsequently Montefiore went to Egypt with Adolphe Cremieux, the illustrious spokesman of French Jewry, to persuade Mehemet Ali, pasha of Egypt and ruler of Syria, to dismiss the ritual murder charges. Their success (although some of the Jewish prisoners were now dead) helped reassure the Jewish people of a better future than in the medieval past.

"The guilt must be equally shared by those who delivered up an innocent people into his hands."

THE RESULT of my enquiries I will briefly submit to you. That two men, the Padre Tommaso and his servant, are missing, is beyond dispute. There is not the least reason to believe that the servant is murdered or dead; there is but little evidence that the Padre has been murdered, and not the slightest that he was murdered by Jews; on the contrary, evidence *a priori* is entirely in their favour, and that extorted by torture, if fairly considered, is equally so . . .

I need not allude to their [the Jews'] ceremonial and moral law; both are equally abhorrent of the act imputed to them; but perhaps they [the accused Jews] were fanatics influenced by an inward light stronger than their law? Fanaticism is not usually found among such men as Solomon Murad and Meyer Farki, with their compeers, the leading men of a highly respectable and wealthy community, as was evident from the appearance of their families even in distress . . .

What testimony is there then to overcome these probabilities? Confession wrung from mortal agony and unsupported by circumstantial evidence! Their enemies do, to be sure, appeal to certain circumstances, such as the identity of the extorted confession itself: true, I believe it to be so perfectly identical as to lose all character of independence. But there were other circumstances. There were animal remains found twenty-five days after the friar had disappeared, in a running sewer in closer proximity to a butcher's stall than to David Arari's house. There was said also to be the mark of fire on the white marble pavement of the same gentleman's court. I saw it not, though the stone was pointed out. This mark, which did not exist, was supposed to be caused by the burning of the padre's clothes, but there were certain stains on a wall which might be blood; I thought they might be anything else rather. Again, with the aforesaid animal remains there was found a piece of cloth such as might identify it with part of the friar's cap. Is this circumstance consistent with the burning of his apparel, or did they spare that part only which would most easily lead to detection?

The dullness of such reasoning defeats its malice. And this is [the type of] evidence for the charge procured by the bastinadoing [beating] of 120 persons, in several instances to death. I think its meagerness proves the negative, viz. that the poor victims had nothing really to confess . . . But might not the accused have brought forward positive evidence in their favour? One person did come forward to prove that he had seen the friar in another part of the town subsequently to the date of the supposed murder. He was bastinadoed to death—a consummation not likely to encourage other witnesses to come forward; and indeed the Jews assert that Moslems of the first rank in Damascus, if they dared speak, could have established an alibi for them in many cases . . .

But it is indeed too unreasonable and unjust to lay on the pasha of Damascus the whole blame of these proceedings, unequalled in atrocity since the days of the fourth Antiochus. The guilt must be equally shared by those who delivered up an innocent people into his hands; indeed their share is greater. He may plead that he was obliged to do these things by the nature of his office. The persecutors of the Jews cannot even shelter themselves under such a plea as that. Indeed, if they be blameless, then is the Spanish Inquisition blameless also; the auto-da-fé being, in the last result, certainly the result of the civil power.

Although I trust you will persevere in your meritorious exertions for the sake of humanity and truth, yet, as you ask my opinion as to the practicability or prudence of proceeding at once to Damascus, I must say that I do not think it advisable . . .

From *Diaries of Sir Moses and Lady Montefiore*,
edited by L. Lowe

HERMAN MELVILLE Writes of Jerusalem, 1857

No spot on earth is more precious to Jews than Jerusalem—the symbol and repository of Jewish religious emotion and spiritual unity. Every morsel of information about this sacred city is eagerly devoured by a people who yearn to know all of its long and eventful history. One such morsel is found in a journal kept by the famous American writer, Herman Melville, on an eighteen-day visit to Palestine (January 6–24, 1857), during a trip to Europe and the Middle East.

Not intended for publication, Melville's journal consists of hastily noted observations and reactions, but even these give frequent evidence of literary genius. While Melville often complains of the circumstances, he was obviously moved by what amounted to a "pilgrimage" to sites laden with meaning for adherents of Judaism, Christianity, and Islam. The journey is thought to have inspired his *Clarel,* a long narrative poem in which a group of English and American pilgrims of varying religious backgrounds travel from Jerusalem to Bethlehem.

The journal reveals the desolation of the Holy Land in the mid-nineteenth century, as well as the depressed status of the Jews, who were forced to live inside walled towns and villages. Reading Melville's comments on the hopelessness of the Jewish future in Palestine (in the last paragraph of his journal), one realizes anew how amazing was the immigration of the *Biluim* (early Zionist settlers) less than twenty years later and the founding of agricultural colonies in Palestine, not to mention the astounding story of the creation of a modern Jewish state.

"And how are the hosts of Jews scattered in other lands to be brought here? Only by a miracle."

JANUARY 4th., 1857. Sailed from Alexandria for Jaffa. Second class passage. Many deck passengers, Turks, etc. . . .

Jan. 6th. Early in the morning came in sight of Jaffa . . . Landed, not without some danger,—boatmen [Arabs] trying to play upon my supposed fears. Cunning dogs!—Employed a Jew dragoman to take me to Jerusalem.—Crossed the plain of Sharon in sight of mountains of Ephraim. Arrived at Ramlah and put up at [alleged] hotel. At supper over broken crockery and cold meat, pestered by mosquitoes and fleas, dragoman said, "Dese Arab no know how to keep hotel." I fully assented. After horrible night, at 2:00 in the morning in saddle for Jerusalem. . . . Got to Jerusalem about 2:00 P.M. . . . Hotel overlooks on one side pool of Hezekiah [balconies], is near the Coptic convent, is on the Street of the Patriarchs leading out of Street of David . . . view of battered dome of Church of Sepulchre and Mount Olivet [The Mount of Olives] . . .

Jan. 18th. Quitted Jerusalem . . . Stayed at Greek convent at Ramlah. No sleep. Old monk like rat. Scurvy treatment . . .

Jan. 19th. Rode from Ramlah to Lydda. A robbery of a village nearby, by party of Arabs, alarms the whole country. People travel in bands . . .

Jan. 20th. I am the only traveler sojourning in Joppa. I am emphatically alone, and begin to feel like Jonah . . .

Jan. 21st. Could not sleep last night for the fleas . . . In the afternoon called upon Mr. and Mrs. Saunders . . . , the American missionary.—Dismal story of their experiments. Might as well attempt to convert bricks into bride-cake as Orientals into Christians. It is against the will of God that the East should be Christianized.

Jan. 24th. (Saturday)—Bravo! . . . the Austrian steamer is in sight . . . Thus then will end nearly six days in Joppa . . .

From Jerusalem to Dead Sea, Etc.

Over Olivet by St. Stephens Gate to Bethany—on a hill—wretched Arab village—fine view— . . . Brook Kerith—immense depth—black and funereal—Valley of Jehosophat—grows more diabolical as approaches Dead Sea—Plain of Jericho—looks green [part of it] an orchard, but only trees of apple of Sodom [dust-filled pods] . . . Where Kerith opens into Plain of Jericho looks like Gate of Hell . . . village of Jericho—ruins on hillside . . . tent the charmed circle, keeping off the curse . . . Ride over mouldy plain to Dead Sea . . . foam on beach and pebbles like slaver of mad dog—smarting bitter of the water—carried the bitter in my mouth all day—bitterness of life—thought of all bitter things—Bitter it is to be poor, and bitter to be reviled, and Oh bitter are these waters of Death, thought I . . . nought to eat but bitumen and ashes with dessert of Sodom apples washed down with water of Dead Sea . . .

Rainbow over Dead Sea—heaven, after all, has no malice against it.

Barrenness of Judea

Whitish mildew pervading whole tracts of landscape—bleached—leprosy—encrustation of curses—old cheese—bones of rocks—crunched, gnawed, mumbled . . . rubbish of creation.

No moss as in other ruins—no grace of decay—no ivy—the unleavened nakedness of desolation . . . Over lofty hills to Bethlehem . . . saw Jerusalem from distance—unless knew it, could not have recognized it—looked exactly like arid rocks . . .

Jerusalem

Hillside view of Zion—loose stones and gravel as if shot down from carts. The mind cannot but be sadly . . . affected with the indifference of Nature and Man to all that makes the spot sacred to the Christian . . .

Warder Crisson of Philadelphia—an American turned Jew—divorced from [former] wife—married a Jewess, etc.—Sad . . .

In Jehosophat, Jew gravestones lie as if . . . flung by a blast in a quarry. So thick, a warren of the dead—so old, the Hebrew inscriptions can hardly be distinguished from the wrinkles formed by Time . . .

In pursuance of my object, the saturation of my mind with the atmosphere of Jerusalem . . . I always rose at dawn and walked without the walls . . . Daily I could not but be struck with the clusters of townspeople reposing along the arches near the Jaffa Gate . . . They, too, seemed to feel the insalubriousness of so small a city pent in by lofty walls obstructing ventilation . . . I would stroll to Mount Zion, along the terraced walks, and survey the tombstones of the hostile Armenians, Latins, Greeks, all sleeping together . . . Along the hillside of Gihon . . . and higher up my eye rested on the cliff-girt basin, haggard with riven old olives, where the angel of the lord smote the army of Sennacherib . . . [*II Kings* 18:17, 19:33]

Had Jerusalem no peculiar historic association, still would it, by its extraordinary physical aspect, evoke peculiar emotion in the traveler . . . I have little doubt, the diabolical landscapes of the great part of Judea must have suggested to the Jewish prophets their ghastly theology.

. . . The Cave of Jeremiah is in this part. In its lamentable recesses he composed his lamentable Lamentations . . .

Stones of Judea

We read a good deal about stones in Scripture . . . Monuments and memorials are set up of stones; men are stoned to death; the figurative seed falls in stony places; and no wonder that stones should figure so largely in the Bible. Judea is one accumulation of stones—Stony mountains and stony plains; stony torrents and stony roads; stony walls and stony fields; stony house and stony tombs; stony eyes and stony hearts. Before you and behind you are stones. Stones to right and stones to left. In many places laborious attempts have been made to clear surface of these stones. You see heaps of stones here and there; and stone walls of immense thickness are thrown together, less for boundaries than to get them out of the way. But in vain; the removal of one stone only serves to reveal there stones still larger, below it . . .

The Hills

Are stones in the concrete. Regular layers of stone walls [loose] seem not the erections of art but mere natural varieties of the stony landscape. In some of the fields, lie large grotesque rocks—all perforated and honeycombed—like rotting bones of mastodons.—Everything looks old . . .

No country will more quickly dissipate romantic expectations than Palestine—particularly Jerusalem. To some the disappointment is heartsickening, etc. Is the desolation of the land the result of the fatal embrace of the Deity? Hapless are the favorites of heaven.

In the emptiness of the lifeless antiquity of Jerusalem the emigrant Jews are like flies that have taken up their abode in a skull.

Christian Missions, Etc.

A great deal of money has been spent by the English Mission in Jerusalem. Church on Mt. Zion estimated to have cost $75,000 . . . The present bishop . . . seems a very sincere man and doubtless does his best . . . But the work over which he presides . . . is a failure—palpably. One of the missionaries confessed . . . that out of all the Jew converts but one he believed to be a true Christian . . . Also said many things tending to the impression the mission was as full of intrigue as a ward-meeting or caucus at home.

I often passed the Protestant school, etc., on Mt. Zion, but nothing going on . . . Only place of interest was the Grave Yard . . .

At Joppa, Mr. and Mrs. Saunders from Rhode Island . . . sent to found an agricultural school for the Jews . . . but miserably failed. Jews would come, pretend to be touched, etc. . . . then —vanish.

Mrs. Minor of Philadelphia—came . . . to start a kind of agricultural academy for Jews . . . A woman of fanatic energy and spirit . . . returned to America for contributions . . . returned with implements, money, etc. Bought a tract about mile and half from Joppa. Two young ladies came with her from America . . . Not a single Jew was converted either to Christianity or Agriculture . . .

Deacon Dickson of Groton, Mass., . . . caught the contagion from Mrs. Minor's published letters. Sold his farm . . . and came out with wife, son, and three daughters, about two years ago.—Be it said, that all these movements combining Agriculture and Religion . . . are based upon the impression . . . that the time for the prophetic return of the Jews to Judea is at hand, and therefore the way must be prepared for them by Christians, both in setting them right in their faith and their farming—in other words, preparing the soil literally and figuratively . . . The following talk ensued—

H. M. "Have you settled here permanently, Mr. Dickson?"

Mr. D. (with a kind of dogged emphasis) "Permanently settled on the soil of Zion, Sir."

H. M. to Mr. D. "Have you any Jews working with you?"

Mr. D. "No, can't afford to have them. Do my own work, with my son. Besides, the Jews are lazy and don't like work."

H. M. "And do you not think that a hindrance to making farmers of them?"

Mr. D. "That's it. The gentile Christians must teach them better. The fact is the fullness of Time has come. The gentile Christians must prepare the way."

Mrs. D. (to me) "Sir, is there in America a good deal of talk about

Mr. D's efforts here?"

Mr. D. "Yes, do they believe (basically) in the restoration of the Jew?"

H. M. "I can't really answer that."

Mrs. D. "I suppose most people believe the prophecies to that effect in a figurative sense—don't they?"

H. M. "Not unlikely." Etc., etc., etc.

. . . The whole thing is half melancholy, half farcical—like all the rest of the world . . .

Sir Moses Montefiore—This Croesus visited Palestine last year, bought a large tract on the hill of Gihon and walled it in for hospital grounds.

A huge man of 75, he was carried to Jerusalem from Joppa, on a litter borne by mules. They fleeced him sadly, charging enormous prices for everything he bought. Sir M. seems to have the welfare of his poor countrymen near his heart, and it is said, purposes returning here for life.

The idea of making farmers of the Jews is vain. In the first place, Judea is a desert with few exceptions. In the second place, the Jews hate farming. All who cultivate the soil in Palestine are Arabs. The Jews dare not live outside walled towns or villages for fear of the malicious persecution of the Arabs and Turks.—Besides, the number of Jews in Palestine is comparatively small. And how are the hosts of them scattered in other lands to be brought here? Only by a miracle . . . Mr. Wood saw Mr. Dickson going about . . . with open Bible, looking for the opening asunder of Mount Olivet and the preparing of the highway for the Jews.

From the journal of Herman Melville

SIR MOSES MONTEFIORE Intercedes in the Mortara Affair, 1858

It was incredible that in the mid-nineteenth century the Catholic Church would forcibly abduct a Jewish child—but such was the case. On June 26, 1858, six-year-old Edgar Mortara of Bologna, Italy, was kidnapped from his parents so that he could be reared as a Catholic. Church authorities insisted that the lad was irrevocably a Catholic because he had been privately baptized by his housemaid when he had been seriously ill. The fact that his parents knew nothing of this act made no difference.

The Church's behavior, so crudely violent and in contradiction to its own doctrine that "secret" or "forced" baptism was null and void, shocked the world. Even Catholic monarchs like Napoleon III of France and Francis Joseph of Austria beseeched the pope to return the boy to his parents. Jewish leaders all over the world vehemently objected to the abduction, but in vain. The Church rejected the chorus of arguments heard 'round the world.

Among those who worked to dramatize and publicize the injustice of the Mortara affair was the eminent English Jew, Sir Moses Montefiore, then president of the Board of Deputies, the chief governing body of English Jewry. He contacted influential figures all over the world in the hope of bringing pressure on the Church, and even planned a trip to Rome to plead with the pope himself for Edgar Mortara's freedom.

In the next selection from the diaries of Sir Moses and Lady Montefiore, we see the efforts of the English statesman to rectify the wrongs done to the boy.

Moses Montifiore, at age 100. (The Jewish Encyclopedia, *Funk & Wagnalls*)

"They protest most strongly against baptism without the consent of the party baptised."

THE COMMITTEE met on the day of their appointment, and at once determined to appeal for cooperation to the Central Consistory of the Israelites of France, and to the central Jewish authorities at Amsterdam. They further determined to memorialise the British government, soliciting its powerful intervention, and feeling well assured of its humane and friendly sympathy. The committee further resolved to transmit to the press copies of communications received from Turin, and they have every reason to feel grateful to the press, particularly in England, France, Germany, and the United States, for its able and humane assistance.

At a subsequent meeting the committee determined to transmit a report of the case, as it had appeared in the *Times* newspaper, to every member of the Catholic clergy throughout the United Kingdom, and about 1800 of such reports were circulated accordingly.

The committee, through the medium of the president, have also appealed for cooperation to the Jewish congregational bodies in the principal cities and towns of Germany and the United States of America, and they rejoice to be able to report that their appeal has been zealously responded to, and that various bodies of their co-religionists are taking active measures to seek redress for the grievous wrong . . .

"It is well known," the Board of Deputies announced, "that the Committee of the Evangelical Alliance and other religious societies of the Protestant community have manifested great interest in this unhappy case. They have on various occasions conveyed to this committee the expressions of their kind sympathy, and the committee are assured that the humane and zealous interposition of these important bodies may be relied on.

"Although, as will have been seen from the correspondence which has been published in the daily press, the British government is unable to assist the case by a direct intervention, its views thereon are emphatically pronounced, and the committee offer their grateful acknowledgments for the prompt attention and great kindness they have received from the Earl of Malmesbury and Mr. Fitzgerald throughout the communications which have taken place between your committee and the foreign office.

"The committee are strongly urged to appeal personally to the emperor of the French by means of a deputation from your body, and from the Jewish congregations in the principal states of Europe and America, under the hope that His Imperial Majesty, conscious that the public opinion has declared itself indignantly against an outrage so disgraceful to the present age, will exercise his powerful influence with the papal government, so as to induce it to restore the young child, Edgar Mortara, to its bereaved parents, and to denounce the repetition of any similar practice.

"The committee, however, feel that they would not be justified in the adoption of so important a step without bringing the matter under the attention of the General Board, and have resolved to report thereto their proceedings to date, and to seek therefrom further instructions. They protest most strongly against baptism without the consent of the party baptised.

"In this particular case the committee have purposely abstained from entering into the full details of the abduction and of the subsequent events relating thereto. To do this would be to extend this report beyond reasonable limits. The committee are in possession of important documents and voluminous correspondence, extracts from portions of which have from time to time appeared in the press. After a careful consideration of these documents, your committee have strong grounds for believing that the alleged baptism never took place. If it did, it was administered by the menial and illiterate servant girl Morisi, when she was herself a child only fourteen years old, and under circumstances which appear to render it invalid, even by the Roman canonical laws. It is quite clear the child, from its tender age [twelve months], must have been unconscious of the act; that up to the date of its abduction it had been nurtured in the faith of its parents, and so far from there being any truth in the statement that Edgar Mortara rejoices in his adoption into the Catholic faith [a statement which, considering the still tender age of the child, is manifestly absurd], it yearns incessantly for the restoration to its home—while, alas! if report speaks truly, its unhappy mother has been bereft of reason, and its father, prostrated in spirit, is about to emigrate from the scene of his recent afflictions.

"The case in itself is one deserving of the sincerest commiseration; but, when viewed with reference to its bearings on society at large, it appeals irresistibly to all; and the civilised world will indeed be wanting in energy and wisdom if it permit the nineteenth century to be disgraced by the retention of the child in contravention of the laws of nature, morality, and religion, and most especially it behooves the Jewish community to exert itself to the utmost in so urgent a cause, so that if it fail it may have at least the consolation of knowing that it has done its duty, while if, under the blessing of the Almighty God, it succeed, it may rejoice not only because the sorrows of an afflicted family will thereby be alleviated but also because a moral victory will have been achieved, the advantages of which will be recognised and prized by every friend of humanity, law, and order throughout the world."

Moses Montefiore, President.

From *Diaries of Sir Moses and Lady Montefiore*,
edited by L. Lowe

RABBI DAVID PHILIPSON Looks Back on the Hebrew Union College Dedication, 1875

By 1870 the American Jewish community was made up of people from many different countries and backgrounds. Rabbi Isaac Mayer Wise believed that to hold them together American-born and American-bred rabbis were needed. He maintained that Judaism could survive here only if led by men "educated in America . . . filled with the free spirit of America" who "combined a modern American education with a knowledge of Jewish lore." He worked indefatigably to establish a seminary to train such men.

Rabbi Wise's first effort to found a rabbinical school, Zion College in Cincinnati, lasted only a few years. After the Civil War, another school, Maimonides College in Philadelphia, survived six years and graduated one student. Rabbi David Einhorn's plans for a seminary in New York also failed. Finally, Wise realized that a national organization was needed to support a theological school. In 1873, the Union of American Hebrew Congregations was created to unite synagogues all over the country. In two years the Hebrew Union College opened in Cincinnati under auspices of the Union, with a faculty consisting of Wise and an assistant and with a student body of nine.

The Hebrew Union College was truly a pioneering venture, for nothing like it existed. It has flourished and grown, and today it is the rabbinical center of American Reform Judaism.

This description of the dedication services was written by a member of the college's first graduating class.

". . . We wish to keep our students home and raise them as genuine Americans on the virgin soil of American liberty."

THE LONG looked for day finally dawned. The dream of a quarter of a century began to be realized when on Sunday, the third of October, 1875, the formal opening of the Hebrew Union College took place in the beautiful temple of the Bene Yeshurun Congregation, at Eighth and Plum Streets [Cincinnati, Ohio]. The multitude that filled the brilliantly illuminated house of worship little reckoned at how historic an occasion they were assisting. Isaac M. Wise knew it full well but possibly even he did not realize completely the amazing task to which he had set his hand. It was a real work of salvation for Judaism in America. Within the past half century he has been frequently called the "master builder" of American Judaism. And that in truth he was. His determination, his persistence, his struggle, his faith were finally justified and rewarded. But it was only the beginning. The great tests and trials were still to come. Many doubters and mockers were still in the land. But what of that? Sufficient to the day was the joy thereof. The first rung of the ladder of achievement was being ascended. The difficult first step had been successfully taken.

The active participants in that historic event were Bernhard Bettmann, the president of the Board of Governors, the Reverend Dr. Isaac M. Wise, the Reverend Dr. Max Lilienthal and the Reverend Dr. S. S. Sonneschein of St. Louis, Mo. The speakers sensed the epoch-making significance of the event and stressed the responsibility that would lie upon the persons who were blazing the new path in American Israel's onward journey. Bernhard Bettmann, who served as president of the Board of Governors with singular ability and devotion from the day of its founding until February 1, 1910 . . . said in his inaugural address: . . . "While it is hoped that from this college will depart the future rabbis and teachers of the American Israel . . . a most cordial welcome is extended to any one that may want to seek its benefits, no matter what may be his or her religion, present position or future purposes in life . . . We shall be happy to have amongst us the followers of other creeds, not for the purpose of making proselytes of them—for that has always been and still is repugnant to the spirit of Judaism—but that they might understand the parent faith from which their own religion sprang, and enjoy a literature equal to that of Greece and Rome. We confidently count upon the attendance of some of the daughters of Israel, so that . . . may be revived the glory of those ancient days when the *Keser Torah*, the crown of knowledge of the law, encircled many a Jewish woman's brow."

The Reverend Dr. Max Lilienthal who had stood shoulder to shoulder with Isaac M. Wise during all these years . . . stressed the American note . . .

"We could have adopted the plan proposed by several good men, of sending those who wish to devote themselves to the Jewish ministry to Germany, where the master minds of Jewish literature and theology are . . . and where Jewish colleges already are fully established . . . But we do not want any ministers reared and educated under the influence of European institutions; we intend to have ministers reared by the spirit of our glorious American institutions; men who love their country above all, men who will be staunch advocates of civil and religious liberty as the men who signed the Declaration of Independence understood it—men who are ready to defend this priceless gem against all and any encroachments, and hence we wish to keep our students at home and raise them as genuine Americans on the virgin soil of American liberty."

When the founder arose to speak, a great hush fell on the assembled multitude. There was a feeling that the occasion for him was beyond adequate expression . . . Too deeply moved to speak at any length, Isaac M. Wise said that he lacked words to do justice to his feelings. As far as in his power lay he would carry out the hope of Israel that God's law should be magnified and glorified, with all the enthusiasm of his soul and he would strive to raise high the standard of learning and intelligence in this college, to bring down to us the *Shechinah* [Presence of God]. He called the occasion *Chag lAdonai,* a solemn feast of the Lord which we celebrate. And such indeed it was! . . .

From "The History of the Hebrew Union College, 1875–1925,"
by David Philipson, in Jubilee Volume Special, 1925,
of *The Hebrew Union College Annual*

DR. H. PEREIRA MENDES Recalls the Beginnings of the Jewish Theological Seminary, 1885

The Jewish Theological Seminary of America, today the center of Conservative Judaism and a major force in American Jewish life, was founded in 1886 by a small group of rabbis and laymen as a counterpoise to what they regarded as the "excesses" of Reform Judaism. The Pittsburgh Rabbinical Conference of 1885, led by Kaufmann Kohler of the Central Conference of American Rabbis, had adopted a platform that outraged many adherents of traditional Judaism. They objected particularly to the abolition of circumcision for proselytes, rejection of the dietary laws, limiting of Hebrew to a minor role in the liturgy, conducting of Sabbath services on Sunday, and denial of Jewish national aspirations for their homeland in Palestine.

Although the rabbis who left the Central Conference regarded themselves as traditional Jews, their traditionalism was quite different from that of their parents and of the new Jewish immigrants from Eastern Europe. Hence they called themselves "historical" or "conservative" Jews rather than "orthodox." They accepted some practices introduced by Reform Judaism, as family pews, mixed choirs, and in some cases even organ music. However, the differences between Conservatism and Reform were soon made quite clear. The United Synagogue of America, formed in 1913 to unite all Conservative synagogues, reaffirmed the authority of the *Talmud* as a guide to Jewish practice, emphasized traditional observance of the Sabbath and dietary laws, expressed hope in Israel's redemption as a nation, and maintained Hebrew as the fundamental language of prayer.

The new seminary was supported mainly by English speaking traditional Jews, most of them Spanish, Portuguese, Hungarians, and second-generation Germans. Among them were Dr. Sabato Morais, rabbi of Philadelphia's famed Mikveh Israel Congregation, who became the seminary's first president, and Dr. H. Pereira Mendes of New York's Spanish and Portuguese Synagogue, whose recollections of the seminary's beginnings are reported here.

The creation of Reform and Conservative rabbinical seminaries made clear to American Orthodox Jewry the need for a rabbinical academy of its own. In 1886 the first *yeshivah* in America was established, the Yeshiva Eitz Chayyim. It was followed in 1897 by the Yeshiva Rabbi Isaac Elchanan Theological Seminary in New York, with which it eventually merged. Under imaginative leadership, the *yeshivah* developed an academic high school, a teachers' institute, a college of liberal arts and sciences, a graduate school, and the Albert Einstein Medical School, achieving university status in 1945. Today Yeshiva University is the key institution of the Orthodox Jewish community.

With the establishing of rabbinical schools by all three branches of Judaism, American Jewry was prepared to produce its own leadership.

". . . in order that the Shechinah, *the Divine Presence, might be manifest in our midst in America."*

IT IS true I am one of the few survivors of the group of rabbis and laymen who gathered fifty years ago, under the leadership of that Jewish-hearted and far-visioned watchman of Israel, the late Reverend Doctor Sabato Morais (Be his memory ever blessed) . . . His vision of a house of learning as the fortress for defense of Israel's truths was transmuted into the actuality of the seminary, our seminary, to promote in America God's purpose with Israel . . .

. . . My first thought is that the seminary was founded for the glory of God, His glorification. Then what right have I . . . to respond unless I can evolve some thought that shall glimpse His glory and glow with His glorification?

I shall speak of the past . . .

The "beginnings of the seminary" must be sought amid the echoes of the Pittsburgh Conference of 1885. That conference, convened by earnest Reform rabbis, adopted resolutions objectionable to the Orthodox and Conservative groups. The resolutions came to be called "The Pittsburgh Platform."

Fifty-one years have softened the asperities it occasioned. Be it far from me to revive any!

But to understand "the beginnings of the seminary" we must revert to the atmosphere of Jewish public opinion in those stirring days . . .

Today we can well take a calm and a reasonable view of the whole situation.

Article 3 of that platform formally rejected "all such ceremonies as are not adapted to the views and habits of modern civilization." That sounded plausible, but it took action pointing to abolition of the ceremony of the Abrahamic rite for Jewish proselytes. It countenanced Sunday services under certain conditions. It recommended that each rabbi read "only such section of the *Pentateuch* as he thinks proper, but with regard however to the regulations of the Jewish calendar." I quote from the *Jewish Encyclopedia*, Vol. 4, p. 215.

Apart from the clamor of *hoi polloi* thus born, many calm and thoughtful Conservative and Orthodox rabbis belonging to our New York Board of Jewish Ministers met for consultation. Among these were such rabbis as Doctors Alexander Kohut, Aaron Wise, Henry S. Jacobs, F. de Sola Mendes, Moses Maisner, Bernard Drachman. I had the honor of being secretary of the Board at the time.

Outside of New York, men like those giants of Jewish thought, Doctors Sabato Morais and Marcus Jastrow in Philadelphia, were not idle; and . . . earnest and sturdy champions like Rabbis

Bettelheim, Schneeberger, Schaffer, and Meldola de Sola proclaimed their sympathies.

Prominent laymen gathered around them, Doctors Cyrus Adler, Aaron and Harry Friedenwald, S. Solis Cohen, with others like Hon. Mayer Sulzberger, Simon M. Roeder, and of my own congregation, Hon. Adolphus S. Solomons, Hon. Joseph Blumenthal, Edgar Phillips, David M. Piza . . .

One day, Dr. Sabato Morais, a man whom I had learned to hold in high esteem, a man older than my honored father, called on me in New York. He proposed changing our action at meetings (debates, press-communications, accusations, recriminations, effervescence and indignation with no tangible result) into action that might mean, under God . . . the preservation of historical and traditional Judaism . . . and its ethical values by establishing a Jewish institute of learning to educate and inspire rabbis who would stand "for the Torah and the Testimony," as cried our prophet of old. (*Isaiah* 8:20)

. . . He proposed that he and I, as heads of the oldest congregations in the country, take immediate action to awaken the Jewish communities of New York and Philadelphia to the need of the hour, to create a Jewish college or seminary on these lines . . . that we exchange pulpits for this purpose . . .

I eagerly and enthusiastically embraced all his propositions.

I went further. I told him that I considered his proposition . . . so vitally important that, in order that he might stand at its helm . . . I would do all in my power to facilitate . . . his residence in New York; thus . . . to impart to the students his own personal inspiration, his own *ruach Elohim* [spirit of God] through constant close personal . . . contact.

We took immediate action by arranging that he would preach in my pulpit on the approaching *Shabbat Mishpatim,* and I in his, in Philadelphia, on the succeeding *Shabbat Terumah* . . .

On that *Shabbat Mishpatim,* historic in American Judaism, Dr. Morais preached to my congregation in New York.

. . . His very heart and soul were in his theme . . .

Eloquent, too, was the very name of that Sabbath, *Shabbat Mishpatim,* the "Sabbath of the Judgments," so called because of the opening words of the Scripture-lesson of the day, "Now these are the judgments which thou shalt set before them." (*Exodus* 21:1) That was his theme. He preached the sacredness and the eternity of the judgments or ordinances of our God; he "set before his audience the inviolability of laws which, in the judgment of God, were necessary for mankind's welfare . . ."

But with him, words alone did not suffice. We could erect a thousand institutions to teach God's word, His laws and statutes and judgments, but we should in our institution transmit the spirit as well as the word . . . "My spirit which is upon thee, besides my words which I place in thy mouth, shall not depart from thy mouth, nor from the mouth of thy children, nor from the mouth of thy children's children, from henceforth and forever! So saith the Lord!" (*Isaiah* 59:21)

His sermon bore fruit. God blessed his effort. The institution he advocated, our Seminary, became a fact.

The next Sabbath . . . I preached in Dr. Morais' synagogue in Philadelphia. Again the Sabbath and the Scripture portion of the day bore a name singularly significant . . . *Shabbat Terumah,* the "Sabbath of the Offering," is named for the opening words of the *parasha* or Scripture-lesson of the day: "Let the children of Israel bring Me an offering. From everyone whose heart prompts him to give willingly, ye may accept an offering for Me. And let them make for Me a sanctuary that I may dwell in the midst of them." (*Exodus* 25: 2–8)

That was my theme. I pleaded for *Torah* . . . for offerings to build a fortress for *Torah,* but only from the willing-hearted, . . . to erect a sanctifying-center, in order that the *Shechinah,* the Divine Presence, might be manifest in our midst in America.

I well remember that when the Scroll of the Law was placed on the reading desk, Dr. Morais honored me by calling me to read a section of the Scripture-lesson of the Sabbath . . . In courtly fashion he presented me with a silver pointer to guide in reading the lines. I bowed, but I resigned the honor to him. The verses to be read were *Exodus* 25–31ff. They commanded the making of a *menorah,* or seven-branched candlestick, whose beautiful and soft light was to pervade the *mikdash,* the sanctifying center, and whose beams were to reveal the *Shechinah,* the Divine Presence, on earth.

I feel that I acted rightly in handing over to Dr. Morais the honor of announcing the crowning meaning of our proposed sanctuary or seminary, which we fondly hoped would kindle the . . . light of God, the light of the *Torah,* the light for Israel, the light that one day "shall reach all nations of Earth." (*Job* 37:3)

Reflecting on that moment of deep spiritual emotion, the coincidence seemed to me like a whisper of God, suggesting that the proposed seminary be a *menorah,* to carry spiritual light to the world.

For Israel it would mean response to the prophet's cry, "Come let us walk by the light of the Lord." (*Isaiah* 2:5)

From *The Jewish Theological Seminary,*
edited by Cyrus Adler, Semi-Centennial Volume, 1939

THE FRENCH PRESS Reports the Dreyfus Case, 1895 and 1906

The charges against Captain Alfred Dreyfus, a Jewish officer on the French general staff, of selling military secrets to Germany aroused strong emotions all over the world. His arrest on October 15, 1894, signalled a vitriolic campaign in the French press, branding the entire Jewish people as traitors endangering the security of the French nation. Dreyfus' public degradation the following January was accompanied by jeers of "Traitor!" "Judas!" "Dirty Jew!" "Death to the Jews!"

Controversy over Dreyfus' innocence grew even more intense after his imprisonment on Devil's Island. Although the uncovering of new facts cast increasing doubt on Dreyfus' guilt, the army bitterly resented questioning, and the Catholic Church maintained an unrelenting campaign of slander against the Jewish community. Nevertheless, the fight for justice continued, led by such staunch idealists as writer Emile Zola and Colonel Henri Picquart of the French army, despite threats to their lives and well-being. Picquart uncovered proof of Dreyfus' innocence but had trouble inducing his superiors to act upon it. Zola published an angry pamphlet, *J'accuse* (I Accuse), "A cry of the conscience of humanity," which charged the French army with falsifying evidence against Dreyfus.

Although every expression of support for Dreyfus was followed by increased mob violence against French Jews, continuous agitation did force a reopening of the case. The real spy was revealed to be a certain Major Esterhazy, and the documents that had incriminated Dreyfus forged by Lieutenant-Colonel Henri. To avoid trial, Esterhazy fled to England and Henri committed suicide. Finally, Dreyfus was released from prison (1901), and five years later was invested with high military honors.

The Dreyfus case, by exposing the deep-rooted anti-Semitism that underlay the thin veneer of French enlightenment and liberalism, helped to stimulate the modern Zionist movement as a solution to the Jewish problem.

Following are press accounts of Dreyfus' degradation in 1895 and of his vindication in 1906.

"I swear that I am innocent. I swear it."

THE FIRST stroke of nine sounds from the school clock. General Darras lifts his sword and gives the command, which is repeated at the head of each company: *"Portez armes!"* The troops obey. Complete silence ensues.

Hearts stop beating, and all eyes are turned toward the corner of the vast square . . . Soon a little group appears: it is Alfred Dreyfus advancing, between four artillerymen, accompanied by a lieutenant of the Republican guard and the oldest noncommissioned officer of the regiment . . . We see distinctly the gold of the three stripes and the gold of the cap bands: the sword glitters, and . . . we behold the black sword knot on the hilt of the sword.

Dreyfus marches with steady step.

"Look, see how the wretch is carrying himself," someone says.

The group advances towards General Darras . . .

There are cries now in the crowd.

But the group halts . . . The drums beat, the trumpets blow, and then again all is still; a tragic silence now.

The artillerymen with Dreyfus drop back a few steps, and the condemned man stands well out in full view of us all.

The clerk salutes the general, and . . . reads distinctly the verdict: "The said Dreyfus is condemned to military degradation and to deportation to a fortress."

. . . The voice of General Darras is then heard . . .

"Dreyfus, you are unworthy to wear the uniform. In the name of the French people, we deprive you of your rank."

Thereupon, we behold Dreyfus lift his arms in the air . . .

The little group, led by two officers of the Republican Guard . . . begins its march along the front of the troops . . .

Dreyfus holds his head well up. The public cries, "Death to the traitor!"

Soon he reaches the great gateway, and the crowd has a better sight of him. The cries increase, thousands of voices demanding the death of the wretch, who still exclaims: "I am innocent! *Vive la France!*"

. . . A formidable burst of hisses replies to him, then an immense shout which rolls like a tempest across the vast courtyard.

"Death to the traitor! Kill him!"

And then outside the mob heaves forward in a murderous surge. Only by a mighty effort can the police restrain the people from breaking through into the yard, to wreak their swift and just vengeance upon Dreyfus for his infamy.

Dreyfus continues his march. He reaches the group of press representatives.

"You will say to the whole of France," he cries, "that I am innocent!"

"Silence, wretch," is the reply. "Coward! Traitor! Judas!"

Under the insult, the abject Dreyfus pulls himself up. He flings at us a glance full of fierce hatred. "You have no right to insult me!" A clear voice issues from the group. "You know well that you are not innocent. *Vive la France!* Dirty Jew!"

Dreyfus continues his route.

His clothing is pitiably disheveled. In the place of his stripes hang long dangling threads, and his cap has no shape.

Dreyfus pulls himself up once more, but the cries of the crowd are beginning to affect him. Though the head of the wretch is still insolently turned toward the troops, his legs are beginning to give way.

The march round the square is ended. Dreyfus is handed over to two gendarmes, who . . . conduct him to the prison van.

Dreyfus . . . is placed once more in prison. But there again he protests his innocence.

From the French newspaper *l'Autorité,* January 6, 1895

"Lucy Dreyfus is seen, weeping . . ."

WHEN HE had asked that the ceremony should not be held in the large courtyard of the Ecole Militaire, Dreyfus had desired to avoid the too-vivid recollection of the agony he had suffered there. But the somewhat similar shape of the courtyard . . . the movement of troops and regiments of artillery, the pealing of bugles, the clashing of arms . . . brought back the scene before him. Never, not even during those sleepless nights on Devil's Island, had the hallucination been so intense.

His heart beat as if it would burst. He passed again through the agony of his martyrdom . . . He could not see the regiments . . . assembled in his honour. He could see only those regiments which had been assembled to witness his degradation. And he heard, unceasingly, the wild cry of the mob: "Kill him!"

Brigadier General Gillain . . . arrives in parade uniform . . . takes up his position in the centre of the courtyard, and draws his sword. Colonel Gaillard calls: "Officers of the Legion!" Dreyfus and Targe come forward, and stand before the general. "Open the Sentence!" Four trumpet-peals . . . the general is heard . . . calling the names of the two officers. He decorates Targe first . . . Voices are heard: *"Vive la République!"*

"In the name of the President of the Republic, and by virtue of the authority vested in me, Major Dreyfus, I proclaim you Chevalier of the Legion of Honour." The general's sword falls three times upon his shoulder. He pins the cross on the black dolman, and kisses on both cheeks the man of Devil's Island. "You once served in my division," he says. "I am happy to have been entrusted with the mission which I have just discharged." The trumpets sound to close the sentence.

All eyes are turned to two windows. At one of them Lucy Dreyfus is seen, weeping, and at the other is seen the slender silhouette of General Picquart. There are cries: *"Vive Picquart!"* Picquart replies, "No, no,—Dreyfus!" And many voices are raised: *"Vive l'armée! Vive la République! Vive la vérité!"*

The general speaks with Dreyfus, while the bodies of infantry and artillery . . . are massed at the back of the courtyard. The command rings out: "Company column! Forward march! The troops pass amid the blowing of bugles. When the last soldier has disappeared under the arch, the general shakes Dreyfus by the hand again. The spectators press toward him. The cries are raised again: *"Vive Dreyfus!"* . . .

In a choked voice, Dreyfus pleads: "No, no, gentlemen, please . . ." He cannot go any further; only his lips move. Then a young man, breaking through the crowd, throws himself in the arms of Major Dreyfus: "Father! Father!" . . . Every one turns away. Dreyfus weeps.

From *A History of the Dreyfus Affair,* by Theodore Reinach, translated by Maurice Samuel

A DELEGATE Attends the First World Zionist Congress, 1897

The love of the Jews for Zion did not waver throughout the 2,000 years of their exile; nor was their hope of returning to their ancient homeland ever quenched. It was kept alive in their songs and holidays, in the Hebrew language and literature, and above all in their daily prayers. To this day, synagogues are built so that Jews face east—towards Jerusalem—when they pray. In their deeds of charity, too, they remembered Zion, as they sent help to the Jews struggling to maintain themselves in the impoverished land.

Although individual Jews continued to return to *Eretz Yisrael,* there was no organized movement to help the scattered Jewish people settle there.

Such a movement actually emerged in the last decades of the nineteenth century. Called *Chovevei Zion* (Lovers of Zion), it developed branches in every country with a sizable Jewish population and was active from 1879 on. The *Chovevei Zion* were the forerunners of modern Zionism, but they lacked the political structure to make a reality of their plans for colonization.

Then came the Dreyfus case in France, which was covered by a Viennese reporter named Theodor Herzl. Herzl saw in the trial of Alfred Dreyfus the eternal tragedy of Jewish homelessness which left the Jew everywhere a stranger. The Jewish problem would not be solved, he felt, until the Jewish people had a homeland of their own. In 1895 he wrote his astounding book, *Der Judenstaat* (The Jewish State). Translated from the original German into French, English, and Hebrew, it galvanized the Jewish world, and political Zionism was born.

A man of daring vision, Herzl called for a World

Zionist Congress. It convened in Basel, Switzerland, on August 29, 1897—an epochal turning point in Jewish history.

The congress undertook the gigantic task of creating the machinery for a democratic worldwide Zionist organization. Any Jew could belong simply by paying the nominal sum of 50 cents (comparable to the ancient Israelite levy of the *shekel*). Delegates to future congresses were to be selected by the members of the various Zionist groups.

The dominant, towering spirit of the first congress was Theodor Herzl, whose dedication, limitless energy, and self-effacing humility made its success possible. Until his premature death in 1904 at the age of thirty-nine, he was the guiding genius of the movement.

"In Basel I founded the Jewish state." With these prophetic words Herzl summed up the first congress. And he was right. It was the Basel program that set off the remarkable chain of events that was to bring about the Jewish state only a half century later.

The following passages from the diary of a German delegate to the First World Zionist Congress gives his personal reaction to the giant who is known as "The Father of Modern Zionism."

"No member of the commission had in mind anything other than the securing of a homeland through international law . . ."

BEFORE I went to the congress I took a holiday in Switzerland. My impatience to make the acquaintance of the man who had breathed new life into us will be understood; and when I heard that Herzl was likewise in Switzerland, I imagined that I might meet him there somewhere or other. But I had to wait until the congress. If I had seen an early photograph of Herzl I would not have recognized him. Even in his first Paris period his face had the expression of one who had shone with success in the salons

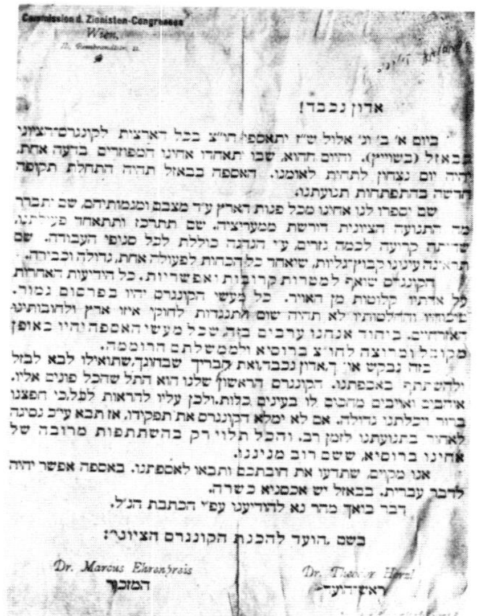

Commission d. Zionisten-Congresses
Wien,

אדון נכבד!

ביום א׳ ב׳ ג׳ אלול ש״ז יתאספו תר״צ בכל הארצות לקונגרס־הציוני
בבאזל (בשוייץ). והיום ההוא, שבו יתאחדו אחינו המפוזרים בדעה אחת,
יהיה יום נצחון לתחית לאומנו. האספה בבאזל תהיה התחלת תקופה
חדשה בהתפתחות תנועתנו.
שם יספרו לנו אחינו מכל פנות הארץ ע״ד מצבם ומגמותיהם, שם יתברר
מה התנועה הציונית דורשת ממעריציה. שם תתרכז ותתאחד פעולתנו,
שהיתה קרועה לכמה גזרים, ע״י הנהגה כוללת לכל סעיפי העבודה. שם
תראינה עינינו קבוץ־גליות, שיאחד כל הכחות לפעולה אחת, גדולה וכבירה.
הקונגרס ישאף למטרות קרובות ואפשריות. כל הידיעות האחרות
על אודותיו קלוטות מן האויר. כל מעשי הקונגרס יהיו בפרסום גמור.
ישיבותיו והחלטותיו לא תהיה שום התנגדות לחוקי איזו ארץ ולחובותינו
האזרחיים. ביחוד אנחנו ערבים בזה, שכל מעשי האספה יהיו באופן
מקובל ומרוצה לחו״צ ברוסיא ולממשלתם הרוממה.
בזה נבקש את כ׳ אדון נכבד, ואת חבריך שבחוגך, שתואילו לבא לבזל
ולהשתתף באספתנו. הקונגרס הראשון שלנו הוא התל שהכל פונים אליו.
אוהבים ואויבים מחכים לו בעינים כלות, ולכן עליו להראות לעל־כי חפצנו
ברור ויכלתנו גדולה. אם לא ימלא הקונגרס את תפקידו, אז תבא ע״כ נסיגה
לאחור בתנועתנו לזמן רב. והכל תלוי רק בהשתתפות מרובה של
אחינו ברוסיא, ששם רוב מנינגו.
אנו מקוים, שתדעו את חובתכם ותבאו לאספתנו. באספה אפשר יהיה
לדבר עברית. בבאזל יש אכסניא כשרה.
דבר ביאך מהר נא להודיענו עפ״י הכתבת הנ״ל.

בשם „הועד להכנת הקונגרס הציוני״:

Dr. Marcus Ehrenpreis
המזכיר

Dr. Theodor Herzl
ראש־הועד

Theodor Herzl's room at the Jewish Agency building, Jerusalem. (Zionist Archives and Library)

Invitation to the First Zionist Congress, 1897. (Zionist Archives and Library)

Caricature of a Jew from the period of the First Zionist Congress. (Zionist Archives and Library) of Parisian society. After the publication of *Der Judenstaat* [The Jewish State] he became a different man. The gentle cheerfulness of the countenance had given way to a profound earnestness, and the dreamy eyes had acquired a look of power. From the moment when he greeted me at Basel, like an old friend, I knew that he was indeed to be the leader of our movement.

At the inns there was a great deal of talk about Zionism and the congress. I found that the non-Jewish public accepted the Zionist plan as something quite natural . . . The congress was to take place in the *Burgvogtei.* But no sooner did Herzl see the room than he refused it. He declared that it was undignified to meet in a hall that was used for dancing and low music-hall turns. Finally the small salon of the casino was found to be suitable.

Herzl was staying at the Hotel Zu den Drei Konigen . . . His appearance filled me with joy and pride; a magnificent man. It had been someone like this that I had imagined during my school days, in thinking of the Trojan hero, Hector. Above all his eyes and mouth impressed me. Spirit was united with strength and goodness, severity with mildness and grace, in features that were both noble and agreeable. He was well above middling height, and his bearing was not inaccurately described as a kingly one. Thus he cast a spell through his personality . . .

At a preliminary conference in the *Burgvögtei,* my attention was drawn by a short man with a full, grizzled beard, lively gestures, powerful forehead, and large, luminous eyes . . . Many people crowded about him. I asked his name and learned that it was Max Nordau. So now I knew the second of the great figures in the movement. A remarkably heterogeneous group of people had gathered round Zionism. Among them were Baron von Manteuffel and the poet Borries von Munchhausen. An English clergyman, the Reverend William Hechler, was of historic importance to the cause of Zionism. At one of the preliminary conferences Herzl warned against two men whom he linked with his Berlin opponents—namely Ussishkin, one of the most important leaders of the Russian *Chovevei Zion,* and the Hebrew author, Sefer

Rabinowitsch. As a result of this distrust Ussishkin was at once forced into the opposition. He had never made a secret of the fact that he did not share the views of Herzl, and had always combated his policy . . .

The speech by Herzl . . . came like a revelation to us and was received with enormous acclaim. He concluded: "Wherever we are and however long it may be until our work is completed, our congress will be noble and serious, for the benefit of the unfortunate, to the harm of no one, and to the honor of all Jews, as worthy of a past whose fame, remote though it may be, is eternal." It was not only what he said that gripped us but also the noble and heart-warming way in which he said it, and the appearance of a man of such towering distinction that he was a credit to all civilized peoples.

The speech by Nordau had an equal effect. His description of the position of the Jewish people in all lands and periods was moving and tragic . . . A nation without a home and without soil under its feet—such, he said, was the moral distress of the Jews which was more bitter even than the physical. The emancipated Jew was rootless, uncertain in his relations to his fellow men, anxious in contact with the unknown, mistrustful . . . He had used up his best energies in the suppression or at least the dissembling of his own character. He never had the straight-forward urge to give himself wholly as he was. Thus inwardly he became crippled, while outwardly . . . he only looked ridiculous . . . Nordau . . . had a horror of the future development of this generation, which morally lacked the support of a tradition, whose spirit had been poisoned by hostility against its own as well as against alien blood, and whose self-esteem was destroyed . . . To find a remedy for this Jewish distress, he said, was the great task of the congress.

Of the greatest importance for the future of the movement were the negotiations about its platform, which has remained unchanged down to the present day . . . There was a draft by Professor Schapira . . . setting forth only the idea of the colonization of Palestine and then the Theses of the Cologne Zionist Society. Out of these Nordau framed the succinctly worded statement: "*The aim of Zionism is the creation of a homeland, recognized by international law, for the Jewish people in Palestine.*" This statement was opposed by Schapira, who emphatically rejected any formulation that would arouse suspicion of an intent to create a Jewish state in Palestine. In order to obtain a unanimous vote the lawyers in the commission proposed the version: "The aim is a *legally secured homeland.*" They were guided by the consideration that this phrasing admitted of the possibility of constitutional law as well as international law, without particularly emphasizing the fact. This phrasing was the one adopted. Nevertheless no member of the commission had in mind anything other than the securing of a homeland through international law . . .

From *Prelude to Israel, the Memoirs of M. I. Bodenheim,* edited by Henriette H. Bodenheim, translated by Israel Cohen

CHAIM NACHMAN BIALIK Cries Out on the Kishinev Pogrom, 1903

The city of Kishinev was quiet on Easter morning of 1903. The calm, however, was shattered by a hitherto unparalleled storm of violence against the Jewish inhabitants. The government had carefully prepared the groundwork for this outbreak by fostering vicious anti-Jewish propaganda, denouncing Jews as enemies of the people, exploiters and bloodsuckers. Highly placed public officials encouraged their maltreatment by letting it be known that the Jewish people stood outside the protection of the law.

The attack began about 1:00 P.M. when a number of youths assaulted Jews and broke windows. The tempo picked up a couple of hours later as twenty-four small bands rushed into the Jewish section of the city, shouting obscene epithets, destroying property, plundering, and striking down all who opposed them. The police remained on the sidelines except to share in the stolen booty. By five o'clock, drunken rioters started on a murder spree that left ten Jews dead. The next day, strangers were armed with axes and clubs and invited to join in the sport. When the Jews undertook to defend themselves, the police intervened to disperse or arrest them. In the course of the day, people of all classes—police, officials, priests, peasants, workers, tramps, women, and children—joined to rob, plunder, and assault. Finally, at five o'clock the soldiers, on orders from St. Petersburg, took up positions throughout the city. They cleared the streets without firing a single shot, making it abundantly clear how easily the whole tragedy could have been prevented.

The final tally showed 49 Jews killed, 90 maimed, 50 injured; 600 shops destroyed, 700 homes ruined;

and over 10,000 people impoverished. The Kishinev pogrom shocked the whole civilized world, which had thought such brutality impossible in a so-called Christian society in the twentieth century.

Realizing that such gruesome acts might befall them tomorrow, masses of Russian Jews came to the sad conclusion that, though their ancestors may have lived there for hundreds of years, they had better leave Russia while they could.

The Russian born Hebrew poet, Chaim Nachman Bialik (1873–1934), proclaimed the ghastly deeds at Kishinev to the world in the poem, *The City of Slaughter*. A portion of this searing poetry follows.

"The fear of death is breathing round thee!"

OF STEEL and iron, cold and hard and dumb,
Now forge thyself a heart, O man! and come
and walk the town of slaughter. Thou shalt see
With walking eyes, and touch with conscious hands,
On fences, posts, and doors,
On paving in the street, on wooden floors,
The black, dried blood, commingled here and there
With brains and splintered bone.
And thou shalt wander in and out of ruins
Of broken walls, doors wrenched from off their hinges,
Stoves overturned, dilapidated hearths,
And singed beams laid bare, and half-burnt bricks,
Where axe and flame and iron yesternight
Danced a wild dance and led the bloody revel.
Then, creep to attics, clamber over roofs,
Peep in where all the black and yawning holes
Appear like ragged wounds that neither wait
Nor hope for healing more in all this world.
Outside, the sultry air is thick with feathers,

And thou shalt think to wade as in a river,
A flow of human sweat, the sweat of anguish.
Thou stumblest over heaps of goods and chattels—
They're just whole lives of men, whole lives of men,
Like broken potsherds, past all mending ever—
Thou walkest, runnest, fallest in the wreckage,
In cushions, tinsel, linings, silk and satin,
All dragged and rent and torn to bits and trampled—
They're holidays and Sabbaths, joy of feast days—
And scarfs and prayer books, parchments, scraps of *Torah,*
The white and holy wrappings of thy soul.
Look, look! they fold themselves about thy feet,
They kiss thy very footmarks in the dust . . .
Thou fleest! whither? back to light and air?
Run, run! the sky will laugh thee, man, to scorn!
The sun will blind thee with its glowing spears,
Acacias hung with tassels white and green
Will poison thee with smells of blood and flowers,
And blossoms and feathers fall on thee in showers.
A thousand, thousand shivered bits of glass
Shall twinkle in thy dazzled eyes—behold!
For now is given thee a wondrous thing,
A twofold gift, a slaughter and a spring!
The garden blossomed and the sun shone bright,
The *Shochet* slaughtered!
The knife was sharp and glistened, from the wound
Flowed blood and gold.
Thou seek'st the shelter of a court! in vain!
A heap of refuse. They beheaded twain:
A Jew—his dog, with hatchets, yesterday,
Toward the centre of the court. This morning
A hungry pig came by and dragged them hither,
And routed, grunting, in their mingled blood.
Let be! tomorrow there will fall a shower
And wash the blood into the drain, and stifle

Its cry to heaven for vengeance; some, maybe,
Has sunk already deep, deep down, and feeds
The thorny tangle of a crooked hedge.
And calmly, like today and yesterday,
The sun will rise tomorrow, in the East,
Its splendour not diminished in the least,
And just as nothing were, pursue its way . . .
Go, half distraught, and scramble to a garret,
And there remain alone in musty gloom.
Alone? the fear of death is breathing round thee!
It fans the dark with black and chilly feathers
And lifts each single hair upon thy head.
Look, here and here, and in between the rafters,
Are eyes and eyes that gaze at thee in silence,
The eyes of martyred souls,
Of hunted, harried, persecuted souls,
Who've huddled all together in the corner,
And press each other closer still and quake;
For here it was the sharpened axes found them,
And they have come to take another look,
And in the apple of each staring eye
To glass once more the picture of their end,
Of all the terror of their savage death,
Of all the suff'ring of their dreary lives
And, trembling like a crowd of startled doves,
They flutter in a cluster to the ceiling,
And thence they gaze at thee with dumb, wild eyes,
That follow thee and ask the old, old question,
The one that never yet has reached to heaven,
And never will:
For what, for what? and once again, for what?
Yes, strain thy neck . . . behold, there is no heaven!
There's nothing but a roof of blackened tiles.
Thence hangs a spider—go and ask the spider!
She saw it all, and she's a living witness,

The old grey spider spinning in the garret.
She knows a lot of stories—bid her tell them!
A story of a belly stuffed with feathers,
Of nostrils and of nails, of heads and hammers,
Of men who, after death, were hung head downward,
Like geese, along the rafter. . . .
And, stifling down the sob within thy throat,
Thou rushest headlong down the stairs and out—
To see again the world of ev'ry day,
The usual sun, outpouring unashamed
A wealth of beams at every guilty threshold,
And lavish of its store on worse than swine. . . .

The City of Slaughter, translated by Helena Frank.
Included in *Selected Poems: Chaim Nachman Bialik*,
translated by Maurice Samuel

DAVID BEN-GURION Arrives Home, 1907

There was never a time since the destruction of the Second Temple when there were no Jews in *Eretz Yisrael* (the Land of Israel). Some communities of Jews had never left. Those who were exiled did not give up the hope of returning, and many made their way back.

Through all the periods of the Dispersion there were Jewish immigrants to the destroyed and desolate land of their ancestors. In the Middle Ages they lived in Jerusalem, Hebron, Acco, Beth Shean, Safed, and in villages in the Galil. Following the expulsion from Spain, there was a new flowering of Jewish culture in Palestine as thousands of Spanish Jews returned. In the sixteenth century and after, Jews settled mainly in the four holy cities—Jerusalem, Safed, Hebron, and Tiberias—where they came to study and pray, and to be buried in the soil of the Holy Land.

But the late nineteenth century saw a new breed of Jewish immigrants to *Eretz Yisrael*—idealistic young Russian Jews who came to rebuild the land with their own hands. One of the first groups (1878) chose the name BILU, which was made up of the first letters of the biblical phrase, *Bet Ya-akov, lechu venelchah* (House of Jacob, come and let us go). Young intellectuals, most of them students at the University of Kharkov, the *Biluim* settled on communal farms and worked the land. They spearheaded the First *Aliyah* (wave of immigration) in the 1880's, which was spurred by the vicious anti-Jewish outbreaks in Russia. It was the birth of a new era, marked by new ideas.

The famous Second *Aliyah*, early in the twentieth century, brought many of Israel's future leaders to the land, among them David Ben-Gurion, who became the first prime minister of the State of Israel. Born David Green, near Warsaw, Poland, he was twenty-two when he arrived in 1907. Steeped in the new Hebrew literature, which stressed the return to the soil and the dignity of labor, he found the life of a Palestinian farmer, despite its difficulties and dangers, full of unceasing excitement and joy. The Turkish authorities in the Holy Land looked askance at the "socialist-minded" young newcomers and sharply limited their opportunities for work. Some left the country in dismay, but others, the *chalutzim* (pioneers) who came with a dream in their hearts, were not to be easily discouraged or deterred from their goal.

In the accompanying account, David Ben-Gurion describes his return. His story throbs with the heartbeat of a strong, idealistic pioneering youth. It is a priceless record of the efforts of brave men to establish a home for their people after centuries of untold wandering and suffering.

"You felt as a partner in the act of creation."

AS SOON as I had disembarked and passed through the Turkish customs, I hurried to Petah Tikvah. Friends pressed me to stay a few days in Jaffa, but I could not restrain an overmastering urge to see a Jewish village, and toward evening of the same day I arrived at the oldest and largest of Jewish colonies.

That night, my first night on homeland soil, is engraved forever on my heart with its exultation of achievement. I lay awake—who could sleep through his first night in the homeland? The spirit of my childhood and my dreams had triumphed and I was joyous! I was in *Eretz Yisrael,* in a Jewish village, and its name was Petah Tikvah—Portal of Hope!

For a year I sweated in Judean colonies, but I had more malaria and hunger than work. All three—work, hunger, and malaria

Founding of Tel Aviv, 1909. (Zionist Archives and Library)

—were new and full of interest. Was it not for this that I had come to the homeland? The fever would visit me every fortnight with mathematical precision, linger for five or six days, and then disappear. Hunger, too, was a frequent visitor. It would stay with me for weeks, sometimes for months. During the day I could dismiss it somehow, or at least stop thinking of it. But in the nights —the long racked vigils—the pangs would grow fiercer, wringing the heart, darkening the mind, sucking the very marrow from my bones, demanding and torturing and departing only with the dawn. Shattered and broken, I would drop off to sleep at last.

But the enthusiasm and joy did not fade. Who worried about malaria in those days? The few who did not suffer from it were a little shamefaced before the rest of us who did!

That was in 1907, at the time of a new *aliyah;* every ship brought more young people. Most of the new laborers settled in Petah Tikvah, and although the farmers there had recently issued a ban on Jewish labor, our numbers grew from week to week.

After a day of work, or maybe of fever, we would gather in the workers' kitchen, or in the sandy tracks between the vineyard and the groves, and sing and dance in a circle, sing and dance arm in arm and shoulder to shoulder.

The interminable hoeing and spading did not satisfy me fully. It was too mechanical and monotonous. The ceaseless thumping and thudding smacked of a factory. I yearned for the wide fields, for waving stalks of corn, for the fragrance of grass, the plowman's song—and I made up my mind to go north to the Galil.

From Judea I came to Sejera. Here, at last, I found the Land of Israel. Nature, people, work—here everything was wholly different, more of Israel; here one inhaled the aroma of homeland at every step.

Sejera almost monopolized the diverse lovelinesses of created scenery with which the land is clad. Mountains surround it and enclose it on every side.

The settlement is built on the slope of a hill—two rows of houses one above the other, encircled by thickets of eucalyptus and pepper trees, and looking from afar like rungs of a ladder mounting to the peak. The farm itself stands there.

The people of the village were as diversified as its environment. Among the fifty-odd farmers and laborers were tall, broad-shouldered Kurdish Jews, as unlettered as their non-Jewish neighbors in Kurdistan; thin, bony Yemenites, highly learned in the Hebrew language and in traditional Judaism; young Russians, disciples of enlightenment and revolution; native-born Ashkenazi [German Jews] and Sephardi [Spanish Jews], who had left the *yeshivot* of Safed and Tiberias to take up the spade and the plow; Russian farmers from the shores of the Caspian Sea, who had embraced Judaism and come to labor in the homeland of their new faith; young *Sephardim,* educated in the schools of the Alliance Israelite. This motley community had Hebrew, Arabic, Aramaic (spoken by the Kurdish Jews), Yiddish, Russian, French, and Spanish. But this miniature "ingathering of exiles" was cemented and made one by a firm and powerful bond—the land and its cultivation. In Sejera—and in those days it was unique of its kind—there was nothing but Jewish labor, the labor of the farmers themselves and their children; even the farm, which belonged to the Jewish Colonization Association (ICA), employed only Jewish workers.

The officials and laborers lived on the hilltop; the villagers, the farmers, lived below, on the slope; but the relations between the two sections were very cordial. Almost all the farmers were young men who had formerly worked as laborers on the farm, and when they acquired land of their own, went on working it themselves. We, the workers, would meet them often, in the field and at home. There was no sign here of the rift that divided farmers from laborers in Judea. On Sabbaths and festivals we would celebrate together, and on workdays we would meet in the fields, plow side by side and help one another.

Here I found the environment that I had sought so long. No shopkeepers or speculators, no non-Jewish hirelings, no idlers living on the labor of the others. The men plowed and harrowed their fields and planted the seed; the women weeded the gardens and milked the cows; the children herded geese and rode on horseback to meet their fathers in the field. These were villagers, smelling wholesomely of midden and ripening wheat, and burned by the sun.

The work, too, was more satisfying. There was none of the deadening monotony that attends the rigors of the hoe in Judea. You follow and guide the plow, turn the sod and open furrow after furrow; and soon the very soil you plowed and planted would clothe itself in green. Before your very eyes it would bring forth its crop. No sooner were the rains over than the grain would ripen, and out you would go to reap the harvest and carry the yield to the threshing-floor. You felt as a partner in the act of creation.

From *Sound the Great Trumpet*, edited by M. Z. Frank

COLONEL MEINERTZHAGEN Witnesses a Pogrom, 1910

As this eyewitness account by a British officer indicates, the barbaric attacks on Russian Jews should have shocked all civilized people. What made these pogroms even more insufferable was that the government incited them, determined their duration, and did not suppress them until sufficient blood had been spilled and enough property had been ruined. The pogroms, which were part of the government's calculated attempts to destroy its Jewish population, were the major reason for the mass exodus of Russian Jews in late nineteenth and early twentieth centuries.

"There is no word in the English language to describe such vile and bestial behaviour."

I HAVE BEEN shocked beyond belief. I have seldom been so angry and yet so impotent as I have been today. I would never have believed that human beings could behave worse than the most savage and cruel wild beasts; worse, because their behaviour was intended to be cruel and brutal, and what they did was done with relish; I witnessed a pogrom in the streets of Odessa.

I was having dinner with our Consul General Smith when it started. There was running and shouting in the streets. Smith and I went to the front door of the consulate and saw people running excitedly in all directions and much hysterical shouting. Smith said, "I fear this is a pogrom: we had one here some years ago. We must keep off the streets as the Russians become quite irresponsible and the police become immobile. Now you will witness one of the vilest facets of the Russian character." We watched. The streets were well lit and we could see well in both directions; there was also a small square in front of the house.

Russians, many with bludgeons or knives or axes, were rushing all over the place, breaking open barricaded doors and chasing the wretched Jews into the streets where they were hunted down, beaten, and often killed. One old man was axed on the head quite close to us. I was longing to interfere and beat up some of these Russian wild beasts, but Smith restrained me—fortunately. A young woman chased by a Russian rushed frantically into the consulate and collapsed on the door mat; her pursuer pulled up short on seeing us. I abused him in English. Smith said, "For God's sake, don't provoke them; they're mad!" Another Jewish youth was chased, beaten into the gutter, viciously kicked, robbed, and left unconscious. By this time, the streets were in an uproar, but not a policeman was in sight. A large window of a store was smashed and the shop entered, looted, and its goods thrown into the street.

The climax arrived when a Russian passed the consulate dragging a Jewish girl about twelve years old by her hair along the gutter; she was screaming and the man was shouting. I have no doubt she would have been outraged and then murdered. I could not help it, I heard old Hales [headmaster of a private school] whispering, "Do something!" So I dashed out, kicked the Russian violently in the stomach with my heavy Russian boots and landed him a good blow on the jaw; he went down like a log, and I carried the child into the consulate. Smith said, "We shall get into trouble for this." Trouble, indeed, when compared with the fate of this child! I am overcome with anger and compassion this evening.

Smith has been in Odessa for ten years. He tells me that some years ago when the Russian revolution was in full swing, it was decided to have a pogrom in Odessa. Many Jews were warned of their impending danger and succeeded in bribing the revolutionary leaders not to molest them, but some four hundred Jews were nevertheless killed. The pogrom, which lasted three days, was organized by the minister of the Interior, in order to demonstrate to the Czar that the people were not yet fit for self-government. On the first day of the pogrom all the police were withdrawn from Odessa . . . for three days. After that time, an order went forth that the military must stop the massacres; this was effected in a few hours. Some of the rioters, on being shot in the streets, bitterly complained that they had not had the full three days promised by the authorities! Smith assured me that the above was strictly accurate and that a full report with proof had been sent at the time to our foreign office.

I am deeply moved by these terrible deeds and have resolved that whenever or wherever I can help the Jews, I shall do so to the best of my ability. There is no word in the British language to describe such vile and bestial behaviour.

From *Middle East Diary,* by Col. R. Meinertzhagen

DAVID ZASLAVSKY Observes the Beiliss Trial, 1911

Menachem Mendel Beiliss was a simple and obscure Jewish watchman of a brickyard in Kiev. He was catapulted to international notoriety, however, by a vicious and baseless charge of ritual murder. He was accused of murdering thirteen-year-old Andrei Justchinski, whose body was found near the brickyard in March, 1911.

Investigation established clearly that Justchinski had died in the home of the mother of one of his friends, a den of thieves, fences, and murderers, because he knew too much about their infamous activities. Beiliss' innocence was so patent that it took the government two years to contrive sufficient falsified evidence to charge him with ritual murder "aided and abetted by persons unknown."

The entire civilized world reacted with revulsion and horror to this blatant perversion of justice. Opening of the Russian archives later revealed the extent of the government's deceit, forgery, and depravity. The charges of the prosecution were so baseless that even the carefully selected jurors could not submit a verdict of guilty. The jurors succumbed to the tremendous pressures placed upon them only to the extent of declaring that although Beiliss was innocent ritual murder had occurred.

Beiliss was obviously being used as a means of attacking the entire Jewish people. The government had arranged the case for the express purpose of vilifying all Russian Jewry. It stands forth as one of the most flagrant attempts to violate elementary justice.

Placard published in Russia on the fifteenth anniversary of the Beiliss trial. The Beiliss family is in the center, other pictures are of leading defense personalities in the trial. (YIVO Institute for Jewish Research)

". . . all the peasants and burghers who, with their simple and naive arguments, tore apart the web in which the prosecution tried to enmesh Beiliss."

WE WRITE these lines before the ritual expertise has begun. Actually, we can say that the trial is over . . .

Shrouded in fog there stands behind us a multitude of hazy witnesses, a small segment of the sea of humanity, one corner of Russia, which was transferred to the courtroom . . . Doctors, professors, lawyers, officials and poets, artisans and laborers, policemen and criminals, Jews of all strata of society, rich manufacturers and ordinary workers, journalists, judges, "burghers," residents of out-of-the-way little streets of a large city; one way or another they all convereged on Beiliss . . .

I remember the peasants, gray dumpy figures in old-fashioned clothes. In court, they looked like savages who had stumbled into the city for the first time. They were unable to answer simple questions. They had no accurate reference to determine time . . . The calendar and its months had not yet entered their consciousness and they reckoned time by saints' days . . . All of them were so unenlightened and ignorant; more unenlightened and ignorant than the peasants in the jury box who, as I write these lines, are racking their brains with the difficult question: "How can we translate the word *sair?* Is it a goat, a Roman, or just any Gentile?"

Here is what is remarkable. Through the court there paraded dozens of peasants, approximately a hundred "burghers," residents of the Kiev suburbs. Simple, insignificant Russians. They were all asked leading questions about the Jews, and yet we did not hear one word of enmity toward or hatred of Jews from them. Of course, the exceptions were the "unionists" (members of the Black Hundreds), members of the "two-headed eagle," the police spy Polishchuk and Gendarme-Colonel Ivanov . . . and the old grandmother of the murdered boy . . .

For more than two years there had been pogrom agitation . . .

Such an extraordinary, incomprehensible, puzzling killing should have aroused and incited the mob. Yet the masses did not prove to be saturated with the poison of anti-Semitism . . . All Beiliss' neighbors . . . spoke in favor of the accused . . . and none of them gave evidence of a desire to take revenge against the Jew, to do him harm. The accusers . . . actually incited them against Beiliss, but nothing came of it.

Lukianovka—where Beiliss lived—is a suburb almost entirely populated by Russian "burghers." Jews have no official permission to live there . . . Tcheberiak's home was a merry little house, right next to Dobjanski's tavern, where thieves and procurers used to gather. Near Tcheberiak's house lives Mifle, her lover, a man with a shady past. A little beyond that is the hangout of Adele Ravitch, the one who sailed for America right after the murder, in whose possession stolen revolvers were found and who undoubtedly was connected with the murder. This little criminal household lived as an ordinary "burgher" family . . .

Nevertheless, despite two years of ritual incitement, the prosecution did not succeed in instilling confidence in Beiliss' guilt. We know how the detective Polishchuk worked in this direction. With whisky and money, he was able to get only the witnesses Volkovna and the Schachovski couple. The beggar woman, however, repudiated her perjured testimony in court, and the lamplighter Schachovski's testimony was contradictory and confused, but nobody would believe such a seedy drunkard anyhow. It looked as if there was nothing easier than to prejudice simple shrewd "burghers" against the Jews by using ritual propaganda. Nevertheless, it did not succeed. On the contrary, many testified with open sympathy for Beiliss and, when the court visited the scene of the murder, Beiliss, who was taken there under guard, was warmly greeted by his Christian neighbors. Not only did no perjured witnesses (who played an important role in ritual murder trials of the past) come forth, but the cobbler Nakonechi, the intellectual among the Lukianover residents, warmly and with conviction defended Beiliss . . .

There were almost no workers at the trial. The saddlemaker

Gorbotko and the brickmaker Bobrovski were the only ones. The saddlemaker, a tall strong middle-aged fellow, presented his evidence calmly. He was asked questions whose answers could have implicated another saddlemaker, the Jew Gulko . . . The saddlemaker, however, refused to cooperate and gave clear and simple answers. Bobrovski made an impression as a civilized, well-read, conscientious worker. He was supposed to testify that the factory was in operation on the 12th. It is well-known how much the prosecution counted on this. Bobrovski was aware of the trick, however, and destroyed the prosecutor's carefully made plans . . .

We cannot list all the peasants and burghers who, with their simple and naive arguments, tore apart the web in which the prosecution tried to enmesh Beiliss. One thing we can say: among the simple crowd . . . the pogrom and ritual agitation found no fertile ground, no supporters. As soon as one of the people spoke, the voice of truth was heard, but the anti-Semitic lie, hatred of Jews or Beiliss was heard either from a student, a detective, a clergyman, a landowner, an official, or a professor. On the side of the reactionaries and their ritual aims, there were a suitable legal researcher, a suitable prosecutor, a suitable judge, obedient officials, professors, conscienceless clergymen, common police spies, and, for everything, capable students. In short, all the elements of the Russian intelligentsia who gladly jeopardized their honor and conscience to preserve or further their careers.

Among the real, simple Russian people who live on the earnings of their labor, the reactionaries could not find one person who would sell his honor and conscience for money, emoluments or a good job.

From the newspaper *Die Zeit,* St. Petersburg, Russia,
October 26, 1913

VLADIMIR JABOTINSKY Serves in the Jewish Legion, 1917

Near the end of World War I, a Jewish unit was formed within the British army. Known first as the Jewish Legion, and later as the Judaeans, the troop fought as Jews in its own closed formations—for the first time in 1300 years. They carried the blue-and-white ensign of the Palestinian *yishuv* (Jewish community), used the *Magen David* (the Star of David) as their insignia, and spoke and issued military commands in Hebrew.

Such a troop had been advocated for years by Vladimir Jabotinsky, the militant Zionist writer who believed that the Jews should join with the British for the conquest of Palestine. Many Russian Jews in England and America responded to his call to arms. The British government, glad for the support of world Jewry in the critical year of 1917, approved Jabotinsky's proposals and helped recruit Jewish regiments. Lieutenant-Colonel John Henry Patterson, their commandant, praised the courage and fortitude of the Jewish soldiers, who played an important role in the British campaign in the Holy Land.

The Jewish Legion met with strident opposition from many quarters, both Jewish and non-Jewish. Some Zionists feared the outcry of anti-Semites. Many English Jews felt that Jews should fight under the English ensign alone. The greatest hostility came from the Egyptian Expeditionary Force, which despised all things Jewish. The British general staff itself soon displayed a desire to disband the battalion.

Despite harassment and hazing, the Jewish Legion remained alive. It survived an assignment to the Jordan Valley during the murderously hot summer (where British soldiers were normally sent for only brief periods of duty) under the ceaseless guns of Turkish snipers. It performed brilliantly at Um-esh-Shert, Nimrin, and Es-Salt, pinning down the Turkish army in Transjordan.

Although the Jewish soldiers were highly praised by the commanding generals, the English and Egyptian newspapers printed nothing on their achievements. Nonetheless, the valor of the Jewish Legion reflected honor on the entire Jewish community.

"There was great enthusiasm among the young people, some of whom had broken through the Turkish border patrols, and had arrived at Petah Tikvah asking, 'Where is the legion?'"

WE LEFT Southhampton for France—Egypt—Palestine. It took us ten days to traverse France and Italy. But they were not difficult days. One inevitably gained the impression that both France and Italy had been created for the express purpose of insuring the comfort of English soldiers . . .

Every two days we stopped for a day and a night at rest camps . . . like villages of barracks and tents, with . . . a chemist, a hospital, a concert-hall, even a *kalabush*—the name given by our Zion Mule Corps boys, under Egyptian influence, to the military prison. Our battalion possessed a first-class concert orchestra . . . It must be added that their repertoire contained nothing even remotely Jewish—except for *Hatikvah* [the Jewish national anthem], which, at Colonel Patterson's orders, concluded every concert.

Of our thirty officers, twenty were Jews—transfers from other regiments. Most of them had at that time heard very little about Zionism; the Officers' Mess, after meals, often had the appearance of a discussion-evening of the good old days in Minsk or Kishinev. Are the Jews a nation? What is nationality? Can one be a Zionist and a British patriot at the same time? They often tried to drag me into the discussion—but I had long forgotten how one "proves" such problems. I left this honor to younger Zionist "recruits."

The *padre,* Reverend Mr. Falk, held out bravely against . . . a whole regiment of skeptical lieutenants, who pleaded that being a Zionist had nothing to do with eating kosher food. He stood like a rock by his principle. "It isn't a question of eating. It is the principle that the Jew must always fight against all temptation, control and discipline himself at every step, and build a Zion of purity in his heart before building a Zion for his people."

The best Zionist was the colonel [Patterson]. His arguments were convincing . . . Gideon, Deborah, King David, Migdal, the moon in the valley of Ajalon . . . The *padre* tried to prove that Patterson was not even a general Zionist but a Mizrachist [religious Zionist]! And it is a fact that the colonel saw to it—how, I do not know—that every Saturday should find us in a rest camp; in the morning we would have synagogue parade, with all the officers and men, even Christians, standing with their hats on, with the Zionist flag flying . . . with the Scroll of the Law given to us by the Portsmouth community, and with the concert choir singing all the prayers, and *Hatikvah* and the English anthem at the end. The Reverend Mr. Falk would deliver a sermon, with consistent brilliance . . .

We did not stop at any of the big towns, and saw no Jews. Only once, in Italy . . . when we were marching with our flag to the railway station, an old man suddenly rushed out from a gate, and, pointing at himself, shouted: *"Yehudi! Yisrael! Eviva!"*

In Taranto . . . Patterson and Falk went to a cabinetmaker . . . and ordered an ark of the finest wood. At the Sabbath parade, the scroll was placed in this ark with much ceremony, and the colonel said to the men, in all seriousness: "With this talisman on board, we need have no fear of German submarines."

The voyage occupied less than two days . . .

The Sephardic [Spanish Jewish] community in Alexandria gave us a rousing welcome. Again I found our old friends of the

"*Gabbari*" days . . . "The Zion Mule Corps was our son, the Jewish Legion is our grandson," they said.

They arranged an impressive service, attended by the governor, generals, allied and neutral consuls and Arab notables.

The same happened in Cairo . . . The English high commissioner, Sir Reginald Wyndham, took the salute of the marching battalion . . . and listened to *Hatikvah* at the salute . . . Far away still were those gloomy days of 1919 when General Money, the military governor of Palestine, in the presence of important Jewish, English, and Arab personalities, remained seated when *Hatikvah* was played!

. . . According to military regulations, all letters written by the men must be scrutinized by an officer . . . I was the only one who could read Hebrew and Yiddish. As a result, I was ordered to look through all the letters not written in English. It was then that I discovered that there were several Lithuanians in our battalion—Lithuanian Christians. They had previously worked in a coal mine somewhere near Glasgow and, when called up, had asked to serve with us . . .

In the hundreds of Jewish letters . . . there always came the main items: "How are the children?" "How are Hannah's teeth?" and "Joe's measles?" "Don't be lonely, dear. Have you installed the gas in the kitchen?" Here you found an indescribable love, not of a country, or of a town or a street, but of home and family. I often wonder whether this love is not better than patriotism. For is it not the true foundation of patriotism? Give these people a "home," not in a strange country where they are immigrants of yesterday, but a home where the house and the street and the town and the country are interwoven with one another, bricks in the same building, where you cannot break one without disturbing all—and you will perhaps have created the psychology of Bar Kochba's Zealots . . .

We were waiting for new arrivals. Before our departure from England we had received a telegram from New York, signed by Brainin, Ben-Zvi and Ben-Gurion, informing us of the recruiting campaign for the legion in America. The Greek government had announced that volunteer-recruiting would be permitted in Salonika. A message came from Buenos Aires signed by Vladimir Herman: "English consent obtained." And a recruiting office had been opened in Egypt itself.

But the most encouraging news had come from Palestine. Hardly had the train entered the railway station at Cairo, when a khaki-clad young man ran up to me. "My name is Aloni," he said. "I have been sent from Tel Aviv to welcome the legion on behalf of the Palestine volunteers."

And he told me of a great movement in that part of Palestine which had already been liberated—Jerusalem, Tel Aviv, and Jaffa, and the colonies of Judea; and even in the north, which was still in the hands of the Turk—in Zichron-Jacob and Hedera, in Haifa, and in the colonies of Upper and Lower Galilee—there was great enthusiasm among the young people, some of whom had broken through the Turkish border patrols and had arrived at Petah Tikvah asking, "Where is the legion?"

One morning Patterson told me to pack: "I have been given permission to go to Palestine with you."

In the train neither of us slept . . . not so much because of my excitement as because of the colonel's. It is difficult to describe what it means to a Protestant to "live through" such names as Sinai, Gaza, Palestine.

In his childhood he had sat by the fire for hours every Sunday, quietly listening to his father read chapters of the Bible. Suez Canal! . . . to Colonel Patterson it was a personal memory, bringing back to him a picture of his old home, and the beautiful Bible stories . . . the crossing of the Red Sea, Moses with his patriarchal beard, Pharaoh's iron chariots, pillars of fire and smoke.

. . . Around us was always the desert, here and there relieved by tufts of grass . . . And suddenly a new world, a green eucalyptus wood followed by vineyards, white houses with red roofs in the distance—a piece of Europe.

I heard the colonel ask the inspector, a soldier, "What place is this?"

"Doyran."

Here I had a taste . . . of that attitude to Jewish works which had become a tradition with Allenby's staff. Doyran? It was our colony, Rehovoth. Doyran is the name of an Arab village not even mentioned on the map. But Allenby had instituted this tradition. To him "Petah Tikvah" was "Mulebis," "Beer-Jacob" was "Bir-Salem." . . .

We alighted at Beer-Jacob . . . The colonel went to meet the commander-in-chief, and I was taken to Tel Aviv. In the evening we exchanged impressions. Mine were pleasant; his were not. For I had visited the bride, a poor bride awaiting the coming of the bridegroom, believing devoutly all the while that he loved her; Patterson had visited the bridegroom's rich father.

I had found Jaffa and Tel Aviv in a state of unbounded enthusiasm . . . Then Tel Aviv was a town of 3,000 inhabitants . . . a few score houses surrounding the *gymnasium* [secondary school]—a clean, westernized suburb for intellectuals . . .

Approaching the town I met a ten-year-old boy . . . He told me the latest news: 40,000 Jewish soldiers were coming in English ships; at the head of this army was General James Rothschild, the baron's son. I had not the heart to tell him that so far we were but one battalion. But I had to tell my friends in Tel Aviv . . .

But their enthusiasm was created by something which completely overshadowed even our legion—their own volunteer legion. Its initiator and leader was Moses Smilansky, a man of forty, a well-known Hebrew writer (*Hawaja Musa*) . . . Berl Katzenelson, later editor of *Davar*, Yavnieli, who years ago first brought Yemenites to Palestine, Dov Hos, Eliahu Golomb, and many others today prominent in the Labor movement were the leading spirits . . .

"How many are you?" I asked.

"Nearly fifteen hundred. One-third are girls who want to

serve as a *Red Magen David* [Red Star of David, comparable to the Red Cross] group, though many of them hope that the English will agree to create a regiment of Amazons."

. . . They arranged an improvised parade of the Jaffa volunteers . . . One glance was sufficient to show what excellent material we had—slim, alert, with impatient eyes; though sunken cheeks testified to the years of hunger under Turkey.

These were the tidings I brought to Colonel Patterson. His story was of an altogether different kind.

General Allenby had exhibited much coldness . . . He had inherited from Kitchener a strong antagonism to "fancy regiments" . . . But Patterson emphasized one thing: it was not Allenby himself who was the chief opponent, but his chief of staff, a certain General Louis Bols—who two years later did nothing to prevent the Jerusalem pogrom.

Unhappily silent, we paced to and fro on the dusty road among the cactus bushes. Looking back . . . one can see . . . a prophetic introduction to the Military Administration. On the one side, enthusiasm, hope, preparedness for any sacrifice, impatience to fight and to create; on the other, cold, skeptical eyes and a strange reproachful attitude, opposed to . . . everything not routine . . .—like Zionism.

But the colonel was not one of those who remain depressed for long . . .

"It doesn't matter," he said. "We have had greater difficulties. It will be all right. I am certain that the commander-in-chief will still change his mind."

There was truth in what Patterson said, even too much. For not once but ten times did Allenby change his mind, about both the legion and the whole Zionist question.

Several weeks afterward he gave his consent to recruiting in Palestine, then again delayed the matter months; promised to create a Jewish brigade with Patterson as general, then withdrew his promise, though it was in black and white in a letter.

It is a notorious fact that the strongest of soldiers are often weak and influenced with utmost ease. As a general, Allenby was a good strategist—at any rate, they say so and I am not qualified to judge. But . . . they made him a statesman as well. And here he showed himself strong only as an "executive"—the executor of the council of others . . . a big "motor car" which can be driven by anybody with a little skill and luck. This combination is always dangerous. A man who . . . had a reputation for power and strong will (Allenby's subordinates . . . called him the "Bull of Bashan") deep down in his heart did not know what to do and must of necessity seek counsellors . . . Usually only those who suit themselves to the "Bull of Bashan" legend can influence him, for they help him appear as terrible as his reputation . . . Allenby seemed anti-Jewish but was probably not even anti-Zionist—he was scarcely the type to have any theoretical attitudes at all . . .

His government . . . went on entrusting him with important functions (Egypt after the War!), which, in my humble judgment, he mismanaged. Years later I asked an Englishman . . . "How is it? Don't they know he is not suited to the role?"

He replied, "The English people always like a man to be big, handsome, and not too bright."

From *The Story of the Jewish Legion*, by Vladimir Jabotinsky, translated by Samuel Katz

CHAIM WEIZMANN Gives the Inside Story of the Balfour Declaration, 1917

During World War I, British victories over the Turks raised the hopes of Zionists everywhere. They recalled that when Theodor Herzl launched political Zionism England had been the only nation that displayed sympathy with Jewish national aspirations. If England liberated Palestine from the Turks, might she not restore it to the Jews as a national homeland?

Excitement mounted at news that the British government was indeed considering a pronouncement which would promote Zionist hopes. France and Italy indicated that they would respond favorably to such a statement. The major opposition came from a powerful minority of upper-class British Jews who feared that a Jewish national homeland might damage their status as English citizens.

The Zionists' principal spokesman was Dr. Chaim Weizmann, then a highly respected scientist who taught chemistry at the University of Manchester. It was largely through his efforts that a suitable statement was finally issued.

After long negotiations, the government published its declaration on November 2, 1917. It took the form of a letter from the secretary of state for Foreign Affairs, Lord Arthur James Balfour, to Lord Lionel W. Rothschild, who was to bring it to the Zionist organization. The Balfour Declaration put "His Majesty's Government" on record as favoring "the establishment in Palestine of a national home for the Jewish people." To placate anti-Zionists, it affirmed "that nothing shall be done which may prejudice . . . the rights and po-

Hebrew University amphitheater, Mt. Scopus, Jerusalem, where General Rabin was honored. (Israel Government Tourist office)

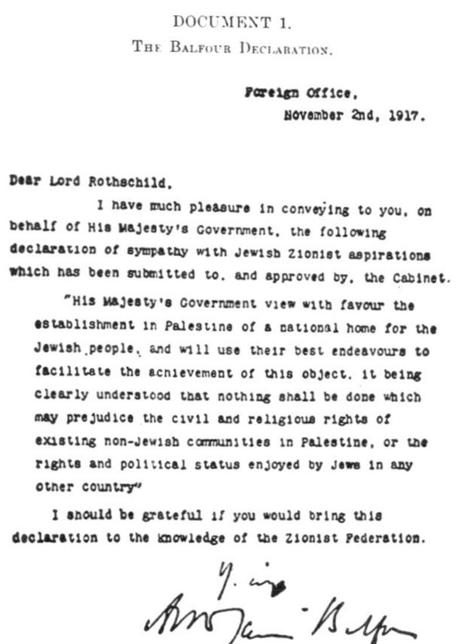

DOCUMENT 1.

THE BALFOUR DECLARATION.

Foreign Office,
November 2nd, 1917.

Dear Lord Rothschild,

I have much pleasure in conveying to you, on behalf of His Majesty's Government, the following declaration of sympathy with Jewish Zionist aspirations which has been submitted to, and approved by, the Cabinet.

"His Majesty's Government view with favour the establishment in Palestine of a national home for the Jewish people, and will use their best endeavours to facilitate the achievement of this object, it being clearly understood that nothing shall be done which may prejudice the civil and religious rights of existing non-Jewish communities in Palestine, or the rights and political status enjoyed by Jews in any other country"

I should be grateful if you would bring this declaration to the knowledge of the Zionist Federation.

The Balfour Declaration. (Zionist Archives and Library)

litical status enjoyed by Jews in any other country."

Although the declaration was not as strong as some had hoped for, it was a momentous step forward which lifted the hearts of Jews throughout the world. In the accompanying document, Chaim Weizmann tells the exciting inside story of the Balfour Declaration.

"We entrusted our national and Zionist destiny to the War Office and the Imperial War Cabinet . . ."

AN EXTRAORDINARY struggle developed within English Jewry in the half-year which preceded the . . . Balfour Declaration—a struggle which probably had no historic parallel anywhere. Here was a people which had been divorced from its original homeland for some eighteen centuries, putting in a claim for restitution. The world was willing to listen . . . and one of the Great Powers was prepared to lead in the act of restitution . . . And a well-to-do, contented and self-satisfied minority, a tiny minority, of the people . . . exerted itself with the utmost fury to prevent the act of restitution . . . Itself in no need . . . , this small minority struggled bitterly to deprive the vast majority of the benefits of a unique act of world conscience . . .

. . . On May 20, a special conference of . . . Zionist societies of Great Britain was held in London. I had been president of the Zionist Federation for about a year . . .

. . . At that time the whole world—and the Jews more than anyone else—had been thrilled by the overthrow of the czarist regime in Russia . . . "Some of us . . . and especially some of our opponents," I told the conference, "are very quick in drawing conclusions as to what will happen to the Zionist movement . . . Now, they say, the great stimulus of the Zionist movement has been removed. The Russian Jews . . . do not need any places of refuge . . . Nothing can be more superficial, and . . . more wrong . . . The sufferings of Russian Jewry never were the cause of Zionism. The fundamental cause of Zionism was, and is, the ineradicable national striving of Jewry to have a home of its own—a national center, a national home with a national Jewish life . . . A strong and free Russian Jewry will appreciate more than ever the strivings of the Zionist organization."

I was speaking the simple truth. The great outburst of enthusiasm with which the Balfour Declaration was received in Russia, the great revival of the Zionist movement, . . . was a stirring demonstration of the Jewish national will to live . . . I said: "It is a matter of deep humiliation that we cannot stand united in this great hour . . . We do not want to offer the world a spectacle of a war of brothers. We are surrounded by too many enemies to be able to afford that luxury. But we warn those who will force an open breach that . . . we shall not allow anybody to interfere with the hard work we are doing, and we say to our opponents: 'Hands off the Zionist movement!' "

As I suspected, the attack had been prepared. Four days later, on May 24, the Conjoint Committee . . . published a long statement in the *London Times,* violently repudiating the Zionist position and urging the government against favorable action on our demands . . . Mr. Edwin Montagu (by then secretary of state for India) and others—were afraid of having their patriotism challenged. The *London Times,* in a rather remarkable leading article, answered: "Only an imaginative nervousness suggests that the realization of territorial Zionism . . . would cause Christendom to turn round on the Jews and say, 'Now you have a land of your own, go to it.' " . . . It caused something like consternation among the assimilationists. It was a magnificent presentation of the Zionist case . . . "We believe it [Zionism] in fact to embody the feelings of the great bulk of Jewry everywhere . . . The importance of the Zionist movement is that it has fired with a new ideal millions of poverty-stricken Jews cooped up in the ghettos of the Old World and the New."

. . . On June 13 . . . I wrote Sir Ronald Graham: "It appears desirable from every point of view that the British government give expression to its sympathy and support of Zionist claims on Palestine." . . . And a few days later I went, together with Sir Ronald and Lord Rothschild, to see Mr. Balfour . . . and put it to him that the time had come for the British government to give us a definite declaration of support and encouragement. Mr. Balfour promised to do so and asked me to submit to him a declaration which would be satisfactory to us.

. . . The Political Committee . . . busied itself with the preparation of the draft . . . We were careful to stay within the limits of the general attitude which prevailed among the leading members of the government. This is something to be borne in mind . . . The final formula . . . which Lord Rothschild handed to Mr. Balfour . . . on July 18, 1917, ran . . .

"His Majesty's Government, after considering the aims of the Zionist Organization, accept the principle of recognizing Palestine as the National Home of the Jewish people and the right of the Jewish people to build up its national life in Palestine under a protection to be established at the conclusion of peace, following upon the successful issue of the war.

"His Majesty's Government regard as essential for the realization of this principle the grant of internal autonomy to the Jewish nationality in Palestine, freedom of immigration for Jews, and the establishment of a Jewish Colonization Corporation for the reestablishment and economic development of the country.

"The conditions and forms of the internal autonomy and a charter for the Jewish National Colonization Corporation should, in the view of His Majesty's Government, be elaborated in detail and determined with the representatives of the Zionist Organization." It is only fair to note . . . opposition within the ranks of the non-Zionists . . . The heads of the Conjoint Committee had acted without the knowledge and consent of the constituent bodies, the Board of Deputies of British Jews and the Anglo-Jewish Association, in issuing the anti-Zionist statement to the *London Times*. A vote of censure . . . actually forced the resignation of Mr. Alexander and a number of his colleagues . . .

On August 17, I was able to write to Felix Frankfurter, in the United States: "The draft has been submitted to the Foreign Office and is approved by them, and . . . also meets the approval of the Prime Minister Lloyd George."

. . . There cannot be the slightest doubt that without outside interference—*entirely from Jews!*—the draft would have been accepted early in August . . . substantially as we submitted it.

Around September 18, I learned that our declaration had been discussed at a cabinet meeting from which both Mr. Lloyd George and Mr. Balfour were absent, and that . . . Edwin Montagu had caused withdrawal of the item from the agenda . . . I received a letter from Lord Rothschild in which he said: "I have written to Mr. Balfour asking for an interview . . . Do you remember I said to you, as soon as I saw the announcement . . . of Montagu's appointment, that I was afraid we were done."

I did not feel as desperately as Lord Rothschild, but the situation was unpleasant . . . On the 19th, I received the utmost encouragement from Balfour. He told me that his sympathies had not been changed by Montagu. I was able to . . . cable Brandeis:

"Following text declaration has been approved Foreign Office and Prime Minister and submitted War Cabinet: 1. His Majesty's Government accepts the principle that Palestine should be reconstituted as the National Home of the Jewish people. 2. His Majesty's Government will use its best endeavors to secure the achievement of this object and will discuss the necessary methods with the Zionist Organization."

I added that it would be of great assistance if the text . . . received the support of President Wilson and of Brandeis.

To Lord Rothschild, Balfour expressed the same unwavering firmness . . . Lord Rothschild wrote to me . . . "I said I had evidence that a member of the cabinet was working against us. He [Balfour] hastily said: 'He is not a member of the cabinet, only of the government, and I think his views are quite mistaken.'"

On the twenty-first I had another talk with Smuts—a member of the War Cabinet—and obtained from him the expected reiteration of his loyalty. At the same time we were trying to counteract the attacks of the assimilationists . . . in pamphlets, in the press, and in person-to-person propaganda, as well as in the cabinet. On the 28th I talked again with Lloyd George, who put our memorandum on the agenda of the War Cabinet for October 4. And on the third I wrote to the Foreign Office for transmission to the War Office:

"We cannot ignore rumors . . . that the anti-Zionist view will be urged . . . by a prominent Englishman of the Jewish faith . . . We . . . respectfully point out that in submitting our resolution *we entrusted our national and Zionist destiny to the Foreign Office and the imperial War Cabinet* in the hope that the problem would be considered in the light of imperial interests and the principles for which the entente stands. We are reluctant to believe that the War Cabinet would allow the divergence of views . . . to be presented to them in a strikingly one-sided manner . . . We have submitted the text of the declaration on behalf of an organization which claims to represent the national will of a great and ancient though scattered people . . . after three years of negotiations with prominent representatives of the British nation."

. . . The next day I came to the office of Mr. Kerr, Lloyd George's secretary, and I had the temerity to say: "Mr. Kerr, suppose the cabinet decided to ask me some questions . . . would it not be well for me to stay here and be in readiness?" To this he replied kindly, even compassionately: "Since the British government has been a government, no private person has been admitted to its sessions. So you go back to your laboratory, Dr. Weizmann, and everything will be all right."

I did not go to my laboratory. I could not have done any work. I went, instead, to the office of Ormsby-Gore, close by . . . I learned too late that I might have done something.

When the Palestine item was laid before the War Cabinet, Edwin Montagu made a passionate speech . . . The vehemence

. . . the implacability of his opposition, astounded the cabinet. I understand the man almost wept . . . Balfour and Lloyd George suggested that I be called in, and messengers were sent for me. They looked for me high and low—and I happened to be a few doors away in Ormsby-Gore's office. I missed a great opportunity—due entirely to Philip Kerr . . . Montagu's opposition, coupled with the sustained attacks of that tiny anti-Zionist group . . .—their letters to the press, pamphlets . . . their feverish interviews with government officials—was responsible for the compromise formula the War Cabinet submitted to us a few days later.

. . . On the seventh of October I wrote to Kerr . . . expressing my chagrin and bewilderment at the attention paid by the British government to a handful of assimilated Jews, in their opposition to . . . the deepest hope of millions of Jews whom we, the Zionists, represented. On October 9, I could cable to Justice Brandeis:

"The cabinet . . . suggested following amended formula: His Majesty's Government view with favour the establishment in Palestine of a National Home for the Jewish race and will use its best endeavours to facilitate the achievement of this object; it being clearly understood that nothing shall be done which may prejudice the civil and religious rights and political status enjoyed in any other country by such Jews who are fully contented with their existing nationality and citizenship.

". . . It is essential to have not only president's approval of text but his recommendation to grant this declaration without delay. Further your support and enthusiastic message from American Zionists and also prominent non-Zionists most desirable to us. Your support urgently needed."

A comparison of the two texts . . . shows a painful recession from what the government itself was prepared to offer. The first declares that "Palestine shall be reconstituted as the National Home of the Jewish people." The second speaks of "the establishment in Palestine of a National Home for the Jewish race." The

. . . second introduced the subject of the "civic and religious rights of the existing non-Jewish communities" in such a fashion as to impute possible oppressive intentions to the Jews and can be interpreted to mean such limitations on our work as completely to cripple it.

. . . The cabinet actually did not know what to do with the obstructionist Jews . . . In the end it decided to send the text to . . . four anti-Zionists and four Zionists . . . with a letter which . . . stated that "they [the government] would like . . . the views of representative Jewish leaders, Zionist and non-Zionist."

We, on our part, examined and re-examined the formula . . . but did not dare to occasion further delay by pressing for the original . . . In replying . . . I said: "Instead of the establishment of a Jewish National Home, would it not be more desirable to use the word 're-establishment'? By this small alteration the historical connotation with the ancient tradition would be indicated . . . May I also suggest 'Jewish people' instead of 'Jewish race.' " (This last suggestion actually came from Mr. Brandeis.)

It goes without saying that this second formula, emasculated as it was, represented a tremendous event in exilic Jewish history—and that it was as bitter a pill for the Jewish assimilationists as the recession from the original . . . was for us. It is one of the *ifs* of history whether we should have been intransigeant and stood by our guns. Should we then have obtained a better statement? Or would the government have wearied of these internal Jewish divisions and dropped the whole matter? Again, the result might have been such a long delay that the war would have ended . . . and then all the advantage of a timely decision would have been lost. Our judgment was to accept, to press for ratification. For we knew that the assimilationists would use every delay for their own purposes . . . On October 16, Colonel House, acting for President Wilson, cabled the British government America's support of the declaration. This was one of the most important factors . . . in deciding the British government to issue its declaration.

On November 2 . . . Balfour issued the famous letter known

as the Balfour Declaration. It was addressed to Lord Rothschild. . . . I had suggested Lord Rothschild rather than myself . . . The text read:

"His Majesty's Government view with favour the establishment in Palestine of a National Home for the Jewish people and will use their best endeavours to facilitate the achievement of this object, it being clearly understood that nothing shall be done which may prejudice the civil and religious rights of the existing non-Jewish communities in Palestine or the rights and political status enjoyed by Jews in any other country."

While the cabinet was . . . approving the final text, I was waiting outside, this time within call. Sykes brought the document out to me, with the exclamation: "Dr. Weizmann, it's a boy!"

Well—I did not like the boy at first. He was not the one I had expected. But I knew that this was a great departure . . .

From *Trial and Error*, the autobiography of Chaim Weizmann

GENERAL ALLENBY Enters Jerusalem, 1917

The entrance of General Allenby into Jerusalem on December 11, 1917, signaled the termination by the British of Turkish control over the Holy Land. Jews all over the world viewed the event as a prelude to the end of their long exile. For now Britain's promise of the creation of a Jewish state, as published in the Balfour Declaration, could be realized. The entrance of General Allenby was looked upon by the Jews as the logical next step in the drama whose climax would be eventual fulfillment of the age-old dream of a return to Zion. Christians, too, regarded his arrival as an event of great significance, because it was the first time that Palestine had a government controlled by Christians since the epoch of the Crusades.

The following eyewitness account by Bertha Spafford Vester, a member of a Christian missionary family, conveys the peak excitement and exuberant spirit of that important historical moment which helped to bring an end to World War I. It is interesting to contrast her view of Allenby with that of Vladimir Jabotinsky in *The Story of the Jewish Legion,* quoted earlier.

"In a photograph of this ceremony the chief rabbi stands beside the grand mufti."

ON DECEMBER 11 the commander-in-chief, General Allenby, made his formal entry into Jerusalem. The great general rode on horse-back as far as the Jaffa Gate. The gate had been closed for some time. Before the visit to Jerusalem of Kaiser Wilhelm II of Germany in 1898, the Turks . . . had made a breach in the old

Street named after General Allenby, in Tel Aviv, over fifty years ago. (Zionist Archives and Library)

rampart wall so that carriages could enter the city. The kaiser had entered on a white charger wearing the gorgeous white Uhlan uniform with the dazzling and burnished helmet surmounted by the German eagle, but even that was not spectacular enough for him. Whatever uniform His Majesty put on was the signal for the rest of his military entourage to copy; but as some of his suite were more imposing in stature than he was, he had made himself unique by wearing a white-and-gold *kaffiyeh* [Arab headdress] under the spreading eagle, and over his white uniform was a white silk *abayah* [a loose outer garment] with gold threads that sparkled in the sunlight . . .

How different was this solemn and dignified entrance of General Allenby, who, to do honor to his Master, walked into the Holy City as a pilgrim.

First in the procession came Colonel Barton, postmaster general of Cairo, who had hurriedly come to Jerusalem to be the first military governor.

The commander-in-chief, preceded by his aide-de-camp, had on his right the commander of the French detachment and on his left the commander of the Italian detachment. Following were the Italian, French, and American military attachés and a few members of the general staff . . . Guards of honor marched in the rear.

The procession entered the Jaffa Gate, walked past the Grand New Hotel, which was our hospital, turned to the right toward [Mt.] Zion, and on the steps of the citadel in the shadow of the Tower of David, part of which dates from David's time, and another part which was standing at the time of Christ, the proclamation was read.

This proclamation, which was read in English, French, Arabic, Hebrew, Greek, Russian, and Italian, announced that order would be maintained in all the sacred sites of the three great religions which would be carefully guarded for the full use of the worshipers—that the people might pursue their lawful business without interruption.

Throughout the ceremony no allied flag was flown. After the short ceremony the chief notables and ecclesiastics . . . in Jerusalem were presented to General Allenby. In a photograph of this ceremony the chief rabbi stands beside the grand mufti. After the reception the commander-in-chief left Jerusalem by the Jaffa Gate. Outside the gate he mounted his horse and rode away . . . The photographs showing General Allenby leaving Jerusalem on a horse, with the city wall as a background, had difficulty in passing the censor, but it was finally released because the rampart wall at his back proved he was leaving the city, not entering.

Palestine had a so-called Christian government for the first time since the crusaders were driven out by Saladin. The inhabitants . . . expressed their gratitude for being delivered from the Ottoman yoke. Church bells rang . . .

During the ceremony I was on the balcony of the Grand New Hotel. John Whiting . . . asked whether I would mind giving my place to James McBey. Of course I minded, but I could not refuse the official artist a good place to make the sketches for his famous painting of the historical entry of General Allenby. I looked over his shoulder, and I knew I was fortunate indeed to be witnessing one of the great events in history . . . The whole Christian world outside of Germany and Austria was jubilant. People in the streets were crying at their deliverance. I saw a Jew embrace a Greek priest, and his tall, clerical hat went askew in the exuberance of fraternal feeling. Truly we could sing with the Psalmist, "Then were our mouths filled with laughter and our tongue with smiling . . . the Lord hath done great things for us, therefore we are glad."

I never recall this day without remembering John Finley's words:

"The earth's free nations now will bring
Their genius to its glorying,
And they who sat in darkness sing
Fore'er of thee, O Allenby!"

From *Our Jerusalem: An American Family in the Holy City*,
by Bertha Spafford Vester

JULIUS ROSENWALD Gives J.D.C.'s First Million, 1917

By the twentieth century, American Jewry had developed a number of its charitable institutions, both local and national. As one of the largest and most favorably situated Jewish communities in the world, it also recognized its responsibility to its less fortunate brethren in other countries. Following the talmudic precept, "All Jews are responsible for one another," they created relief agencies to assist persecuted and suffering Jews in other lands, Zionist funds to help build the Jewish homeland, and educational organizations in support of *yeshivot* (academies) and scholars abroad.

There have been many great American Jewish philanthropists, but few exceeded Julius Rosenwald in generosity. A native of Springfield, Illinois, he came to head the mail-order merchandising firm of Sears, Roebuck and Company. Joining it in 1893, he raised its annual income to $50,000,000 within a decade. Rosenwald supported many causes, Jewish and non-Jewish, often in aid of the American Negro. He was so beloved by the Negro people that in many homes his picture was displayed next to Abraham Lincoln's.

During World War I, Rosenwald served as chairman of the Council of National Defense, which mobilized United States economic resources for defense. His many activities in behalf of the Jewish community made his voice one of the most influential in American Jewry.

One of Rosenwald's most significant gifts was a million-dollar contribution launching the 1917 campaign of the Joint Distribution Committee. His generous act, which exceeded any previous contribution, moved

American Jews to donate $10,000,000 to J.D.C. that year. It made possible a tremendous program of relief and rehabilitation of victims of war and persecution.

"We seemed both under the spell of a common great purpose."

ALL THROUGH the night I kept rehearsing the speech I was to make to him. I doubt whether I closed an eye all the way from New York to Washington. I sketched the most gloomy picture of the state of things abroad, drawing largely on my overwrought imagination and on a printed copy of Dr. Magnes' Carnegie Hall address. And I lay in bed repeating it silently until I knew it by rote and was almost in tears myself over its tragic details . . .

When I arrived at the Willard Hotel I made for the Rosenwald suite. I was received with the usual cordial hospitality. I was asked to join the family at breakfast, but this was no occasion for broaching my project. There were one or two other guests with us at the table. I did, however, manage to convey to my host that I had something of importance to talk about to him and he assured me that he would make time for it late in the evening . . . The meal was given over to small talk about the forthcoming inaugural celebration. Mr. Rosenwald insisted on getting me tickets . . .

For the remainder of the day I was left with nothing to do but contemplate the trying business ahead of me. A friend . . . succeeded in reducing still further the little self-possession that was left me. He thought the whole mission absurd and fantastic. Happily I had the good judgment later in the day to take Mrs. Rosenwald into my confidence. She listened to my recital with a quizzical smile . . . and when I had finished said quietly, "It is, I confess, a rather ambitious mission . . . I suspect Mr. Rosenwald will throw you out of the window when you broach it to him." Involuntarily I glanced down on the pavement below. "It is not very serious," I said with a forced smile. "It won't be so much of a fall." We talked about other things, or rather . . . Mrs. Rosenwald did. She took considerable delight in mocking my brooding seriousness; all of which was exceedingly fortunate for me, otherwise the suspense and uncertainty might have unnerved me altogether.

It was getting late and I dared not leave my post lest he appear while I was gone and retire . . . before I returned. For the first time I had a taste of a detective's life and I found it unsavory. Whether or not I was to succeed as a money-gatherer the future might tell, but for the moment I learned that man-hunting was distinctly out of my sphere. And meanwhile the hour for the last train to New York was drawing nearer and nearer . . .

At 11 o'clock, however, Mr. Rosenwald appeared in the company of two senators. He stopped at the hotel desk for his mail and, never hesitating an instant, I approached and touched his shoulder. He hailed me cordially and unsuspectingly. With his arm around me, he . . . proceeded to introduce me . . . and to tell my life history. One of the legislators was from my own state of Missouri; and . . . he fell into reminiscence. Did I know this one or that one? Did I recall the last political battle between the forces of light and the powers of darkness in Kansas City? . . . Did I say I had been instrumental in floating that magnificent organization called the Board of Public Welfare? . . . And all this while, I was rehearsing anew what I was to say to the man I had been shadowing an entire day, assuming that I could get him alone before train time. I squeezed Mr. Rosenwald's arm significantly and whispered that I had something of importance to convey to him. He studied me calmly. "Is it very, very important?" he asked lightly and, before I could give him my emphatic reply, he bade our friends good-night and drew me off to a sofa in a corner of the lobby.

"Well, tell me all about it," he said as we sat down. I glanced up at him and my entire harangue on which I had spent so much arduous toil and thought evaporated. I heard myself, to my own great surprise, telling him in the very simplest and unadorned style that a campaign for ten million dollars was about to be launched; that it needed some powerful dramatic stimulus to start it off effectively and to end it successfully; that a committee had determined that nothing but a great single gift would serve and that he alone could make that gift. I dwelt hardly at all on the state of things abroad, merely indicating in a matter-of-fact way what he was well aware of, that the condition of the European Jews was growing increasingly worse, and that therefore a renewed effort on a much greater scale than had ever been tried must be initiated. He listened to me without comment while my appeal was gathering momentum and climbing from argument to argument to climax. I had had hundreds of conversations with Mr. Rosenwald, but I had never before asked him for contributions of any sort, and never before had I seen a face so transparent and serene and yet so profoundly thoughtful. I kept praying, as I talked, that he might not break in. We seemed both under the spell of a common great purpose and I knew that as long as the spell was not broken the future of the undertaking was assured. As I concluded with my specific request for a round million, his earnestness deepened. He said, "Do you think it will do any good?" I nodded and was about to make a highly-colored forecast . . . when he added: "Very well, I will do it. You may go back to New York and tell them that I'll do it."

From *This Thing of Giving,* by Henry H. Rosenfeld

SIR HERBERT SAMUEL Receives an Aliyah, 1920

The Jewish struggle to reestablish a homeland in Zion extended almost 2,000 years. Every step that seemed to bring the Jews closer to their dream was an occasion of great joy. One such event was the appointment by the British of Sir Herbert Samuel as high commissioner of Palestine—the first Jewish governor of the Holy Land since 70 C.E.

Samuel was a highly respected Jewish leader with years of government experience. His appointment reassured many Jews that England sincerely intended to carry out the goals of the Balfour Declaration. Hence, his first visit to the synagogue in Jerusalem, where he received an *aliyah* (call to go up to read a portion of the *Torah*), was a highly emotional experience: the Jewish settlers who crowded the synagogue felt that the messianic redemption was surely at hand.

In truth, Samuel's administration was disappointing. Although personally committed to the cause of Jewish statehood, he was forced to carry out his government's policy of pacifying the Arabs who were fomenting violence from one end of the land to the other. As a result, large parcels of land that should have gone to the Jews were distributed to the Arabs who remained as truculent as ever in denying to the Jews any right to a homeland in Palestine. The Jewish settlers, nonetheless, retained their enthusiasm and hope.

In this excerpt from his *Memoirs*, Sir Herbert Samuel tells of that morning in 1920 when he was called to the *Torah* in Jerusalem.

"Have mercy upon Zion, for it is the home of our life . . ."

THE MOST moving ceremony that I have ever attended was on my first visit, after my arrival in Jerusalem, to the old and spacious synagogue in the Jewish quarter of the ancient city. As it was the Sabbath, I had walked over from Government House so as not to offend the Orthodox by driving and found the surrounding streets densely thronged and the great building itself packed to the doors and to the roof mostly by older settlers, some of those who had come to live, and to die, in the Holy City for piety's sake. Now, on that day, for the first time since the destruction of the Temple, they could see one of their own people governor in the Land of Israel. To them it seemed that the fulfillment of ancient prophecy might at last be at hand. When, in accordance with the usual ritual, I was "called to the Reading of the Law" and from the central platform recited in Hebrew the prayer and the blessing "Have mercy upon Zion, for it is the home of our life, and save her that is grieved in spirit, speedily, even in our days. Blessed art Thou, O Lord, who makest Zion joyful through her children" and when there followed the opening words of a chapter of *Isaiah* appointed for that day "Comfort ye, comfort ye my people, saith your God. Speak ye comfortingly to Jerusalem, and cry unto her, that her warfare is accomplished, that her iniquity is pardoned"—the emotion that I could not but feel seemed to spread throughout the vast congregation. Many wept. One could almost hear the sigh of generations . . .

From *Memoirs* of Hon. Viscount Herbert Samuel

SHOLEM SCHWARTZBARD Defends His Assassination of Petlura, 1926

On May 25, 1926, in Paris, Sholem Schwartzbard, a watchmaker who had originally come from the Ukraine, shot down Semyon Petlura, the chief of the Ukrainian Republican army. Petlura had led 493 pogroms against the Jews and had commanded the Battalion of Death which butchered 1600 Jews within a few hours at Proskurov. A priest, dressed in his vestments and with his crucifix in hand, who had tried to persuade the mob to cease their wanton killing, likewise lost his life. On the following day Petlura's men slew five hundred more Jews at the nearby village of Felshtin.

The Ukrainian leader had publicly declared that he disapproved of these excesses and would punish those responsible, but no action was ever taken against them, and Petlura is reputed to have sanctioned the atrocities privately. He also aided in the publication of a newspaper whose avowed aim was the death of all Jews in the Ukraine.

In the testimony at Schwartzbard's trial for the assassination of Petlura, one of the witnesses revealed that, of the 500,000 Jews who served in the Russian army, 70,000 had been killed. When the facts of Petlura's part in the slaughter of multitudes of Russian Jews were laid before the court, the French jury exonerated Schwartzbard of the murder charge.

"Judge me, my judges."

PARIS, TUESDAY, May 25, 1926, half past three in the afternoon. The car in which I had suddenly found myself honked and barely managed to drive through the dense throng, with people screaming on all sides: "Kill him, kill him!"

"Murderer!"

"Lynch him!"

"He's not a Frenchman, but a foreigner!"

"He should be torn limb from limb!"

Out of the tumult comes the weak voice of my escort, the policeman, trying with all his might to ward off the crowd: "Let him alone. We have laws to take care of this . . ." The car moves slowly, the mob surges forward . . .

"Drag him out!"

"Lynch him. Kill! Kill!" Finally the car breaks through . . . Rescued! Just barely saved! The chauffeur drives at full speed . . .

"The devil!" says the policeman, as if to himself. "That was a wild mob. They would not have given me kid-glove treatment either." He wipes the sweat from his face and straightens his uniform.

. . . Then, turning to me, "Well, you got beaten up, eh?"

"Nonsense."

"Some nonsense," he says ironically. "That mob could have torn you apart right there. You really got off well."

"I've been through worse."

The car came to a halt. We were at the Odeon police station. We went into a room where two clerks sat, their heads buried in books. My escort greeted them and reported, "Murder."

No one answered, no one stirred, the clerks continued what they were doing, as if nothing had happened . . . For them that was no news. My escort pondered, then took me into another room, where a man sat at a table, his back to me. Probably a stenographer, I thought. The policeman greeted him and reported, "Murder." The man did not even turn his head . . .

The policeman did not know how to begin; . . . he told me to sit in a corner . . .

The silence lasted a few minutes. All at once he said to me, "Empty your pockets—everything. The suspenders, the shoe laces, the garters, the belt, everything."

A door opened and a man entered—in his forties, medium height, with a large shiny forehead and a bald pate, a friendly face, and two black searching eyes . . . My escort jumped to attention, taut as a string, greeted him, and reported: "Inspector, murder at the corner of Racine and Boulevard Saint-Michel."

But the inspector was not interested and went out. Several policemen came in, changing duty. My escort told them what a tough job he had just had.

"What about?" one of them asked . . .

"Murder," my escort replied . . .

"Whom?"

"I don't know, and I didn't ask. Some old bean pole. Right in the street. Imagine, I'm standing at my station, all of a sudden I hear shots. I run in the direction of the shooting and I see this body stretched out on the sidewalk and this fellow standing over him with a revolver . . . empty except for the last bullet, which jammed."

"Great!" the others beamed. One turned to me.

"Wouldn't you have spared him even that last bullet?"

"Lucky for you the revolver didn't jam at the first bullet," commented another . . .

"When you arrested him, did he resist?" someone asked.

"No. He stood there calmly and gave me the revolver."

"And the crowd attacked him?"

"And how! As soon as they saw I had taken his revolver, they attacked like hornets and would have torn him to pieces. I got some of it, too, but he got the better part. Lucky someone from the department came in a car. Even then, the crowd began to fight with sticks."

"Oh, people are like wild animals," someone commented. "If they see danger, they scatter like flies. Don't we know the mob?"

"That's just what it was like," assented my escort. "When they heard the shooting, they dispersed in all directions. Afterward, they wanted to lynch him . . ."

. . . All the time . . . I sat in a corner, resting from the blows . . . My head ached badly and my face was inflamed. My eyes were burning and swollen. But my heart did not fail me. It beat calmly and quietly as usual. I felt . . . liberated from an enormous oppressive burden; instantly I felt good and relaxed. I followed their conversation without particular interest, as if it were not about me, and became aware of them only when they began to inspect me.

"Who is it that you killed?" one asked me.

"He was a Ukrainian general. Petlura was his name."

"What kind of bird is he?"

"A general, the leader of a barbarous army."

"That's good," a policeman responded.

"Once in a while they ought to know the taste of death, too," another commented, "instead of only sending others to break their heads. So it was a political act. That's not so terrible."

"He probably was a real bastard," said a second.

"Not worse than most of that rank," philosophized a third.

"Are you sure he was the right one? You didn't shoot someone else by mistake?" one of the police asked me.

"I think not."

The last question, so innocently put, upset me. I felt disturbed. Perhaps? Who knows? . . . I tried to remember various details, but my head was not working. Had I made a mistake? Was it possible I had been wrong all along? What a calamity! What a crime! Suppose I had killed an innocent person? . . . My heart, which a few moments before had been relaxed, began pounding violently. Fear and despair seized me. I wiped off the sweat and tried to banish the frightful thoughts . . .

The inspector came in . . . and told me to follow him into his office. He sat at his desk and showed me a chair facing him. "Now we have time to talk."

"I am ready." I felt feverish, as if intoxicated, my eyes blurry, but I tried to control myself.

"Now, tell me, why did you do this deed?"

For a while I was silent. I felt everything I had to say was concentrated in one word and I blurted it out: "I am a Jew!"

"An Israelite," the inspector corrected me. "Proceed."

Slowly, with a beating heart I began to tell about the Jewish calamity, the horrible tragedy that had befallen us in the Ukraine, the massacres and pogroms, beginning with the bloody days of Chmielnitsky down to Petlura.

The inspector sat with his head bowed and kept writing, recording.

"All right," he said. "But I want to know who this Petlura is. All that stuff about the seventeenth and eighteenth centuries is pretty old. We are now living in the twentieth century. Tell me about the murdered man. Who was he?"

"In short, he was the second Haman. The first wanted to destroy the Jewish people and this one most brutally destroyed a great part."

The inspector smiled.

"Yes, yes. Put in your report . . ." I urged him, but inside the painful question comes up again: Did I make a fatal mistake? Just then my arresting policeman entered.

"Inspector, I have come from the hospital. The wounded man died. His identity papers were found. He is called Semyon Petlura."

Then I was right! I had shot not an innocent man but the murderer Petlura . . . After all, I had never seen the beast . . . Despite all my investigations, it was impossible to find out anything about him. My numerous acquaintances in Jewish and non-Jewish circles could not satisfy my curiosity. When I first learned in a Russian newspaper that Petlura was in Paris, I could not rest. I began chasing around, searching, investigating. Many people thought my inquiries peculiar, and some even mocked me, inquiring whether perhaps I planned to kill him . . . Sometimes I became sick at the petty comments of friends who suspected something, who tried to dissuade me, saying that I should leave his punishment to other hands, not ruin my life . . . But the knowledge that this murderer was alive and well, and so near, would not let me rest. Ceaselessly I looked for his traces . . . Most of all, I suffered in the quiet night hours, lying on my bed and thinking . . . It was impossible to conceal my sufferings from my wife . . .

"Why are you crying?" she used to ask.

I would pull myself together . . . "What gives you such a notion? My eyes are watering from my work." . . .

Several months passed in dreadful suffering . . . All I could find out was that Petlura went about incognito, had a younger brother, and was a frequent visitor in certain Jewish homes . . .

Then the lucky chance came. A Ukrainian paper . . . printed a photograph of Petlura with Pilsudski . . . For a time I was not yet quite certain that the person whom I had seen several times and heard speaking Ukrainian was Petlura. When finally I decided it was he, I found him several times in the company of a woman and a little girl. The fear of hurting an innocent victim restrained me. When chance brought us together when he was alone, I was so struck with my luck that I abandoned any opportunity to check my information, and I raised my arm to punish . . .

On hearing that he was in truth Petlura . . . a heavy burden rolled off my heart . . . Everything seemed to me radiant and beautiful. I felt . . . like one born anew—like a young man in love who loves the whole world. Even though I had never felt any liking for the police, I wanted to embrace the policeman who brought me the news, to kiss him and press him to my heart.

The Speech I Did Not Make

My judges:

Whenever I read the chronicles of world history, my heart bleeds each time I encounter human injustice . . . The most pitiless enemy of any human being is another human being . . .

I cannot contain my tears when I recall the great sufferings which our people endured the last centuries in the Ukraine, that vale of tears. For 300 years Jewish blood flowed without halt on Ukrainian soil. In 1648, Hetman Bogdan Chmielnitsky and his Cossacks drenched the Ukraine with our blood. They slaughtered old people, tore little children limb from limb, raped women and strangled them afterward. This massacre lasted until 1654, and 500,000 Jews met their death in the severest agonies.

. . . A Polish Memoirist Describes This Epoch

"When Kievan Ataman Charchevsky entered Kanev, the Cossacks massacred all its Jews. It was their custom thus to entertain themselves. In Nemirov . . . Cossacks lashed hundreds of Jews together and drowned them. Little children were ingeniously severed in half . . .

"In Tulchin all the Jews were assembled and ordered to be baptised. With one voice they cried out: 'Hear, O Israel, the Lord our God, the Lord is One.' "

. . . The Cossacks assaulted the Jews, cut off their hands and feet, raped women in the sight of their husbands, smashed children against walls to crush their skull, carved open the bellies of pregnant women and forced cats in . . .

They desecrated synagogues, ripped apart *Torah* scrolls, and sent entire towns up in flame and smoke . . .

That was the first time these wild Ukrainian creatures emerged in the arena of world history.

In 1768 . . . Chmielnitsky's descendants, Ivan Gonta and Maxim Zheleznyak duplicated the atrocities . . . The heartless and soulless Haidamacks began their orgies and demons' dances in Lisyanka. Archimandrite Melchizedek Yavorsky gave them the blessing of the sword and promised them complete absolution if they would slaughter the unfortunate Jews. The hordes charged out and destroyed the Jewish communities in Uman, Zabotin, Chihirin, Smela, Kanev, and Cherkassy.

In his poem *Haidamacks,* Shevchenko described . . . a new Bartholomew's massacre brutally enacted in 1768 by the Haidamacks and Cossacks in Uman . . . Cooling their hatred of Jews and Catholics in streams of blood, the Haidamacks found, in a Jesuit monastery . . . two children their chief Gonta had had by a Polish Catholic woman. They brought the children to their father, saying:

"You have sworn to destroy all Jews and Catholics, regardless of age or sex. Before you stand your own two children reared by the Jesuits!"

Gonta did not waver; with his own hand he stabbed his children.

Under the light of the conflagration which they had set, the Haidamacks feasted and celebrated their victory. Amid the ruins and heaped-up corpses they abandoned themselves to fiendish orgies . . . lacking none of the usual ingredients: vats of wine, wild dancing, and virtuous Jewish daughters abducted to be violated . . .

Our tragedy is intensified when poets and historians glorify these grisly deeds. The barbarous epic of sadism committed by animals in the guise of men evokes no pity for our martyrs, . . . no regret. For these poets and historians, too, the Jews are creatures without legal protection, scapegoats, animals to be driven and slaughtered with gratification. Historian Kostomanov, novelist Gogol, and poet Shevchenko depicted these scenes of horror in tranquil tones and lauded the heroes who did these deeds. The victims appear to them as comical creatures. The Haidamacks boasted that they were heroes because they were cruel. They were thought vigorous because they were not deterred from butchering infants in their cradles.

. . . The ghastly acts committed by the Haidamacks of Ataman Petlura in 1918, 1919, and 1920 in their cruelty and evil surpassed the earlier deeds . . .

I need only recall that dreadful time for a shudder to pass over my body. The hideous visions pursue me always, though I strive to ward them off . . . Pogrom scenes I witnessed float before my eyes and at night keep me awake. I jump up from sleep and cannot shake off the bloody nightmares.

All the remembrances of my life are gruesome, as is our whole history of martyrdom. My anguish grows greater when I cannot aid my suffering brothers and sisters. There are times when private sorrows disappear in public woe, like a drop of water in the sea. But as for him who suffers for humanity, his sorrows continue and are vast as the world . . .

The blood of the innocent and of the martyrs demands justice and vengeance.

My life was the theater of all misfortunes and afflictions . . . At the end of July, 1919 I arrived in Zhidowska-Grebla, two days after the Haidamack pogrom. The first Jewish home I entered looked as if it had suffered an earthquake. Two old women sat on the ground and lying next to them an old man, his face bloodied, his eyes bloodshot, blood still running from his bandaged head, and from him issued one lament, "My God, my God, why hast Thou forsaken me?"

In that town, eight of fifteen families were completely annihilated. A widow with six children, whose husband had fallen at the front, was violated and then strangled.

In Cherkassy on the Dnieper, the first Jew I encountered told me: "We have just buried a thousand victims of the last pogrom. All lie in one mass grave. One gets accustomed to calamity . . ."

At the end of August, when I was in Kiev, Petlura's advance guard entered. They murdered all the Jews they met on their way. In the center of Bolshaya Vasilkovskaya Street, I saw the corpse of a young man stretched out on the pavement, and, her head on his dead body, a woman lamenting for her one and only son. Hoodlums shouted obscenities, mocking her despair . . .

Kozyr-Zyrko, Petlura's aide . . . selected thirty old Jewish men for his amusement . . . and ordered them to sing and dance. The Haidamacks were free with their whips and revolvers, mocking, deriding, goading the dancers. When one Jew or another broke out in a lament, the torturers beat them . . . Then they shot all the old men and piled the bodies in a heap.

Palenko, another of Petlura's aides, told a Jewish delegation in Kiev: ". . . Do you think that for a few damned Jews I would disrupt my boys' amusements?"

And the great Petlura himself stated: "Do not make a quarrel between me and my army."

In all the cities they posted placards with insults, hatred, and threats against the Jewish population: "You, cursed people, whom all nations despise . . ."

They forced unfortunates to eat their excrement. They shoveled earth over them and buried them alive . . .

In Tripole on the Dnieper, after the fifth pogrom . . . forty-seven corpses of the old, the sick, and the children were left lying in the street, and no living soul remained after them. Dogs began to pick at the bodies and pigs to nibble. Finally, a Gentile who used to work for Jews, out of pity, dug a grave and buried them. The Haidamacks learned of it and for that they murdered him.

In Ladyzhin only two Jewish girls remained alive. They were raped, their noses bitten by sadists, and infected with venereal disease. They came for help to a hospital in Kiev.

Intoxicated with blood and hatred, the twentieth-century descendants of Chmielnitsky, Gonta, and Zheleznyak completed the mission of their ancestors. Are these the flag-bearers of the New Testament, of civilization, and of hope for a nobler mankind?

Judge me, my judges.

From *The Golden Tradition,* edited by Lucy S. Dawidowicz

PIERRE VAN PAASSEN Tells the Truth about the Massacre at Hebron, 1929

In 1929, savage Arab attackers fell upon the Jews of Hebron with sticks, knives, daggers, and firearms. The raiders attacked on a Sabbath evening when the Jews were unprepared to defend themselves, even murdering those at prayer in the synagogue. Students and faculty of the local talmudic academy were killed.

The outbreaks, which spread to Safed and Jerusalem, had been sparked by the frenzied preaching of the Jerusalem *mufti* in the Moslem mosque on the previous Friday against the Balfour Declaration. The extent of the massacres was made possible by the inaction of the British police who could not be found anywhere on the night of the raids. The government authorities not only failed to protect the Jewish community but also obstructed subsequent investigation by suppressing evidence of the horrid tortures and mutilations perpetrated by the Arabs on their Jewish victims.

The incident deepened the chasm between Jews and Arabs and weakened confidence in the British government. The succession of official enquiries threatened for a long time to persuade the British to scrap all intentions of building a Jewish national home on Palestinian soil. World Jewry responded by contributing large sums of money to help the victims.

This eyewitness account by Pierre van Paassen, a long-time Christian friend of the Jewish people, gives the true facts on the Hebron massacre.

"Both the men and women were horribly mutilated."

ONE DAY in September of that year, on a Sabbath eve, the Arabs of Hebron were brought to a point of such frenzied hatred against the Jews that they invaded the synagogue and slaughtered all the men and women at prayer there. Later they asked the Jewish community's forgiveness, explaining that about a hundred or so of the worst elements in town had become terribly excited by the agitation of the Jerusalem *mufti* [religious head] against the British mandate which aimed at the setting up of a "national home for the Jewish people in Palestine."

The *mufti's* campaign was directed, in his own words, "not against the pious and non-political Jews in the land, who had always lived in peace and harmony with the Arabs," but against the new Zionist settlers who were entering (by right, let it be said) under the aegis of the British administration. This should have meant security for the Jews of Hebron, for they were an old and established community, who had never had any trouble with their Moslem neighbors and who were not Zionists in the *mufti's* sense of the word.

Even so, when whipped up by the *mullah's* [preacher] inflammatory sermon . . . some young men . . . invaded El Cortijo, the quarter where the Jews had peacefully lived for ages. Captain Saunders was absent that evening, conferring . . . on the tumult which had broken out . . . elsewhere. There had been a murderous attack in Safed and in the old quarter of Jerusalem, two other areas inhabited by "non-Zionists."

After killing the Jews in the synagogue, the Arab mob in Hebron went down the road . . . where stood a *yeshivah,* a Jewish theological seminary, and massacred both students and professors. Only two or three escaped . . . After this the mob . . . attacked the house of the local rabbi, called Slonim, where a number of men and women had taken refuge . . . But the Arabs came in through the windows . . . and made short shrift of the thirty-eight persons in the room. Their throats were slit and both men and women were horribly mutilated.

Certain citizens of Jerusalem . . . communicated with me at seven o'clock in the evening of the same day and asked me to come with them to the scene of the pogrom. They were Dr. Felix Dantzier and Dr. Abraham Ticho, two physicians, and Marek Schwartz, a former artillery officer in the Austrian army . . . and Mr. Abraham Goldberg, who represented a Yiddish language newspaper in New York . . .

Driven by Schwartz' chauffeur, Menachem Katan, an ex-member of Colonel John Henry Patterson's Jewish Legion which fought at Gallipoli, at Jericho and Megiddo under Allenby, we raced out to Hebron and saw the whole ghastly scene by lamp-light: the slain students . . . the dead men in the synagogue and the thirty-eight slain in Rabbi Slonim's house . . .

I must say here, for the matter was raised in an official communiqué by the Palestine government and led to most unpleasant consequences for me personally, that the two doctors and I found that the dead in Slonim's house had had their genital organs cut off; in the case of the women, their breasts. This was really nothing very extraordinary: it was the usual practice of Arab mobsters in those days, and still is.

There wasn't a British policeman or soldier to be seen in all Hebron that night of death. The door of Rabbi Slonim's house stood wide open and we just walked in. By the light of flashlights we examined the rooms where the slain men and women lay about, stiff, as if frozen in all the attitudes of horror. Mr. Goldberg turned away and went out weeping. I walked into the kitchen and saw there the body of one more woman. While I bent over to look at her face, my attention was diverted by the crying of an infant. I . . . finally traced the wailing to a small cupboard under the sink . . . Some mother, perhaps the woman lying on the kitchen floor, just before dying had pushed her child amidst the pots and pans . . . under the sink.

. . . We pried open the cupboard door. We found a little boy, probably from six to eight weeks old . . .

. . . The baby was delivered to an Orthodox orphan asylum in Jerusalem at twelve midnight. He grew up, I am happy to say, to splendid manhood and, as an officer in the Israeli army, covered himself with glory in the Judeo-Arab war in 1948. I have kept in touch with him all these years and he once did me the honor to come all the way to New York to see me.

Strange to say, the Palestine Administration, while admitting that the peaceful Jewish community of Hebron had been virtually exterminated, formally denied that the slain men and women had been either tortured or mutilated. Having broken the telegraphic secret and read the dispatch which I sent late the night of the massacre to the *New York Evening World,* Sir Harry Luke, the chief secretary, thought fit to make a denial of the mutilations. The government's communiqué . . . citing me as an atrocity-monger and anti-British agitator, appeared in . . . the *Jerusalem Post.* Judge Jonah J. Goldstein of New York, who had arrived in Jerusalem a few days before, asked the government what the meaning was of shielding the Hebron murderers . . . acquitting them beforehand of the charge of mutilation. Sir Harry did not answer. He had the bodies removed and interred post haste.

The morning after the massacre, I was back in Hebron at six o'clock. I found the town occupied by a company of the King's African Rifles, the so-called Green Howards, and a sentinel with fixed bayonet in front of Rabbi Slonim's house. The boy would not let me in. "They're cleaning up in there," he said. "Only government officials are permitted to enter." I went to the synagogue to find that the bodies had already been removed. The only evidence of the pogrom . . . was a blood-soaked prayer book and a set of leather prayer straps. I picked them off the floor and stuck them in my pocket. I still have these gruesome momentos in my possession and plan to restore them to the Jewish community of Hebron on the day when their city, the city of David and Abraham, is restored to the people of Israel.

. . . I met Captain Saunders on the main street of Hebron . . . in the company of Captain Joseph Cafaretta, of the Palestine police . . . They wanted to know where I was going. "I am going to the mosque," I said, "to see the *imam*" [a religious leader].

Saunders advised against it. "You will have to pass through the bazaar," he warned. "It isn't safe this morning; the Arabs are in an ugly mood. There are no more Jews left in Hebron. Arab business is ruined as a result. There may be trouble."

"Give me your helmet," I said. "I will look like a British officer and nobody will harm me." We exchanged helmets and I . . . went on to the Haram Al Khalil.

"Ah, there is Your Highness at last," said Moulay Effendi. "It took you a long time to come back."

"Three years," I said.

"To be sure, three years, it is a long time," he agreed. "Have you come to hear Abraham's voice this time?" he asked with a laugh. "If you have . . . you've come at the wrong time."

"How so? Have the ghosts been laid?"

"No, but the people here in Hebron are afraid."

"Afraid of what?"

"Someone spread the rumor that our Father Abraham is angry, that he will ask an accounting for the death of the Jews killed last night . . ."

"Well, what do you say to that?"

"It's nonsense," replied Moulay Effendi.

"You mean Abraham is not angry?"

"I didn't say that," the *imam* corrected me. "The *hadjees,* the faithful, stayed away from prayer this morning. They dare not come near the mosque. Isn't it pitiful, such superstitions? . . . Would you care to make a slight contribution to the fund for Hebron's widows and orphans? . . ."

I made my contribution and returned to the police station . . . Some seventy persons had been arrested, Captain Cafaretta said . . .

"It will be impossible to identify any of the actual rioters," said

Cafaretta. "But the whole thing could probably have been avoided by firing a few shots in the air . . ."

"Were you in town last night?" I asked Cafaretta.

"I was," he said.

"Then why didn't you fire a few shots?" I asked, pointing to the pistol in his belt.

"You have no business in Hebron," the governor of Jerusalem, Sir Edward Keith-Roach, broke in angrily. "You are hereafter to confine your operations to Jerusalem."

"You don't want any embarrassing witnesses around, do you?" I said. "Do you know that the Arabs last night were shouting: 'The government is with us!' when they went in for the kill?"

A few days later I was given twenty-four hours' notice to quit the mandated territory of Palestine on the charge of spreading "anti-British propaganda and . . . false rumors concerning the Arabs of Hebron . . ."

I sailed on the *Lotus* from Beirut but was back . . two years later. By then everybody had forgotten my "anti-Britishness" and "atrocity-mongering." Winston Churchill, who was apprised of my expulsion, commented: "This man is a British subject. Every British subject has the right once a week to tell his government to go to hell."

From *A Pilgrim's Vow*, by Pierre Van Paassen

HENRIETTA SZOLD Greets the First Youth Aliyah Ship, 1934

Early in the 1930's the doom of German Jewry was sounding. The fanatic Adolph Hitler led his National Socialist German Workers Party (Nazis, for short) to power and became dictator of Germany in 1933. Finding the small Jewish community a convenient scapegoat, he blamed it for all of Germany's ills. Anti-Jewish legislation was followed by physical persecution and internment in concentration camps from which few returned.

Some German Jews fled at the first signs of trouble. Others, with faith in the country they loved, believed the Nazi madness would pass and waited until too late. The majority were bottled up inside Germany because there was no place to go: England (despite her promises in the Balfour Declaration) had halted the flow of Jewish immigration to Palestine to a trickle in order to placate the Arabs, and many other countries had immigration quotas.

In 1934, Youth Aliyah (Youth Immigration) was formed by world Jewry to save Jewish children in Germany from certain death by bringing them to *Eretz Yisrael*—a daring and successful venture. Later its efforts were extended to Nazi-occupied countries and even to concentration camps. By the end of World War II, Youth Aliyah had rescued over 17,000 children, and by 1954, 62,000.

Youth Aliyah was organized and led by seventy-four-year-old Henrietta Szold who obtained special permission from the British to bring the children to Palestine—the crowning achievement of a lifetime of service to her people. A worthy daughter of the famous Baltimore rabbi, Benjamin Szold, she had worked ardently in behalf of the Jewish Publication Society and had founded Hadassah, whose members esteemed her a saint. This great woman, who is called "A Mother in Israel," inspired the work of Youth Aliyah until her death in 1945.

In the following selection, Miss Szold describes the arrival of the first shipload of German Jewish children in Haifa on February 19, 1934. The letter shows how careful preparation in Germany as well as thoughtful and understanding arrangements in *Eretz Yisrael* brought joy and hope to what was essentially a heart-breaking situation—for these boys and girls had just left home and parted forever from their beloved parents.

"They burst spontaneously into Hebrew song . . ."

Bulletin No. 2
February 25, 1934

ON MONDAY, February 19, on the steamship *Martha Washington* of the Lloyd Triestine Line, the first group of boys and girls organized for settlement in Palestine by *Judische Jugendhilfe,* the federation of German Jewish youth organizations, arrived at the recently opened port of Haifa. There were forty-three of them, eighteen girls and twenty-five boys. An older comrade, Hanoch Reinhold, their trainer and leader, accompanied them . . .

The arrangements at the dock were in the hands of the director of the Haifa Branch of the Immigration Department of the Jewish Agency. He was assisted by volunteers, representatives of various public bodies, as the Central Bureau of the Jewish Agency for the Settlement of German Jews in Palestine, the Social Service Bureau of the Haifa *Kehillah* [Community], the Haifa Section of the *Hitachdut Olei Germania* [Union of German Immigrants], and . . . of the *kevutzah* [communal settlement], Ain

Youth Aliyah group dancing the hora on landing at Haifa, Israel. (Zionist Archives and Library)

Youth Aliyah children arriving on the S.S. Negba. (Zionist Archives and Library)

Harod, future home of the young people. Everything from quarantine to customs . . . to the first meal on Palestinian soil, moved flawlessly—except the weather. The vessel came in under a heavily shrouded sky, driven by a gale with pelting rain . . . The merciless wet could not dampen the enthusiasm of the young travelers nor the joy of the grandparents, brothers, sisters, aunts, and friends who were on hand to greet them. All of them . . . swiftly adopted the point of view of the Palestinian farmer, who was rejoicing in the blessed downpour, after the devastating drought of the past three years . . .

. . . Amid suitcases of every conceivable shape, size, and material, there stuck up flagpoles and cellos and mandolins and . . . bicycles. In addition, some of the boys and girls had chunky rucksacks strapped to their backs. In spite of careful preparations, the numerous willing and expert helpers, and the courtesy of the officials, the formalities stretched out over hours . . . until long after 7:00 P.M. Finally, in the dark and through the rain, stimulated by the hope of the first square meal of the day, the troop trotted gayly across the new wharf to the Workingmen's Kitchen . . . Seated at the long T-table, they burst spontaneously into Hebrew song, a gift from their youth organization training.

. . . The group was to have spent the night at the *Bet ha-Olim* [Immigration Station] of the Jewish Agency, in Bat Galim, the seaside suburb of Haifa, but . . . it was filled with immigrants who had just arrived from Europe . . . Emergency arrangements had to be made . . . Eighteen of the young people were . . . guests at a hotel on Mt. Carmel; the rest for a nominal fee at two of the new children's houses recently established, also on Mount Carmel, by their German compatriots . . .

The opportunity was thus granted to the new Palestinians . . . to view one of the most beautiful spots of their new home, the ravishing combination of the sea and mountain of the Haifa headland. Fortunately, Tuesday morning the sun broke through the pall of clouds, allowing the unique beauty of the scene to emerge . . .

At the railroad station the intimate scenes of the dock repeated themselves—relatives more or less acclimated to Palestine mingled with the new recruits and . . . good cheer prevailed.

. . . On the railway journey of about 1¾ hours, there was much craning of necks and darting from windows on one side of the train to the other, to catch a glimpse of Nahalal, Kfar Yehoshuah, Yagur, Kfar Yecheskel, and finally the twin *kevutzot* of Tel Joseph and Ain Harod. All these were names not unknown to the boys and girls, also a gift of their youth organization training. They greeted them as acquaintances and, when the crossroad sign of Ain Harod and Tel Joseph hove into sight, they sang out merrily, "Main Station of Ain Harod!" Again they broke into song, responding to the greetings of the older pupils of the Ain Harod and Tel Joseph school who had come . . . to welcome them . . .

All the way up to the settlement, the troop was met by members of the *kevutzah* streaming down to catch a first glimpse of the new contingent added to the six hundred, among them ninety from Germany, which constitute the co-operative community of Ain Harod . . . In front of the crowded veranda . . . the ubiquitous photographer snapped the scene.

The travelers were hurried into the dining-room for lunch and again . . . they sang out lustily one Hebrew song after the other, their hosts joining in. After the meal came the inevitable *hora* [circle dance] . . .

At the order of the leader Reinhold, calm fell upon the dancers . . . in order to assign rooms . . . The business was well-planned and executed, another evidence of the preliminary camp and group discipline practiced by the organizations in Germany which are taking care of the Youth Aliyah . . . Then the troop was marched off to the storerooms to disengage sheets and pillows and pillow-cases . . . from suitcases and trunks . . .

The thoughtful . . . Ain Harod hosts made even this first routine act . . . a festive ceremonial. The boys and girls were guided to the storehouse, not by the most direct route but via the incubators, the workshops, and the stables, thus familiarized at once with the lay of the land . . .

The boys and girls will be housed in wooden barracks until the permanent concrete houses are completed, in about two months . . . On the second day, the rest of the baggage arrived, the rooms were stocked and beautified with equipment provided by loving hands at home. Within they lost all semblance to barracks and assumed a homelike cozy air.

Meantime the teachers . . . were discussing details of a plan long ago laid out for work and study . . . study half the time, work the other half. For the first six months the studies will center about the Hebrew language, the geography of Palestine, the history of Israel, and the Bible. The work will introduce them by means of the lightest tasks gradually to all details of the *kevutzah* life . . . There will be planned walks to neighboring settlements—applied geography lessons—and lectures and supervised reading . . . For the Sabbath, a *mesibbah,* a gathering, was being organized, with song, dramatic scenes, and readings . . . A committee has been appointed to work out with the young people self-government methods . . .

. . . The group should have consisted of sixty-one instead of forty-three boys and girls. Ten had been denied certificates because they had passed their seventeenth birthdays . . . No candidate over seventeen by a single day was allowed a certificate [by the British]. The effort is being made to induce the government to permit a less rigid interpretation . . .

From *Henrietta Szold: Life and Letters,* by Marvin Lowenthal

A GIRL Escapes from Babi Yar, 1941

The Nazi slaughter of tens of thousands of Russian Jews at Babi Yar, a ravine near Kiev, is one of the most heartbreaking chapters in the shameful saga of German anti-Semitism during World War II. On September 29–30, 1941, Jewish men, women, and children were herded together by the German army which occupied Kiev and shot *en masse.*

The name, "Babi Yar," came to world attention twenty years later when the talented Russian writer, Yevgeny Yevtushenko, wrote a poem about the horrors that occurred there. The Soviet government repudiated Yevtushenko's contention in the poem that the massacre was principally anti-Semitic, declaring that Ukrainians and other nationalities had also died there.

A novel published in 1966, *Babi Yar,* by Anatoly Kuznetsov, a non-Jew who was twelve when the massacre at Babi Yar took place, vividly documents the tragic end of Kiev's Jewish community. The impressive array of eyewitness evidence which the author marshaled in his work prompted the Soviet government to change its position on the events at Babi Yar and to erect a monument in Kiev as a memorial to the victims of Nazi inhumanity but not at Babi Yar.

The novel concentrates on the true experiences of Dina Mironovna Pronichev, a survivor of the Babi Yar massacre who at this writing is an actress with the Kiev Puppet Theater. The following excerpt from the novel begins after Dina has read the Nazi orders that all Jews appear on September 28 at an intersection near Kiev's cemeteries in the northern part of the city.

"My child, we are going to pay our last respects to God."

SHE HAD gone to read the order, read it quickly, and left; no one lingered long or started conversations near the posted orders.

There were discussions and conjectures everywhere all day and evening. Her father and mother were now feeble; her mother had just left the hospital after an operation . . . Everyone wondered how the old lady could leave. Dina's parents were sure that every one would be put on trains . . . and sent to Soviet territory.

Dina's husband was a Russian [Gentile]. Her surname was Russian and, furthermore, she did not look Jewish at all. They decided that her parents would leave, and Dina would see them off . . . but she would remain with her children, come what may.

She was at her parents' place before 6:30 in the morning. No one in the building was asleep. The people leaving were saying good-by, promising to write, and turning their apartments, things, and keys over to neighbors.

. . . Artem Street was complete bedlam. People with bundles, others with baby carriages, various two-wheeled vehicles, horse-drawn carts, and occasionally even trucks were standing there . . .

A good many people were seeing them off; neighbors, friends, relatives, Russians and Ukrainians all helped them . . .

They reached the cemeteries only after lunch. She remembers that on the right was the long, brick wall of the Jewish cemetery. Across the roadway were a wire entanglement and anti-tank obstacles, with a passage in the middle; a line of Germans was standing there . . . and there also were Ukrainian *Polizei* . . .

A strapping, energetic, middle-aged man in an embroidered shirt and a drooping, Cossack-style mustache was conspicuously in charge at the entrance. The mob poured past him into the passageway, but no one came back, except for an occasional *izvozchik* [driver], with his cab empty . . .

It was all completely incomprehensible. Dina set her parents down at the gate of the cemetery and went to see what was happening up ahead.

Like many others, she had been thinking that there was a train there. Some firing was audible close by, a plane was circling low in the sky; the general mood was anxious and panicky.

"It's war, war! They're sending us far away, where it's quieter."

"But why only the Jews?"

. . . Dina elbowed her way through the crowd, growing more and more worried, and then she saw that everyone in front of her was piling up his things. Garments, bundles, and suitcases went into the pile on the left, and food on the right . . . People were being let through in groups of ten . . .

"Ah, the things are going in the baggage car, of course. We'll sort them out when we get there."

"How can we sort them out there? There are so many, they'll simply be divided evenly."

Dina became terrified. This was nothing like a railroad station. She did not yet know what it was, but with all her heart she sensed that people were not being shipped out . . .

Especially odd were the bursts of machine-gun fire nearby. Her mind still boggled at the idea that these were executions. In the first place, there were such enormous masses of people! Such things just do not happen. And then, what was the reason for it? . . .

But if the Jews were not being shipped out, what on earth was going on?

Dina says that at that moment she felt only some kind of animal terror . . .

People were being stripped of their warm things. A soldier went up to Dina and took off her fur coat quickly, adroitly, and without any words.

Then she rushed back. She found her parents at the gate and told them what she had seen.

Her father said, "Daughter, we don't need you any longer. Go away, dear."

. . . Rather a lot of people were there, struggling to get permission to go back . . . The mustached man in an embroidered shirt was yelling. Dina elbowed her way to him and began to explain that she had been seeing people off, and that she had children in town, and ought to be released.

He demanded her passport [state-issued identification papers]. She took it out. He looked at the heading, "National Grouping," and screamed in Ukrainian, "Hey, you dirty little Jew! Get back!"

Then Dina finally understood that people were being executed.

She tore her passport into bits . . .

Although she no longer had her fur coat, she began to feel that she was suffocating . . . Some people were sitting on their bundles and having lunch. She thought, "How can they eat? Is it possible that they do not understand even now?"

Then those in charge began ordering, shouting . . . and moving them further on; the ones in the rear were shoving, and the result was unimaginable . . . Dina lost her parents in the chaos; . . . they had been sent off with a group further along. The line stopped in front of her.

They stood. They waited. She craned her neck to grasp where her father and mother had been taken. Suddenly, a most enormous German came up to her and said, "Come sleep with me. I'll let you go."

She looked at him as if he were a psycho, and he went away. Finally, her group was let through.

. . . The Fascists stood in ranks along the sides. In front of them appeared files of soldiers with dogs on leashes. Dina heard some man behind her saying, "Children, help me get through, I'm blind."

She took the old man around the waist and started walking alongside him.

"Pop, where are they taking us?" she asked.

"My child," he said, "we are going to pay our last respects to God."

At that moment, they entered the long passage between the

two ranks of soldiers with dogs. This corridor was narrow, some five feet in width. The soldiers were standing shoulder to shoulder; their sleeves were rolled up and they all had rubber truncheons or big sticks.

Blows showered down on the people passing by.

There was no way to hide or dodge. From left and right, the most vicious blows showered upon their heads, backs, and shoulders and at once drew blood. The soldiers were shouting, "*Schnell! Schnell!* [Quick!]" laughing merrily, as if having a good time; they were trying to hit sensitive places as hard as they could.

Everyone began shouting; women started screaming . . . She saw people fall. The dogs were loosed on them immediately. The people picked themselves up, but a few remained on the ground; others were shoving from behind, and the crowd was . . . tramping on them.

. . . Dina . . . raised her head high and walked without bending, as if made of wood. Apparently she was injured, but she barely felt it and had only one idea rattling in her mind: "Don't fall, don't fall."

The maddened people fell onto a grass-covered area surrounded by troops. Underwear, shoes, boots, and other clothing were strewn about the grass.

The Ukrainian *Polizei* . . . grabbed people, thrashed them, and shouted in Ukrainian: "Clothes off! Hurry! Hurry!"

Whoever dallied was stripped . . . by force, kicked, beaten with brass knuckles and truncheons by the *Polizei* who were drunk with malice and in a sadistic rage. Clearly this was done to prevent the mob from coming to its senses. Many naked people were completely covered with blood.

From the direction of those who were undressed and being led off, Dina heard her mother shouting to her. "Darling, you don't look like one. Save yourself, dear."

Resolutely, Dina went up to the *Polizei* man and asked where the *Kommandant* was. She said that she had been seeing someone off and had gotten here by accident.

He demanded her identity papers. She began to reach for

them, but he took the purse himself, and looked all through it; it contained money, her workbook, and her trade union card (which did not indicate her national grouping). Her surname, "Pronichev," convinced him. He did not return her purse, but pointed to a small hillock where a group of people were sitting. "Sit there," he said in Ukrainian. "They'll shoot the Jews and then we'll let you go."

Dina went up to the hillock and sat down. Everyone there was quiet, stunned . . .

Everyone there had been seeing people off.

. . . The nightmare was taking place in front of them, as on a stage. Group after group of screaming and unmercifully beaten people were falling out of the corridor, taken by the *Polizei,* thrashed, stripped, and so on endlessly . . .

They drew up the naked people in rows and led them to a passageway dug in the steep wall of sand . . . Sounds of shooting came from that direction . . .

Dina sat for a long time with her head buried in her shoulders, afraid to look at her neighbors . . .

It grew dark.

Suddenly, an open car drove up carrying a tall, graceful, and very elegant officer with a riding crop in his hand. An interpreter was beside him.

"Who are these?" the officer asked the *Polizei* man through the interpreter, pointing at the hillock where about fifty people were sitting.

"Those are our people," answered the *Polizei* man. "They didn't know. They have to be let out."

Then the officer shouted loudly, "Shoot them at once! If even one gets out and tells . . . not one kike will come tomorrow." . . .

"Well now, come on! Get moving! Get up!" shouted the *Polizei* men.

The people got up like drunks. It was already late. Maybe that was why this group was not made to undress . . .

. . . They passed through a corridor cut through the wall, and came to a sandpit with almost vertical sides. It was already half dark. Dina saw the sandpit with difficulty. Everyone was sent to the left, hurrying in single file along the narrow overhang.

On the left was a wall, on the right was a large hole. The overhang was apparently cut specially for the executions; it was so narrow that the people walking along it instinctively pressed against the wall to avoid falling.

Dina looked down, and her head began to spin. Below was a sea of bloody bodies. On the opposite side of the sandpit . . . light machine guns had been set up. Several German soldiers there had lit a campfire on which they were cooking something.

When the entire file had been driven out onto the overhang, one of the Germans moved away from the campfire, took the machine gun, and began shooting.

Dina felt rather than saw the bodies falling off the overhang and the path of the bullets approaching her. The idea flashed in her mind: "In a moment, I'll . . . in a moment." Without waiting for that moment, she threw herself down . . .

When she fell, she felt no blow or pain. At first, she was washed all over with warm blood, and blood flowed along her face, as if she had fallen into a bath of blood. She lay with her arms spread out and her eyes closed.

She heard some belly-sounds, moans, hiccups, and wailing around her and beneath her; many were not yet dead. The entire mass of bodies, barely noticeably, was moving, sinking, and yielding from the motion of the living heaped on top.

Soldiers went out on the overhang, looking down with their flashlights, and taking pistol shots at those who still seemed to be alive.

She heard the Germans close by, over the corpses. They came down, bent over, took things from the dead, and from time to time shot at those moving . . .

One SS man stumbled on Dina, and she seemed suspicious to him. He flashed a light, raised her up, and began to hit her. But she hung limp without giving any signs of life. He kicked her in the breast with his boot, and stepped on her right arm so that it crunched, but walked on.

Several minutes later she heard a voice above say, "Hey, come on, let's put some dirt on them!"

The shovels began to clang, the dull sound of sand hitting the bodies came closer, and finally piles of sand began falling on Dina.

She did not move until they covered her mouth. She was lying with her face up, breathing in the sand, suffocating, and then she floundered in wild horror, ready to be shot rather than buried alive.

She began to push the sand away with her left hand, which was uninjured; she was choking and was about to have a coughing fit but with a final effort choked it back. Finally she got out from under the sand.

. . . Apparently they had only shoveled on a little dirt and gone away. Dina's eyes were full of sand. It was pitch dark and the smell was oppressive.

Dina noticed a wall of sand close by. She picked her way slowly toward it, and then stood up and began making holes in it with her left hand . . . while pressing against the wall. She lifted herself up inch by inch and risked falling every second.

There was a bush up above. She groped for it and then clung to it desperately. When she had crossed the edge of the ridge, she heard a still voice which almost caused her to throw herself back: "Auntie! Don't be afraid! I'm alive, too." It was a little boy in a sleeveless shirt and shorts. He had crawled out just as she had. He was trembling.

"Sh! Quiet!" she said to him. "Crawl after me." And they crawled without speaking or making a sound.

They crawled for a long time, slowly, accidentally running into precipices, turning, and apparently crawled all night because it was growing light. Then they found bushes and crept into them.

They were at the edge of the big ravine. Not far away they

saw the Germans, who had begun sorting out the things and piling them up. They had dogs, fidgeting on leashes. Sometimes trucks drove up for the things . . .

When it grew light, they saw an old woman running with a boy of six behind her shouting, "Gramma, I'm scared!" . . . Two German soldiers caught up with them and shot them . . .

The Germans were constantly walking, now above and now below, and chatting loudly. There was continual shooting somewhere very close by . . .

She and the boy were lying down; they forgot themselves and fell asleep. The boy said that his name was Motia, that none of his relatives remained alive . . . Dina looked at his frightened face and somehow thought that if she managed to save herself she would adopt him.

Toward evening she began to have hallucinations: . . . When Dina came to her senses, Motia was sitting over her and weeping, "Auntie, don't die, don't leave me."

With great effort she realized where she was. Because it was already dark, they moved out from the bushes and crawled farther . . . Sometimes she forgot herself and raised herself up. Then Motia would cling to her and press her to the ground.

They had not had anything to eat or drink in over a day . . .

So they crawled another night until it began to grow light. There were bushes in front of them and Motia crawled out to reconnoiter . . . If all was well there, Motia was supposed to move a bush. But he shouted piercingly, "Auntie, don't come out! Germans here!"

Shots rang out, and they killed him on the spot.

Fortunately, the Germans did not understand what Motia had been shouting. She crawled back along the sand. Then, somehow, mechanically, she made a small hole and began to cover it up conscientiously, making a funeral mound, imagining that she was burying Motia . . . She began to weep . . .

It grew light, and Dina discovered that she was sitting and swaying on the road, that there were fences on the left and an alley . . . It turned out to be a garbage dump. She dug herself into the garbage, threw all sorts of rags and paper over herself, and put a torn woven basket over her head in order to breathe beneath it.

Thus she lay, holding her breath. Germans passed once, stopped and smoked.

Only when it was completely dark did she move out . . .

She crawled for a long time . . . Toward morning she saw a little house with a shed behind it . . . She had hardly crawled in when a dog yelped in the yard . . . A sleepy housewife came out and shouted, "Quiet, Spotty!"

She looked into the shed and saw Dina. The housewife's face was sullen. She began questioning Dina about who she was and what she was there for, and Dina lied that she had come from the foxholes, had gotten lost, and decided to spend the night in the shed . . .

"And where were you?" asked the woman in Ukrainian.

"Near Belaia Tserkov," Dina answered in the same language.

"Near Belaia Tserkov? Well, well!"

Dina's appearance, of course, was horrible: she was covered with caked blood, mud, and sand. She had lost her shoes in the sandpit and torn her stockings.

Neighbor women came out at the noise and formed a circle around Dina.

An officer appeared almost at once.

He looked over and nodded, "*Komm.*"

And he went forward on the path . . . but looked around to see if she was coming. She folded her arms over her breast and shrank inwardly. She felt cold, her right arm hurt (it was bloody) and her legs hurt (they were badly battered).

They entered a one-story brick house, where about 20 soldiers were having breakfast . . . Dina wanted to sit down on the chair in the corner, but the officer began to yell and she sat down on the floor.

Soon the Germans began to take their rifles and disperse. Only one soldier remained . . . He gave Dina a rag, indicating that she should wipe off the big window . . . Through the window, Dina saw that she had been crawling round and about the *Yar* and had come back to the place from which she had fled.

The soldier began talking quietly. Dina understood him, but he thought that she did not, and he tried to explain: "You get this straight . . . The authorities have left. I'm giving you a rag so that you can scram. Wipe the window and look for a place to scram to. Yes, get this straight, *Dummkopf!*"

He spoke compassionately . . . She moved her head with an uncomprehending expression.

The soldier angrily shoved a broom at her and sent her to sweep up the next little house which was empty. Dina began sweeping and was ready to run when noise and wailing were heard. An officer appeared, bringing in two girls of fifteen or sixteen.

The girls were yelling and sobbing. They threw themselves on the ground and tried to kiss the officer's boots. They begged him to make them do anything he liked, only not to execute them. They were wearing identical, clean, dark dresses, and braids.

"We are from the children's home," they shouted. "We don't know what our national grouping is. We were taken there when we were infants."

The officer . . . ordered them and Dina to follow him.

They went out to the same field where they had undressed. As before, piles of shoes and clothing were lying around. Thirty or forty old men were sitting to one side . . .

A girl in an army blouse and greatcoat sat next to Dina, saw that she was trembling from the cold, and covered her a little with the greatcoat . . . The girl's name was Liuba, she was nineteen. She had been in the army and had been captured.

A truck came up with Soviet prisoners of war. Each had a shovel . . . The prisoners began to list the old people and to herd them into the truck. . . .

One German was in the cab, another in the back . . . and four *Polizei* men were posted along the sides.

The truck began to back out . . . A German jumped out, and four *Polizei* men remained: two in the cab and two at the sides . . . Dina and Liuba began to talk things over. They had to jump. The guard would shoot . . . At least death would be sudden . . .

They drove off quickly. Liuba used some of her greatcoat to cover Dina. They weaved along the streets . . .

Covered by the greatcoat, Dina rolled across the tailgate of the truck and jumped when it was going fast. She fell against the pavement and hurt herself . . . but those in the truck did not notice anything.

Or might it have been that they did not wish to?

Passersby surrounded her. She began mumbling that she had been in the truck and had wanted to get off near the market, but the driver did not understand, so she jumped. They believed her and did not believe her. But she saw human eyes around her. They took her quickly into a courtyard.

Half an hour later she was at her brother's wife's, whose national grouping was Polish. All night long they heated water and wet her slip where it had been sticking to her wounds.

From *Babi Yar*, by Anatoly Kuznetsov,
translated by Edgar H. Lehrman,
as quoted in *The New York Times Magazine*, December 11, 1966

A NAZI COLONEL Sees a Mass Extermination at Belsen, 1942

A new word was coined during the Nazi era—genocide. The dictionary defines genocide as "the use or user of deliberate, systematic measures toward the extermination of a racial, political, or cultural group."

The Nazis introduced genocide to the world. Adolf Hitler, the mad dog of Europe, expected literally to destroy the entire Jewish people. As country after country fell to his armies, their Jewish residents were rounded up and transported to death camps. The plans of the Nazi dictator would be realized with his conquest of the world—confidently outlined in his book, *Mein Kampf* (My Struggle)—the United States included. How close he came to fulfilling his insane dream is seen in the fact that, before he was stopped, he had wiped out one-third of the world's Jewish population.

It is no simple matter to kill thousands upon thousands of human beings: it takes careful planning and organization. The Nazis methodically carried out their grisly task with the vaunted German efficiency and ingenuity.

How did their death machine work? How did the German overseers execute tens of thousands of Jewish captives a day?

One technique is disclosed in the following account of mass death at the notorious Belsen camp in 1942, as witnessed by Colonel Kurt Gerstein, an SS colonel. He was officially a part of the apparatus to annihilate the Jews. At great risks to himself and to his family, he tried to disclose to the world Hitler's extermination policies.

Yad Vashem, memorials to the victims of the holocaust, Jerusalem. (Israel Office of Information)

"All you have to do when you get into the chambers is to breathe in deeply."

A TRAIN arrived from Lemberg [Lvov]. There were forty-five cars containing 6,700 people, 1,450 of whom were already dead. Through the gratings on the windows, children could be seen peering out, terribly pale and frightened, their eyes filled with mortal dread . . . The train entered the station, and two hundred Ukrainians wrenched open the doors and drove the people out of the carriages with their leather whips. Instructions came through a large loudspeaker telling them to remove all their clothing, artificial limbs, glasses, etc. They were to hand over all objects of value at the counter . . . Shoes were to be carefully tied together, for otherwise no one would ever again have been able to find shoes belonging to each other in a pile that was a good eighty feet high. Then the women and girls were sent to the barber who, with two or three strokes of his scissors, cut off all their hair and dropped it into potato sacks. "That's for some special purpose or other on U-Boats, for packing or something like that," I was told by an SS-Unterscharfuhrer . . .

Then the column moved off. Headed by an extremely pretty young girl, they walked along the avenue, all naked, men, women, and children, with artificial limbs removed. I myself was stationed up on the ramp between the [gas] chambers with Captain Wirth.

Mothers with babies at their breasts came up, hesitated, and entered the chambers of death. At the corner stood a burly SS man with a priest-like voice. "Nothing at all is going to happen to you!" he told the poor wretches. "All you have to do when you get into the chambers is to breathe in deeply. That stretches the lungs. Inhaling is necessary to prevent disease and epidemics." When asked what would be done with them, he replied: "Well, of course, the men will have to work building houses and roads, but the women won't need to work. They can do housework or help in the kitchen, but only if they want to." For some of these poor creatures, this was a small ray of hope that was enough to make them walk the few steps to the chambers without resistance.

Most of them knew what was going on. The smell told them what their fate was to be. They went up the small flight of steps and saw everything. Mothers with their babies clasped to their breasts, small children, adults, men, women, all naked; they hesitated, but they entered the chambers of death, thrust forward by the others behind them or by the leather whips of the SS [Storm Troopers]. Most went in without a word . . . Many were saying prayers. I prayed with them. I pressed myself into a corner and cried aloud to my God and theirs. How gladly I should have gone into the chambers with them; how gladly I should have died with them. Then they would have found an SS officer in uniform in their gas chambers; they would have believed it was an accident and the story would have been buried and forgotten. But I could not do that yet. First, I had to make known what I had seen here. The chambers were filling up. Fill them up well—that was Captain Wirth's order. The people were treading on each other's feet. There were 700–800 of them in an area of 270 square feet, in 1,590 cubic feet of space. The SS crushed them together as tightly as they possibly could. The doors closed. Meanwhile, the rest waited out in the open, all naked. "It's done exactly the same way in winter," I was told. "But they may catch their death!" I said. "That's what they're here for," an SS man said . . . The Diesel exhaust gases were intended to kill those unfortunates. But the engine was not working . . . The people in the gas chambers waited, in vain. I heard them weeping, sobbing . . . After 2 hours and 49 minutes, measured by my stop watch, the Diesel started. Up to that moment, men and women had been shut up alive in those four chambers, four times 750 people in four times 1,590 cubic feet of space. Another twenty-five minutes dragged by. Many of those inside were already dead. They could be seen through the small window when the electric light went on for a moment and lit up the inside of the chamber. After twenty-eight minutes, few were left alive. At the end of thirty-two minutes, all were dead.

From *Pius XII and the Third Reich: A Documentation*,
by Saul Friedlander

TUVIA BELSKY Leads the Jewish Partisans, 1942

Many stories of Jewish valor during the Nazi conquest of Europe have gone untold. Fortunately, we have some records of Jewish resistance to the death and of heroism under unspeakable circumstances. A proud and noble chapter in this record of courage was written by the Jewish Partisans, a band of fighters from Byelorussia and the Ukraine who had escaped the invading Nazis and became part of the underground resistance movement.

In 1942 Tuvia Belsky's parents and two of his brothers were murdered by the Nazis. Tuvia and his remaining brothers took to the forest, where he organized the Jewish Partisans that summer. He sent messages to the doomed ghettos, urging those who could escape to join him. The band later functioned as part of the Soviet and Polish Partisans, resisting the Germans in every way possible. Their courage and fortitude lifted the hearts of Jews the world over. They were in turn inspired by reports of the Warsaw Ghetto fighters whose heroism demonstrated the indomitable spirit of the Jewish people.

The Jewish Partisans operated in the forests of White Russia in the vicinity of Novogrodok. Eventually joining forces with the Soviet Partisan brigade led by Viktor Panchenko, they performed numerous deeds of daring. They also gave refuge to a large number of non-fighters, including women and children. When they finally emerged from the forest at the end of World War II, they brought to safety their most precious burden—one hundred ten children.

Belsky writes about his Partisans in a book called *In the Forests,* from which the following is taken.

"Thus will be done to everyone whom Hitler wishes to honor."

WE RECEIVED the news . . . that Russian Partisans had decided to kill us as robbers. The local farmers had complained about us . . . and were believed.

Although I was very careful about preventing robbery, it would be quite difficult to pinpoint the line which divided that requisitioning which sustained our lives and outright robbery. The code of the Partisans provided: all that is essential—is permitted; but appropriation of anything . . . more-than-necessary, is considered robbery.

Of course, the Partisans' conception of the difference . . . was not the same as that of the farmer . . .

. . . I decided to meet the threat head-on. We would go to the Russian Partisans and would try to speak to them.

Yehudah Belsky had an acquaintance among the peasants of Butzkovitz, who knew these Russian Partisans. We sent Yehudah and arranged a rendezvous at one of the outlying isolated settlements.

We went to the meeting—four armed men. We did not go with light hearts . . . The spokesman for the other side was Viktor Panchenko, their head. He went over all that we had heard before and said to us: "We have decided to shoot you."

I started by saying that I was the head of the Soviet Partisan group named for Marshal Zhukov. "If you did not know it until now, you should be aware of it from now on that we are not bandits. Moreover, if you are a true Soviet citizen you must know that our motherland requires that we struggle together against the German-fascist enemy. And our motherland makes no distinction between Jews and non-Jews; the only distinction is between loyal, obedient citizens . . . and undisciplined gangs bent on sabotage and destruction."

"But they tell us that you have been robbing the villages!"

"That we can determine. And if it should prove to be a lie, then we must fight together." . . .

. . . We went to the village of Nagrimov, to one of the peasants who had complained against us. We rapped on the window, and . . . asked for bread. He answered in a whining voice, "There is no bread, beloved brothers, the Jews . . . took everything. They robbed us and went."

Viktor was livid with rage. He drew his gun.

"I'll murder the son of a bitch."

I restrained him. "You'll have plenty of time to do that later. Ask him what they took."

The farmer called the girl who was in the house at the time of the alleged robbery . . . This was her story: The Jews had come last night . . . after midnight and took bread, oil, onions, salt, butter, eggs, as well as the tablecloth . . .

. . . Viktor shouted at the peasant. "From now on, if a Partisan fighter comes to you, pay no attention to the fact that he may be a Jew, or a Russian, or a Pole. Give him food, give him boots, and even a fur coat if necessary. Listen here, a moment ago you were just one step away from death. My friend here prevented me from shooting you. Why did you accuse the Partisans falsely?"

I said to the peasant. "I'm Belsky." This announcement had its effect. It threw a pall of fear and trembling over him.

From that time on, we were on the friendliest of terms with Viktor Panchenko and his men. We divided among ourselves the district provision . . . We did not enter his villages, and he kept out of ours. Viktor would visit us occasionally. A close friendship grew between him and the female secretary of our group . . .

With the harvest . . . of 1942, we were getting ready to destroy the harvest stores of the Germans. They had expropriated the large landholdings and the majority of the cooperative settlements (*kolkhozes*) and had planted the fields for their own needs . . .

We divided the great landholdings between our group and Panchenko's. We set a time for the setting of fires in the whole district . . .

One autumn night, at midnight, . . . fires broke out in all the farms worked by the Germans. Snipers from the Partisan groups shot at everyone who came to extinguish the flames. The skies grew red over the forest and the fields. The farmers knew who was responsible for it and why . . . In our midst there was exultation mixed with fear. We had to expect danger from both sides.

As if the fire were not enough! To this day we do not know how this thing happened . . . Airplanes flew over and dropped bombs on the flaming area . . . evidently, Russian planes returning from a bombing raid . . . guessed the significance of the flames and added their load to the destruction.

The enemy was confounded and amazed. The Partisans—they surmised—are in liaison with the Russian High Command, and they are co-ordinating their operation . . .

The farmers began to look upon the Partisans with greater respect . . .

. . . A decision was reached to kill the mayors of the local towns who were puppets of the Germans as well as village leaders guilty of the crime of collaboration. Groups of four would go out at midnight and assassinate the mayors . . . co-operating with the Germans. Five or six were thus liquidated.

In each group . . . one of us brothers Belsky was always present . . .

. . . [Now] we decided to disturb their foodstock in the villages . . .

We said: "Let us try. We will set an ambush and, when the German trucks . . . pass by, we will attack them." This would be a joint operation with Viktor Panchenko's group. Our group provided twenty-five armed men, with Asahel and me at the head, and the same number came from their group.

The point of attack was on the Novogrodok-Novoelna road,

where the vehicles have to slow down. We would prepare a reception for them. We would be the first attackers, and Viktor's group would serve as reinforcements. If the Germans resisted us, then Viktor's men . . . would attack from the rear . . .

Mothers and fathers of the men in the group could not be prevented from learning of the planned operation. Some of them began to entreat their sons not to go. Wives began to plead with their husbands.

I was compelled to reprove and to threaten to drive the rebels away or to shoot them . . . "We went into the forest not only to eat. Have you already forgotten the slaughter? We ourselves are going out without sparing our own lives, to fight and to avenge! To avenge even at the price of death!"

We went to the place of ambush. We waited in the forests for information from our liaison men in the nearby village of Radyoki . . .

Just before noon, good news reached us. A girl, one of our allies, came from the village and told us that one automobile and one truck were collecting chickens and eggs in Radyoki. Soon they would be returning to Novogrodok . . .

We lay for a half hour, a chain of rifles hidden in the grass and the bushes ten meters from the road. I was in the center of the chain, in order to command my two flanks. Asahel was supposed to shoot at the front tire, and I, at the driver. In 1927 and 1928 I served in the Polish army and was a sharpshooter . . .

The sound of a horn blowing . . . a small, fast car, carrying four officers. We fired and missed! . . . Viktor's group also shot and missed. Less than three minutes later a truck passed by . . . Now we had experience in how to shoot at a moving target. This target was also larger and slower.

Tach! Tach! The truck stopped. We hit the wheels as well as the driver. We showered down a hail of bullets. Eight Germans and Byelorussian police jumped from the truck. They established a position and began to return fire with machine guns.

Suddenly, a charge with a shout . . . of Panchenko's men from the rear . . . The enemy ran. Afterwards we found out that most of them were wounded . . .

We swooped down on the machine guns, the rifles and the boots, on the chickens and the ammunition. We trampled the eggs and the butter, but the sacks of sugar we took. We fired bullets into the gas tanks, setting them on fire. Everything exploded. All this took . . . a few minutes. In our hands remained two machine guns, four rifles, and thousands of bullets. Excitedly we ran into the forest. This was our first victory against an armed unit of the enemy . . .

However, caution demanded that we . . . get as far as we could to the other side of the forest. We walked until dark . . .

One day Viktor told me . . . that in an isolated farm settlement, not far from Abelkevitz, there was a farm on which there was a group of armed Jews who robbed by night and did nothing during the day. The population round about were angry and complaining. They had not yet turned them over to the Germans for fear of the Partisans, but they did ask if he, Panchenko, was protecting them . . . If not they would get rid of them on the spot . . . Viktor was of the opinion that that group—if they wanted to live as Partisans—should join our group. If not, he would eliminate them.

I saw that a large group of Jews was in danger. On the other hand, I saw a possibility to increase and strengthen our fighting force . . .

About twenty of us went out with three machine guns, . . . rifles and pistols. It was a cold and snowy night. With the first light of dawn we arrived at the farm. We began to stand guard. Because of the cold we had to change the guard every half hour. The farmer received us with food. He was very friendly, but . . . he played dumb . . . He swore that there were no Jews on his farm. I explained to him that I did not come to kill them. On the contrary, I myself was Jewish, the commander of a group of Jewish Partisans . . .

My words had no effect. I aimed my pistol at his head. "Come," I said. Then he got softer. "Seek, my friend, maybe you'll find them in the barn." We went into the barn. I spoke in a loud voice in Yiddish: "If the Jews hear, let them answer." There was no sound and no answer.

In one of the corners we found, under straw, a wooden door covering a hole in the ground . . .

Ben-Zion Gulkovitz sprawled on the floor and shouted into the excavation: "Jews, don't be afraid, come out to us!"

No sound. Ben-Zion went down alone and to his amazement he found there an armed group, each man standing at his post, his gun in his hand.

"Friends, Belsky is here, the commander of the Jewish Partisans. Why won't you come out to see him?"

Kessler, the leader, answered: "Okay. We'll go out."

He climbed up from the excavation, fully armed, and gave me his hand in greeting.

"Ah—Belsky, we heard about you. Come down and let's talk." I went down. The Shumanska woman was there with her two sons, formerly the owners of a flour mill in Dvorec. The father also came up to me and greeted me. They were happy. Avraham of Butskov, who knew me, came up and asked:

"Aren't you the son of David of Stankovitz?"

"And who are you? The brother of Meishke? Avreml?"

"Yes."

But the important discussion began after we slept a little and after we ate. I said:

"Here they will kill you, bombarding you with grenades which they'll throw down into your underground. I have a large gang, several hundred. You can live with us. Why don't you take the women, the children, the horses, and everything you can carry, and come to our camp? In the forest you'll be free. There, there is no fear and no ghetto. The accursed ones come from one direction, we run in the opposite direction. We have fighting forces. They won't kill us all. Here your situation is hopeless. Viktor

Panchenko is our friend, but he decided to eliminate you from this place."

Kessler laughed. "We also have rifles, but I wouldn't want to fight against the Partisans" . . .

"You have been alone long enough. This is no place for you. Take everything and let's go. I have prepared a bunker that will be large enough for all of you."

"Give us time to think it over."

"Okay, you have a half hour, but the answer must be definite. I came at great risk to our men . . . We want results." They went out to consult among themselves. They returned and suggested:

"Let us send four men to your camp to see how you live."

"Did you ever study the Bible? Joshua sent spies to Jericho, and they fell into a trap . . . I am ready to take your weapons away from you by force. March to the road!"

Shumanski intervened: "Why should you get angry, Mr. Belsky? Of course, we'll go. But first we want to see what you have."

"I am not a German. You have nothing to examine. A bunker is ready for you, and you'll live like all the Jews. What are you bargaining for? When the *goyim* come, they won't make you any offers."

They saw that I wasn't joking . . . They yielded.

Now another one came up to me, Hanan Pressman. He said:

"Comrade Commander, we're going, but we have here an unsettled account with one of the farmers . . ."

"What's the story?"

"He is the head of the local anti-Partisan guard, and he already turned over to the Germans twenty Jews, including women and children . . ."

This matter appealed to me. It would be good to pay off such a villain, and very good for the . . . neighborhood to know that the lives of Jewish women and children cannot be taken lightly . . .

Toward evening . . . we went out . . .

It was quiet all around. Only the snow crunched underneath

our feet . . . Near a settlement dogs were barking. We had good horses and we made rapid progress. The order was: "The whole family is to be destroyed . . ."

When we reached the house, I placed guards at each of the windows . . .

Ben-Zion knocked and called to open the door. At first there was no answer but, when the blows became stronger, a voice was heard: "Why are you making so much noise? I am coming to open."

A bald farmer opened the door. We asked him if there were any strangers there. He assured us there were none. In this large room the entire family slept in beds along the walls . . .

Pesach sat on the bed near the farmer.

"What's new?"

He answered in rhyme in White-Russian: "Live we will, and Jews we'll kill."

. . ."How many Jews did you kill so far?"

"I don't kill. It doesn't pay to dirty one's hands. I turn them over to the police, and they finish them."

"How many Jews did you already turn over?"

"Four days ago a woman, two children, and two men. Several weeks ago—eleven men . . . Two more several days ago. We chased them on horses. From one we took a gun . . ."

And he added: "The woman and the children and the man I first locked up in my storeroom . . . all night. In the morning they were nearly frozen. I tied them up like sheep and led them to the police in Dvorec."

I went up to the farmer and said: "Listen, you are a man . . . How does your conscience allow you to take living human beings and turn them over to certain death at the hands of the murdering Germans?"

"What are you talking about? Hitler made a law and we must obey it." . . .

"What do they pay you?"

He mentioned a sum . . .

At this point Pesach let fly the first blow to his cheek, saying: "I am also a Jew."

I said: "Enough playing around." I restrained them. I tried to continue to question him but he saw that the end had come and he stopped speaking . . .

After our men had slain everyone in the house I said to them: "Thus will be done to everyone whom Hitler wishes to honor." I remembered the verse from the *megillah*. I wrote a large announcement in Russian: "This family was wiped out for collaboration with the Germans and for turning over Jews to them." And I signed it "Belsky's Group."

From "In the Forests," by Tuvia Belsky,
in *A Tower from the Enemy*, edited by Albert Nirenstein

A SURVIVOR Relives the Warsaw Ghetto's Last Stand, 1943

One of history's unforgettable episodes of human heroism was the resistance of the Warsaw Ghetto against the Nazis in 1943. The 60,000 defenders were the only survivors of over 400,000 Jews who had been crowded three years before into an area that normally held half that number. Rations were so meager—a daily bowl of soup, frequently boiled from straw—that multitudes succumbed to starvation every day. In addition, medical care and hygienic facilities were withheld. The Jews could find work only in the armament factories and related businesses which the Nazis operated inside the ghetto under conditions of virtual slave labor. Nevertheless, the Jews struggled to maintain an organized communal life with worship, education of the young, and aid to those in dire need.

In 1942, the Germans decided to remove the ghetto altogether by "resettling" the inhabitants—which meant sending them to gas chambers. No one was sure what happened to the six to ten thousand Jews who were taken away each day, but, as rumors of their fate increased, Jewish resistance stiffened. At the beginning of 1943, the Jews commenced their active opposition to the deportation, despite German vengeance.

This was but the prelude, however, to the blood bath which began on April 19, 1943, and completely consumed the ghetto within a month. On that night, which happened to be the first night of Passover, the Nazi soldiers who came for the daily quota of Jewish families were met by guns and explosives that had been smuggled in. Despite fearful retaliation, every Jewish man, woman, and child fought with valor and dedication until all were liquidated. After forty-two days of fierce struggle, the Germans announced that "the former Jewish quarter of Warsaw is no longer in existence."

The following account was written by Ziviah Lubetkin, one of the few survivors of the death grapple of the Warsaw Ghetto.

"Tell about our fight; tell of our loneliness; tell about our last stand. Tell! Tell!"

THE GHETTO was burning. For days and nights it flamed, and the fire consumed house after house, entire streets. Columns of smoke rose, sparks flew, and the sky reflected a red, frightening glow. Nearby, on the other side of the wall, citizens of the capital strolled, played, and enjoyed themselves. They knew that "the Jews were burning." . . . Sparks scattered and a house outside the ghetto would catch fire. But these fires were immediately extinguished. Only in the ghetto no one hastened to put out the flames, to come to the rescue . . .

This was the ghetto of the largest Jewish community that had ever existed in Europe. Within its walls the last remaining Jews, still numbering tens of thousands, were trapped. Some days before, in April 1943, the Germans had planned to send this remnant in death cars to Oswiecim and Belsitz, as they had previously sent hundreds of thousands . . . But this time they met with opposition. Units of the "Fighting Jewish Organization" manned the street corners and the ruins, planting land mines and hurling grenades into the files of German troops. Taken by surprise, the Germans retreated. They attacked the next day and the next, but each time they met with resistance. After ten days of battle, they did not dare to enter the ghetto.

Then the Germans set fire to the ghetto, first from airplanes and then on the ground, at the four corners. They celebrated from afar . . .

It was not the triumph they had planned. With their last vital

Monument memorializing the holocaust, Philadelphia. (Sculptor, Natan Rapoport)

energy the Jews found shelter behind every wall, among ruins that could no longer burn . . . Men, women, and children crawled out from underground hiding places and wandered about, loaded with their last bits of food, blankets, pots. Babies were carried . . . older children trailed after their parents, in their eyes an abyss of suffering and a plea for help . . .

Below the smoldering ruins . . . at a depth of five meters, hundreds of us lay in absolute darkness on the floor of a bunker. Not a ray of daylight could penetrate—only the clock told us that outside the sun was setting. Here, on Milah No. 18, was the headquarters of the Fighting Jewish Organization. When night fell and the city beyond . . . was silent, the streets of the ghetto would awake. Those . . . in the bunkers got up and crawled out from the depths . . .

Each night . . . Jews would roam the streets, searching for families and friends. And each night we saw how much smaller our numbers grew. We were gradually vanishing, and the terror of inactivity gnawed at our spirit . . .

The Jewish combat units were not the only occupants of Milah No. 18. Our real landlords were the "Chumps." They had been part of the Warsaw underworld—thieves and even murderers—and had originally built the bunker, a spacious and astonishingly well-equipped underground dugout with electric light . . . and a well . . . There were luxuries: a reading room and a game room.

The leader of the gang was Shmuel Asher, a broad and fleshy Jew who ruled his henchmen with an iron hand. But he did not hesitate to share his supplies with us and was especially tender with the children . . . Now the place was densely crowded with three hundred persons. He had treated our fighters with cordial respect and put everything he had at our disposal. "Our strength is still with us," he told us, "and my men are trained to open locks. At night we can walk quietly without being observed. We can climb fences and walls, and all the paths and holes of the ghetto are well-known to us . . ."

The Chumps proved very useful. They guided us at night to spy out the German positions. And when the ghetto was nearly all burned, and it was hard to distinguish . . . the streets, one of the thieves would lead us confidently, climbing like a cat through the wreckage. Every sundown, Shmuel Asher would put on his shining boots, hang two pistols at his belt, and crawl out to forage for food. The hole he squeezed through just fitted his mighty torso. Later on, it became much too wide for his wasted body . . .

The ghetto swiftly crumbled away. Starvation and the discovery of bunker after bunker by patrolling Germans took their toll . . .

Sometimes, while walking through the ruins, silence all about, one suddenly heard a low, despairing moan. We would search the rubble. To call aloud was dangerous and . . . the wounded person would fall silent, afraid we might be Germans. Once I found a woman and her child . . . more dead than alive. More than once, the wounded begged: "Kill me!" . . . but we lacked the heart . . .

During one of these days I visited Geffner's bunker and was confronted with a deep silence. It was a great shock. No one was in it, all had been captured by the Germans . . .

At first this bunker had housed the fighter units of Shlamek Schuster and Henick Guttman. One day the bunker was suddenly attacked by the Germans. They shouted an order to surrender. Guttman acted quickly. He assumed the Nazis would not fire at a girl, so he sent Dvorah Barn out first. For a split second, the Germans were immobilized, amazed at her beauty and daring. She used this moment to throw a hand grenade and they scattered in fright. Our fighters then came out and attacked. Guttman was wounded and Eiger died, but many Germans paid with their lives. As he lay dying, Eiger shouted to his comrades, "It's a shame to waste pistols. Take my pistol!"

Unfortunately . . . it took too long to find a new refuge . . . and the Germans returned to the bunker, threw in grenades, and ten of the fighters, among them Dvorah Barn, were killed. Guttman was carried to Zechariah's bunker; when that was attacked, too, he died with the others. He was one of the best men in our movement . . . His men all loved and obeyed him with a steadfast devotion.

. . . Contact with the city was completely cut off. Some days before we had sent groups through the sewers and a secret tunnel, but no word had come from them. Any mission to the Aryan side was terribly risky. With great luck a messenger might . . . get through, but, if he did, who would give sanctuary to a hunted Jew? . . . And our friends among the Gentiles had not yet found hiding places for us.

We had no choice but to continue sending groups through the sewers . . . It was better than remaining here to die of hunger and suffocation. If only a few got through, it would be worth while . . .

Tovyah Buzhikovski answered our doubts. There was a guide in the other bunker who could lead us safely through the labyrinth . . . In desperation we brushed aside all fears and made a plan. A group of ten would go into the sewers. They would emerge at night and hide in the ruins of abandoned houses on the Aryan side. Once there, comrades with a gentile appearance would try to find the ones who had gone before and together work out an escape. I was to accompany the group . . .

Final preparations were made. We dressed, took our weapons, and parted from our friends. Would we ever see each other again? Outwardly we were calm; we smiled and even joked. Handshakes were exchanged. We grasped our pistols and left.

One by one, we crawled on our bellies out of the bunker . . . Above ground, we drank in the fresh air with open mouths. In a whisper the guard posted outside told us. "There is firing from the left; on the right it is quiet and you can go that way." . . .

Tensely and cautiously, our fingers on the triggers of our pistols, we proceeded . . . Here and there we met survivors . . . "What is to be done?" they asked. "There is no more food. Everything is burned." Oppressed by a feeling of futility, we nevertheless said some heartening words . . .

At Franciskanska No. 20 . . . there was an emotional reunion with our friends. It was some time since we had heard from them. There was much to tell them for they had no radio and could get no news. This bunker had once been surrounded by the Germans and nearly wiped out, but the survivors, 160 out of the 300, had escaped into the sewers. Unable to find a new shelter, they had returned . . . to the old bunker, hoping the enemy would think they had killed everyone and not bother to attack again.

We found the guide . . . After leading the group to the exit from the sewers, he was to return to teach the way to one of our men; then the next night he would escape to the Aryan side with the second group. For the trip each person was given a bag with a piece of sugar and a few dried crusts.

They were to emerge from the manhole on Belinska and take cover in a group of houses . . . blasted by the 1939 bombardments. Once there, Pavel and Helen Shipper, whose appearance was Aryan, were to . . . try to contact our comrades outside. Carefully we taught them the addresses and telephone numbers. The others were to wait in the bombed buildings until they returned. In a day or two another group would leave. These would be at the exit at nine in the evening and there wait for the signal —three consecutive raps—that the first group had got to safety and that they could come out. The exit was in the middle of the street, in full view—a dangerous spot.

Murmurs of farewell, handshakes. Then, one after another, the comrades jumped into the tunnel . . . We could hear the water splash with every jump. Each had a candle to light his way. They disappeared, and their splashing footsteps soon were no longer audible.

Two and a half hours later, two of them returned; one was the guide. They told us how they had reached the street. It was silent.

But as soon as they had closed the manhole and started to return, they heard shots on the street above. Had the shots been fired at our comrades? They couldn't be sure . . .

That night, Chaim P . . . , Marek Edelstein, and I started back to our bunker . . .

When we reached our bunker, I hardly recognized the place. I thought we'd made a mistake . . . We dashed to all six entrances but they were unrecognizable and there were no guards. We screamed the password but there was no answer. Then in a nearby yard, among the shadows, we found some of our comrades, . . . weak and trembling . . . wrecked people. The Germans had descended upon them and only a few had escaped . . .

When the Germans called out, the Chumps and the civilians surrendered, but none of our fighters . . . The Germans announced that everyone who came out would be taken to work; others would be shot at once. Our comrades entrenched themselves near the entrance and waited with weapons ready . . . Finally the Germans began to send gas into the bunker. They let in a small quantity of gas, then stopped, trying to break their spirit with a prolonged suffocation. A terrible death faced the one hundred twenty fighters.

Aryeh Wilner was the first to cry, "Come, let us destroy ourselves. Let's not fall into their hands alive!" The suicides began. Pistols jammed and the owners begged their friends to kill them. But no one dared take the life of a comrade. Lutek Rotblatt fired four shots at his mother but, wounded and bleeding, she still moved. Then someone discovered a hidden exit, but only a few got out . . . The others slowly suffocated in the gas. Thus the best of the Jewish fighters met death, one hundred in all; among them Mordechai Anilewitz, our handsome commander whom we all had loved.

Twenty-one had escaped; of these eighteen were fighters. Some were wounded . . . Others were suffering from the gas. We felt now that death was certain for all of us . . .

Here was buried our last hope; we moved away, a file of spiritless bodies, to find a place for the handful of wounded and weakened comrades.

On our way, we stopped at Zechariah's unit to tell what had happened . . . Zechariah flared out, "Then what are we waiting for? Let us all go out against them, in the middle of the streets, in the light of day. Let's fire at them and fall ourselves and let the end come!"

This was my last meeting with Zechariash—as everyone called him. There was not a Jew in the ghetto who did not know, love, admire him. He was the one who had brought us . . . the first German rifle . . . A German had caught him; he pretended to surrender and raised his hands. Then he pulled out his pistol, shot his captor, took the rifle . . .

When we reached our new headquarters we slumped to the floor and lay as if paralyzed . . .

Responsibility for the survivors stirred us into action. Another group must be sent through the sewers. No one wanted to go. In our despair we wanted to stay right there and end our lives together . . . At last ten comrades were ordered to go, with them the two who had returned the night before.

We wept at their leaving. And each of us thought: what testament shall I send to dear ones, to the world, to coming generations, to comrades in the longed-for land? One after another we murmured, "Tell about our fight; tell of our loneliness; tell about our last stand. Tell! Tell!"

I lay on my pallet, exhausted and unable to sleep after the terrible day . . .

Then I saw the two guides. I was dazed. What were they doing here? . . . Breathing excitedly, they told us that in the sewers they had found . . . Kazhik, and that he was waiting for us . . .

They had returned to lead us to the others waiting in the sewer . . . We felt no joy. Just the day before, death had seized 100 who might have come with us now and been saved . . .

It was hard to leave the ghetto, the dead. The thought of forsaking Zechariash's and Josef Farber's units tormented us. We had arranged to meet them the following day. Now at dawn there was no opportunity to contact them . . . if we emerged in the light we would only give them away to the enemy. Logic told us that nothing could be done now, that we had to go . . .

With heavy hearts we descended into the sewer . . . I felt the water splash around me . . . I was overcome by a dreadful nausea there in the cold, filthy water. I felt that nothing—not even freedom—was worth this.

Very few could come with us. The aged and the children would only die on such a trip. They did not even ask to go along. Sixty people crawled through the narrow sewer, bent almost in half, the filthy water up to their knees. Each held a candle. We half-walked, half-crawled for twenty hours . . . without stopping, without food or drink, in that terrible cavern. Hunger and thirst weakened us . . . The eighteen who had survived the catastrophe at Milah No. 18 had not yet recovered from the gas. Some of them were unable to walk and we dragged them through the water . . . More than once, one of us would fall and beg to be left lying there. But no one . . . was abandoned . . .

Early the following morning we reached a spot under Frosta Street on the Aryan side . . . Kazhik and his Polish companion lifted the sewer lid and vanished. We sat in the water and waited. That day we had no word from them . . .

The idea of returning to the ghetto and leading out the others seized us. Many volunteered for the mission. But only two were assigned. One was Shlamek Schuster, a youth of about seventeen. There was no one better suited for the daring job . . . He had saved his unit from a burning house surrounded by Nazis . . . He had broken through a wall of Germans by flinging hand grenades, and when they recovered he had already cut a path for himself and his comrades. He was now to be joined by Yorek Blons, an older comrade . . . They left before evening.

It was not until midnight that the comrades from the Aryan side contacted us. The lid over the sewer was lifted and some soup and bread were handed down. We could scarcely touch the food; only thirst troubled us. Yehuda Vengrover, still weak from gas, could not bear his thirst. He had bent down in the sewer and drunk from it. Who knows whether this was not the cause of his death? When we reached the forest the following day, he fell to the ground and died within a few minutes.

The comrades on the outside—among them a Pole whom the P.P.R. (Polish Labor party) had appointed to assist the Jewish Fighting Organization—told us that they could come for us in the morning. We told them that two comrades had gone back to fetch the others . . . and we would not stir till they came . . .

Above us the life of the street went on as usual. We listened to street noises, heard the gay sounds of children playing . . .

In the morning our messengers, Shlamek and Yorek, returned, their faces distorted with suffering. All the sewer passages to the ghetto had been blocked. Shlamek acted like a man insane with grief.

In our sorrow we prayed that everything would come to an end. Physical and spiritual strength were ebbing. Then at ten o'clock we heard a noise and soon the tunnel was flooded with such a bright light as we had not seen for many days . . . Sure that the Germans had discovered us, we rushed further into the sewer. But it was our comrades . . . They called to us excitedly and began to help us climb the ladder. Near the exit stood a truck. In a few minutes, all forty persons got on the truck, it moved away, and another pulled up.

Now when we saw each other by daylight—dirty, wrapped in rags, smeared with the filth of the sewers, faces thin and drawn, knees shaking with weariness—we were overcome with horror. Only our feverish eyes showed that we were still living human beings. We stretched out on the floor of the truck so as not to be seen from the street, each with his weapon. In this manner the truckload of armed Jewish fighters proceeded through the very heart of Nazi-occupied Warsaw on May 12, 1943. The Pole Kasczed, our ally, sat near the driver and directed him while in the truck Kazhik stood upright, visible to all. We who lay below were calmed by the expression on his face . . .

. . . Several times a whispered command was given—"Weapons ready! We see Germans!" . . . The most difficult minutes came while trying to cross the bridge which leaves the city. German sentries near each bridge . . . searched every auto. Our truck wandered from one street to another, and when the driver noticed that careful examination was being made at a bridge he would turn back to look for another exit. At the fourth bridge, we succeeded in crossing safely in the confusion of heavy traffic. Thus we reached the Mlochini Forest, seven kilometers from Warsaw.

Our escape had been organized by our comrades on the Aryan side . . . The action was carried out by only three Jews and one Pole. Two of them stood at either end of the street, and with the aid of weapons prevented anyone from entering it. A Polish policeman accidentally appeared on the scene and one of our comrades shouted, "Get out of here or I'll shoot!" He fled for his life.

. . . Our comrades had phoned a transport company to send two trucks to Frosta Street to transport some wooden shoes. When the trucks arrived . . . our comrades, armed, came up to the drivers and said, "There are no wooden shoes here. We have a group of Jewish fighters. You must take them to the forests outside Warsaw. Otherwise we shall kill you." They obeyed . . .

Throughout the trip we worried about the others who had remained in the sewer . . . By the time they reached the exit the comrades outside had no longer been able to hold back the traffic in the street. The driver of the second truck became frightened and left his cab. There was time only to tell them, "Follow the sewer to the exit in the nearest street. We will come to get you later." But they had apparently tired of waiting and came up out of the sewer. Immediately the entire neighborhood was surrounded by Germans, who . . . threw grenades into the sewer. When the twenty had come into the street there was a terrible and prolonged hand-to-hand battle between our handful of hungry and weakened people and the German troops. Amazed admiration was expressed by the Poles for this handful of Jewish boys and girls who dared break out into the city to fight the Germans. Legends were woven about this encounter in which all the young Jews met their death.

We did not know where we were being taken, but when we approached the forest we found ourselves among friends. A group of fighters from the small ghetto, Tebens-Schultz, ran out to greet us. They too had escaped . . . about ten days before. They had already mourned us, believing that we were lost and that they were the last survivors . . .

. . . They at once brought us warm milk . . . About us was the green forest and a beautiful spring day. It had been a long time since we had known a forest, spring, and the sun. All that had been buried and restrained in our frozen hearts now stirred. I burst into tears.

Soon there was a new sorrow. Even as we were excitedly talking, Yehuda Vengrover lay down on the ground. Still weak from the gas, Yehuda was now dying, and in a few minutes his eyes closed forever.

For hours we sat silent till one comrade arose and began to dig a grave . . . In our hearts we felt that we were the last survivors of a people that had been exterminated. We . . . felt that the end had come for all our people and that we were the last, the smoking and dying embers . . . Our future was veiled in darkness and we felt superfluous and alone, abandoned by God and man. What more could be done that we had not done?

We lay down on the ground, but could not sleep. We thought of the mystery of the world and man, we remembered the murder of our people, the beloved dead comrades who were part of the ashes of our burned souls. The heart wondered and asked, wondered and asked—but there was no answer.

From "The Last Days of the Warsaw Ghetto," by Ziviah Lubetkin, translated by Shlomo Katz, as quoted in *Commentary,* 1947

A MAJOR Speaks to Soldiers from Judea, 1943

During World War II, the Jews of Palestine fought valiantly with the allies against Nazi Germany. Although there was no conscription in the Holy Land, 25,000 Jews volunteered for the British army. The Arabs in the country, although twice the number, contributed less than 10,000 men, and the other Arab nations were at best neutral and often openly aided the Nazis. When Italy entered the war on the side of Germany, thereby obstructing Allied traffic in the Mediterranean Sea, the role of Palestine's Jews became crucial.

Jewish participation in the war was motivated not only by Germany's enmity against the Jews but also by the Jewish teaching that freedom is the foundation and capstone of the human personality. It was similar to the struggle which the Jews had waged 2,000 years before to free the Holy Land from Roman tyranny. In memory of their victory against those ancient defenders of liberty, the Romans had erected the Arch of Titus overlooking the Forum in Rome. On the inner panels of this arch is carved the victory procession, carrying the holy vessels plundered from the Temple in Jerusalem.

Now a detachment of victorious soldiers on the Island of Malta were preparing to enter vanquished Rome. In the following selection, their officer, Major Louis Rabinowitz, encourages his men to walk proudly under the Arch of Titus since their achievements have vindicated the cause of their ancestors.

"March through it with flags flying and bands playing."

MALTA, JUNE 1943; I am addressing a detachment of a Palestinian unit in the centre of the island. After my address there are questions. One of them asks in all seriousness:

"Can you please advise us what our attitude should be toward the Arch of Titus when we get to Rome?"

I look at him blankly.

"Does not *Adoni ha-Rav* know that Jews do not walk through that arch, erected to commemorate the destruction of the Temple?"

I confessed my ignorance of that fact.

"Should we avoid it, or march ceremoniously through it? Or perhaps we could have it removed to Palestine?"

My heart throbs with an uncontrollable emotion.

"March through it," I said. "March through it with flags flying and bands playing if you can get them. March through it proudly and with heads erect, for you have wiped out that defeat." And with tears more of pride and joy than of sorrow welling into my eyes, I sat down.

From *Soldiers from Judea,* by Major Louis Rabinowitz

A BRITISH OFFICER Helps Free Bergen-Belsen, 1945

When the conquering Allied armies rolled into Germany, the notorious concentration camps came into their hands. Although the Germans tried to hide what had been going on, they were not able to dispose of the camps and their prisoners fast enough. The soldiers who liberated the pitiful survivors in these places of human degradation and destruction found themselves shocked beyond all belief.

The German concentration camps will remain forever a symbol of the depths of man's inhumanity and depravity. One of the worst camps was Bergen-Belsen, where over 55,000 inmates were crowded together amidst filth and disease. Their diet was below starvation level, water was scarce and often polluted.

The prisoners at Bergen-Belsen came from many backgrounds. Russian farmers, French students, Polish soldiers, and Hungarian physicians were interned here as well as Jews. The Allied liberation in April, 1945, was an unbelievable act of salvation to men and women who had long ago despaired of any future. Unfortunately, their joy was dampened by a typhus epidemic that made a quarantine necessary, but they could still rejoice in the arrival of food and medical supplies and in the halt to the crematorium.

The following first-person story by a British officer of the Allied take-over at Bergen-Belsen reveals the dulled moral sensitivity of the Germans who ran these camps.

"You've made a fine hell here."

April 15, 1945

"IF WE agree to by-pass this place, Belsen, the Germans are talking about giving us the bridge at Winsen," said the lieutenant. We were studying the operations map outside the divisional commander's caravan.

It was April 12, the hedges were sprouting and the dust was rising on the roads . . .

"What's Belsen?" I asked.

"It's a concentration camp. Typhus is apparently rife there, and Himmler has sent a personal representative to talk about sealing the place off."

"Sounds a bit odd."

"H'm, does, doesn't it?"

I left Division H.Q. in my loud-speaker car . . . I was more preoccupied with the intentions of the brigadier of 159 Brigade, who had asked us to talk through the loud-speaker to the enemy, than with mysterious negotiations about a concentration camp . . .

Winsen had been taken twelve hours when we drove in . . .

At Brigade headquarters a staff officer stopped us . . .

"A message has just come through from division. They want you to go forward with your loud-speaker into this place, Belsen."

Col. Taylor, commanding the 63rd Anti-Tank Regiment, had the job of camp commandant of Belsen Camp. He was understandably preoccupied when I called on him . . . Sixty thousand "political prisoners," some SS [Storm Trooper] personnel, and a raging epidemic of typhus . . .

He showed me a copy of the truce between the general commanding 8th British Corps and the German army commander at Bergen-Belsen. Under its terms an area round Belsen was to be treated as "neutral," i.e., no shots would be fired into or out of this zone. A battalion of German infantry and a Hungarian regiment would remain to guard the perimeter of the camp . . . And about fifty SS men . . . would await the British commandant, to hand over the camp.

My instructions were to drive forward with the leading British tanks, enter Belsen Camp, and make an announcement by loud-speaker . . . to tell the inmates that, although they were liberated from the Germans, they must not leave the camp because of the danger of spreading typhus . . . But they were to be assured that food and medical aid were being rushed up with all possible speed.

We . . . took the main road northeast. Here we caught up with the long cavalcade of tanks, scout cars, and Bren carriers of the 23rd Hussars . . .

The Belsen neutral zone was clearly marked with white notices, "Danger Typhus," and in five minutes we reached the first of these boards . . . Turning the next bend in the road we saw the camp entrance—a single pole across the roadway with wooden huts on either side. A group of smartly dressed officers stood waiting in front of it . . . Glancing at the uniforms we picked out the forked lightning badge of the SS, the khaki of a Hungarian captain wearing three rows of medals, and the fieldgrey of the *Wehrmacht* [German army].

The group of soldiers saluted as I got out, and I asked one of them, an SS *Hauptsturmfuhrer* [chief Storm Trooper], what was the state of the camp. He was a powerfully-built man, fat-faced, with a scar across one cheek, and he answered simply, "They are calm at present."

"I propose to go in and make a loud-speaker announcement," I said.

The Hungarian captain stepped forward and said in a voice of extreme solicitude, "I shouldn't. Seven people a day are dying here of 'fleck typhus.' " The fat-faced SS officer, Josef Kramer, added quickly, "They're calm now. It would be unwise to risk a tumult." I remembered the purpose of the "truce," which was to prevent the spread of typhus . . .

A desultory conversation started . . .

"What type of prisoners have you got in here?" I asked Kramer.

"Homosexuals and professional criminals," he said, "as well as some *Bibel Forscher* [biblical scholars]." He watched me carefully . . .

"And political prisoners?"

"Oh yes, there are the *Haftlinge* [half-breeds]," he said in a friendly confiding sort of way.

"What's the total?"

"Forty thousand in this camp and 15,000 in the overflow camp . . . up the road."

. . . A few minutes later Colonel Taylor pulled his jeep up in front of us. I asked for confirmation of my orders to enter the camp.

"Go in and make the announcement," he said, and drove on up the road . . .

I told Kramer to open the gate. He looked taken aback. "I can't do that without authority from the *Wehrmacht* commandant." I waved to him to lift the barrier. The barrier went up. "Stand on the running-board," I said, and he mounted it. "You have to guide us round the camp . . ."

We swung through the almost deserted front compound . . . and two hundred yards further reached a high wooden gate with criss-cross wiring. It reminded me of the entrance to a zoo.

Once through the gate this resemblance was strengthened. On the left . . . stood row upon row of green wooden huts, and we came into a smell of ordure—like the smell of a monkey-house. A sad blue smoke floated like a ground mist between the low buildings.

. . . I had not imagined it like this. Nor had I imagined the strange simian throng, who crowded to the barbed-wire fences . . . with their shaven heads and obscene penitentiary suits, which were so dehumanising.

We had experienced gratitude and welcome in France, Belgium, and Holland. We had been surrounded in Paris, embraced and thanked . . . But the half-credulous cheers of these almost lost men, of these clowns in their terrible motley, who had once been Polish officers, land-workers in the Ukraine, Budapest doctors, and students in France, impelled a stronger emotion, and I had to fight back tears . . .

As we rolled on through the camp, crowds of prisoners began to surge through the barbed wire into the thoroughfare. "Now the tumult is beginning," Kramer said.

Suddenly a German soldier began firing his rifle into the air. Gradually he lowered the muzzle until it was firing only just over the heads of the prisoners. I ran across to him and covered him with my revolver.

"Stop shooting," I said.

He stopped firing. But suddenly a dozen striped figures jumped into the crowd, hitting again and again with sticks and packing-case strips.

No leaps in a ballet could have astonished me as did these kangaroo jumps. They were like prancing zebras, these creatures in broad-striped garments, careening here and there, smiting to left and to right . . . Why did they [the mob] not strike back, defend themselves . . . ?

Half-way across the road I saw a thin creature on his back trying to ward off blow after blow from a thick stick.

I tried to understand what I saw. Could these "policemen" be the political prisoners suppressing criminals among the inmates . . .

I did not know that they were hut-leaders "keeping order" for the SS, nor that the stampeding mob was making for the kitchen . . . I did not understand that mortal starvation conditioned all happenings in the camp.

. . . We came out through a second wire gate opposite the smaller of the two women's camps. Crowds of women, all in the hideous penitentiary garb, lined the roadside. One of them called out in French, "You must deliver us. It is frightful, this camp."

I went to her and she said: "We are four hundred French women here—all political prisoners. You must deliver us."

We turned and came up the main thoroughfare. The men were still cheering and one wraith-like figure, with a crutch, threw it down and fell on his knees as our car passed, clasping his hands in thanksgiving. We . . . entered the larger women's camp and began our announcement.

In a few seconds the car was surrounded by hundreds of women. They cried and wailed hysterically, uncontrolledly, and no word from the loud-speakers could be heard . . .

We drove back to the main entrance. Kramer jumped off the runningboard and I said to him, "You've made a fine hell here."

"It has become one in the last few days," he replied.

Half a mile up the road we saw the first concrete buildings of the Panzer Training School. A dozen or so of these formed an overflow camp, housing 15,000 men . . .

Our announcement here was again drowned by the cheering . . .

Ceremony and an attempt at an "official front" were being staged at the *Kommandantur* [headquarters] . . . The two German colonels talking to Colonel Taylor were dapper and immaculate and very conscious of their role as trustees of the "Belsen truce." . . . A British medical officer came in.

"There have been some casualties down at the concentration camp."

. . . The telephone rang. A German captain answered it then turned to us. "It appears that a loud-speaker went into the camp and that it has started a disturbance."

Colonel Taylor said to Colonel Schmidt: "Who is causing casualties? Under the agreement only SS administrative personnel may be in the camp and they should be unarmed."

"They may have pistols," said Colonel Schmidt with a shrug . . .

Colonel Taylor ordered the German colonels to go with us immediately to the camp.

Kramer came up and saluted as we alighted . . .

"Tell him that all SS must hand in their arms within half-an-hour," said Colonel Taylor to me. I did so.

"Without arms I can't be responsible for the camp," answered Kramer.

"No, but you can show the British officers how it's administered."

"I can't enter the camp unarmed."

"In that case, tell him," said Colonel Taylor, "he can keep his arms for the present but that for every inmate of the camp who is shot one SS man will be executed."

I asked Kramer why he needed . . . arms in the camp. He answered, "To protect the food-stores." "What reserve of food was there?" "For two days." "What meals did the inmates get?" "Turnip soup in the morning and evening. Bread as often as possible." . . .

Colonel Taylor demanded the personal documents of the 40,000 prisoners.

"They have all been destroyed."

"On whose authority?"

"That of the *Hauptwirtschaftsamt* [Chief Economic Bureau] in Berlin."

. . . A German army captain . . . hurried up . . .

"The kitchens are being stormed," he said.

"Come on, let's see for ourselves," said a British officer.

The British party, about six officers and a few NCO's, walked towards the huts, Kramer and the German army officer walking in front.

. . . The cheering began again. Hundreds of pyjama-clad figures were milling about on the highway. There were cries of "How do you do?" and "God save the King." . . . The sound of shots rang out from the far end of the camp.

Half-way down the main highway stood the kitchen, a long wooden shed with thirty large cauldrons. This was the kitchen which "had been stormed." . . . Only the SS supervisor was there.

"I see no storming going on," I said.

The SS supervisor lifted the lid of one of the cauldrons and pointed to the level of the soup . . . about a foot below the top.

"All that has been taken," he said.

"And you call that 'storming the kitchen'?"

I noted down this SS man's name as a trouble-maker and went out to Kramer.

"Is this the extent of your 'riot'?" I asked.

"No, there's also been an attack on the potato patch."

"Take us there."

Kramer led us through the tall wire gate at the end of the camp. In front stood the dismal little crematorium of brick, with its thin chimney . . . On our right an undulating straw patch. Dusk was falling, but there was movement on the patch of straw. The emaciated figure of a woman, her face yellow, her eyes shining like coals, was kneeling there. With her hands she was pulling up the straw, striving to uncover the potatoes underneath.

Kramer turned to me. "You see what I mean."

. . . The chief medical officer pointed to something on the ground. "That fellow's in a bad way," he said.

I looked . . . and saw a man lying there with blood running over his face.

"He ought to be got on to a stretcher."

I turned to the nearest SS man. "Get a stretcher—at the double!" He trotted away.

Suddenly we heard screaming coming from the potato patch. Lying on the straw was a man in great agony. He was jerking the upper part of his body up and down. Soon he became still and his screaming stopped.

As we walked on we came to another body, then to another, then to another . . .

Sergeant C. came over to me. "Why shouldn't Kramer carry one of these people away?" he asked.

I looked at Kramer. "Pick up that man and take him to the hospital!"

Kramer flushed, threw back his head, and stepped a pace back. He still felt himself "the commandant of the camp."

"Pick up that man!" I covered him with my revolver. Kramer came forward and stooped. I pushed my revolver into his back. He hoisted the body over his shoulder and ambled away.

It was pitiable to think of these men shot like rats on the very day of liberation. At first I thought: Could they not have restrained themselves and waited just three hours for the camp to be taken over? But such reflections were unimaginative and childlike. In their delirium of hunger they had lost the power to reason. Words like "liberation," "tomorrow," "wait" had lost all meaning for them. They were consumed by the famine which was burning them up, possessed only by the wild urge to eat and survive . . .

When Kramer returned the potato patch was swarming with women. The British soldiers urged them with gestures to go back to their huts. Three white-faced, bright-eyed women called out, "Good-night, boys!" It was like some fantastic closing-time . . .

As we walked back . . . the men of the 63rd Anti-Tank Regiment were coming in . . .

Curious reflections suggested themselves on this first evening in Belsen Camp. What had possessed Kramer and his fifty "administrative SS" to await the coming of the British? They must have had innumerable opportunities to escape into the dark forest. Did they not understand that they were courting death?

Undoubtedly their SS superiors . . . had made great play with "the truce" and hoodwinked these dull-witted ruffians into the belief that they could "work their passage" with the British by helping to clean up the typhus-ridden camp.

It is a strange commentary on their utter ignorance of all Western standards and codes of morals and behaviour, that they should have believed their collaboration would be accepted. It also indicates the extent to which their sense of wickedness had been dulled by years of brutish crime. Kramer was revealed afterwards as the man of the "selection" at Auschwitz. Here he had stood before the crematorium as truckloads of human cattle were unloaded, motioning frail young women and their children towards the gas chamber, and more robust men, able to work, into the camp. His nostrils must have been unaccustomed to anything except the stench of death.

But this grotesque attempt at collaboration was perhaps indicative of something else. Had the racial teaching of Himmler's schools really succeeded in making these SS men regard Jews and *Haftlinge* as species of poisonous rats? Did they really feel no more concern at the shooting through the stomach of a beautiful Jewish girl, or the death from slow starvation of an innocent man, than a normal person might feel at the similar fate of a rat? It is possible . . .

From *Belsen Uncovered,* by Derrick Sington

A NEWSMAN Sees Ten Nazi Leaders Pay for Their Crimes, 1946

The Nuremberg Trials were a historic "first." President Harry S. Truman predicted that they would "stand in history as a beacon to warn international brigands of the fate that awaits them." He believed that the trials, which lasted ten months, had set a precedent that would become a basic principle in international law.

Not everyone agreed that the verdicts passed against twenty-two Nazi leaders by the International Military Tribunal were good. Some argued that the trials were unprecedented and unfair, because men were being tried for deeds committed before any international authority had made them crimes. Others maintained that the defendants had violated the most elementary and basic principles of international morality by which man lives.

Finishing on October 1, 1946, the tribunal condemned twelve to death, seven to prison, and freed three. The condemned included some of Hitler's most notorious lieutenants: Hermann Goering, the ex-Reichsmarshall; Joachim von Ribbentrop, the former foreign minister; Alfred Rosenberg, the party theorist; and Julius Streicher, the infamous Jew-hater. After appeals for clemency or for death by firing squad had been denied, preparations were swiftly made for hanging the condemned on October 16.

The grim story of the execution was reported in a press dispatch filed by Kingsbury Smith, European general manager of the International News Service, one of eight reporters from Allied countries permitted to witness the hangings.

"Now it goes to God!"

Nuremberg, October 16

EX-REICHSMARSHALL Hermann Wilhelm Goering cheated the gallows of Allied justice by committing suicide in his prison cell . . . Despite the fact that an American security guard was supposed to be watching his every movement, the crown prince of Nazidom managed to hide, chew, and swallow a vial of cyanide of potassium.

Goering swallowed the poison while Colonel Burton C. Andrus, American security commandant, was walking . . . to the death-row block to read to the condemned Nazi leaders the International Military Tribunal's sentence of death. In an hour . . . Goering was scheduled . . . to lead the parade of death to the scaffold.

None of the condemned men had been told that they were to die this morning. How Goering guessed this was to be his day of doom and how he managed to conceal the poison on his person is a mystery that has confounded the security forces.

. . . The ten other condemned princes of Nazidom were hanged in . . . the small gymnasium inside one of the prison yards of the Nuremberg city jail.

The executions took approximately one hour and a half . . .

The only one to make any reference to Nazi ideology was Julius Streicher, the arch Jew-baiter . . . He appeared in the execution hall, which had been used only last Saturday night for a basketball game . . . at 12½ minutes after two o'clock.

An American lieutenant colonel . . . entered first . . . followed by Streicher. Inside the door, two American sergeants closed in on each side of him and held his arms while another sergeant removed his manacles and replaced them with a leather cord.

The first person whom Streicher saw upon entering the gruesome hall was an American lieutenant colonel who stood directly in front of him while his hands were being tied behind his back . . .

This ugly, dwarfish little man [Streicher], wearing a threadbare suit and a well-worn bluish shirt buttoned to the neck but without a tie, glanced at the three wooden scaffolds rising up menacingly in front of him. Two of these were used alternately to execute the condemned men while the third was kept in reserve.

After a quick glance at the gallows, Streicher glared around the room, his eyes resting momentarily upon the small group of American, British, French, and Russian officers on hand to witness the executions.

By this time Streicher's hands were tied securely. Two guards, one to each arm, directed him to the gallows on the left. He walked steadily, . . . but his face twitched nervously. As the guards stopped him at the bottom of the steps for official identification, he uttered his piercing scream, "Heil Hitler!"

His shriek sent a shiver down the back of this International News Service correspondent, who is witnessing the executions as sole representative of the American press.

As its echo died away, another American colonel standing by the steps said sharply, "Ask the man his name."

In response . . . Streicher shouted, "You know my name well!"

The interpreter repeated his request, and the condemned man yelled, "Julius Streicher."

As he mounted the platform Streicher cried out, "Now it goes to God!"

After getting up the thirteen steps to the eight-foot-high and eight-foot-square black-painted wooden platform, Streicher was pushed two steps to the mortal spot beneath the hangman's rope.

This was suspended from an iron ring attached to a crossbeam which rested on two posts. The rope was being held back against a wooden rail by the American army sergeant hangman.

Streicher was swung around to face toward the front. He glanced again at the Allied officers and the eight Allied correspondents representing the world's press. With burning hatred in his eyes, Streicher looked down upon them and screamed, "Purim Fest, 1946!" [a reference to a Jewish holiday commemorating the hanging of Haman, biblical anti-Semite and oppressor of the Jews].

The American officer at the scaffold said, "Ask the man if he has any last words."

When the interpreter had translated, Streicher shouted, "The Bolsheviks will hang *you* one day!"

As the black hood was adjusted, Streicher was heard saying, "Adele, my dear wife."

. . . The trap was sprung with a loud bang. With the rope snapped taut and the body swinging wildly, a groan could be heard distinctly within the dark interior of the scaffold.

It was originally intended to permit the condemned to walk the seventy-odd yards from the cells to the execution chamber with their hands free, but they were all manacled in the cells immediately following Goering's suicide.

The weasel-faced Ribbentrop . . . uttered his final words while waiting for the black hood to be placed over his head. Loudly, in firm tones, he said, "God save Germany!" He then asked, "May I say something else?" The interpreter nodded. The former diplomatic wizard of Nazidom, who negotiated the secret German nonaggression pact with Soviet Russia on the eve of Germany's invasion of Poland, and who approved orders to execute Allied airmen, then added, "My last wish is that Germany realize its entity and that an understanding be reached between East and West. I wish peace to the world."

The ex-diplomat looked straight ahead as the hood was adjusted. His lips were set tight.

Next in line was Field Marshall Wilhelm Keitel, symbol of Prussian militarism and aristocracy. He was the first military leader to be executed under the new concept of Allied international law—the principle that professional soldiers cannot escape responsibility for war crimes by claiming they were merely carrying out orders of their superiors.

Keitel entered the death arena at 1:18 . . . while Ribbentrop was still hanging . . . He could not, of course, see the ex-foreign minister, whose body was concealed within the first scaffold and whose rope still hung taut.

Keitel . . . held his head high while his hands were being tied and walked erect with military bearing to the foot of the second scaffold, although a guard on each side held his arms. When asked his name he answered in a loud sharp tone, "Wilhelm Keitel!" He mounted the gallows steps as he might have climbed to a reviewing stand to take the salute of the German army . . . At the top of the platform, Keitel looked over the crowd with the traditional iron-jawed haughtiness of the proud Prussian officer. Asked if he had anything to say, he looked straight ahead and spoke in a loud voice: "I call on Almighty God to have mercy on the German people. More than two million German soldiers went to their deaths for the fatherland. Now I follow my sons."

Then, while raising his voice to shout, "All for Germany," Keitel's black-booted uniformed body plunged down with a bang. Observers agreed he had shown more courage on the scaffold than he had in the courtroom . . .

There was a pause in the grim proceedings.

The American colonel directing the executions asked the American general representing the Allied Control Commission if those present could smoke. An affirmative answer brought cigarettes into the hands of almost every one of the thirty-odd persons present . . .

In a few minutes an American army doctor and a Russian army doctor, both carrying stethoscopes, walked to the first scaffold, lifted the curtain, and disappeared within.

They emerged at 1:30 A.M. and spoke to a short, heavy-set American colonel wearing combat boots. The colonel swung around and, facing official witnesses, snapped to attention to say, "The man is dead."

Two GI's quickly appeared with a stretcher, which was carried up and lifted into the interior of the scaffold. The hangman, a sergeant, mounted the gallows steps, took a large commando-type knife out of a sheath strapped to his side, and cut the rope.

Ribbentrop's limp body with the black hood still over his head was speedily removed and placed behind a black canvas curtain. This all had taken less than ten minutes.

The directing colonel turned to the witnesses and said, "Lights out, please, gentlemen," and then to another colonel, "O.K." The latter went out . . . to fetch the next man.

This creature was Ernst Kaltenbrunner, Gestapo chief and director of the greatest mass murder Europe has seen since the Dark Ages.

Kaltenbrunner, master killer of Nazidom, entered the execution chamber at 1:36 A.M. wearing a sweater beneath his double-breasted coat. With his lean, haggard face furrowed by old dueling scars, the terrible successor of Reinhard Heydrich had a frightening look as he glanced around the room.

He was nervous and he wet his lips as he turned to mount the gallows, but he walked steadily. He answered his name in a calm, low voice. When he turned around on the gallows platform he first faced a U.S. Catholic army chaplain attired in a Franciscan habit. Asked for his last words, he answered quietly, "I would like to say a word. I have loved my German people and my fatherland with a warm heart. I have done my duty by the laws of my people and I am sorry my people were led by men who were not soldiers and that crimes were committed of which I have no knowledge."

This was strange talk from a man whose agent, Rudolf Hoess, had confessed at a previous trial that under Kaltenbrunner's orders he gassed 3,000,000 human beings at the Auschwitz concentration camp.

As the black hood was about to be lowered, Kaltenbrunner, still in a low, calm voice, used a German phrase which means, "German good luck."

His trap was sprung at 1:39 A.M.

Field Marshall Keitel had been pronounced dead at 1:44 A.M., and three minutes later guards had removed his body. The scaffold was made ready for Alfred Rosenberg, master mind of the Nazi race theories, who had sought to establish Nazism as a pagan religion.

Rosenberg was dull and sunken-cheeked . . . his complexion a pasty brown. But he did not appear nervous, and walked steadily to the gallows. Apart from giving his name and replying "No" to . . . whether he had anything to say, he did not utter a word. Despite his disbelief in God he was accompanied by a Protestant chaplain, who stood beside him, praying.

Rosenberg looked at the chaplain once but said nothing. Ninety seconds after he had entered the hall he was swinging from the end of a hangman's rope . . .

. . . Kaltenbrunner was pronounced dead at 1:52 A.M. Hans Frank, the *Gauleiter* of Poland and former SS general, was next in the parade of death. He was the only one of the condemned to enter with a smile on his lips.

Although nervous and swallowing frequently, this man, who was converted to Catholicism after his arrest, seemed relieved at atoning for his evil deeds. He answered to his name quietly and when asked if he had any last statement replied in almost a whisper, "I am thankful for the kind treatment during my captivity and I ask God to accept me with mercy."

He closed his eyes and swallowed as the black hood went over his head.

The sixth man . . . sixty-nine-year-old Wilhelm Frick, former Nazi minister of the Interior, entered at 2:05½ . . . He seemed to be the least steady of any so far and stumbled on the thirteenth step of the gallows. His only words were "Long live eternal Germany" . . .

Following . . . removal of Frick's corpse at 2:20 A.M., Fritz Sauckel, the slave-labor director and one of the most bloodstained men of Nazidom, faced his doom.

Wearing a sweater with no coat and looking wild-eyed, Sauckel proved to be the most defiant of any except Streicher. Here was the man who drove millions into bondage on a scale unknown since the pre-Christian era. Gazing around the room from the gallows platform, he suddenly screamed, "I am dying innocent. The sentence is wrong. God protect Germany and make Germany great again. God protect my family."

The trap was sprung at 2:26 A.M. and, like Streicher, this hate-filled man groaned loudly as the fatal noose snapped tightly . . .

Ninth was Colonel General Alfred Jodl, Hitler's strategic adviser and close friend. With the black coat-collar of his *Wehrmacht* uniform turned up at the back as though hurriedly put on, Jodl entered the death house with obvious nervousness.

He wet his lips constantly and his features were drawn and haggard as he walked . . . Yet his voice was calm when he uttered his last six words on earth, "My greetings to you, my Germany."

At 2:34 Jodl plunged into the black hole of the scaffold's death. Both he and Sauckel hung together in the execution chamber until pronounced dead six minutes later.

Czechoslovakian-born Seyss-Inquart was the last actor in the ghastly scene of Allied Justice. He entered the death chamber at 2:38½ A.M., wearing the glasses which made his face familiar and despised in all the years he ruled Holland with an iron hand and sent thousands of Dutchmen to Germany for forced labor.

Seyss-Inquart looked around with noticeable signs of unsteadiness and limped on his left clubfoot as he walked to the gallows. He mounted the steps slowly, with the help of guards. When he spoke his last words, his voice was low but intense: "I hope that this execution is the last act of the tragedy of the Second World War and that the lesson taken from this world war will be that there should be peace and understanding between peoples.

"I believe in Germany."

From an International News Service dispatch, October 16, 1946

MEYER LEVIN Films the Underground to Palestine, 1946-47

The American writer, Meyer Levin, went to Europe after World War II to film the illegal movement of Jewish DP's from their confinement camps to Palestine. The operation, as well as each individual station along the "underground" route, was called *Brayha* (the author's choice for the word *brecha*) from the Hebrew verb meaning "to flee." Indeed, the Hebrew tongue, incomprehensible to most non-Jewish Europeans, was the language in which the secret tactics and strategies of the *Brayha* were communicated across the continent.

The *Brayha* was run by a small number of dedicated Jews who labored day and night to return their forlorn and forsaken brethren to the ancient home in Palestine without being caught by local police units. The refugees had to spend weeks, often months, in fearful transit from one place to another under the cover of night, over little-used roads, and often on foot. Coordinating center for *Brayha* was Munich, where such organizations as ORT, the American Jewish Joint Distribution Committee, the Jewish Agency, and the Central Committee on Jewish Refugees had representatives.

Levin's cameraman complained about the author's growing personal involvement in the events he witnessed. The journey, he said, was becoming a "pilgrimage" instead of a film project. The following excerpt from Mr. Levin's volume, *In Search*, is indeed a verbal pilgrimage on the route of one of the noblest humanitarian undertakings in human history.

Some 4,000 Jews held demonstrations against disembarkation of "Exodus" refugees on Hamburg docks, at DP camp of Bergen-Belsen, Germany. (Zionist Archives and Library)

"For you this is not a film project; this is a pilgrimage."

. . . FINALLY I was back on the roads I had traveled with the Fourth Armored Division, back at last to do the job that had been crying out in me to be done . . .

Venya had given me a note scribbled in Hebrew to Ernst, the *Brayha* chief in Munich. All through Europe it was to be like that —a word or two on a scrap of paper, or just a verbal contact, "See Amos, he'll arrange everything." Beside each Ernst, each Amos, there was a telephone, and all across Europe the *Brayha* operated in a very simple code—Hebrew. Presumably, a few Hebrew-speaking controls at Europe's central switchboards could have supplied full information about the illegal movement of refugees.

There was a street in Munich that had become the post-war capital for the Jews of Europe . . . There was the ORT, the AJDC, the Jewish Agency, the Central Committee of Jewish Refugees —and the street itself was filled with wanderers from all over Europe, on their confused searches . . .

We found Ernst in a back bedroom on the second floor of the Jewish Agency house . . . with an innocuous-looking, chubby little man named Ephraim. We were to meet Ephraim everywhere—on the stairs of the Jewish community headquarters in Prague, at a *Brayha* truck station in Vienna, in an office in Paris; and he was always hurrying off—to Marseilles, Rome, Munich, Bratislava. For Ephraim was the *Brayha*. He carried in his head all the financial accounts, in a dozen different constantly shifting currency values; he knew last night's population of every *Brayha* station, every camp.

I often wondered how this man managed to flit around Europe, passing through the Iron Curtain as though it were gauze, and going in and out of the military zones . . . Once Ephraim showed me his credentials. He was in Europe as a representative of the Volunteer Fire Brigade of Haifa!

Only another Jew from Palestine could know that the Volunteer Fire Brigade . . . was a *Haganah* [self-defense] center. Ephraim was supposedly in Europe studying municipal fire-prevention methods.

There was indeed a big movement scheduled from Munich, Ernst informed me . . . We could watch the first phase at the Austrian zone border . . .

Ernst sent a guide with us—Yitzhak the Yugoslav, a handsome, loquacious lad who had "been in the *Brayha* even before it was the *Brayha*," for he had been moving Jews out of Europe since the war.

We got into the Austrian zone easily enough by virtue of our American papers and car. In Salzberg, Yitzhak guided us to a ramshackle house . . . operated officially as a small DP camp. In the yard were a half-dozen GMC trucks . . .

This was a *Brayha*, for the word was used for each unit as well as for the whole movement. The little DP camp housed a trucking unit of the underground railways. The drivers were tough, half-wild DP's who climbed out of their army cots several nights a week to make clandestine trips over side roads, carrying truck loads of men, women, and children to the zone border. The refugees were then walked across the border, to be picked up by trucks on the other side and taken to another DP camp . . . for the next stage of the journey.

. . . The technique depended on bluff and complaisance and sometimes pure nerve; it has been born out of necessity and perfected in two years of operation.

At midnight the movement began. The trucks rolled across Salzberg to a huge DP camp on the other side of the city; there, the passengers were waiting.

They were transients, lodged for a few days in a "permanent" camp, a one-time army camp made up of the usual rows of barracks . . . Over the door of this building hung a sign in Hebrew—*Bruchim ha-Baim* [Welcome]. Literally, "Blessed be those who come here."

Within was an astonishing sight. A few hundred people were sprawled on the floor, as though poured out of a dump truck . . . A man lay under a table, his head on his knapsack; some lay curled around their suitcases; some on tables, on benches, others sat against the wall. There a mother sat with her three children around her, asleep, the youngest babe hugging a sleeping cat. The room was filled with the tired bawling and whimpering of babies and young children, the shushing . . . of the mothers . . .

. . . At last, a lad in a zipper-jacket climbed onto a bench . . . and began to call out names from lists in his hand . . . The trucks backed up to the opening, and they clambered aboard.

Though their heavier belongings were forwarded by other trucks, . . . every refugee was be-bundled and be-hung, carrying rucksacks, valises, bags, packages . . . They pushed onto the trucks, doubled under huge knapsacks, their arms loaded. And some of the women had infants slung from their necks . . .

For a time the trucks rode on the *autobahn* [highway]. Then they switched off their lights and took a sideroad. It was like wartime driving now, in blackout; only, instead of a fear of blundering into the enemy, we were afraid of running into American MP's.

At last the trucks halted. We were on a little road in the woods. The people were hurried off the vehicles and formed into a line. "You won't be able to see even the person in front of you—hold onto each other," the guide admonished.

The *Brayha* boys stationed themselves at the head, and alongside the column.

We took our places in the file. Filming was, of course, out of the question. Perhaps on another night we would be able to film the first part of the movement . . . And somewhere we would . . . duplicate this walk through the forest, shooting day for night.

I would never be able to approximate the real thing . . . For I could never reproduce the silent obedience and tension . . . this line threading in the night through the forest, with six-year-old children walking, clinging to their mothers, the children too with their bundles and burdens. I tried to lift one little boy's pack from him and he fought me as though I were a brigand, all silently . . . What world could ever be safe for a child grown out of this terror?

In the utter darkness . . . each clung to the blackness before him, stumbling onward; branches whipped our faces, one after another the same branch against the entire line of people.

A baby cried, and the guide ran alongside, muttering angrily, "We told you not to take babies in arms!" Later I learned that all women with infants should have waited for a truck that went by a more circuitous route, carrying mothers and babies . . . But the women always feared they would be separated from their husbands. And so they slipped through with the main group, carrying their babies.

. . . We moved on in the utter dark, feeling a small surprise each time our lifted foot touched solid earth again.

There was a patch of thinner woods where we could once more make out shapes. Before me was a man bent double, gasping, stumbling under a tremendous pack; . . . his face, sweat-covered as he desperately dragged himself onward with all his possessions. Then I saw the woman with the three children; she was carrying the youngest, and the two tots clung to her sides so that the whole group of them made a strange monumental form in movement through the forest.

In that moment an anguished hatred arose in me, pure bile and bitterness against the entire world, the whole rotten putrid human race that could drive its own beings into this. What were these people? They were just any people from anywhere, just a number of families and splinters of families scooped up from St. Louis Avenue in Chicago as well as from Jassy and Bucharest and Wrotzlaw; they were the same little launderers and grocery store keepers and machinists and peddlers and peddlers' wives. Why were they crawling here through this forest with their children . . . why? And what border was it? A zone border. From one American military zone of occupation into another . . . What cursed, stupid world could cause such fruitless, inexcusable indignity! And how many times had they walked through border forests, and how many times had they yet to do it? These very same people, crawling across Europe, patiently, without rage!

Tereska was walking alongside a shrunken little woman huddled in many sweaters, who kept moaning, "Where is my husband? maybe he got lost altogether"—for they had been separated some ways back in the darkness.

We came out of the woods into a field . . . the actual border. The guide took little sections across, half-crouched, running.

I walked for a little while with Tereska. She had taken the pack of the woman in all the sweaters, who was breathing heavily . . .

André, our cameraman, was just behind us, striding easily.

We crossed a dirt road. The guides led the group into a clearing. We made out the forms of several large trucks . . .

There was a little boy . . . wearing an east-European cap and boots; he had a canteen and blanket slung around him. "Mama, my feet are cold even in the boots," he said. "Is it still far to go to *Eretz Yisrael?*"

The trucks carried us to another ex-army camp, this time in Germany. Here there was only a barrack into which scarcely a third of the people could crowd. The rest huddled in the corridor or remained outside in the cold . . .

Most of them had bits of provisions with them, and those who weren't too tired opened their sacks . . . and ate. The others fell asleep where they were.

Yitzhak took us to the drivers' quarters . . . Some of us stretched out on the floor. André paced.

At dawn we drove back in the truck to Salzburg, and I hurried to a military hotel and secured a room for my cameraman. But at lunch he said we would have to have a serious talk. He didn't think I could work (on the film) with the necessary objectivity. "For you this is not a film project," he declared, "this is a pilgrimage."

. . . André agreed to complete this trip, filming the convoy into France. Then we would have to hunt up another cameraman . . .

On the following night another group was to pass the same border. We returned to the starting camp and persuaded the *Brayha* leader to let us film the vast room with the waiting refugees . . . and the departure of the trucks.

As a precaution, I stopped in to see the army commander of the camp. He was a sergeant, middle-aged, bored, and a little bewildered at being in charge of these thousands of Jews. Oh, they gave no trouble, he said; it was a model camp, they ran their own affairs, they were clean. But he was lonesome for an American voice and insisted that I sit drinking beer with him.

Then the sergeant unburdened himself. He had got himself a nice girl here in this camp, nice little woman; all he did was take her to dance at the service club . . . But what happens? The camp committee . . . forbids her going out with him. Why is that? Why are these people so high and mighty?

I had to smile inwardly at the curious form of this recurrence of the tale of the gentile ruler and the daughters of Israel. I wondered in what myriad forms and circumstances this tale had been repeated, through the centuries, and I imagined the community elders of the time of Esther disputing, and at last giving in, deciding that for the sake of the people the girl had to be sent to lie with King Ahasuerus. And I imagined the angry tumultuous little committee here at Camp Bialik, disputing whether a DP from Roumania should be permitted to go on dates with this Sergeant Ahasuerus, and this time they had decided no, for in the end such relations always became troublesome.

I sympathized with the sergeant; and at last . . . I hurried off to set up my lights . . . With 220-volt wiring, 110-volt bulbs had to be used in pairs; this required hasty rewiring at times, and I had already blown one bulb . . . when a self-effacing little man asked whisperingly whether he could help, saying he was an electrician . . . All evening long he worked with us, anticipating every need, moving the lights as the camera moved, improvising, making-do . . . Our meagre equipment had to serve in three or four ways at once—it was a task for a half-dozen helpers—and he pressed men into his service, showed them in a second how to aim the lights properly, leaping from one to another, training the beams like a long-experienced head-electrician in a studio. When we were done he wound up the cables professionally and disassembled the spots, putting them wistfully away.

Here he had rotted for a year and a half, living with his wife and two children in a curtain-partitioned room shared with two other families. His wife was sickly . . . So they were waiting . . . "Do you think they need electricians, there?" he asked with the same secretive whisper.

I said the whole country ran on electricity, that vast hydro-electric projects were in prospect, that electricians would be like gods in the land. "We'll go!" he whispered. "Soon, we'll go."

The sergeant watched complacently as we filmed the departure of the trucks. He, of course, knew that the movement was not regular. But he let them run their own affairs: some came, some went, the camp total was about the same . . .

Only, they might have been decent enough to let him have the girl.

We returned in the morning for a general view of the camp; a CIC man was there, talking to the sergeant. Where was our permit to film?

I wondered whether this was because I hadn't got the girl for Ahasuerus . . . For a couple of hours I squatted in the public relations office in Salzburg. The officer put through a call to Vienna . . . Fortunately, the film control chief had known me in Hollywood . . .

In Munich the mass of refugees were being assembled in a transient barracks . . . to be moved in a "legal" IRO train to France . . . A thousand transients were accommodated in two huge lofts. They became "legal" as they arrived there, for the *Brayha* workers of Munich had a group visa waiting for them. Such visas were issued periodically by the French; officially the refugees were in transit to some South American republic. Actually everyone knew they were destined for Palestine.

A list of names was required for each group visa. The Amoses and Ernsts simply invented names as needed. When the refugees arrived, the names were parcelled out to them, each receiving a little identity card that conformed . . . with a name on the visa . . .

In the morning they were taken to a railroad siding where a boxcar train was waiting. IRO officials, social workers from the AJDC, and uniformed Jewish Agency workers walked along the tracks, watching the results of their labor as the families clambered aboard. Several of these organizational officials were actually in the *Brayha*.

In each freight car was a little stove and a pail and a jerrycan of water. A worker from the AJDC assured me, "Oh, they'll fix themselves up comfortably enough, with their blankets and their coats and their bundles. Don't worry, they're used to it. They know how to make themselves comfortable."

It was true that not many of these same people had memories of boxcar transports, for those who had been taken to Auschwitz in such cars were for the most part dead . . . Most of this batch were recent arrivals from Roumania.

And even if one remembered those boxcars, it had to be admitted that the IRO was far more humane than the Gestapo. There were the little stoves; and only twenty or thirty people in a car—room enough for everyone to lie down, if the people fitted themselves carefully. Besides, there was no risk. They were leaving the dark countries at last.

From *In Search*, autobiography, by Meyer Levin

THE TEL AVIV RADIO Broadcasts the News of the Exodus, 1947

England turned a deaf ear to appeals from Jewish victims of Hitler who sought refuge in Palestine. To curry favor with the Arabs, who controlled the Suez Canal and oil, the British adamantly refused entry to thousands of refugees who faced certain death in Germany. In desperation, many Jews tried to enter illegally. Many perished on the way.

One of the tragic consequences was the sinking of the *Struma,* a ship carrying 769 men, women, and children who had set out from Roumania in February, 1942, to find haven in *Eretz Yisrael.* The *Struma* was not fit for an ocean voyage, but it was the only alternative to the Nazi gas chambers. Denied asylum in Istanbul by Turkey, and refused admission to Palestine by Britain, the passengers had to remain aboard the unseaworthy ship which split apart five miles from Turkish shores. All but two of its human cargo went down with it.

At the end of World War II, efforts to find a home for the displaced Jews of Europe brought tremendous pressures on Britain to admit them to Palestine. Reluctantly, England allowed 1,500 Jews a month to settle in the land of their ancestors. It organized an Anglo-American Committee of Inquiry to study the matter but refused to implement its recommendations that 100,000 Jews be admitted immediately into the Holy Land. This callousness toward the plight of these helpless Jews created great antagonism to England whose leaders, especially Ernest Bevin, the foreign secretary, were accused of anti-Semitism.

The British established camps on Cyprus where illegal immigrants were interned upon capture. In the summer of 1947, when the British attacked the ship, *Exodus 1947,* upon its arrival at the shores of Palestine, they committed an atrocity even worse than deportation to Cyprus: the ship's 4,500 passengers were sent back to the German concentration camps from which they had fled.

A radio program from Tel Aviv on July 17, 1947, gave a first-hand account of the tragedy of the *Exodus 1947.*

"The ship looked like a matchbox that had been splintered by a nutcracker."

Tel Aviv. July 17, 1947, 10:00 P.M.

A TAUT VOICE is heard broadcasting in a fine American accent to all of Palestine on *Kol Yisrael* [the Voice of Israel], the *Haganah* secret radio:

"This is the refugee ship, *Exodus 1947*. Before dawn today we were attacked by five British destroyers and one cruiser at a distance of seventeen miles from the shores of Palestine, in international waters. The assailants immediately opened fire, threw gas bombs, and rammed our ship from three directions. On our deck there are one dead, five dying, and one hundred twenty wounded. The resistance continued for more than three hours. Owing to the severe losses and the condition of the ship, which is in danger of sinking, we were compelled to sail in the direction of Haifa in order to save the 4,500 refugees on board from downing."

Next morning as the broadcast is being repeated at 7:30, the Jews of Palestine, still under the British mailed fist, spontaneously with one mind and heart closed store and shop, shut down factory and motor, and "struck" in protest against British terror and in-

"Exodus 1947." Jewish refugees singing Jewish national anthem on upper deck. (Zionist Archives and Library)

justice. Later that day the port of Haifa became an armed camp. Gunners, paratroopers, sailors, and marines in steel helmets and battledress, panzer cars, sten guns, and hospital stretchers—all were in readiness to meet the "invader."

Off on the horizon a black and broken hulk of a boat was seen being tugged into port. About her, the lean and trim and proud British destroyers heaved and panted like hounds after a long chase cornering their prey.

As the vessel approached shore the words *Haganah Ship - Exodus 1947* were seen on her side. Above her masts the blue-and-white flag of Zion floated in defiance. The appearance of the formidable "foe" which had challenged and dared the might of the British navy is described by an eyewitness:

"The ship looked like a matchbox that had been splintered by a nutcracker. In the torn, square hole, as big as an open blitzed barn, we could see a muddle of bedding, possessions, plumbing, broken pipes, overflowing toilets, half-naked men, women looking for children. Cabins were bashed in; railings were ripped off; the lifesaving rafts were dangling at crazy angles."

Once long ago, before it was sold as scrap, the boat had carried Sunday excursion crowds on trips about Chesapeake Bay.

"Amidst the blare of the loudspeakers ('Come off quietly, women and children first'), the smashing of glass bottles which the refugees took along in which to keep their drinking water, and the explosion of depth bombs by the British to ward off underwater swimmers who might attach floating mines to damage the ships, the slow weary march of unloading began from the *Exodus* on to the prison boats."

Seen through the eyes of the same eyewitness:

"The pier began to take on the noise and smell and animal tragedy of a Chicago slaughterhouse. The cattle moved slowly down the tracks."

Was this the long awaited day of *aliyah* [immigration] to the Land of Promise—land of their dreams after the hideous Nazi nightmare, the living death of Auschwitz, Dachau, and Treblinka? Was this the day which they hoped would reunite them with their families . . . ? Were they to be . . . sent off to another concentration camp on the hot island of Cyprus? Were they to wait another two years behind barbed wire and under the ever-present scrutiny of armed guards and searchlights? *Exodus 1947!* It culminated a period of fifteen years of a mass exodus from Europe. *Exodus 1947*—but another link in the sad history of the wandering of a persecuted people.

But these unfortunates lived to see the shores of their longed-for land. Their brethren on the *Struma* had not been as "lucky" . . .

The Struma

Go back six years. December 16, 1941. It is the third black year of the war. The scene this time is the crescent harbor of Istanbul, Turkey. On the port side of a leaky boat, a large sign readable to the people of Istanbul and to the prim world diplomats in the Turkish capital read, SAVE US. The cry came from almost eight hundred refugees jammed in a boat built for one hundred. The passengers on the *Struma* had sailed through waters infested with submarines and mines. They were fleeing blood-soaked Europe—for Palestine—anywhere. But they had no passports and visas. Now they were waiting for the world to open a door—to open its heart. But no. They were illegals. Turkey wouldn't let them land. Britain wouldn't let them go to Palestine. The diplomats of the world looked on: "Sorry. We can't let you in. Sorry! Sorry!"

A week later a tug was sent to pull the *Struma* out to sea. Five miles out the *Struma* split apart and went down. Only two passengers swam to shore. Only two remained alive. The others—70 children, 269 women, 428 men—found their eternal rest on the bottom of the Bosporus.

Had the *Struma* been an enemy ship, its passengers would have been interned. But they were Jews . . . DP's . . . illegal immigrants. . . .

From a broadcast of the Tel Aviv radio, July 17, 1947

ZEEV SHAREF Attends the Declaration of the State of Israel, 1948

On April 2, 1947, Great Britain, unable to resolve the Palestine issue, had turned it over to the United Nations. The General Assembly had appointed a Special Committee on Palestine (UNSCOP), made up of representatives from Australia, Canada, Czechoslovakia, Guatemala, India, Iran, Netherlands, Peru, Sweden, Uruguay, and Yugoslavia, to study the issue.

After hearing testimony on the Jewish problem, the Displaced Persons' camps in Europe, and Arab attitudes, UNSCOP recommended the partitioning of Palestine into two states, one Jewish and the other Arab. The Jews would receive areas in which they were the bulk of the population (most of the coastal area, part of Galilee, the Negev desert). Because it contained sites sacred to three faiths, Jerusalem was to belong to neither but would be administered by the United Nations.

The ensuing debate aroused worldwide interest. It would determine whether the ancient struggle of the Jewish people to recover their homeland would finally end or whether they would continue to wander over a hostile world seeking temporary haven. England declared that it would not support any plan unacceptable to either Jews or Arabs and that come what may it would relinquish its mandate over Palestine in May, 1948. The United States favored the UNSCOP report, as did the Russians, who were pleased to hasten the decline of British power in the Middle East. On November 29, 1947, the General Assembly voted 33 to 13 to divide Palestine into two sovereign states.

The United Nations decision filled world Jewry with joy and gratitude. The miracle of miracles had happened—the Jews could go home.

". . . The return to Zion is born amid travail."

IT WAS a day like any other day. We moved about our duties as usual but as if in a dream. Mingled joy and dread filled us, the present and past were fused. Vision and reality were indistinguishable; the days of the Messiah had arrived, the end of servitude under alien rulers. We hurried . . . toward the Tel Aviv Museum hall, the precious document in hand—our hearts resounding the sing-song chant of the *rebbe,* the teacher, in our boyhood *cheder* [religious class], telling of the great things reserved for the righteous and the just by divine ordainment . . . What had loomed in the distant future, as nebulous as a dream, now became transposed into the present; and we had been privileged to witness the day. Past chapters had been sealed, new chapters were beginning—the days of the Third Jewish Commonwealth.

The guard around the building was strict, cordon within cordon, and pressing against them a multitude of people hastening from all directions. . . .

Below the steps to the museum entrance stood an honor guard of cadets of the Jewish army's officers' school, their white belts gleaming. The small hall was specially decorated . . . [with] works by Jewish artists, Minkowsky's *Pogroms,* Marc Chagall's *Jew Holding a Scroll of the Law,* S. Hirshenberg's *Exile,* among others. A large portrait of Theodor Herzl hung . . . against a blue-and-white backdrop flanked by the blue-and-white flags. When had he said: "The Jewish state is essential to the world. It will therefore be created"?

The hall was packed . . . Movie cameramen and newspaper

photographers from other countries . . . with their arc-lamps and flash-bulbs. . . . Newspapermen and reporters . . . The peoples of Europe and America, to whose culture the Book of Books was integral, were turning their eyes to the tiny corner in which . . . its prophecies [were] being fulfilled.

Beneath Herzl's likeness sat the eleven members of the National Administration and the secretary. The other fourteen . . . were at a table in the center. . . .

Ranged in a semi-circle were members of the Zionist General Council, mayors and party leaders, rabbis and *yishuv* elders, writers, artists, newspaper editors, members of the *Haganah* [self-defense] Command, representatives of the national funds and economic organizations, district representatives and municipal councilors . . . young and old, rustic and urban, teachers and former pupils. . . . The people of Jerusalem were missing; none had come from Haifa and the north, or from districts south of Rehovot, because of the interrupted communications.

Exactly at four o'clock Ben-Gurion rose, rapped the gavel on the table, and the gathering rose. Spontaneously they began to sing *Hatikvah* [the national anthem; literally, "The Hope"] not according to plan. It was to have been played by the Philharmonic Orchestra, concealed on the upper floor. . . .

Ben-Gurion said: "I shall now read to you the Scroll of the Establishment of the State. . . ."

His face shone. . . .

"The Land of Israel was the birthplace of the Jewish people—here came Joshua ben-Nun and King David, Nehemiah and the Hasmoneans.

"Here their spiritual, religious, and national identity was formed. Here they achieved independence and created a culture of national and universal significance.

"Here the prophets and Ezra the Scribe and the men of the Great Assembly wrote and gave the Bible to the world."

A profound sigh seemed to well up out of the words: "Exiled from the Land of Israel the Jewish people remained faithful to it in all the countries of their dispersion, never ceasing to pray and hope for their return and the restoration of their national freedom"; and You remembered the prayers—*for our sins and iniquities were we banished from the land . . . O Almighty Father, gather us in from among the Gentiles . . . and bring us unto Zion Your city in gladness. . . .*

"Impelled by this historic association, Jews strove throughout the centuries to go back to the land of their fathers and regain their statehood" . . . 1,800 years of exile and wandering, eighteen centuries of ceaseless striving to return to the Holy Land and become a people once more; Israel's staunch struggle against the pressures of Christian Byzant; the fugitives from Mahomet's sword fleeing to the land of their origin and the others coming after the Arab conquest to found in Jerusalem a home for their genius; the merciless destruction of the Jewish community by the crusaders and the victory of Saladin over the crusading empire inaugurating a new epoch of settlement; Rambam [Maimonides] comes to the land with his disciples . . . ; the persecutions in Western Europe and the expulsion from Spain bringing new streams, and Don Joseph Nasi's experiment in Galilee . . . ; the Polish *Chasidim,* the vicissitudes, and the abysmal poverty.

But a new spirit sweeps through the Diaspora; the urge to return assumes practical shape and the new epoch of *Shivat Zion,* the Return to Zion, is born amid travail—

"In recent decades they returned in their masses. They reclaimed the wilderness, revived their language, built cities and villages. . . ."

These were the builders of Petah Tikvah, the men and women of the *Bilu* movement from Russia, the founders of Rehovot and Hadera, the pioneers of the Second *Aliyah* and the stalwarts of *Hashomer,* the earliest watchmen, the builders of Tel Aviv and Hadar Hacarmel and the new Jerusalem.

". . . The First Zionist Congress . . . proclaimed the right of the Jewish people to national revival in their own country"—

the right that was acknowledged by the Balfour Declaration, in its turn incorporated in the Mandate of the League of Nations.

Two articles of the mandate are mentioned—"explicit international recognition to the historic connection of the Jewish people with Palestine and their right to reconstitute their National Home." It was this recognition which led to the *Yishuv* growing eightfold or tenfold in number. Only a "National Home" was given, but the royal commission under Lord Peel agreed that "National Home" meant a Jewish state. And a higher tribunal, the community of the world's nations, eventually recognized the right of the Jewish people to a state.

A . . . catastrophe befell the Jews of Europe, and the millions who were led off to slaughter were mute testimony to the imperative need of a Jewish state . . . as if to say, had the state existed, the calamity would not have befallen and millions . . . would have been spared. . . . The Jewish community volunteered in the last world war to fight against the forces of evil and by their blood purchased the right to be among the founders of the United Nations. . . . But the Jewish population of Palestine, which gave so much . . . was not given the right, because it was not a state.

Ben-Gurion continued reading. The Resolution of the General Assembly of the United Nations adopted on 29 November 1947, requiring the establishment of a Jewish state in Palestine, put emphasis upon the legal premise: "This recognition by the United Nations of the right of the Jewish people to establish their independent state is unassailable." For the United Nations had done nothing more than to acknowledge an existing right—"the natural right of the Jewish people to lead, as do all other nations, an independent existence in its sovereign state."

After the preamble . . . he paused for a moment, and then in a raised voice continued:

"Accordingly we, the members of the National Council, representing the Jewish people in Palestine and the World Zionist movement, are met together in solemn assembly today, the day of termination of the British Mandate for Palestine; and by virtue of the natural and historic right of the Jewish people and of the Resolution of the General Assembly of the United Nations.

"We hereby proclaim the establishment of the Jewish state in Palestine to be called *Medinat Yisrael* [the State of Israel]."

At these words the entire audience rose to its feet and burst into prolonged hand-clapping. All were seized by ineffable joy, their faces irradiated.

The chairman read the seven articles arising out of the declaration . . . [concluding]: "With trust in Almighty God, we set our hand to this declaration, at this session of the Provisional State Council, on the soil of the homeland, in the city of Tel Aviv, on this Sabbath eve, the fifth of *Iyar*, 5708, the fourteenth day of May, 1947."

He added: "Let us stand to adopt the Scroll of the Establishment of the Jewish state."

. . . Rabbi Y. L. Fishman delivered the benediction of "Who hath kept and sustained and brought us unto this day," which the aged rabbi did in a trembling voice choked with emotion. . . .

Ben-Gurion . . . read the "Proclamation" of the Provisional State Council. At the passage revoking the legal enactments arising out of the "White Paper". . . the storm of applause broke again.

Yes, it is true, an established fact: our own state. It has the power to enact laws and here we are legally repealing sections so-and-so of the Immigration Ordinance 1941 and . . . of the Defense (Emergency) Regulations 1945.

Suddenly the full impact of what had been done came home . . . —the significance of the creation of the state.

Consider what had happened: *the mass parades of protest against the White Paper, the bitter struggle, the refugee ships . . . the hunger-strikes, the death of young men and women in the flower of their radiant youth, appeals to the British High Court, executions on the gallows, and still the "White Paper"*

. . . And now the Council of State writes Finis to the bitter struggle by a stroke of the pen: . . . the White Paper is . . . dead and the Royal Navy can no longer halt refugee ships nor banish their storm-tossed human cargoes, the monthly quota of 1,500 immigrants is no more, come one come all now freely and unhindered—yes, that was the meaning of the state. . . .

The "Proclamation" was adopted by acclamation. . . .

As the signing of the document ended, *Hatikvah* was struck up by the orchestra; and . . . it seemed as if the heavens had opened and were pouring out a song of joy on the rebirth of the nation. The audience stood motionless, transfixed. . . .

"The State of Israel is established! This meeting is ended!"

It had taken thirty-two minutes in all to proclaim the independence of a people who, for 1,887 years, had been under the servitude of other nations. . . .

People embraced . . . tears of rejoicing streamed; yet there was grief for sons who had fallen and sons whose fate was in the womb of the future—grief and dread locked in the innermost recesses of the heart.

Outside thousands had gathered. . . . The streets of Tel Aviv were filled with crowds. . . .

Copies of *Day of the State,* jointly issued by all newspapers combined . . . were grabbed from shouting newsboys.

Music played by the *Voice of Israel* lilted from radios in open windows. Overhead, planes dropped leaflets urging subscription to the Independence Loan. . . . City employees posted placards announcing that recruiting for the services would go on throughout the Sabbath and into the night. . . .

Among the notices posted was one by *Haganah*. . . .

"The enemy threatens invasion. . . . The security forces are taking all necessary measures. The entire public must give its full help.

"1. Shelters must be dug in all residential areas and the orders of Air Raid Precautions officers must be obeyed.

"2. Mass gatherings in open areas and streets must be avoided.

"3. Every assistance must be given to . . . security forces in erecting barriers, fortifications, etc.

"No panic. No complacency. Be alert and disciplined."

. . . I waited for the first copies [of the Proclamation] and took two, one of them for David Ben-Gurion. When I brought it to him, he asked, "What's new in the city?"

"Tel Aviv is rejoicing and gay," I answered.

He returned soberly: "I feel no gaiety, only deep anxiety as on the 29th of November, when I was like a mourner at the feast."

From *Three Days,* by Zeev Sharef

CHAIM WEIZMANN Recounts the Recognition of the Jewish State, 1948

How would the world react to the creation of the Jewish state? Would diplomatic recognition be granted to the new government of Israel?

These questions worried the leaders of the State of Israel during that period of uncertainty and anxiety which preceded the end of the British Mandate on May 15, 1948. Chaim Weizmann, the great scientist and statesman who had succeeded in procuring the Balfour Declaration in 1917, also played a crucial role in diplomatic recognition of Israel by the United States.

Recognition by the United States was considered all-important, since many smaller states were waiting to see what it would do before they made their own decision. Weizmann's written invitation to recognize the Jewish state was favorably received by President Harry S Truman. Truman's positive response helped solidify the new country's position when she most needed it, for the armies of five hostile neighbors waited at her borders to destroy her virtually before she began to exist.

During that first hectic day, Weizmann's innumerable labors for the creation of a Jewish state were given public recognition—the new government named him the first president of the State of Israel. The drama and excitement of these critical days are contained in Dr. Weizmann's own words.

Israel's first president, Chaim Weizmann, presenting Sefer Torah to President Harry Truman. (Israel Office of Information)

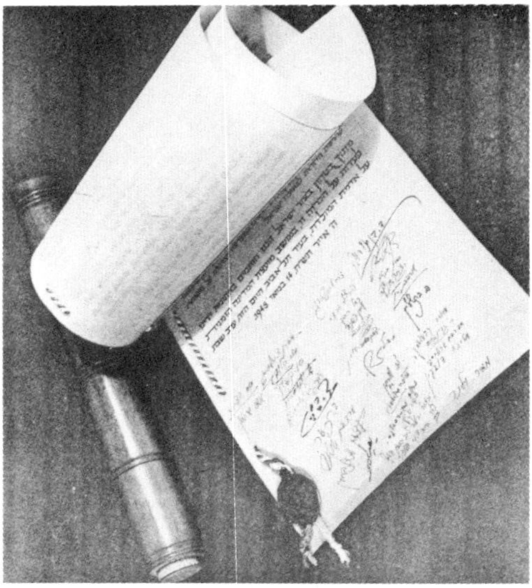

Israel's Proclamation of Independence. (Photo, Weissenstein, Zionist Archives and Library)

"I dedicate myself to service of land and people . . ."

IN THE EARLY part of May, Mr. Shertok left for Palestine . . . and I affirmed my intention of going ahead with a bid for recognition of the Jewish state as soon as it was proclaimed. On May 13, I addressed the following letter to the President of the United States [Harry S Truman]:

Dear Mr. President:

The unhappy events of the last few months will not, I hope, obscure the very great contributions which you, Mr. President, have made toward a definitive and just settlement of the long and troublesome Palestine question. The leadership which the American government took under your inspiration made possible the establishment of a Jewish state, which I am convinced will contribute markedly toward a solution of the world Jewish problem, and which I am equally convinced is a necessary preliminary to the development of lasting peace among the peoples of the Near East.

So far as practical conditions in Palestine would permit, the Jewish people there have proceeded along the lines laid down in the United Nations Resolution of November 29, 1947. Tomorrow midnight, May 15, the British Mandate will be terminated and the provisional government of the Jewish state, embodying the best endeavors of the Jewish people and arising from the Resolution of the United Nations, will assume full responsibility for preserving law and order within the boundaries of the Jewish state, for defending that area against external aggression, and for discharging the obligations of the Jewish state to the other nations of the world in accordance with international law.

Considering all the difficulties, the chances for an equitable adjustment of Arab and Jewish relationships are not unfavorable. What is required now is an end to the seeking of new solutions which invariably have retarded rather than encouraged a final settlement.

It is for these reasons that I deeply hope that the United States, which under your leadership has done so much to find a just solution, will promptly recognize the provisional government of the new Jewish state. The world, I think, will regard it as especially appropriate that the greatest living democracy should be the first to welcome the newest into the family of nations.

Respectfully yours,
Chaim Weizmann

On the fourteenth of May the President and his advisers were in constant consultation on the Palestine issue . . . In Palestine the British Mandate had only a few more hours to run [Palestine time is seven hours ahead of Washington time]. On the same day representatives of the *Yishuv,* convoked in Tel Aviv, proclaimed to the world the rightful independence of the Jewish state to take effect as of the hour of the termination of the British Mandate.

At a few minutes past six o'clock, American time, unofficial news reached Lake Success [then the site of the United Nations] that the Jewish state had been recognized by the government of the United States. The delegates were incredulous . . . The United States delegation was unaware of any such decision. Finally, after much confusion, Professor Jessup rose to read the following statement from the White House:

"This government has been informed that a Jewish state has been proclaimed in Palestine and recognition has been requested by the provisional government itself. The United States recognizes the provisional government as the *de facto* authority of the new State of Israel."

This historic statement must be regarded not only as an act of high statesmanship; . . . it set the seal on America's long and generous record of support of Zionist aspirations.

On May 15 a great wave of rejoicing spread throughout the Jewish world. We were not unmindful of the dangers which hung over the new-born state. Five Arab armies were at its frontiers, threatening invasion; our forces were not yet properly organized; we were cut off from international support. But the die was cast . . . We were now face to face with the basic realities, and this was what we had asked for. If the State of Israel could defend itself, survive and remain effective, it would do so largely on its own; and the issue would be decided . . . by the basic strength and solidity of the organism which we had created in the last fifty years.

May 15 was a very full day. Recognition was extended to the State of Israel by the Soviet Union and Poland, to be followed shortly by several countries of Eastern Europe and South America. Great Britain remained silent, and I received reports that Mr. Bevin was bringing pressure to bear on the British Dominions and Western Europe to withhold recognition. However, I bethought myself of one surviving author of the Balfour Declaration and addressed a cablegram to General Smuts. This was closely followed by South African recognition.

On this same day, amidst the avalanche of messages from Tel Aviv, there was one signed by the five Labor Party leaders . . . David Ben-Gurion, Eliezer Kaplan, Golda Myerson [Golda Meir], David Remez, and Moshe Shertok:

"On the occasion of the establishment of the Jewish state we send our greetings to you, who have done more than any other living man toward its creation. Your stand and help have strengthened all of us. We look forward to the day when we shall see you at the head of the state established in peace."

I answered:

My heartiest greetings to you and your colleagues in this great hour. May God give you strength to carry out the task which has been laid upon you and to overcome the difficulties still ahead. Please accept and transmit the following message to the *Yishuv* in my name: "On the memorable day when the Jewish state arises again after two thousand years, I send expressions of love and admiration to all sections of the *Yishuv* and warmest greetings to its government now entering on its grave and inspiring responsibility. Am fully convinced that all who have and will become citizens of the Jewish state will strive their utmost to live up to the new opportunity which history has bestowed upon them. It will be our destiny to create institutions and values of a free community in the spirit of the great traditions which have contributed so much to the thought and spirit of mankind.

Chaim Weizmann

Two days later, when I was resting in my hotel from the fatigue of the preceding weeks, a message reached me that the provisional council of state had elected me as its president . . . A few hours later the same message was repeated over the radio and was picked up in the adjoining room where my wife was entertaining friends. Almost at the same moment Aubrey Eban [Abba Eban], then one of our younger aides at the United Nations and at this time of writing the brilliant representative of Israel before that body—and, I might add, one of its most distinguished members—came in with some friends from Madison Square Garden where the Jews of New York were celebrating at a mass rally which I could not attend because of ill-health. They brought definite confirmation of the report. That evening my friends gathered in our hotel apartment and raised glasses of champagne in a toast to the President of Israel.

. . . The minister of Justice, Dr. Felix Rosenblueth, had proposed my election. Mr. Ben-Gurion, prime minister and minister of defense, had seconded it. He did not conceal the many differences of opinion which had divided us to say: "I doubt whether the presidency is necessary to Dr. Weizmann, but the presidency of Dr. Weizmann is a moral necessity for the State of Israel." I quote these words . . . only as an indication of the essential unity of purpose which underlay all those struggles of ideology and method in our movement . . . I cabled Ben-Gurion:

Many thanks your cable May seventeenth. Am proud of the great honor bestowed upon me by provisional council of government of State of Israel in electing me as its first president. It is in a humble spirit that I accept this election and am deeply grateful to council for confidence it has reposed in me. I dedicate myself to service of land and people in whose cause I have been privileged to labor these many years. I send to provisional government and people of Israel this expression of my deepest and most heartfelt affection, invoking blessing of God upon them. I pray that the struggle forced upon us will speedily end and will be succeeded by era of peace and prosperity for people of Israel and those waiting to join us . . .

My first official act as president of the State of Israel . . . was to accept the invitation of the President of the United States to be his guest in Washington and to take up the usual residence at Blair House. I traveled to Washington by special train and arrived to find Pennsylvania Avenue bedecked with the flags of the United States and Israel. I was escorted to the White House by representatives of the United States government and by Mr. Eliahu Epstein, whom the provisional government had appointed its envoy to the United States . . . I expressed our gratitude to the President . . .

. . . It had been my intention to go to England . . . I now felt no longer free to do so. Arab armies were attacking Israel . . . spearheaded . . . by the Arab Legion of Trans-Jordan, equipped by British arms, financed by the British treasury, trained and commanded by British officers . . . Their main operations were directed against the Holy City. The Hebrew University and Hadassah Medical Center were under bombardment; Jewish shrines . . . which had survived attacks of barbarians in medieval times, were now being laid waste . . . I had always believed that an anti-Zionist policy was utterly alien to British tradition, but now . . . the ideals of the State of Israel, and the policies of Great Britain, under Mr. Bevin's direction, were brought into bloody conflict . . . I felt it to be a bitter incongruity that I should not be able to set foot in a country whose people and institutions I held in such high esteem, and with which I had so long sought to link the Jewish people by ties of mutual interest and cooperation. I decided to arrange my affairs in France . . . then proceeded to Switzerland for a much-needed rest before I went on to Israel to assume my duties.

Here, in the quiet of Glion, I write these closing lines to the first part of a story which is . . . hardly begun . . . the New History of Israel.

Glion, Switzerland
August, 1948

From *Trial and Error,* the autobiography of Chaim Weizmann

YAD MORDECAI Fights to the Death, 1948

In 1943 a group of Jewish settlers from Poland and Galicia, many of them survivors of the Warsaw Ghetto, went down into the Negev. There they founded a *kibbutz* they called Yad Mordecai (literally, "Memorial to Mordecai"), in memory of Mordecai Anilewicz, the heroic commander of the Warsaw Ghetto uprising. On a small patch of arid land the refugees, who averaged twenty-eight to thirty years of age, began to rebuild their lives in the land of their people, resolved that never again would they be strangers at the mercy of others in a strange land.

But two years later the blow fell. On May 15, 1948, the British pulled out of Palestine. The next day the armies of seven Arab states struck the new-born state of Israel, in defiance of the United Nations decision. On May 18 Yad Mordecai was attacked by an Egyptian army marching up the coast to Tel Aviv. The settlers would not abandon the piece of land that was the realization of all their hopes. And once again the world stood by while they fought and died.

The colony's diary, portions of which follow, tell the story of their hopeless stand against a huge, well-equipped force. After five days the remnant of Yad Mordecai managed to withdraw from its smoking ruins. They swore that they would some day return.

Their last-ditch fight was typical of the life-and-death struggle of the State of Israel against its massive enemy. The world expected the tiny Jewish state to be overwhelmed quickly, but it put up an incredible battle for its life. When the war was over, the Arabs had been defeated and the State of Israel lived. How had they managed to win their War of Liberation? The Israelis give the answer in two words: *En bererah*—"No choice."

The Arab attack had an unanticipated result. Radio broadcasts by the Arab Higher Committee had urged the Arabs in the Jewish part of Palestine to leave until the invading armies had destroyed the Jews. Although the Jews urged them to remain (in Haifa, sound trucks went through the streets assuring them of protection), almost a million fled. Thus was born the Arab refugee problem which still plagues the Middle East. Those who remained are Israel's present-day Arab citizens, about ten per cent of its population.

The survivors of Yad Mordecai kept their promise: they returned. The *kibbutz* stands today, once more carrying on in the spirit of their fallen leader.

"Here too we had stood, as only a man is able to stand."

Tuesday, May 18

DOWN the road from our settlement . . . went a small Red Cross car driven by Grisha. He had been sent to evacuate those who had been wounded in an Egyptian attack. En route he was stopped by the Egyptians who told him they would not recognize international law and refused to permit the evacuation of the wounded. Grisha was forced to return. On his homeward trip he observed a large military force preparing to attack Yad Mordecai. He quickly roused the *kibbutz* but before they were able to reach their posts the attack began. An enemy plane dove suddenly out of the sky, dropped its bombs, and began strafing. Neither the bombs nor the bullets caused any serious damage. That night the children were miraculously evacuated. . . .

Wednesday, May 19

The murderous attack began in all seriousness . . . Air raid! Two spitfires flew over the *meshek* [farm] and dropped bombs. A fire spread in the hay-loft and in the machinery shed. *Chaverim* [members] ran about, trying to put out the fire and save the machinery. . . . More bombs fell and it became obvious that it was not worth while to attempt to extinguish it in one place only to see it start again in another. With grief we helplessly watched as the fire consumed the fruits of our years of labor.

We turned our machine guns and rifles upon the planes, with no success. The air raid lasted two hours after which we had intended to investigate our damage. But . . . enemy cannon on the eastern and southern hills started a concentrated, systematic bombardment. . . . Twenty-five hundred cannon shells were fired at us without interruption for twenty-four hours straight. The Egyptians probably intended to subdue us through this intensive bombardment alone but they were to be sadly mistaken.

The first victims fell; Avraham K., one of the members of the group called "*Cherut*" [Freedom] training and waiting for the day when they could settle on their own *kibbutz*. Moshe B., . . . who handled the Spandau machine gun, was killed when a shell splinter struck him in the neck. He left a wife and two daughters. Yitzchak, the eternal optimist even during the battle, was killed instantaneously. . . . Mundek . . . had been in the war in Poland and had fought at Stalingrad. He was telling the *chaverim* that he had never experienced such intensive fire even in the worst days on the Russian front when a shell blew his head off.

Our water tower was blasted; the fuel . . . was set on fire. Clouds of smoke rose from the *meshek*. The second barn burned to the ground. . . . The cows were hit and lay dead and dying all over the yard. What a horrible sight! To stand and watch helplessly. . . .

In spite of the destruction and the sacrifice of human lives, in spite of the fact that we were cut off from electricity and water, we were determined to defend our *meshek*. . . . The first wave of Egyptian infantry approached. About sixty men stormed Post No. 1. Others attempted to isolate this post from the others. The pillbox itself was out of commission but the *chaverim* continued their fight from the adjacent trenches. Tzvi, the commander of our front line, took a terrific toll of the enemy with his rifle. Marc Siegal succeeded in breaking up the attack by using a hand grenade. The enemy retreated leaving behind many dead and wounded. They returned, attacking more savagely. But . . . we once more disposed of them with our rifle fire.

. . . We had lost six *chaverim* killed and one seriously wounded. We estimated the enemy losses at, at least, 105 men. . . .

Thursday, May 20

In the early morning the bombardment began again. The . . . shelters built against light machine gun fire were badly hit and very dangerous to enter. The three underground air raid shelters were used as hospitals. . . . The defenders were in the trenches day and night. No one thought of rest, for the lack of reserves made it impossible to relieve anyone. The *chaverim* stood at their posts, nerves taut, watching for signs of an enemy advance. . . .

At 11:00 o'clock there began a rain of fire that surpassed even that of yesterday. During three hours volleys of three to four shells at a time fell at intervals of less than a minute. It was impossible to raise one's head to survey the immediate vicinity. The enemy fire . . . destroyed three outposts . . . but reached the very heart of the trenches as well. Tzvi and Marc, who yesterday cut down the enemy so bravely and coolly, were hit by a direct shell. Meir Finkelstein and David Reiter of the first settlers of the *kibbutz*; David Glickson, the quiet and thorough worker

. . . all were destroyed by bombs. Mundel Halpern, whose two legs were amputated and suffered greatly but silently for he did not wish to bother anyone, died in the underground hospital . . . conscious to the end.

After this death-dealing barrage . . . the Egyptians renewed their infantry assault. Again they stormed our positions and we responded with passionate molten anger and at the same time with cool military understanding. Exceptional bravery was shown by Musa Hamam when he rose out of the trenches to command the battle. . . . He lost his life. Tzvi S., who came from Outpost No. 6 to help in the most threatened sector, raised himself to shoot and was slain by an Egyptian bullet. Victor, a practical, experienced military man, got a bullet in his mouth and died. The defenders were near exhaustion but they threw back the enemy with heavy losses. . . . In the midst of . . . the most deadly bombardment the first aid nurse worked removing the wounded, giving first aid. . . .

For forty-eight hours we did not close our eyes and repulsed attack after attack. It was impossible to clean the weapons. . . . The sand covered everything. There was no telephone connection between the posts and . . . the women transmitted orders from one position to the other, at . . . risk of their lives.

During the night a small unit of *Palmach* [Israeli striking forces] succeeded in entering our besieged *kibbutz*. They were a group of courageous people, ready for battle, who had spent the last day and night nearby listening to the bombardment. . . . But when they arrived . . . they couldn't believe their eyes. . . . That night tired *chaverim* worked all night making the trenches deeper, digging connecting trenches and bunkers. . . .

Friday, May 21

The people who spent forty-eight hours in the trenches were relieved. But there was no place to rest. The shelters were filled with the wounded and with command and supply posts. Kitchen crews also worked here. The *chaverim* went back to the trenches to try to find a little rest in spite of the burning sun and the enemy fire. . . .

. . . We knew that with such an overwhelming superiority in weapons the enemy should be able to wipe out a small place like ours within a very short time. We steeled ourselves to the last ditch defense and sent out a call for help. But no help arrived. The dead animals lay all about us but it was impossible to bury them. We faced the danger of an epidemic. For the third day we were not able to wash ourselves.

In the afternoon, the enemy placed five big guns on the eastern hills and opened fire. We were unable to understand the purpose of this fire. . . . The buildings were all destroyed and no one could be seen in the yard.

Before evening the riddle was solved. Under cover of cannon fire the enemy transferred a convoy of one hundred twenty vehicles to the north. We faced the danger of being surrounded and cut off from the *Yishuv* [the Jewish community]. Our situation became worse. The injured were unable to receive adequate medical treatment. The doctor, an elderly man, lost his strength running from one position to another. The ammunition was decreasing. . . . The promised outside help had not yet arrived. The enemy now occupied all of the strategic positions around us and we faced . . . attack from all sides. . . .

Saturday, May 22

Physical exhaustion increased. The enemy maintained pressure on all of our positions. The southern sector was in their possession and in the west all of our outposts were destroyed. In our possession were two or three posts in the northern and eastern sectors. The destruction was performed by the enemy according to plan. The machine guns using tracers showed the cannons the target. The shells fell five meters from the defenders and they faced annihilation without even being able to meet the enemy man to man. The order of the day was not to leave the trenches. The pressure of the enemy after a while became somewhat weaker. The defenders now had the opportunity to use the connecting trenches and to visit the injured. . . .

How had we lost the pill box? It was a position that we were very proud of, believing that it would withstand even a hit from a two-inch mortar. The pill box had been heavily shelled and Yitzchak, the command of the post, injured in the head and close to collapse, ordered his men to withdraw, taking all of the guns and ammunition. One of his men, Zelig, with a paralyzed leg, succeeded in taking a box of ammunition while retreating. . . . All of them reached our lines safely with all of their arms. We ourselves wondered what was the source of this spiritual and physical strength which enabled us to repulse for four days and nights the unceasing enemy attacks.

Sunday, May 23

We are very troubled today. This is the fifth day and no help has reached us. There was not even an attempt to divert the enemy in order to give us a little rest. For the fifth day we drank filthy water, the stench of dead corpses permeated the air, and there was no opportunity to bury the cows, the dogs, the chickens, and the ducks. The condition of the injured became worse. No surgeons around and the Red Cross did not appear. The representatives of Egyptian civilization do not recognize international institutions. . . .

In the afternoon the cannons renewed their concert. . . . We decided to invite the position commanders to a conference to find out what the chances were of breaking through to evacuate the injured and non-combatants. Before evening enemy tanks approached. The *chaverim* were alerted. . . . Our heavy machine gun had been hit and was out of action. The other automatic weapons were covered with sand—as a result of the bombings. However, in spite of this we stormed the tank with grenades and rifles.

It was a hard battle. The tank was followed by Egyptian soldiers firing as they came. Once more our *chaverim* performed exceptionally heroic deeds. Shmulik, with a hand grenade in his hand, ran to the tank and threw his hand grenade at it. He was slain. Nissim, from the *Palmach,* who was in charge of the *Piat* (anti-tank gun), was badly injured and died. Zvi Kestenbaum, the operator of the *Spandau,* who for the past few days could be seen running from position to position constantly under fire, appeared here too . . . but before he was able to shoot he was killed. Clarus, wandering with his mortar from place to place, received a bullet through his heart. Tzvi, from the *Palmach,* the young boy in charge of the Bren gun, who was not afraid of anything and had always appeared wherever needed, lost his life too. But the tank was put out of action and the corpses of many Egyptians lay on the ground beside it. . . .

This attack had been repulsed but our *chaverim* were in bad shape . . . hardly able to fight. Almost all of our ammunition was exhausted. The best of our fighters had fallen. All of the outposts were destroyed. We were unable to relieve *chaverim* that had been fighting in hand-to-hand combat less than a half hour ago. The number of our casualties had grown.

The situation was very clear. . . . We must either surrender . . . or risk an evacuation in order to save the women, the youth, and the remnants of our exhausted fighters. We chose the second alternative despite the extreme danger. Thanks to the *Palmach* and its *Panzers* the task was performed quickly. Only one *chaver,* one *chavera* [feminine member], and one injured person fell into the hands of the enemy.

When we saw our *chaverim* falling during the battle we did not weep. But then, as we said good bye to our *meshek* the tears came to our eyes. Our greatest, most creative force and energy were invested in this place and here it had stood, magnificently, between the hills and the desert. Here too we had stood, as only a man is able to stand. Here we had given everything that is in the realm of man to give. To this place we shall return! The earth of Yad Mordecai, saturated with the blood of our loved ones, will live again under our hands!

From *Youth and Nation*, August, 1948

AN AMERICAN ARCHEOLOGIST Identifies the Dead Sea Scrolls, 1948

A young Arab herder looking for a goat in the spring of 1947 came upon the greatest biblical discovery of modern times. In a large cave off the west shore of the Dead Sea, in broken jars, he spotted rolls of leather wrapped in black cloth. The *sheikh* of his tribe took them to an antique dealer in Bethlehem and then, hoping for a better price, to the bishop of the Syrian monastery of Saint Mark in Jerusalem, who bought them for thirty-seven Israeli pounds (about $150 at that time).

In February 1948, the scrolls were brought for evaluation to Dr. John C. Trever of the American School of Oriental Research in Jerusalem. Amazed to discover that they included passages from the *Book of Isaiah,* Dr. Trever photographed them column by column. Reports of his study excited biblical scholars everywhere. The scrolls appeared to be biblical documents much older than any others extant.

Subsequently, the scrolls were brought to the Oriental Institute in Chicago, where further testing proved conclusively that they were written about 100 B.C.E., about 1,000 years before the "final text" of the *Tanach.* Hence, the Dead Sea Scrolls, as they are called, bring scholars much closer to the original text of the Bible. They also are a treasury of information about Jewish history, Hebrew, the geography of Israel, and the background of Christianity.

In the following first-hand account, Dr. Trever tells how the scrolls came to his attention and how he discovered their significance.

One of the caves in the Judean Desert which have yielded ancient manuscripts hidden more than eighteen centuries ago. (Israel Government Tourist Office)

Dead Sea Scroll, parchment from the Book of Isaiah. (Israel Office of Information)

"The more we unrolled, the harder it became for me to conceal my excitement."

SUNDAY MORNING, February 15, 1948, Dr. Millar Burrows, director of the American School of Oriental Research in Jerusalem, . . . left for a two-week trip to Iraq. . . . Dr. Burrows had appointed me acting director *pro tem*. . . .

The following Wednesday afternoon Omar, the cook, came to my room saying that someone was calling . . . about some "ancient Hebrew manuscripts." A bit skeptical of the expression "ancient Hebrew," I went to the telephone to find that Father Butros Sowmy, the head monk of St. Mark's Assyrian Orthodox Monastery in the Old City of Jerusalem was the caller. He said that while working in the library of the monastery . . . he had come upon five scrolls in ancient Hebrew about which their catalogue carried no information. . . . Since we had been avoiding visits to the Old City, I asked him if he would bring the scrolls to the school the next afternoon at 2:30. . . .[1]

Promptly at 2:30 the next day, Father Sowmy appeared with his brother, Ibrahim. . . . Opening their small leather suitcase, they showed me five scrolls wrapped in newspapers and a small fragment (4½ x 6½ cm.). Carefully they unwrapped one of the smaller rolls, which has since proved to be a part of the Sectarian Document (now called the "Manual of Discipline"). It was so brittle that they opened it only a little for me to see. Meanwhile Father Butros took out the largest one . . . I took the large one and, finding it much more pliable, . . . began slowly to unroll it. It was rolled with the end of the manuscript on the outside, and the last two columns, being on a single sheet of parchment, had become separated from the rest when the thread with which it had been sewn had disintegrated. The last column of writing covered only five-eighths of the available

---

[1] What actually had happened regarding the call has now been published in the author's *Untold Story of Qumran*, Old Tappan, Revell, 1965, which the reader will want to consult for the complete story.

space and was badly worn from handling in ancient times. I unrolled about a dozen columns, peering intently for positive indications of authenticity, not yet sure that what I was seeing was not a forgery, though the scrolls had every appearance of great antiquity. The script, though obviously Hebrew, looked strange to my inexperienced eyes.

Remembering the box of slides in my desk on "What Lies Back of Our English Bible?" I thumbed through them for the section on early Hebrew manuscripts. One glimpse at the picture of the British Museum Codex from the ninth century (Or. 4445) assured me that these scrolls were far older. The next slide was of the Nash Papyrus. . . . The similarity of the script was striking, but the picture was too small to help much. Since my cameras were at the Museum of the Department of Antiquities, I could not take a picture for study. Father Sowmy, however, permitted me to copy several lines by hand. . . .

While I copied the passage, they related to me a few details about the origin of the scrolls. Some wandering Bedouin, . . . they said, chanced upon a cave near the north west shore of the Dead Sea, high up on the cliffs. The cave had partially collapsed. . . . Some jars containing the scrolls were crushed. . . . Seeing the scrolls protruding from the fallen debris, the Bedouin pulled them out and tore off the cloth wrappings, revealing the ancient contents. They took them to the Moslem *sheikh*[2] in Bethlehem, hoping that he would buy them. The *sheikh* . . . suggested that they take the scrolls to the Assyrians in Bethlehem. When the Assyrians saw them, they called their metropolitan, Athanasius Yeshue Samuel, in Jerusalem. He offered to purchase them . . . and thus they came into the library of St. Mark's Orthodox Monastery in Jerusalem[3]. . . .

After copying two lines just as they appeared, I unwrapped

[2] Apparently they were referring to Ali Subh.

[3] When this account was originally written I deliberately telescoped the story told that first day with what was revealed later to avoid reference to the fact that an incorrect story was told to me at first.

the other scrolls. . . . Three were written on a coarse, yellow parchment, though the largest one (the *Isaiah* scroll) was thinner and showed more evidence of wear. The other two were on a deep brown leather, both showing signs of considerable deterioration. . . .

As soon as the monk and his brother had left, I set to work on the passage which I had copied. . . . A phrase repeated twice in the first line was perfectly clear . . . It seemed somewhat unusual, so I explored the Hebrew dictionary with its columns of references . . . and soon came upon a few references to this very phrase. A quick reference to the passages mentioned soon led me to *Isaiah* 65:1. What I had copied was there word for word!

Sleep was almost impossible that night. Numerous questions flooded my mind. How long was the large scroll? How much of *Isaiah* was there? Could it be authentic? Those few evidences of a corrector's hand on the last twelve columns seemed a certain argument for authenticity. But how could such a perfect manuscript be as old as the Nash Papyrus? . . . [It was considered the oldest text until the finding of the scrolls.]

None of us had dared venture into the Old City for months, but the next morning I found a good excuse to go! To gain admittance an Arab pass, received a few days before, had to be stamped by the Jaffa Gate division of the Arab Higher Committee. Miss Basimah Faris, acting secretary of the school, offered to take me there and afterwards to the Assyrian Monastery. She had difficulties convincing the Arabs guarding the Jaffa Gate that I should be admitted, but we soon were at the Arab office. There further arguments ensued, but my pass was stamped. We had little difficulty probing our way through the maze of passages to the Assyrian Monastery, where Miss Faris left me, assured that a guard from the monastery would conduct me safely out again . . . Father Butros appeared to introduce me to the metropolitan, Athanasius Yeshue Samuel, his superior. I found them both delightful people to meet. The Assyrians . . . seemed delighted to learn that their large scroll was *Isaiah*. Had I derived a date for them . . . ? they asked. I assured them that it would be some time before such a statement could be made. Then I launched into the matter of photographing them for preservation, publication, and further research. They informed me that only very rarely was anyone allowed to photograph anything in their library. My heart sank, but I tried a new attack. Did they realize that by photographing them and getting them widely distributed, their monetary value would be greatly increased—witness the Codex Sinaiticus? This argument seemed to appeal to them. . . . They finally accepted my invitation to bring the scrolls the next morning to the school, where all my equipment would be easily accessible.

Then they brought out the scrolls. . . . Eagerly I looked for other indications of authenticity. In several columns there were large insertions in a different hand. In one case three separate hands were apparent. The more we unrolled, the harder it became for me to conceal my excitement! Before we were halfway through, every shadow of a doubt had disappeared. . . . Finding what looked like the upper part of the first column, I copied out once again what I saw. . . .

It was not until after lunch that there was a moment to examine the lines copied out in the morning, but it was a new thrill to see, word for word, *Isaiah* 1:1! Much of that afternoon was occupied in making plans and arrangements for . . . photographing the scrolls the next day. Unfortunately the power lines were damaged in the afternoon, leaving the school without electricity . . . With two kerosene lamps close beside us, Dr. Brownlee and I huddled over a small table to study the form of the script and gather references to readings about ancient MSS. He found the reference to Dr. W. F. Albright's article about the Nash Papyrus, which I remembered having read a few years before, in the *Journal of Biblical Literature* for 1937 (Vol. 59 pp. 145ff.). I remembered the photograph in the front of I. M. Price's *The Ancestry of Our English Bible*, and quickly we had these before us. By midnight, we were certain in our own minds that the *Isaiah* scroll was as old or possibly older than the Nash Papyrus! . . . It all seemed incredible. . . .

Before dawn on Saturday I was at my desk again. . . . I had only thirty-six sheets of film of the proper kind. Everything was in readiness if only the lights would come on! The metropolitan and the monk arrived at 9:30, and we invited them down . . . to the laboratory where everything was in readiness —except electricity . . . I moved the easel prepared for the scrolls over to the window and took a test shot there, but just then the lights came on to stay, so I hastily moved the equipment back again to the flood lights and took another test shot. . . . The results were perfect. We had counted fifty-four columns in the *Isaiah* scroll; this made it necessary to put two columns on each sheet of film. The scroll is twenty-four feet long, made up of seventeen sheets of parchment sewn together. By noon it was obvious that we could not finish even the one scroll, and we begged the Assyrians to stay for lunch. Dr. Brownlee dashed to the kitchen to see if Helen could take care of two extras, and she obliged. By the time she called us to lunch, I had finished about forty columns. . . .

We returned to the laboratory to face the problem of repairing those first thirteen columns preparatory to photographing. It was an exciting adventure fitting the pieces together like a jigsaw puzzle. To avoid any possible damage to the writing, all the repairing had to be done on the back, and this made the task even more difficult. All the Scotch tape available gave out just as we finished the *Isaiah* scroll. We cut long strips of paper in which to roll the manuscripts. . . . Working feverishly, we completed all the repairing and photographing of the *Isaiah* and *Habakkuk* scrolls by 4:15 P.M., when a taxi called to take the Assyrians home. They consented to leave with us two of the other three scrolls and a small fragment. . . .

Sunday afternoon I went to work to repair these other scrolls and discovered that they fitted together perfectly to make a complete scroll of eleven columns (the "Manual of Discipline"). . . .

The fourth manuscript was in such bad condition that I could do no more than photograph it as it was, without attempting to unroll it. . . . The small fragment photographed is so badly preserved that it can be read only with great difficulty.[4]

. . . By Tuesday afternoon our work on the Sectarian Document scroll was completed and Dr. Brownlee and I started for the Old City to return this scroll. . . .

As quickly as possible we made prints from some of the negatives made on Saturday to send to Dr. Albright in America. . . . Once these were off we settled down to making prints of all the negatives and to study further the script and texts from the pictures. . . .

Meanwhile, as the end of the mandate approached, conditions were steadily growing worse in Palestine. We knew that we must leave soon for our own safety, but there was much yet to be accomplished with the scrolls. . . . Always the Assyrians were most cordial and helpful. . . . It was a joy to work with them. . . . The first set of negatives on the *Isaiah* scroll was not adequate for publication purposes, so I urged them to let me try again. Then arose the problem of getting films. . . . Finally after almost a week of constant searching, I found a little shop in the Old City which could provide some outdated portrait film in this size. Not satisfactory, to be sure, it had to do. . . .

In view of the conditions, we decided to press the metropolitan for permission to unroll the fourth scroll, to get it recorded also. . . . Father Butros . . . opposed the action, feeling that we had plenty to do with the others. The metropolitan assured me, however, that he would get the manuscript to us in the States. . . .

[4] It proved to be an interpretation of *Genesis*, now called the *Genesis Apocryphon*, and was published in 1956 by N. Avigad and Y. Yadin in *A Genesis Apocryphon.*

The patriarch had already urged him to pay a visit to the Assyrian communities in America. . . .

On March 15 an air letter arrived from Dr. Albright. . . . We were delighted to learn that out of his profound knowledge came confirmation of our analysis of the dating of the scrolls! In his usually exuberant manner he said, "My heartiest congratulations on the greatest manuscript discovery of modern times! There is no doubt in my mind that the script is more archaic than that of the Nash Papyrus . . . I should prefer a date around 100 B.C. . . . What an absolutely incredible find! And there can happily not be the slightest doubt in the world about the genuineness of the manuscript." . . .

. . . On March 18 we invited the metropolitan to visit the school for further discussions. . . . For the first time, then, he was made aware of the real significance of his manuscripts. He was delighted!

. . . By the middle of March there was much uncertainty about every form of transportation. . . . Returning from town the day before Good Friday (March 26), I was told that the Assyrians had sent their guard to the school with a taxi to take me to the monastery. It was urgent, they said. . . . I hastened to the Old City, filled with forebodings. . . . When the metropolitan greeted me . . . with a smile, however, all my concern vanished. He took me into his office and handed me a folded sheet of paper. Within the fold was a piece of one of the scrolls! Instantly I recognized it as a portion of the *Habakkuk* scroll; for the color of the leather on which it was written, the script, the size, and the shape all coincided. The edges were eaten away by worms, as was the beginning of that scroll, and it looked exactly like the missing right-hand part of the first column. . . .

Already jubilant over this newest addition to our valuable finds, I was made even more happy when the metropolitan informed me that Father Butros had left that morning with all the manuscripts, to take them to a place of safety outside Palestine. . . .[5]

. . . Thus I left Jerusalem on Monday morning, April 5, to fly from Lydda to Beirut, with the assurance that we had done everything possible to ensure the safety of the manuscripts and to prepare for their ultimate publication for the scholarly world.[6]

From "The Discovery of the Dead Sea Scrolls," by John C. Trever, in *The Biblical Archaeologist*, September 1948

---

[5] This statement has unfortunately often been misinterpreted to mean I rejoiced that the scrolls were illegally removed from Palestine. I had recommended their being taken to the Assyrian Monastery near the Jordan River to get them out of the war-ridden Jerusalem, but the Assyrians decided to take them to Beirut.

[6] In America, I learned with great sorrow that during the heavy fighting in the Old City that followed the end of the mandate, the Assyrian Monastery was badly damaged and Father Butros Sowmy killed.

AN AMERICAN PILOT Flies Yemenite Jews to the Promised Land, 1948

The creation of the Jewish state left Moslem rulers in Arab countries in an angry mood which portended ill for their Jewish populations. Many Jews whose lives and property were threatened emigrated when certain Arab governments offered the opportunity to those who were willing to leave almost all their possessions behind.

Practically the entire Jewish community of Yemen decided to settle in Israel. Denied access to all land and sea routes, they were rescued by an airlift aptly termed "Operation: Magic Carpet." The pious Jews from Yemen regarded their deliverance by plane a literal fulfillment of the ancient promise that God would redeem His people on "wings of eagles."

The Yemenite Jews, swarthy and fine-featured, were part of an ancient Jewish community founded before the destruction of the First Temple. They are for the most part a hard-working, religious, and gifted people. Most of their history has been marked by the twin evils of poverty and persecution. "Operation: Magic Carpet," however, was the beginning of a new life for them.

This eyewitness account, by an American pilot who flew the Yemenites to Israel, describes this momentous act of deliverance, its impact on the Yemenite Jews and on the flyers.

Operation: Magic Carpet. Immigrants from Yemen crowd every inch of space in a forty-passenger plane for the trip to Israel, January 1950. (Zionist Archives and Library)

". . . How many centuries they . . . had waited for this moment."

THE CAR drew up alongside our faithful skymaster on the hot desert airfield at Aden. We could see our patient passengers waiting in the shade of the outstretched wings. There were about one hundred fifty in the group, about half of them children, many dressed in colorful Arabian costumes, flowing robes, and stunning headdresses.

I was struck with their stunted, wizened appearance. Many were emaciated from the ordeal of their long trek from Yemen and, although they had already received considerable care at Hashed Camp, it was clear that they . . . would need a good deal of care when they arrived in Israel. It was clear to me now how we could carry so many of them and still not be overloaded.

Most of them were barefoot, but some wore tennis shoes provided by the camp at Hashed. They had very dark hair, rather wiry, and many, including the men, wore it in curls and sidelocks with ringlets down about their ears. Most of the men were bearded and many looked as though they might have stepped right out of the pages of the Old Testament. They sat under the wing, some of them smoking water pipes which stood about three feet high. . . . If they were excited about the trip it certainly was not apparent from their actions. The women and children also sat around in small groups, the children quietly disciplined to remain with their parents and keep out of the way of the ground crews. Their interest in the aircraft appeared casual and they did not wander around, touching and fingering the strange marvel of flight, as might have been expected. It seemed as though they accepted this great metal bird poised on the desert as a part of the Bible and prophecy in which they were so well versed.

They presented a strange picture, squatting in groups on the sand. Some wore the exquisite silver filigree jewelry for which the Yemenites are renowned—bracelets, earrings, and necklaces.

Many were beautiful, deeply tanned, with fine features and aristocratic faces. They were deeply religious, and . . . many were carrying with them their Bible scrolls, some probably hundreds of years old. They had little else. . . .

One swarthy fellow, barefoot in a red and white headdress and brown and white striped robe approached me while I was inspecting the craft . . . I could see his black curls hanging inside his headdress. He had dark features, bushy eyebrows, piercing black eyes that flashed in the bright sunlight and a hawk nose. He held out to me the most beautiful silver filigree bracelet I had ever seen, probably the only thing he owned besides his clothes. I could not understand what he said, but I'm sure he wanted to sell the bracelet. Unfortunately I did not take advantage of the opportunity. . . .

Before long they climbed the wooden ramp to the main door of the skymaster and were seated on the plywood benches. An attendant who spoke Yemenite Arabic and also knew some English remained with them in the cabin.

One by one the engines were started, and thus began our first flight back to Lydda Airport. The takeoff demanded much of the straining engines in the hot desert air, and almost all of the runway was used up before we were airborne. The load of passengers was noticeable in the performance of our plane, and our rate of climb was low. . . . We finally leveled off at 9,000 feet and after cruise power was set and all was functioning in good order, I took leave of the cockpit for a look at our passengers. Upon opening the door, I saw a scene of crowded tranquility. Most of the passengers had been lulled to sleep by the droning engines. Some were staring through the windows in a relaxed manner, perhaps looking for the Promised Land which they would not see until another seven hours had passed. What a short link of time in the chain spanning thousands of tortured years ere their return! An eternal link forged from the ultimate in a modern technology and fitted to an ancient prophecy which even now was drawing up the anchor of a forgotten age. I thought of the marvel of flight . . . and wondered what they thought of it. I saw one woman thoughtfully touching the circular frame of a window, her delicate fingers vibrating in tune with the quivering pulse of the plane. A mechanical phenomenon, explained in the intricate formulae of vibration mechanics, but, to her, was it perhaps evidence of a living pulse coursing through the great eagle that was winging her homeward?

The return flight was quite beautiful, flying up the middle of the Red Sea toward the Gulf of Aqaba. The sky was a clear, turquoise blue and, below, an occasional ship could be seen plying its way along the sea lanes where three millennia before the ships of King Solomon had sailed. As we droned along in the sky, I thought of the patient people in the cabin behind us . . . and how many centuries they and their ancestors had waited for this moment. No more blocks to their return to Israel now. . . . This time no Red Sea would have to part. . . . We were high above, and somewhere down there, west of Suez, there was a crossroads in the sea where only time separated two epochs of history.

Presently we were flying up the Gulf of Aqaba past the rugged terrain of the Sinai Peninsula. Off our left wing in the distance I could see Mt. Sinai, where Moses received the Ten Commandments, which even now were riding with us on ancient Yemenite parchments, and where the Lord had called unto Moses saying, "Ye have seen what I did unto the Egyptians and how I bare you on eagles' wings and brought you unto Myself." Suddenly I understood . . . the attitudes of the other pilots I had met on the airlift and their quiet devotion to their work in this inspired airlift. I became at this moment an integral part of "Operation: Magic Carpet."

Late afternoon and fatigue can do queer things to a pilot, even two in the cockpit at the same time. We were descending over the Negev Desert toward Lydda when what appeared to be Lydda Airport came into sight. We called Lydda Tower and were cleared to land, although we were advised they did not have us in sight. This meant nothing to us until, as we swung into final approach and were over the end of the runway, we realized too late and with embarrassing suddenness that we were landing on the wrong airport. It turned out to be Aqir Field, an Israeli military airfield. . . .

During the landing rollout on the runway I could see a number of varied types of aircraft on either side of the field. These were of the primary basic and advanced trainer category such as Piper Cubs, BT-13 basic trainers, and AT-6 advanced trainer types. Nowhere, however, could I see evidence of planes of up-to-date combat capability, and I was amazed to think that the Israeli air force had been able to carry on a successful war in the air with such modest equipment. The courage and skill of the Israeli pilots must have been great indeed to have done so well with so little. As we came to a halt, a military jeep loaded with Israeli air force brass raced over to our plane, and it required some rather talented explanation to account for our predicament. The officers were very understanding, however, and in fact took a rather humorous view of the situation, although perhaps a little too much so to suit our ruffled pride. . . . We were permitted to depart for Lydda where we landed about ten minutes later. . . .

Our Yemenite passengers deplaned in orderly fashion, their shining, radiant faces portraying their joy in being at last in the Promised Land. As if in a dream they quietly proceeded to the JDC center at the airport. . . . For these good people the prophecy of Isaiah had been fulfilled: "But they that wait for the Lord shall renew their strength; They shall mount up with wings as eagles; They shall run, and not be weary; They shall walk, and not faint." (*Isaiah* 40:31)

From *I Flew Them Home*, by Edward Trueblood Martin

SIMON WIESENTHAL Finally Tracks Down Adolf Eichmann, 1960

The passion for justice has been a dominant theme in Judaism ever since the Ten Commandments were given. Justice requires both the protection of the innocent and the punishment of the guilty. To this end Simon Wiesenthal, a compassionate and sensitive Jew, has devoted his life. He tracked down Nazi war criminals in order to bring them before the bar of justice.

Wiesenthal, who was born in 1908 in Buczaca, Poland (originally part of the Austro-Hungarian Empire), survived a Nazi concentration camp. Allied troops found him lying in a ward full of corpses when they liberated the Mauthausen Concentration Camp on May 5, 1945. Virtually his entire family had died in Nazi gas chambers. The horrors he had seen and his grievous personal losses motivated Wiesenthal's relentless search for those responsible for this colossal crime.

His task was not easy. Nazi sympathizers, unfriendly government officials, and the human capacity to forget have erected obstacles at every turn. Nevertheless, his Jewish Documentation Center in Vienna led to the capture of almost 1,000 notorious Nazis, including the SS officer who arrested Anne Frank. Wiesenthal is quite the opposite of the "ruthless hunter" and "obsessive avenger" that he has been called. He has served rather as the conscience of humanity which must not forget the horrors of the past lest they be repeated in the future.

In the following pages, Simon Wiesenthal recounts his patient and tireless pursuit of Adolf Eichmann, whom he located after a sixteen-year search.

"How do you like that? Some of the worst criminals got away."

MY HOBBY [stamp collecting] . . . gave me a new clue in the Eichmann case when I was at the end of my wits.

Late in 1953, I met an old Austrian baron in the Tyrol, who invited me to his villa near Innsbruck. We were both ardent philatelists and the baron wanted to show me his collection. I spent a pleasant evening with him, admiring his stamps. Afterward we had a bottle of wine and talked. The baron was a decent old man, a life-long monarchist and devout Catholic. He listened with deep interest when I told him about my work. He knew of some big Nazis in the Tyrol who were back in high positions, "as though nothing had changed." It was shocking, he said.

The baron got up and opened a drawer full of envelopes, which he had saved for their unusual stamps. While looking through the pile he told me of a friend in Argentina, a former German lieutenant-colonel who had not gone higher in the Wehrmacht because he was known as an anti-Nazi. Last year he had gone to Argentina, where he now worked as an instructor in Peron's army.

"He just sent me a letter," said the baron, handing me the envelope. "Beautiful stamps, aren't they? I asked him whether he met any of our old comrades down there. Here is what he writes:

" 'There are some people here we both used to know. You may remember Lieutenant Hoffmann from my regiment and Hauptmann Berger from the 188th Division. . . . Imagine whom else I saw—and even had to talk to twice: *dieses elende Schwein Eichmann, der die Juden kommandierte* [this awful swine Eichmann who commanded the Jews]. He lives near Buenos Aires and works for a water company.'

"How do you like that?" said the baron. "Some of the worst criminals got away."

I said nothing, afraid that the baron might notice my excitement . . . I casually asked to look at the letter, pretending to be interested in the new Argentine stamps. I reread the passage about Eichmann and memorized each word. Later, in my hotel room, I wrote the words down. . . . My elation was short-lived, though. Suppose we found a man who looked like Eichmann living near Buenos Aires and working for a water company—improbable though this was—how could we get him? What could I, a private citizen half the world away, do? The Germans were a strong political force in Argentina where Peron's army was being trained by Germans; Argentine industries were run by German experts and Argentine banks supported by German capital.

Eichmann must have felt quite safe in Argentina, or he wouldn't have sent for his family. Perhaps he had powerful friends there. . . .

I realized that my work as a private investigator had now come to an end. From here on more powerful people would have to take over. Arie Eschel, the Israeli consul in Vienna, had asked me to prepare for the Jewish World Congress a complete report on the case. I wrote a report that began with the first mention I'd heard of Eichmann and ended with the passage from the letter the Austrian baron had received. I added Eichmann's photographs, copies of his personal letters, samples of his handwriting. I sent one copy to the Jewish World Congress in New York the other to the Israeli consulate in Vienna.

There was no answer at all from Israel. Two months after I'd sent off the material, I got a letter from New York. A Rabbi Kalmanowitz wrote that he had received the material and "would appreciate Eichmann's exact address in Buenos Aires." I replied I would send a man to South America if they would defray his travel expenses and give him five hundred dollars. Rabbi Kalmanowitz wrote that they had no money.

It was time to give up. Obviously, no one cared about Eichmann. The Israelis had more reason to be concerned about Nasser. I closed the Documentation Center in March 1954, had all files packed . . . and sent them to the *Yad Vashem* Historical

Archives in Jerusalem. I kept only one large file for myself, the Eichmann file.

Five years later, on the morning of April 22, 1959, I was going through the Linz newspaper *Oberosterreichische Nachrichten.* On a back page there was an obituary notice for Frau Maria Eichmann, Adolf Eichmann's stepmother. Underneath were the names of the survivors. Adolf Eichmann was not among them, but the last name was Vera Eichmann. People usually don't lie when they write obituary notices. It said "Vera Eichmann." Apparently Frau Eichmann had been neither divorced nor remarried. I cut out the obituary notice and put it on top of my Eichmann file.

Late in August 1959, a telephone call from Linz reached me in Murten, Switzerland, where I was spending the holidays with my family. I was told that several people had seen Adolf Eichmann in Altaussee. . . . I reported the news to the Israeli ambassador in Vienna and decided to return at once. My wife was unhappy; she said, quite rightly, that we still had twelve days of vacation all paid for. Why did we have to leave? I said we *had* to leave. . . .

Times were changing again. In recent weeks, the Israeli papers had published new stories about Eichmann, reporting on his crimes and speculating on his whereabouts. There were also many trials of Nazi criminals in Germany and Austria these days. My letter to the Israeli ambassador had arrived at the right moment. He sent it to Jerusalem and gave a copy to the Federation of Jewish Communities of Austria in Vienna. They informed the Austrian minister of the interior. He asked the authorities to get in touch with me. Eichmann was still on the Austrian "wanted" list.

After my return to Linz I talked to my friends. Of course it wasn't Adolf Eichmann who had been seen in Altaussee but one of his brothers—the usual Altaussee rumor. But things began moving now. Two young men from Israel, whom I shall call Michael and Meir, came to see me. There was great interest in the case there; they asked me to continue where I had left off in 1954. In Frankfurt am Main, the prosecutor preparing the trial of SS men from Auschwitz told me that Eichmann led the list of accused criminals and asked for my cooperation. . . . I was deeply involved once more. . . . I went to the Tyrol, hoping to get from the old baron the name of his friend in Buenos Aires who had written the letter six years ago. But the baron was dead and his stamp collection had been sold.

Next I sent one of my men to see Frau Eichmann's mother. Frau Maria Liebl was not very friendly but admitted that her daughter had married a man named "Klems" or "Klemt" in South America. She said she had no address for them and received no letters. She asked my man to let her alone.

I sent what information I had to Israel. On October 10, 1959, I had a message. . . . They had investigated in South America and found the address of Frau Eichmann, who was said to live "in fictitious marriage" with a German named Ricardo Klement. I was sure that it was a real marriage—that Frau Eichmann lived with her husband Adolf Eichmann. Otherwise the Eichmann family in Linz wouldn't have listed her as Vera Eichmann in the obituary notices. The Eichmann boys lived in Buenos Aires with their parents. It occurred to me that they would probably be registered there at the German embassy, since they would soon reach military age. I asked a friend to make a cautious inquiry. He notified me that the Eichmann boys had indeed been registered there, under their real names. (An embarrassed official later claimed that he "had not known these were the sons of Adolf Eichmann.")

On February 6, 1960, the *Oberosterreichische Nachrichten* in Linz published the obituary of Eichmann's father, Adolf Eichmann. . . . Among "daughters-in-law" it again said "Vera Eichmann." . . . Adolf Eichmann had been devoted to his father. . . . There was an outside chance of Eichmann's coming to the funeral. I was told that the funeral would take place in five days "because the family expects relatives from abroad." . . .

Michael and Meir . . . had to get the right man. They urgently needed a picture of Adolf Eichmann as he looked today. We had no recent picture; but perhaps could get something almost as good. . . . I went to the cemetery and looked at the location of the grave. . . . I took a train to Vienna and talked to two friends, expert photographers, at the Presseklub. I asked them to come to Linz and photograph the Eichmann family . . . during the funeral. . . . They must remain unseen.

They did a fine job. Hiding behind large tombstones at a distance of about two hundred yards, they made sharp pictures of the funeral procession, although the light was far from perfect. That night I had before me enlarged photographs of Adolf Eichmann's four brothers. . . . Adolf had not come. . . .

I took the old picture of Adolf Eichmann made in 1936, twenty-four years ago. . . . I took out a magnifying glass and studied the features of the five brothers. Many people had told me that Adolf Eichmann most closely resembled his brother Otto. Looking at the photographs through the magnifying glass I suddenly understood why so many people had sworn they'd seen Adolf Eichmann in the past years in Altaussee when they had seen one of his brothers. They all looked very much alike. The family resemblance was astonishing. . . .

. . . Adolf Eichmann's face must have gone through the same evolution as the faces of his brothers. I cut from the photographs the faces of the four brothers at the funeral and the face from the old picture of Adolf Eichmann. I shuffled the faces like playing cards and threw them on the table. Somehow a composite face emerged: perhaps Adolf Eichmann.

When Michael and Meir came to see me again, I performed the Eichmann card trick. "This is how he must look now. Probably closest to his brother Otto. All five brothers have the same facial expression. Look at the mouth, the corners of the mouth, the chin, the form of the skull."

Michael shook his head, staring at the pictures. "Fantastic."

Meir grabbed the pictures. "May we take them?"

Suddenly they were in a hurry. I didn't want to detain them, not for a second. . . .

On Monday, May 23, 1960, Prime Minister David Ben-Gurion told the Israeli *Knesset* [Parliament] that Eichmann . . . was in an Israeli prison. A few hours later, I had a cable of congratulations from the *Yad Vashem* in Jerusalem.

Some time after, I met one of my former "clients." He had once been a prominent SS man. Now he often comes to my office for a quiet chat about the bad old days. He came in, clicked his heels, shook hands, and said: "Congratulations, Herr Wiesenthal. *Saubere Arbeit* [Nice work]."

He meant it, too.

From *The Murderers Among Us,* by Simon Wiesenthal

GIDEON HAUSNER Talks about the Eichmann Trial, 1962

Karl Adolf Eichmann was an Austrian Nazi from Linz, the hometown also of Adolf Hitler. From the very beginning he headed the Jewish Office of the Gestapo which had complete control over all questions related to the Jewish people. At first the office engaged in the lucrative trade of swapping Jews for money and essential goods. Eventually it became an agency to organize the slaughter of six million Jews.

Eichmann's reports to Hitler proudly announced the success of his mass extermination procedures. He was responsible for the "final solution" to the Jewish question—total annihilation of European Jewry. According to a co-worker, Eichmann declared that "he would leap laughing into the grave because the feeling that he had five million people on his conscience would be for him a source of extraordinary satisfaction." Nevertheless, apparently with second thoughts about jumping into the grave, Eichmann clung to life in an American internment camp from which he escaped in 1945, in Argentina, and during his trial by an Israeli tribunal for crimes against the Jewish people and against humanity.

The trial, which adhered closely to established legal procedures, disclosed to a shocked and incredulous world the extent of German barbarism. Israeli law prohibits capital punishment except for cases of treason. The court, however, determined that although there was no adequate punishment for crimes so heinous anything less than the death penalty for Eichmann would have been a travesty.

The trial of Adolf Eichmann helped teach a new

generation, which was too young to remember World War II, what the Jews had undergone and the true meaning of the State of Israel.

The following account of certain aspects of the case was written by Gideon Hausner, attorney general of Israel.

"There is nothing I have to regret. Had we killed the eleven million Jews as contemplated, however, I would have been happier."

SHORTLY AFTER Eichmann was caught in Argentina and brought to my country, I realized he might attempt to plead insanity. To be ready for such a maneuver, I ordered him examined by psychiatrists. One of the many tests given him was the famous one invented by the Hungarian psychologist, L. Szondi. The accused is shown a long series of photographs. In each group are pictures of a convicted murderer and a proven sadist. The subject is asked to select from each group two photographs of people who attract him and two who repel him. Eichmann was given the test ten times in forty days . . . a total of two hundred forty times.

The important thing about the test, of course, is the interpretation of the results. . . . We decided to have the results sent to the inventor himself, Professor Szondi. It was not revealed who the subject was.

Doctor Szondi's reply astonished me. He started by saying that he never analyzed tests of people who had not been identified for him but that when he'd glanced briefly at the results they were so extraordinary that he performed a complete analysis. The subject, he declared, revealed in all phases "a man obsessed with a dangerous and insatiable urge to kill, arising out of a desire for power." In every group of photographs he had unerringly picked out the murderer and the sadist as people who appealed to him. According to Doctor Szondi, this had never happened to him in his twenty-four years of practice as a criminal psychologist, a period in which he'd tested more than 6,000 criminals.

Other psychiatric tests . . . confirmed that we had on our hands a dangerous, perverted, sadistic personality. . . . However, they also confirmed he was legally sane and responsible for his actions. Eichmann's feeling about Jews started with anti-Semitism and developed into much more. In the end it was no ordinary hatred. In order to hate, one must feel. It is impossible, for example, to hate a chair or a table. And to Eichmann, Jews were nothing more—in fact, far less. In short, he was the final, undiluted product of the murderous Nazi regime—a man chosen because of his special qualities to perform the grisly task of exterminating 6,000,000 Jews. And he did his job so well that he was once able to say that, although Germany had lost the war, nonetheless "I can joyously jump into my grave, knowing my mission has been fulfilled."

Humanity deserves the fullest possible picture of a system of government and of a man able to spread a deadly dragnet over most of Europe and scoop up millions of men, women, and children for slaughter in one of the greatest crimes of all time. . . .

. . . There were many like him, and he had legions of assistants. . . . Many millions of Germans were aware of what was going on. The regime started by indoctrinating the German people with notions of racial superiority and the denial of moral duties toward their fellow men. "Thou shalt not" ceased to exist for them. Next, they instilled hatred and contempt for aliens. Later . . . they were ready to embark on mass slaughter.

. . . Although we were trying a single murderer, we were also exposing the whole Nazi movement and anti-Semitism at large. . . .

Prior to that fateful morning when the trial started in Jerusalem, I had never laid eyes on Eichmann. My first glimpse of him, however, was a shocker.

I already knew a good deal about him, of course. I had collected and examined documents. . . . I had talked with witnesses—most of them his intended victims—and I had read statements he had made during the long police interrogation. I also knew a good deal about how he functioned as a Gestapo—Nazi secret police—official in the hierarchy, in direct charge of "the final solution of the Jewish problem"—that is, death. . . .

I was fully aware of his ruthlessness. I had seen numerous pleas addressed to him to spare the lives of certain Jews. Some had been written even by Nazi big shots who, for reason of bribery or economic policy, wished certain Jews temporarily spared. Eichmann's reply to all such requests had been a resounding "No!" On one occasion, he even bucked Hitler himself. The *Führer* [Leader], late in the war, made a concession to the wavering government in Hungary to allow 8,700 Jewish families to leave, provided the rest of the Hungarian Jews—about 400,000—were handed over to the Nazis. Eichmann was so outraged at the possibility of this tiny remnant of Jewry escaping that he actually appealed to Hitler to change his decision and finally got the *Führer* to do so.

Eichmann frequently came to grips with high officials who felt that winning the war was more important than annihilating Jews. Toward the end . . . military men insisted that Germany needed every man, every rifle, and every railroad train. They did not want these diverted to concentration camps. They wanted the Jews to be put to work. . . . However, in the teeth of all this pressure, Eichmann stubbornly managed to keep his death juggernaut rolling, killing as many as 18,000 Jews a day. There was no stopping him.

. . . I half expected to encounter some of the arrogance, some of the posture, and some of the diabolic strength of this Gestapo leader.

The shocker . . . was that I saw none of these things. In fact, Eichmann looked like nothing much at all. The man facing me was the kind you might rub elbows with in the street any day and never notice. He was nondescript, in his middle fifties, balding, lean, of dark complexion, and of medium height. The first unusual thing one noticed was a twitch around his mouth which gave his face a strange, almost grotesque appearance. Only his narrow eyes behind the heavy eyeglasses disclosed his real personality. When he was cornered on some particularly slippery ground, those eyes would light up with bottomless hatred. Once, when this happened, my assistant tugged at my robe and whispered, "Did you notice his eyes? They frightened me."

But such moments were rare. Almost immediately Eichmann was able to revert to his usual, gray, nondescript appearance. . . .

According to Israeli law, after the pretrial interrogation, an accused man must be shown *in advance* every piece of evidence, every document, every statement of every witness who will testify at the trial. Unlike American prosecutors, Israeli ones cannot introduce anything the defense doesn't know about.

Eichmann made the most of this situation. He studied the hundreds of things we planned to introduce and memorized most of them. . . . He made extensive notes, turning his glass cubicle into a one-man office. He even had a special microphone in his bulletproof "office" by which he could communicate with his counsel, Dr. Robert Servatius.

. . . Eichmann carefully constructed a picture of himself best calculated to save his life. If—as was proved—Jews were segregated, starved, looted, tortured, turned into slave workers, and eventually destroyed in camps, Eichmann's portrait of himself never varied: he was a mere clerk arranging train schedules and other minor details. . . . He maintained that he never displayed any initiative or made independent decisions; he was always acting under orders.

. . . We proved that Eichmann displayed a lot of initiative and authority. For example, we introduced a handwritten memo from a German official who said that when he asked Eichmann what to do with the Jews in Belgrade he got the reply, "Shoot them on the spot!" Another Nazi official wrote that Eichmann had "agreed" to exterminate Jews by poison gas rather than by shooting. These obviously were not the decisions of a mere train scheduler.

We also introduced Eichmann's orders showing how he diabolically lulled his victims into a feeling of confidence that nothing would happen to them if they only "behaved themselves"—that is, wore the yellow badge proclaiming their Jewishness, turned over their property to the state, and quietly took the special trains to the "work camps" which were actually extermination camps. We showed how Eichmann's orders were so skillfully thought out that most Jews were unaware of what was really happening to them until they were on the point of being gassed. Even at the entrance to the death chambers, the victims were told they were merely to be disinfected. Small children were handed pieces of candy to keep them quiet.

All these things were done at Eichmann's behest. Nonetheless, he insisted that in everything he was merely acting under orders. When a document proved that he was acting on his own authority, he took the last retreat: he branded it as a forgery!

Knowing the evidence that we had, Eichmann still half expected somehow to escape with his life. In fact, just before the cross-examination he said to one of his guards, "So long as Mr. Hausner sticks to the documents, I am on safe ground." But, when particularly damaging admissions were elicited from him in questioning, he remarked that he never expected cross-examination to be like this, adding, "I don't like the attorney general."

The portrait Eichmann presented in court rarely brought out his total lack of remorse. Four years prior to the trial, when Eichmann had a long discussion in Argentina with the Dutch journalist, Willem A. Sassen, he declared, "There is nothing I have to regret. Had we killed the eleven million Jews as contemplated, however, I would have been happier." (The figure of 11,000,000 referred to the total European Jewish population, including those in Russia, Great Britain, Ireland, Switzerland, Turkey, and other countries which the Nazis optimistically expected to get their hands on when they won the war.) . . .

It became increasingly clear that the only things that really mattered to Eichmann were the formalities. The true significance of his unbelievable acts never bothered him. . . . We had a striking example of this. . . .

One evening . . . we were previewing in the courtroom some films we wished to introduce as evidence. Some depicted shattering scenes of helpless victims being loaded on trains like cattle. Others, surreptitiously shot inside the camps, showed all the ghastly details of mass slaughter. There were pictures of naked men, women, and children being lined up before the Nazi execution squads. . . . We witnessed one wave of writhing corpses after another fall into the deep open grave dug beforehand by the victims themselves.

Finally came scenes of the liberation when thousands of bodies had to be shoveled by bulldozers into mass graves for fear of infection. They were pictures of unspeakable horror—the kind that turn one's stomach. . . .

The courtroom was almost empty at the time. The judges were not there nor was the general public admitted. The defense counsel, Doctor Servatius, and the accused were in their usual places. Suddenly, Eichmann, who had been watching the films calmly and unperturbed, never lowering his gaze or missing a scene, started an agitated argument with his guards. Everybody expected an objection as to the truthfulness of the pictures. . . . However, the reason was quite different. He had noticed people sitting in the seats reserved for the public and, on being told that they were journalists, he protested against having been brought to the courtroom in slacks and a sweater instead of the dark blue suit provided him for the trial.

Another incident underlined the man's unusual concern with externals.

One evening he developed a rheumatic pain in his right arm. It hampered the putting on of his earphones to get the simultaneous translation of the proceedings in German. He asked the doctor for medicine to relieve the pain at once so that he would put on the earphones in the usual way. "I don't want to appear clumsy in my movements," he explained. The doctor complied. . . .

I doubt whether Eichmann ever entered the courtroom without first neatly adjusting his tie or patting his hair in order. . . .

In all this, Eichmann was true to the Gestapo type, which Dr. G. M. Gilbert, the Long Island University professor who was the prison psychologist at the Nuremberg trials of the Nazi war criminals, summed up: "An inhuman, murderous robot, quiet and correct in military bearing, functioning intellectually on a high level of mechanical efficiency, utterly devoid of human empathy."

Eichmann gave a droll illustration of the way this mechanical man operates. One morning he was given by mistake six slices of bread for breakfast instead of the usual two. He ate all six. When the guard asked whether he'd like six in the future, he replied: "Oh, no. Two are quite enough. But when you give me six, I have to eat them." On another occasion he asked that a portion of onions be removed from his tray because the particles got in his dentures. It never occurred to him simply to leave the onions uneaten.

Eichmann's mask was so impassive that it was only such things as his eating habits occasionally gave us a glimpse of how the evidence was affecting him. . . . Before the trial, he was questioned about a secret Berlin meeting in 1939 . . . to arrange that all Polish Jews be concentrated in ghettos near railroad junctions . . . for the "final solution." Eichmann . . . denied that he was there. . . . But, when we produced a document showing that he was one of the sixteen high-ranking Nazis at the conference, he replied, "Of course, it cannot be denied any more that I was there." That day Eichmann . . . asked if he might be excused from having lunch or dinner.

. . . Eichmann remained fanatically hostile to religion. . . . He admitted that he became so infuriated when his wife read a Bible that he snatched it away and tore it to pieces. He refused to take an oath on the Bible, saying that he did not belong to any church. Although he had frequent conversations with the Rev.

William Hall, a Protestant clergyman, he was never reconciled to religion. . . . He died as he lived—a pagan. He had a kind of mystic belief in the unity of the universe and in man's being solely a biological product.

. . . We found him one of the most garrulous prisoners on record. His pretrial statement, recorded on tape, covered 3,564 typewritten pages—the equivalent of six long novels. And this did not include his extensive personal notes, memoirs, observations on documents, charts, etc.

He revealed . . . an astonishing memory. He could remember in smallest detail the books he had read in the twenties, the name of the German consul who had given him a visa in Linz in 1933, the names of all the persons he met on a trip to Egypt in 1937, the price of a meal and a glass of beer at a military canteen twenty-five years before. "A roll was given extra without charge," he recalled.

It was only in matters relating to Jews that he had a lapse of memory. He couldn't remember what he'd seen at extermination camps. . . . He couldn't remember when he had first ordered Jews to their death. And he couldn't remember why it was necessary for him to send three retroactive orders to Poland to "cover" the execution of 750,000 human beings that had already taken place, killings over and beyond the quota prescribed by Berlin. It was, of course, needed to make the Nazi records "legal." His earlier feats of memory had been so stunning that no one could seriously believe he was capable of such monumental lapses.

Time and again I asked Eichmann in court what made him consider the Jews, who were less than 1 percent of the population of Germany, the main "disaster" of the country. His reply was that the Jews were "opponents." Opponents had to be combated.

The idea of solving problems by the physical annihilation of opponents was not new to Eichmann. He once suggested to Gestapo Chief Heinrich Muller that half a million Germans who did not wholeheartedly support the Nazi measures be executed.

At the height of his career Eichmann was a man of towering

arrogance. During the war he strutted across Europe in his smart uniform, topped with the SS cap complete with skull and crossbones. In winter he wore a long leather overcoat on which, according to his own evidence, the brain of a baby was once spilled when he came too near an execution squad liquidating the Jewish population of Minsk in 1941.

His name was whispered in horror throughout the ghettos of Europe. As supreme head of the Gestapo department dealing with Jews, Eichmann had offices in Berlin, Vienna, Prague, Paris, Oslo, The Hague, and other capitals. . . . He operated so deftly that Gestapo Chief Muller was once moved to say, "If Germany had had fifty Eichmanns, we would have won the war!" . . .

In court we saw a totally subdued Eichmann. . . . He knew that creating a picture of a small man, forced . . . into doing things he did not like, gave him his best chance for saving his neck.

. . . I knew that Eichmann was a sly, cunning opponent . . . clever enough to elude his trackers for fifteen long years—in which he'd had ample time to prepare for a trial. . . . Because he destroyed all records of his Gestapo office and because he knew in advance of our documents and witnesses, he had the advantage of being able to allege or deny facts that we could not refute except by general questioning. It was clear, too, that the court of Israel would insist on strict compliance with the rules of procedure and evidence.

Consequently . . . when Eichmann—looking and acting like an insignificant clerk with a faulty memory—appeared before me for the first time that spring morning in Jerusalem, I realized it would not be easy to convince the court that he was indeed the archmonster who presided over the liquidation of 6,000,000 Jews in the shooting pits and gas ovens of the Nazi overlords.

From "Eichmann and His Trial," by Gideon Hausner,
in *The Saturday Evening Post,* November 3, 1962

ELIE WIESEL Attends Yom Kippur Services in Moscow, 1964

When czarist tyranny was overthrown in 1917, the Jews of Russia, who had suffered so long, looked forward to better times. The Communist successors to the Romanovs, however, continue to hamper the practice of Judaism and to fan the flames of anti-Semitism. Although there is little physical persecution of Russia's 3,000,000 Jews—the second largest Jewish community in the world—the USSR does all it can to deter Jews from learning about their heritage and practicing their faith. The godless regime reviles religion as superstition, uses secret police to undermine synagogue activity, and deliberately drives a wedge between the old and the young. The shortage of prayer books and other religious objects and the difficulty of securing *matzah* for Passover also testify to the Kremlin's hostile attitudes.

Unlike other faiths in the USSR, which are permitted to maintain seminaries and to keep in touch with coreligionists in other countries, Judaism has no place to train rabbis and Jews are not allowed contact with Jewish organizations elsewhere. Thus, Russian Jewry faces extinction.

Nonetheless, many Jews of all ages still identify openly with Jewish religious life. Deprived of news about the modern State of Israel, they obtain inspiration and hope from the ancient messianic vision of Zion reborn, where they dream of some day finding their own salvation. Elie Wiesel, the sensitive Jewish writer who survived the Nazi holocaust, reveals the longing of many Russian Jews in this description of his 1964 visit to a Moscow synagogue on Yom Kippur.

"Next year in Jerusalem!"

IF THERE IS one place in the world where the State of Israel is regarded not as a territorial unit operating according to its own laws and within its own borders but as a distant dream filling the veins of reality with sacred blood, that place is the Soviet Union. It is only the Jews of Russia who have yet to be infected with cynicism toward the Jewish state, who still identify the earthly Jerusalem with its heavenly counterpart, the eternal city that embraces a Temple of Fire.

Isolated behind walls of fear and silence, the Jews of Russia know nothing of the secular affairs of Israel. . . . For them the Jewish state is wrapped in a prayer shawl of purest blue. Its citizens are all righteous men and heroes; otherwise, they would not be living there.

It happened on Yom Kippur in the Great Synagogue of Moscow. Outside it was already dark. The last prayer was almost over. Old men wept as the gates of heaven began to close; the Book of Judgment was being sealed—who shall live and who shall die, who shall be set free and who shall be afflicted. Their tears were a last effort to rend the skies and avert some terrible decree.

The hall was tense and crowded; the worshipers perspired heavily, suffocating from the heat and the effects of their daylong fast. No one complained. Outside, a large crowd was trying to push its way in. There was no room, but somehow they would manage. If there were places for two thousand, there would be places for three. An air of expectancy swept over the congregation.

Something was about to happen. They seemed nervous, serious, as if preparing for a dire and momentous act, a collective act that would be remembered forever.

The cantor finished the last prayer for forgiveness. He quickened his pace, as if rushing toward some critical event. "Our Father our King, seal us in the Book of Life. Our Father our King, do it for the sake of the little children." Everyone seemed to be standing on tiptoe. *Kaddish* [the memorial prayer]. Another minute. They counted the seconds. The cantor proclaimed, "*Adonai hu ha-Elohim,* God is the Lord!" Seven times, with the congregation responding after him. The old sexton brought the *shofar* [ram's horn blown on the High Holy Days]. *Tekiah* [the call for a prolonged blast on the *shofar*]. The congregation held its breath. And then it happened. As if in response to a mysterious command from an unknown source, three thousand Jews turned as one body toward the visitors' section, stood up straight and tall, facing the representatives of Israel, looking directly into their eyes, as if trying to read in them their past and their future, the secret of their existence. Then in the awful mounting silence they suddenly burst into a wild spontaneous cry which seemed to issue from a single throat, a single heart: "Next year in Jerusalem! Next year in Jerusalem! Next year in Jerusalem!"

The dramatic intensity of this moment immediately brought to my mind similar occurrences in the Middle Ages when, with a single nod of the head, with a single declaration of faith, Jews sanctified the Name and died. No one had forced them: of their own free will they had repeated an ancient promise, "We shall do and we shall listen." Instinctively, without preparation or prior instruction, they had slipped back hundreds of years. Their silence, like their cry, is to be understood not as a prayer but as an oath of fidelity.

From *The Jews of Silence,* by Elie Wiesel,
translated by Neal Kozodoy

ISRAELIS SPEAK of the Six Day War, 1967

Israel's victory in the Six Day War is one of the most notable feats in Jewish history. Prompted by the blockade of Aqaba, the massing of Egyptian forces in the Sinai Desert, and repeated threats of annihilation by Arab neighbors, Israeli forces achieved a triumph in the great tradition of Joshua, David, and Judah Maccabee. From June 5 to June 10, they took the Gaza Strip, the Sinai Peninsula, the Arab-held land west of the Jordan, and Syrian territory northeast of Lake Tiberias. Even more significant, East and West Jerusalem were reunited, giving the Jews control over their sacred sites for the first time in 2,000 years. The State of Israel again demonstrated its determination and ability to preserve its sovereign rights as an independent state.

Jews all over the world sat glued to radio sets and studied newspapers for every shred of news in this crisis. But what was it like to be in Israel throughout the six days of bitter combat? How did it feel to be part of a tiny state surrounded by vociferous neighbors who made abundantly explicit their determination to drive you into the sea?

Two Israelis tell us. One is Chana Faerstein, an American-born Jerusalem housewife who teaches English literature at the Hebrew University. The excerpts from her diary here give a civilian's view of the Six Day War.

The other is Major General Yitzhak Rabin, chief of the general staff of the Israel army. Reproduced here is a speech by General Rabin in acceptance of an honorary degree from the Hebrew University. Born in Jerusalem in 1922 to American Zionist pioneers, Rabin planned to be a farmer. Instead, circumstance made of him a soldier. A brilliant strategist and a hardened combatant, he is nonetheless a man with a mission. His remarkable acceptance speech shows the unique qualities of the Israeli army, which reflect the uniqueness of its people.

"We didn't win—we survived."

Monday, June 5

A MAN from *Haga,* the civil defense organization, is at the door. "Please tell the tenants of your building to take the prescribed measures immediately: tape and blackout the windows, sandbag the gas apparatus outside. . . . When you hear the siren, shut off the electricity, open the windows, and go down quickly to the shelter."

I am surprised by his urgency. What's the hurry?

"It just started," he says.

"What happened?"

"Does it matter? We are at war."

I switch on the 10:00 news. "An Israeli army spokesman announces: Since the early hours of this morning, heavy fighting has been taking place on the southern front between Egyptian armored and aerial forces which moved against Israel and our forces which went into action in order to check them." . . . I can recognize the experienced grimness on the faces of my neighbors: "We've been through this before." . . .

Dully, mechanically, I start taping the windowpanes with scotch tape and strips of cloth dipped in a homemade paste of starch and then hammering carpets, tablecloths, bedspreads, anything at hand to the window frames. I fill a shopping basket with crackers, chocolate, a canteen, some papers I want to save. "In Europe, when there was trouble," says a neighbor, "we would

The Western Wall, Jerusalem. (Israel Government Tourist Office)

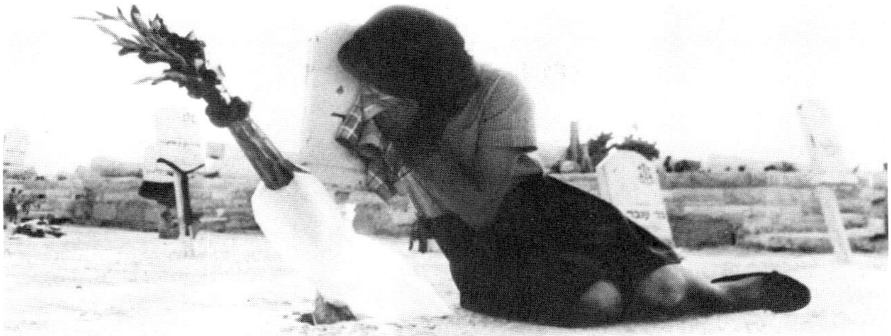

Fallen in the defense of the homeland, June 1967. (Israel Office of Information)

The Jewish Legion, comprising Jewish soldiers from the United States, Canada, England, and Argentina, at the Western Wall, Jerusalem. (Zionist Archives and Library)

In celebration of the twenty-first anniversary of Israel's independence, a special Shalom coin plaque symbolizing Israel's desire for peace is presented to Mayor Walter Washington, of Washington, D.C., by General Yitzhak Rabin. (Israel Office of Information)

tuck away a few coins, a brooch, a pair of earrings—we knew we could always bribe some guard to smuggle us across a border." No trinkets this time. Somewhere in the world you have to plant your feet and make a last stand.

The phone rings. My cousin from Tel Aviv. "Yitzhak is *somewhere* in the south," she says. "Somewhere," *ey-sham,* that vague designation for a military encampment . . . they say Tel Aviv will be bombed, we can expect thousands of civilian dead. Here in Jerusalem, we feel more or less "safe." Eshkol, after all, has just announced that we will not wage war against any state that does not attack us. Hussein may fire a few shots to show he can keep a bargain. . . .

Then, I hear the guns outside. . . . From my window I can see the museum and the *Knesset* [Parliament], on the crests of two facing hills, lift their stone targets to the Jordanian gunners. Below them, the Valley of the Cross, a sloping rocky ground where sheep often graze, is suddenly loud with mortars.

Last Friday night, our whole neighborhood heard bulldozers chewing out gun positions in these hills. The next day, while the field was being cordoned off with barbed wire, I managed to have a look around: ammunition stacked in boxes; trucks and jeeps, camouflaged with netting and tucked behind the olive trees; a few rough pits where the dark snouts of mortars poked out of the dirt. All week the soldiers kept tactfully out of sight; at night their singing would drift up from the valley.

Now they are all out in the open. I see pairs of soldiers stumble uphill with heavy boxes of ammunition between them, while others feed the mortars. I hear the orders . . . "6-2-8-7! Ready, Fire!"—white heat searing a hole in the sky and then the blast, heavy, emphatic, colorless. When they zero in on their target, the soldiers shout and cheer and slap each other on the back. . . .

Kol Yisrael [The Voice of Israel], the radio station, has been playing brassy military marches, disconcertingly unlike the usual innocent fare. Every hour there are news bulletins, often interrupted by strange whining signals which we are told to ignore:

probably some communications code. Suddenly the electricity goes off and, with it, my radio. It is almost better not to hear the news today: dismally precise accounts of enemy attacks and nothing about our own. . . . I can't help hearing the guns blasting outside in the valley and the whistling shells coming our way. What is Hussein up to, after all?

All day, my neighbors keep arriving, with difficulty, from other parts of the city where they were caught when the shooting started. Dvora Barzilay comes from Hadassah Hospital with her sick husband. The hospital was being evacuated of all but the most serious civilian cases. "We watched the volunteers—Israeli teenagers and foreign students—moving the beds down to the shelters, three floors underground. The hospital was ready, waiting. As we were leaving, we saw wounded soldiers, bloody and crudely bandaged, carried in on stretchers."

Ilana Golan, a young mother of two children, was at the main post office. "The machine guns were so close, they rattled the teeth in my mouth." She tells how one postal clerk, hearing the reserves called up over the radio by their code names—*Wedding March, Last of the Just, Close Shave, Alternating Current, Bitter Rice*—abruptly slammed his window shut and disappeared. The forty people in the post office were herded into a large underground shelter. . . . "They told us to stay put but I got out of there and drove like crazy to bring the kids from school. Along the way were people desperately thumbing a ride. I took one woman home; she was whimpering about Treblinka all the way."

Abigail Efroni, a widow of sixty, is principal of a girls' religious school where Civil Defense set up district headquarters. . . . Abigail sent the students home in small groups, escorted by their teachers. Then she settled the eight families who had come . . . for shelter. She prepared food for them, showed them how to use whitewash for sanitation, gave them blankets that her students had collected for the soldiers. At nightfall, the district head of *Haga* . . . drove her home under heavy shelling along with a few remaining teachers. On the way, they had to stop for a convoy of troops: laundry trucks, farm trucks, and busses, daubed with mud for camouflage and packed with soldiers. The streets were almost black. But you could see their faces shining, their eyes. They were singing, "Let us go up and build the wall of Jerusalem."

The only tenants in the building now are women, old men, and children. Sons and husbands are all away at the front. My neighbors have an almost professional wartime manner: they do their worrying in private. Some of them, indeed, have been through four wars. In the course of a few hours, all of us have grown close as a family in trouble. We work together now to finish the shelter: a small cellar room 10 x 12 feet, with thick concrete walls, its narrow slit of a window faced with an iron grating and blocked outside by sandbags. Our assets: one army cot, a few mattresses, chairs and blankets, a small table with a supply of candles, a transistor radio, and a first-aid kit. . . .

. . . A friend from Abu Tor calls me toward evening. The war in Jerusalem began in her backyard today when the Jordanians occupied the United Nations headquarters in no-man's land, just over the hill, and opened fire. "For hours, all we knew was the banging of the guns. We held our breath—and stayed on our bellies. Now it's quiet—whatever that means."

. . . Our mood is grim; there is no dancing in the streets here to touch off the war, as there is in Cairo. Nobody wanted a war. The soldiers were impatient to get home, all of us anxious to get back to work. For the past two weeks, I had been admiring how the human mechanism adjusts itself to new intensities of pressure. "It can't go on like this," we would say, and the next day it would be a little worse. Another border incident, another Arab state up in arms. We would plead with each other, as if at some tribunal of nations: "But you can't just wipe a country off the map." We would joke, bitter Jewish jokes: "Visit Israel—while it's still there!" "Either we win, or—what's so terrible?—only another 2,000 years of exile." And, stubbornly, we would repeat that talismanic phrase, "*Yihyeh tov*—Everything will be all right."

Now we are at war . . . I sit with my neighbors in my apartment, a transistor and a candle on the table between us. Each one of us has somebody at the front lines. . . . The intolerable tension of the last weeks has snapped—and our fate must now be settled one way or the other.

"It can't last long," we comfort ourselves . . . *Tzahal*—the Israel Defence Forces—will come through. But we have no illusions about the price of a victory. . . . The Arab radio has been sufficiently explicit . . . and now, in loud, ungrammatical Hebrew, the Arabs are already crowing over their victories.

"Will the Egyptians use gas?" They did in Yemen. "What would they do with a houseful of women and children?" Not a pretty thought. Our only hope is that the fighting will be carried onto enemy territory. . . .

I can hear the soldiers calling to one another, the mortars answering. A car noses by, its headlights dimmed a ghostly blue . . . The city is black, muffled, lit only by the shells and by a strange profusion of stars.

Tuesday, June 6

The guns did not stop all night. . . . In the morning I hear the news: "We've knocked out four hundred of their planes!" Can it be true? *Kol Yisrael* does not make extravagant claims, like the Arab radio . . . four hundred planes! We are dizzy with relief. . . .

The Arabs claim that we have an "umbrella" of British and American planes. "Well, maybe your Americans did something after all," Ilana teases me. For weeks now all the talk has been about what *my* Americans will do, what promises Eban received from Johnson: "We wouldn't be waiting if there weren't a damn good reason." But most people were skeptical: "Promises? They won't lift a finger. . . . They're too busy in Vietnam." Sure enough, now that war has begun, America plumps for "neutrality."

When there is a lull in the shelling, I take a carton of cigarettes to the troops in the neighborhood. "Hey, here's some ammunition from America!" . . . Everyone has been pampering the soldiers. Before war broke out, the Serviceman's Committee had to call a halt to cake-baking when the soldiers complained of a glut. . . . "Hussein wasn't joking," says the soldier who takes the cigarettes from me. "Yesterday we held fire for awhile, we gave them a chance to stop. We really didn't think Jordan would come in. Don't stick around here, they're bound to find our range soon."

I head for the nearest grocery—if it's open—to buy candles, matches, biscuits, and newspapers. . . . A shell overhead—one of theirs—sends me into a doorway for cover. . . . At the grocery, I find a crowd gathered outside. The local man from *Haga* appears. . . . "Get off the street! Don't you know there's a war going on? Get inside!"

. . . Everyone is talking excitedly—about 1948. "You can't compare it with today; we had no armor, no artillery. We'd fire at the Arab planes with our few guns—like spraying them with Flit!" . . . In Israeli warfare, you come to reckon on a certain margin of miracle.

My neighbors grasp at the papers, avid for news: "Air Force Wins Supremacy as Army Drives into Sinai, Gaza." . . . Anxiety crops out in the pale, tight faces around me. . . . I think of the last weeks, when we were waiting for the "great powers" to do something. . . .

The children . . . are preoccupied with the noises outside: "When you hear *boom-boom,* it's us; when you hear *ssssst,* it's them." They want to know, "Will the sandbags really keep out the shells?" The ten-year-old says proudly: "It's my first war." . . .

Last week we were conscientious about listening to the news, today we have no other reality. . . . *Kol Yisrael* doles out the news like bits of hoarded food, sweet but none too fresh. In 1948, my neighbors tell me, the Arabs used to orient themselves by our news reports; this time, we are wisely letting them believe their own lies.

There is good news from the southern front . . . the strange names send us searching in the atlas. But it is the battles near Jerusalem that really concern us. Latrun, on the road to Jerusalem, Nebi Samwil, Shuafat, Sheikh Jarrah, around the Old City —are in our hands! My neighbors tell me about the bloody fighting over these same places in 1948, the Arab victories that have galled our borders ever since. I look at Abigail, whose husband was killed here by an Arab sniper in the riots of 1937. For many people, the battle today is a chance to settle an old account.

. . . The Arabs are bent on our destruction, puffed up with hate. . . . "Kill the Jews!" But . . . we keep assuring each other—with a bit more confidence today—we have nothing to fear, least of all from the Egyptian front: those officers, who sit like *effendis* [lords] in furnished bunkers, sending their ragged, expendable troops up to the line of fire; troops that panic, shed their boots, and take off into the dunes. . . . They hardly know who put them there. Our soldiers know why they are fighting: "We have no choice; it's a matter of life and death." No one considers the possibility that our soldiers might fail us. "Everything is at stake. The Arabs can afford to lose; we can't."

Wednesday, June 7

I am awakened at dawn by a furious barrage of shelling. My neighbors are out on their balconies, watching the fireworks. "We've completely surrounded the Old City!" says one fine old housekeeper, who in her excitement has started beating the carpets somewhat earlier than usual.

We are closing in on the Old City like a team of archeologists, fussily protective about the holy sites. This display of good breeding makes the fighting all the more difficult for our soldiers. The Jordanian Legionnaires are the best-trained Arab army;

individually they are something to reckon with, barricaded in their stone houses, with their rifles and hand grenades and hidden daggers. "Why don't we just bomb the city and be done with it? They're not being so delicate." In a morning broadcast . . . Hussein goads his soldiers on: "Kill the infidels wherever you can . . . Kill them with your arms, with your hands, with your nails and teeth if necessary." Our losses in Jerusalem . . . will be heavy.

Shortly before noon, the head of *Haga* announces over the radio: "Citizens of Jerusalem! You may now leave your shelters, come out into the fresh air, open your shops. . . . If you hear the sirens, return at once to the shelters." Does this mean that we have taken the Old City? . . . I go out to get the paper: "Security Council Calls Unanimously for Cease-Fire. . . ." "Cairo: We Will Continue to Fight. . . ." "Israel Army 30 km. from Suez." . . . The streets are full of people breathing the fresh air and inspecting the damage. The municipality has supplied quantities of milk in cases, and the grocer is doing a land office business from the middle of the sidewalk. . . .

Judy Blanc, an American who has been living here for many years, is rounding up blood donors and driving them in her station wagon to the *Magen David Adom* [Red Star of David] clinic. . . . The clinic is mobbed. By nightfall the doctors start turning away people: they have twice as much blood as they can handle.

. . . *Tzahal* has taken Sharm el Sheikh on the Strait of Tiran, and this morning, after forty-eight hours of close fighting—the Old City!

Jerusalem is ours! "We had six million allies," says one woman. We listen . . . to an extraordinary account of the conquering army: Rabbi Shlomo Goren, chief chaplain of the armed forces, blowing the *shofar* [ram's horn] at the *Kotel ha-Maaravi,* the Western Wall, and our tough, grimy paratroopers crying openly. . . .

Now that Jerusalem is safe, the soldiers clear out of the valley in a great rousing parade, with all their hardware, followed by two roaring new fire engines from Jordan. The whole neighborhood turns out to cheer, pelting them with cigarettes, flowers, candy. Haggard after three days without sleep, the soldiers are singing, in their hoarse voices, that song about Jerusalem which has become a popular obsession:

". . . In the sleep of tree and stone, Caught in a dream-like thrall—The city that sits solitary, And at its heart—a Wall. Jerusalem of gold, of copper and light: I am the harp of all your songs."

People stream into the streets . . . hugging, kissing, crying *Mazal tov!* [Congratulations!], Newsboys hawk their extras: sheets hastily printed with smudgy photos of the Western Wall. The radio is playing gay Hebrew tunes again, as well as songs improvised during the campaign—one to an old chasidic melody: "Nasser sits and waits for Rabin, ay-ay-ay." Yitzhak Rabin, the chief of staff, a remarkable, modest man, affirms in his quiet voice: "All this the armed forces of Israel did alone and unaided."

. . . We are exalted, dazed, drunk on the air, the stars, the sense of "miracle," that word on everybody's lips. "When the Lord restored the captivity of Zion, we were as in a dream. Then our mouth was filled with laughter and our tongue with shouts of joy. Then they said among the nations, 'The Lord has done great things for them.' The Lord has done great things for us: we are glad." (Psalm 126)

Thursday, June 8

There is mail from the front today. Postcards . . . arrive in a batch, and we share the news with each other. On one side, printed slogans: "Soldier, write home!" "Keep secrets, save blood!" On the other side, those scrawled messages: "*4 June.* Here everything is OK. Morale is high . . . I repeat, nothing to worry about." "*5 June.* The news as you know is not too good but we hope to hold out. . . . My address until further notice, A.P.O.

2900." "*6 June.* I'm fine and healthy . . . Hope you are holding up all right. Be strong." "*7 June.* Well, the war is almost over (a pity it ever started) and I can't wait to get back. . . ."

I have one of the few telephones in the building. All day it is busy with calls for my neighbors; soldiers come in off the street to call their families. The women who do not get messages today comfort themselves, "If you don't hear anything, it's a good sign. . . ."

Today is a holiday—for Jerusalem, at least—and flags are snapping on all the houses. Jordan has agreed to a cease-fire; it won't be long now before Egypt and Syria stop playing their Russian roulette. Everyone is out on the streets, anxious to see how his friends have fared. . . . The post office is open again and there is a long line of people with telegrams in hand: "We Are Safe Thank God It's Almost Over." But the heady sense of deliverance is already beginning to fade. We see prisoners driven through town in open trucks, their eyes blindfolded. In front of the hospitals are knots of people, tense and silent, waiting for the wounded to be brought in. . . .

I visit my friend Tamy in Abu Tor . . . where a border used to be. The barbed wire, the yellow "Stop!" signs, the weeds and ruins of no-man's land are suddenly drained of meaning. You can walk around all four sides of your house now; nobody has his gun sights trained on you. . . .

In Mea Shearim, the Orthodox section . . . little boys in sidelocks wonder at the passing soldiers. Mati shows me the shelter where her family, and six others, stayed: a dank cavelike affair with mattresses on the floor, no light or air. The stench is even now oppressive. . . . "We stayed underground for three days. The old ones didn't stop reciting psalms."

A faded old woman, her face pale and ecstatic, touches my hand. "*Meshiakh vet bald kimmen!*" she breathes to me in Yiddish. "The Messiah is coming soon! My husband told me so it is written: there will be three days of fearful war, the war of Gog and Magog, and we will be saved by miracles, and the whole world will repent and then"—her voice is a shrill whisper—"the Messiah will come!" The ultra-Orthodox are feverish with messianic speculation. Some predict the Messiah will come this very Shavuot [the Feast of Weeks]; some even claim to know who he will be.

Friday, June 9

Shooting continues on the Syrian border. . . . The bulletins have gone cryptic again: "The Syrians are shelling settlements all along the northern border; our forces have gone out to silence the Syrian artillery." Nothing but that sentence repeated every hour, with a choice bit from the Syrian war cry: "The fight has just begun! Kill! Destroy! Wipe Out! Exterminate!" The Syrians are by far the cruelest and least popular of our enemies. "Those Syrian bastards, they started it all. . . ." The Syrians . . . have the strategic advantage of the heights. . . .

Airplanes fly noisily overhead. The children gawk upward like tourists. This is the first time they have seen airplanes in the sky of Jerusalem.

"They're patrolling the border."

"Aw, they're just showing off."

"Stupid! They're on the way to Damascus!"

A group of soldiers remains here on guard. They are mostly reserves, Jerusalemites, young to middle-aged; some . . . from Persia, Morocco, Roumania. These boys have none of the . . . swagger of the military. They look like farmers, not professional soldiers; a few, the regulars, move with the efficiency and grace of athletes. All are in khaki, with scuffed high boots, their uniforms sweaty and wrinkled, their sleeves rolled up, dressed for a job to be done rather than for appearance. . . .

Their discipline shows itself in an instinctive sense of responsibility. When I ask how many mortars were in their detachment they balk indignant: "We succeed because we know how to keep our mouths shut." But they are expansive about their good fortune: "Imagine, we held our ground for three days. . . . The Legionnaires never figured out where we were—or they just don't know how to aim." The erratic, indiscriminate shelling of the Jordanians, in fact, accounts for damage all over the neighborhood. . . .

Beth Hillel, the students' union where Sabbath services are held, is unusually crowded this evening. Rabbi Goren [the army chaplain] gets up to speak. Soldier and fundamentalist, he is dressed in his paratrooper's uniform, a grayish beard bristling over his khaki shirt. I would like to have seen him sprinting toward the wall, a possessed man, the *Torah* in one hand and a *shofar* [ram's horn] in the other, declaiming phrases from The Prophets at the top of his voice. "A great miracle befell us," he begins simply. "A miracle that is by no means supernatural. The miracle is that we have such soldiers, that we have such a people." Goren introduces the president of the state, Zalman Shazar, festive in black suit and holiday top hat. Shazar expounds on the Sabbath hymn, *Lechah Dodi,* in the light of the week's events: "Shake thyself from the dust, arise, put on the garments of thy glory, O My people." . . . We find ourselves repeating all the familiar texts—from The Prophets, the *Talmud,* the prayer book —discovering that the old words have a sudden truth, are not just "literature."

Sunday, June 11

The concert hall last night was brilliantly floodlit. . . . The entrance hall was lined with army cots, blankets, sleeping bags —and the grubby soldiers who had been camping there. . . . There was a moment of silence for the fallen soldiers. Then Mehta conducted *Hatikvah* [The Hope] as if it were Beethoven's *Fifth. Hatikvah,* the national anthem, is much sung these days, by soldiers, rabbis, politicians, and by the people: sung with a fierce solemnity. . . .

After the concert, we heard news of the Syrian cease-fire. . . .

The war was, in its way, as "clean" as the talks are bound to be dirty. Clean as surgery: no wasted flourishes, no gratuitous cruelties; nothing but the sharp end of the knife, cutting in order to save. This war had the dignity of a man facing death and affirming the worth of his life. We didn't win—we survived. The talks will be very different: from the operating table to the Oriental bazaar.

There is an understandable impatience with words here. "The world sat and talked when our lives were at stake. . . . Their talk is empty." . . .

It is a bitter victory. The sense of exaltation—even then, it wasn't triumph—lasted only a few hours. Now we begin to read those black-bordered notices in the newspapers and on the walls of houses: "—who fell in the defense of the people and the land"; "in our battle for survival"; "on the altar of the homeland." On the 11:00 news we hear the number: 687 dead—and then, the stunned weight of Chopin's *Funeral March*. "Only 687 dead," the military experts will say, amazed. "So many!" we say in pain. This country is too small to shrug off its losses.

I cannot forget a soldier I saw in the hospital this morning. Amnon was young, 21 at most. One arm in a cast . . . Under the sheet, a plaster stump in place of a leg . . . There was pain in his smile, beneath the *sabra* [native-born Israeli] diffidence and nonchalance. When he remembered his leg, he said only, "We knew we'd have to pay a price."

Amnon told us how . . . the doctors were operating without a break, how the nurses and volunteers . . . were fussing over the patients. In wartime you learn quickly enough what value a country sets on human life. "We never leave any wounded or dead behind on the battlefield," said Amnon. "Every soldier knows, it's part of the code. That's why we can fight the way we do." I mentioned the pilots who had been rescued so dramatically from behind enemy lines: "They expected it," he said matter-of-fact.

He was indignant about the Syrian soldiers who had been tied to their cannons by their own officers and left to die. Or the thousands of Egyptians wandering now in the dunes of Sinai: those who manage to get across the canal—his friends saw it—are shot by their own men. "They could never win a war," he said; "they don't care enough about life."

What the Israelis have evolved, after all, is a style of life: pragmatic, sinewy, without illusions, without the familiar Jewish pathos—but humanistic to the core. It is a style that has been shaped by crisis and it shows its features nobly in a crisis.

From "Six Days in June: A Jerusalem Diary,"
by Chana Faerstein, in *Midstream*, August/September 1967

"All of this springs from the soul and leads back to the spirit."

YOUR EXCELLENCY, President of the State, Mr. Prime Minister, President of the Hebrew University, Rector of the University, Governors, Teachers, Ladies, and Gentlemen:

I stand in awe before you, leaders of the generation, here in this venerable and impressive place overlooking Israel's eternal capital and the birthplace of our nation's earliest history.

. . . You have chosen to do me great honour in conferring upon me the title of doctor of philosophy. . . . I regard myself, at this time, as a representative of the entire Israel Defence Forces, of its thousands of officers, and tens of thousands of soldiers who brought the State of Israel its victory in the Six Day War. It may be asked why the university saw fit to grant the title of honorary doctor of philosophy to a soldier. . . . What is there in common to military activity and the academic world which represents civilization and culture? . . . I, however, am honoured that through me you are expressing such deep appreciation to my comrades in arms and to the uniqueness of the Israel Defence Forces which is no more than extension of the unique spirit of the entire Jewish people.

The world has recognised that the Israel Defence Forces are

different from other armies. . . . Our educational work has been praised widely and was given national recognition when in 1966 it was granted the Israel Prize for Education. . . .

However, today, the university has conferred this honorary title on us in recognition of our army's superiority of spirit and morals as it was revealed in the heat of war, for we are standing in this place by virtue of battle which, though forced upon us, was forged into a victory astounding the world.

War is intrinsically harsh and cruel, bloody and tear-stained, but particularly this war, which we have just undergone, brought forth rare and magnificent instances of heroism and courage, together with humane expressions of brotherhood, comradeship, and spiritual greatness.

Whoever has not seen a tank crew continue its attack with its commander killed and its vehicle badly damaged, whoever has not seen sappers endangering their lives to extricate wounded comrades from a minefield, whoever has not seen the anxiety and the effort of the entire air force devoted to rescuing a pilot who has fallen in enemy territory cannot know the meaning of devotion between comrades in arms.

The entire nation was exalted and many wept upon hearing the news of the capture of the Old City. Our *sabra* [native Israeli] youth and most certainly our soldiers do not tend to sentimentality . . . however, the strain of battle, the anxiety which preceded it, and the sense of salvation and of direct participation . . . in the forging of . . . Jewish history cracked the shell of hardness and shyness and released well-springs of . . . spiritual emotion. The paratroopers, who conquered the Wailing Wall, leaned on its stones and wept, and as a symbol this was a rare occasion, almost unparalleled in human history. Such phrases and clichés are not generally used in our army, but this scene on the Temple Mount beyond the power of verbal description revealed, as though by a lightning flash, deep truths. . . . Nevertheless we find more and more and more a strange phenomenon among our fighters. Their joy is incomplete, and more than a small portion of sorrow and shock prevails in their festivities. And there are those who abstain from all celebration. The warriors in the front lines saw with their own eyes the price of victory: their comrades who fell beside them bleeding. And I know that even the terrible price which our enemies paid touched the hearts of many of our men. It may be that the Jewish people never learned and never accustomed itself to feel the triumph of conquest and victory and therefore we receive it with mixed feelings.

The Six Day War revealed many instances of heroism far beyond the single attack which dashes unthinkingly forward. In many places desperate and lengthy battles raged. In Rafiah, in El Arish, in Um Kataf, in Jerusalem, and in Ramat Hagolan [the Golan Heights], there, and in many other places, the soldiers of Israel were revealed as heroic in spirit, in courage, and in persistence which cannot leave anyone indifferent once he has seen this great and exalting human revelation. We speak a great deal of the few against the many. In this war perhaps for the first time since the Arab invasions of the spring of 1948 and the battles of Negba and Degania, units of the Israel Forces stood in all sectors, few against many. This means that relatively small units of our soldiers often entered seemingly endless networks of fortification, surrounded by hundreds and thousands of enemy troops and faced with the task of forcing their way, hour after hour, in this jungle of dangers, even after the momentum of the first attack has passed and all that remains is the necessity of belief in our strength, the lack of alternative, and the goal for which we are fighting to summon up every spiritual resource in order to continue the fight to its very end.

Thus our armoured forces broke through on all fronts, our paratroopers fought their way into Rafiah and Jerusalem, our sappers cleared minefields under enemy fire. The units which broke the enemy lines and came to their objectives after hours upon hours of struggle continuing on and on while their comrades fell right and left and they continued forward, only forward.

These soldiers were carried forward by spiritual values, by deep spiritual resources, far more than by their weapons or the technique of warfare.

We have always demanded the cream of our youth for the Israel Defence Forces when we coined the slogan *"Ha-Tovim le-Tayis"*—The Best to Flying—and this was a phrase which became a value. We meant not only technical and manual skills. We meant that if our airmen were to be capable of defeating the forces of four enemy countries within a few short hours they must have moral values and human values.

Our airmen, who struck the enemies' planes so accurately that no one in the world understands how it was done and people seek technological explanations of secret weapons; our armoured troops who stood and beat the enemy even when their equipment was inferior to his; our soldiers in all the various branches of the Israel Defence Forces who overcame our enemies everywhere, despite their superior numbers and fortifications; all these revealed not only coolness and courage in battle but a burning faith in their righteousness, an understanding that only their personal stand against the greatest of dangers could bring victory to their country and to their families and that if the victory was not theirs the alternative was destruction.

Furthermore, in every sector, our forces' commanders, of all ranks, far outshone the enemies' commanders. Their understanding, their will, their ability to improvise, their care for their soldiers, and, above all, their leading troops into battle, these are not matters of material or of technique. They have no rational explanation except in terms of a deep consciousness of the moral justice of their fight.

All of this springs from the soul and leads back to the spirit. Our warriors prevailed not by their weapons but by the consciousness of a mission, by a consciousness of righteousness, by a deep love for their homeland, and an understanding of the difficult task laid upon them: to ensure the existence of our people in its homeland, to protect, even at the price of their lives, the right of the nation of Israel to live in its own state, free, independent, and peaceful.

This army, which I had the privilege of commanding through these battles, came from the people and returns to the people, to the people which rises in its hour of crisis and overcomes all enemies by virtue of its moral values, its spiritual readiness in the hour of need.

As the representative of the Israel Defence Forces and in the name of every one of its soldiers, I accept with pride your recognition.

An address by Major General Yitzhak Rabin at Honorary Doctorate ceremony, Hebrew University, Mt. Scopus, June 28, 1968

ACKNOWLEDGMENTS

1. From *The Holy Scriptures. Jeremiah* 52:3–27. Reprinted by permission of the Jewish Publication Society of America.

2. From *The Bible, A New Translation,* by James Moffat. *The Book of Lamentations* 4:1–22. Reprinted by permission of Harper and Row.

3. *The Book of Psalms 126,* adapted from *The Holy Scriptures.* Reprinted by permission of the Jewish Publication Society of America.

4. From *The Bible, A New Translation,* by James Moffat. *Nehemiah* 2:17–4:23; 6:1–15. Reprinted by permission of Harper and Row.

5. From *The Holy Scriptures. Nehemiah* 8:1–12. Reprinted by permission of the Jewish Publication Society of America.

6. *Mishnah Bikkurim* 3:1–5;8, as quoted in *Post-Biblical Hebrew Literature,* by Ben-Zion Halper. Reprinted by permission of the Jewish Publication Society of America.

7. Translation by Herbert T. Andrews of "The Letter of Aristeas" from *The Apocrypha and Pseudepigrapha of the Old Testament,* ed. R.H. Charles. 1963, Vol. II, pp. 94–122. By permission of the Clarendon Press, Oxford.

8. From *The Apocrypha,* ed. Edgar J. Goodspeed. *The Wisdom of Ben Sirach* 50:1–29. Copyright © 1959 by University of Chicago Press. Reprinted by permission of University of Chicago Press.

9. *The First Book of Maccabees* 2:1–29 from *The Apocrypha and Pseudepigrapha of the Old Testament,* ed. R.H. Charles. 1913, Vol. I, pp. 71–72. By permission of the Clarendon Press, Oxford.

10. From *On the Contemplative Life,* by Philo, as quoted in *Philosophical Writing,* Philo Selections, ed. Hans Lewy, pp. 3, 22–37, 64–90 (end). Phaidon Press, East and West Library, London, 1946.

11. From *The Babylonian Talmud. Seder Nashim, Gittin* 5, ed. Rabbi Dr. I. Epstein. Reprinted by permission of the Soncino Press, Ltd.

12. From *The Wars of the Jews,* by Flavius Josephus. Translated by William Whiston. Book IV, Chapter 4. London, 1818.

13. Novella 146, from the year 553, from *The Cairo Geniza,* by Paul E. Kahle. Published by the Oxford University Press for the British Academy.

14. From the *Karaite Anthology,* by Leon Nemoy. Reprinted by permission of the Yale University Press.

15. From *The Responsa Literature,* by Solomon B. Freehof, pp. 104–5. Copyright © 1955 by the Jewish Publication Society of America. Reprinted by permission of the Jewish Publication Society of America.

16. From *Saadia Gaon,* by Henry Malter, pp. 55–56; 82–83. Copyright © 1921 by the Jewish Publication Society of America. Reprinted by permission of the Jewish Publication Society of America.

17. From *The Jew in the Medieval World,* by Jacob R. Marcus, pp. 287–292. Reprinted by permission of the Union of American Hebrew Congregations.

18. *Ibid.*, pp. 227–232.

19. From *The Island Within,* by Ludwig Lewisohn, pp. 327–339. Copyright © 1928 by Harper & Bros. Reprinted by permission of Louise Lewisohn and the Jewish Publication Society.

20. From *The Jew in the Medieval World,* pp. 247–250.

21. *Ibid.*, pp. 185–188.

22. From *Maimonides Said,* transl. and ed. Nahum N. Glatzer, pp. 22 ff. Reprinted by permission of Nahum N. Glatzer.

23. From *An Anthology of Medieval Hebrew Literature,* by Abraham Millgram, pp. 311–312; 316–317. Copyright © 1935 by Abraham Millgram. Published 1961 by Abelard-Schuman, Ltd.

24. From *The Church and the Jews in the Thirteenth Century,* by Solomon Grayzel. Copyright © 1966 by Hermon Press. Reprinted by permission of the Hermon Press. *The Burning of the Law,* by Meir of Rothenburg. Translated by Nina Davis in *Songs of Exile* (abridged). Reprinted by permission of the Jewish Publication Society of America.

25. From *A Jewish Reader: In Time and Eternity,* ed. Nahum N. Glatzer, pp. 224–232. Copyright © 1946, 1961, by Schocken Books, Inc. Reprinted by permission of Schocken Books, Inc.

26. Introduction to *Commentary on the Book of Joshua,* by Isaac Abravanel.

27. From *The Jew in the Medieval World,* pp. 51-55.

28. From *Roads to Zion,* by Kurt Wilhelm, pp. 15–27. Copyright © 1948 by Schocken Books, Inc. Reprinted by permission of Schocken Books, Inc.

29. From *A History of the Marranos,* by Cecil Roth, pp. 111–116. Copyright © 1941 by the Jewish Publication Society of America. Reprinted by permission of the Jewish Publication Society of America.

30. From *Roads to Zion,* pp. 57–64.

31. From *Abyss of Despair,* by Nathan Hanover. Reprinted by permission of Bloch Publishing Company.

32. From *Anglo-Jewish Letters,* ed. Cecil Roth, pp. 47–48. Reprinted by permission of the Soncino Press, Ltd.

33. From *The History of the Turkish Empire,* by Paul Rycault, 1687. Vol. II, pp. 174–184.

34. From *The Jews of Newport,* by Morris A. Gutstein, pp. 98–103. Reprinted by permission of Bloch Publishing Company.

35. From *An Autobiography,* by Solomon Maimon, transl. J. Clark Murray, pp. 210–215. Copyright © 1888 by Alexander Garner Publishers, London.

36. A letter from Rabbi Schneur Zalman, transl. from the Hebrew by Herbert Weiner. Reprinted by permission of Rabbi Herbert Weiner, and reprinted from *Commentary* by permission. Copyright © 1956 by the American Jewish Committee.

37. From *Jewish Survival in the World Today,* by Abraham Duker. Hadassah, New York City, 1940. Reprinted by permission of Abraham Duker.

38. From *Transactions of the Parisian Sanhedrin Convoked at Paris by an Imperial and Royal Decree,* May 30, 1806, transl. F.D. Kirwan. Copyright © 1807 by M. Diogene Tama.

39. Translated by W. Gunther Plaut from the magazine *Sulamith* as quoted in *The Rise of Reform Judaism,* by W. Gunther Plaut. Reprinted by permission of the Union of American Hebrew Congregations.

40. From *A Source Book on Jewish History and Literature,* eds., Julius Hoexter and Moses Jung, pp. 251–252. Copyright © 1938 by Shapiro, Vallentine & Co., London. Reprinted by permission of Shapiro, Vallentine & Co.

41. From *Diaries of Sir Moses and Lady Montefiore,* Vol. I, ed. Dr. L. Lowe. London, 1890.

42. From Herman Melville, *Journal of a Visit to Europe and the Levant, October 11, 1856–May 6, 1857,* ed. Howard C. Horsford, pp. 124–161. Copyright 1955 by Princeton University Press. Omission of footnotes. Reprinted by permission of Princeton University Press.

43. From *Diaries of Sir Moses and Lady Montefiore,* Vol. II, ed. Dr. L. Lowe.

44. From "The History of the Hebrew Union College, 1875–1925," by David Philipson. Jubilee Volume Special, 1925, *The Hebrew Union College Annual.* Reprinted by permission of Dr. Matitiahu Tsevat, editor.

45. From *The Jewish Theological Seminary,* Semi-Centennial Volume, 1939, ed. Cyrus Adler. Reprinted by permission of the Jewish Theological Seminary of America.

46. From the French newspaper *l'Autorité,* January 6, 1895. From *A*

History of the Dreyfus Affair, by Theodore Reinach, transl. Maurice Samuel. Reprinted by permission of Behrman House.

47. From *Prelude to Israel, the Memoirs of M.I. Bodenheim,* ed. Henriette H. Bodenheim, transl. Israel Cohen. Copyright © 1936 by Thomas Yoseloff. Reprinted by permission of Thomas Yoseloff, A.S. Barnes & Co.

48. *The City of Slaughter,* transl. Helena Frank. Included in *Selected Poems: Chaim Nachman Bialik,* transl. Maurice Samuel. Copyright © 1972 by the Union of American Hebrew Congregations. Reprinted by permission of the UAHC.

49. From *Sound the Great Trumpet,* ed. M.Z. Frank, pp. 61–63. Copyright © 1955 by Whittier Books. Reprinted by permission of Moses Zebi Frank.

50. From *Middle East Diary,* by Col. R. Meinertzhagen, pp. 3–4. Copyright © 1959 by Cresset Press, London. Reprinted by permission of the Cresset Press.

51. From the newspaper *Die Zeit,* St. Petersburg, Russia, October 26, 1913.

52. From *The Story of the Jewish Legion,* by Vladimir Jabotinsky, transl. Samuel Katz, pp. 105–113. Copyright © 1945 by Bernard Ackerman, Co. Reprinted by permission of A.S. Barnes & Co.

53. From *Trial and Error,* the autobiography of Chaim Weizmann, pp. 200–208. Copyright © 1949 by the Weizmann Foundation. Reprinted by permission of Harper and Row.

54. From *Our Jerusalem: An American Family in the Holy City,* by Bertha Spafford Vester, pp. 260–261. Copyright © 1950 by Bertha Spafford Vester and Evelyn Wells. Reprinted by permission of Doubleday and Company, Inc.

55. From *This Thing of Giving,* by Henry H. Rosenfeld. Reprinted by permission of Lessing Rosenwald of Rosenwald Foundation.

56. From *Memoirs* of Hon. Viscount Herbert Samuel, p. 176. Copyright © 1945 by Curtis Brown, Ltd., London. Reprinted by permission of Curtis Brown, Ltd.

57. From *The Golden Tradition,* ed. Lucy S. Dawidowicz, pp. 448–457. Copyright © 1967 by Lucy S. Dawidowicz. Reprinted by permission of Holt, Rinehart and Winston, Inc.

58. Reprinted from *A Pilgrim's Vow,* by Pierre Van Paassen. Copyright © 1956 by Pierre Van Paassen and reprinted by permission of the publisher, Dial Press.

59. From *Henrietta Szold: Life and Letters,* by Marvin Lowenthal, Chapter 15. Copyright © 1942 by The Viking Press, Inc. Reprinted by permission of The Viking Press, Inc.

60. From *Babi Yar,* by Anatoly Kuznetsov, transl. Edgar H. Lehrman, as quoted in *The New York Times Magazine,* December 11, 1966. Copyright © 1966 by The New York Times Company. Reprinted by permission.

61. From *Pius XII and the Third Reich: A Documentation,* by Saul Friedlander, pp. 126–128. Copyright © 1966 by Alfred A. Knopf, Inc. Reprinted by permission of the publisher.

62. "In the Forests," by Tuvia Belsky, from *A Tower from the Enemy,* ed. Albert Nirenstein, pp. 352–362. Reprinted by permission of Orion Press; Giulio Einaudi Editore, Torino, Italy; and Grossman Publishers, Inc.

63. From "The Last Days of the Warsaw Ghetto," by Ziviah Lubetkin, transl. Shlomo Katz. Reprinted from *Commentary* by permission of Shlomo Katz. Copyright © 1947 by the American Jewish Committee.

64. From *Soldiers from Judea,* by Major Louis Rabinowitz. American Zionist Emergency Council, London, 1944. Reprinted by permission of Dr. Louis Rabinowitz.

65. From *Belsen Uncovered,* by Derrick Sington. Reprinted by permission of Mrs. Derrick Sington.

66. From an International News Service dispatch, October 16, 1946. Reprinted by permission of United Press International.

67. From *In Search,* autobiography, by Meyer Levin, pp. 362–372. Copyright © 1950 by Horizon Press. Reprinted by permission of Meyer Levin.

68. From a broadcast of the Tel Aviv radio, July 17, 1947. Reprinted by permission of Kol Yisrael Broadcasting Authority.

69. From *Trial and Error,* pp. 477–482.

70. From *Three Days* by Zeev Sharef, pp. 281–289. Copyright © 1962 by Zeev Sharef. Reprinted by permission of Doubleday and Company, Inc.

71. From *Youth and Nation,* August 1948, pp. 35–38. Reprinted by permission of Hashomer Hatzair.

72. "The Discovery of the Dead Sea Scrolls," by John C. Trever. Reprinted by permission of the American Schools of Oriental Research. This article, first published in the *Biblical Archaeologist,* September, 1948, pp. 46–57, has been corrected and slightly revised, mostly by means of explanatory notes, by the author.

73. From *I Flew Them Home,* by Edward Trueblood Martin. Reprinted by courtesy of the Herzl Press.

74. From *The Murderers Among Us,* by Simon Wiesenthal, pp. 123–128. Copyright © 1967 by Opera Mundi, Paris. Reprinted by permission of McGraw-Hill Book Company.

75. From "Eichmann and His Trial," by Gideon Hausner, in *The Saturday Evening Post,* November 3, 1962. Reprinted with permission of *The Saturday Evening Post,* Curtis Publishing Company.

76. From *The Jews of Silence,* by Elie Wiesel. Transl. Neal Kozodoy, pp. 44–57. Copyright © 1966 by Holt, Rinehart and Winston, Inc. Reprinted by permission of Holt, Rinehart and Winston, Inc.

77. From "Six Days in June: A Jerusalem Diary," by Chana Faerstein, in *Midstream,* August/September, 1967. Reprinted by permission of *Midstream* and Chana Faerstein. An address by Major General Yitzhak Rabin at Honorary Doctorate ceremony, Hebrew University, Mt. Scopus, June 28, 1968. Reprinted by permission of Hon. Yitzhak Rabin.

INDEX